THE CULTURE FACADE

THE CULTURE FACADE

Art, Science, and Politics in the Work of Oscar Lewis

Susan M. Rigdon

UNIVERSITY OF ILLINOIS PRESS

Urbana and Chicago

Manufactured in the United States of America
C 5 4 3 2 1

This book is printed on acid-free paper.

Library of Congress Cataloging-in-Publication Data

Rigdon, Susan M., 1943–
   The culture facade.

   "Publications of Oscar Lewis": p.
   Bibliography: p.
   Includes index.
   1. Poverty—Psychological aspects.   2. Poor.
3. Lewis, Oscar, 1914–1970—Views on Poverty.   I. Lewis,
Oscar, 1914–1970.   II. Title.
HC79.P6R57   1988   305.5′69   87-19063
ISBN 0-252-01495-2 (alk. paper)

This book is dedicated to the memory
of Muna Muñoz Lee
(1920–79)

We have become prisoners of our own categories. In our desire to reduce our materials to their lowest common denominator we have left out some of our most vivid and dynamic material.

Oscar Lewis, 1949

As far as I am concerned, my formulation of a subculture of poverty is simply a challenging hypothesis which should be widely tested by empirical research.

Oscar Lewis, 1967

No generalizations can really encompass the richness and variety of the lives I am attempting to portray in the words of the poor. . . .

Oscar Lewis, 1968

CONTENTS

PREFACE

The sociologist Daniel Lerner once suggested that social science research could profit from the publication of a journal of failed hypotheses, in which scholars would write about how and why their research had not produced the expected results. One hypothesis that could have benefited from such an examination by its author was that which posited the existence of a subculture among poor people, particularly among some urban slum dwellers in capitalist societies. The principal proponent of this thesis from 1958 until his death in 1970 was the anthropologist Oscar Lewis. He called this "design for living" the *culture* (or sometimes the *subculture*) *of poverty*. Throughout the 1960s, and into the 1970s, it enjoyed—or suffered from, depending upon one's viewpoint—considerable notoriety as the subject of numerous articles in social science journals. In fact, so much has been written about the culture of poverty that one may fairly ask what more can—or should—be written on so fragile a construct.

What this study offers that no other critique of Lewis's writing has been able to offer is a review of his work by someone who has had access to all of his field materials and professional correspondence. It grew out of my collaboration with Ruth Maslow Lewis, begun in 1972, to edit and analyze field materials that she, Oscar Lewis, and a large staff of Cubans, Mexicans, and North Americans had gathered in Cuba in 1969–70. (These materials were published in a three-volume series entitled *Living the Revolution: An Oral History of Contemporary Cuba*.) I came to that project with graduate degrees in political science, a specialization in Chinese politics, and a strong interest in the broad issues of development and the study of socialist systems. I had no training in anthropology and had never read anything by either of the Lewises. I had heard Oscar Lewis lecture on the Puerto Rico project in 1966 and had met him once briefly in 1970, just after he returned from Cuba, but my knowledge of his work did not extend much further than an awareness of the culture of poverty concept and his general research approach.

After I began working with Ruth Lewis, whenever time allowed, I read Oscar Lewis's published work. The culture of poverty thesis did not make much sense to me and I immediately put it aside. This was easy to do since in editing the Cuba materials Ruth Lewis and I never seriously considered organizing them around a discussion of the concept. Only one of the project's several studies was devoted to testing the culture of poverty thesis, and these materials were being written up by Oscar Lewis's colleague (and former student) Douglas Butterworth (see *The People of Buena Ventura: Relocation of Slum Dwellers in Postrevolutionary Cuba*).

What I found compelling in Lewis's work, in an era when survey research dominated the social sciences, was his commitment to studying and writing about individuals and a concomitant lack of concern for generality in favor of specificity. In reading his articles on the folk-urban continuum, on comparative method, and on the family study approach, I found, quite unexpectedly, a kindred spirit. I was surprised to discover in these early articles a rejection of the use of models and ideal types for comparing whole cultures. As a student of comparative government in the 1960s, I shared the view of many of my peers that the use of such heuristic devices to compare whole political systems was inadequate and even misleading. We found simple comparisons of "democracies" with "totalitarian" systems as shallow as Lewis had found the comparison of "folk" with "urban" cultures twenty years earlier. His dissatisfaction with the conception of cultural development occurring along a folk-urban continuum paralleled our rejection of the model of a unilinear path to political and economic development. It seemed to me that in both instances the dissatisfaction stemmed from a tendency to confuse the models with real systems and therefore to obscure and understate the specific similarities and differences between systems. It was this general orientation, not any specific technique or piece of writing, that I found most attractive in Lewis's work.

I had the opportunity to examine the raw field materials when Ruth Lewis and I undertook the task of cataloging them for placement in a restricted collection in the archives of the University of Illinois Library. This process eventually encompassed his professional correspondence, research papers, unpublished manuscripts, tape recordings, and transcriptions as well. Examination of these materials left me with two general impressions: first, an increased admiration for the published interviews, especially the care taken in the translation and editing processes in order to keep them as close to the originals as possible; and second, a tremendous disappointment that Lewis allowed and even encouraged the rich and diverse results of his research to be used as evidence of the existence of a culture of poverty. To his credit he never attempted to manipulate the content of the published interviews to be more supportive of his claims for their significance, but this also accounts for many of the contradictions in his writings.

In assessing a large body of data such as this, it was not surprising to find inconsistencies and even contradictions in style and methods in the collection and editing processes, because the materials were gathered over a thirty-year period and because not one or two but dozens of people worked on them. What *was* unusual, and at times stunning, was that even in Lewis's own writings, not infrequently within a single article or letter, there were contradictions. Nowhere are these more evident than in his writing on the culture of poverty.

After noting the disparity between the content of his materials and his theorizing, and how frequently this disparity was called to his attention by critics, I began to think of the culture of poverty as Lewis's nemesis. I undertook this study to explain how he got himself into this position and why, given his own ambivalence about the thesis, he refused to publicly abandon it. I have no independent basis on which to prove or disprove the existence of a culture of poverty and therefore will discuss the thesis only as it appears in Lewis's work. In the introduction to this book I try to establish Lewis's basic orientation toward science and art, as well as toward his discipline, and in a background chapter I attempt to locate in personal circumstance and academic training the origins of his research interests. Chapters 2 through 5 examine the evolution of Lewis's method and the culture of poverty thesis through his major research projects in Mexico, Puerto Rico, and Cuba. Chapters 6 through 8 and the Conclusions are evaluations of his method and the impact of his writings on poverty policy and anthropological research.

Because I have chosen to focus on theory and method, this study is not intended as a full intellectual biography. But because the key to understanding Lewis's research approach, choice of topic, and method of presentation lies in his academic training, political orientation, artistic inclinations, and temperament, I have included what I consider to be the essential, relevant biographical details. Of course, this is a matter of personal judgment; another person might have chosen to include or exclude different material. Thus, it would be logical for a reader to ask whether my decisions were influenced by my privileged access to Lewis's research papers and by my professional association and friendship with Ruth Lewis. The only restriction placed on use of the material by Ruth Lewis was that I protect informants' anonymity. She did not ask for the right of review, but I did give her each draft of the manuscript to read. I was asked to make two deletions from the text but nothing at all from the correspondence in the appendix. I made one of the deletions—some names contained in a footnote. I also engaged in some self-censorship when information was of a sensitive nature—for example, the name of the Communist party organizer who befriended Lewis in adolescence. Where blanket permission was given to quote from correspondence, I used nothing that the letter-writer explicitly said was written in confidence. And, although I have included substantially more biographical material than originally planned and have omitted nothing that in my best judgment was essential to this study, I have not used anything told to me in confidence by Lewis's family or friends.

The field materials and personal papers on which this study is based were not made available to me so that I could write this or any other book on Oscar Lewis, but access to them was not withdrawn when I decided to do so. For Ruth Lewis not to withhold her cooperation required greater restraint than one can appreciate without an understanding of how large a role she played in the research discussed in this book. Furthermore, she knew from the outset that I was in disagreement with the culture of poverty thesis. Did she try to influence my interpretation? Of course she did; I essentially invited her to do so by asking her so many questions. In any case she knows much more about her husband and their work than I do, and it would be extraordinary if she did not assign some credibility to her views on both subjects. However, my conclusions, which are drawn primarily from the archival record and from Lewis's letters to his wife and colleagues, are at odds with Ruth Lewis's interpretations on several points. I asked her to write an epilogue to the book to state the points of difference, but she decided against it. I hope that someday she will write her own evaluation of the work she shared for more than thirty years with her husband.

Acknowledgments

During the decade that I worked intermittently on this book I was aided by a number of people. I received various forms of assistance from the Center for International Studies and the Department of Anthropology at the University of Illinois at Urbana-Champaign, and for this I want to thank in particular the late Joseph Casagrande and Professor Norman E. Whitten, Jr. I am indebted to the staff of the University of Illinois Library Archives, and especially to Professors Maynard Brichford and William Maher, for their cooperation with my research.

I have benefited from conversations and correspondence with several people who worked with Oscar Lewis: his secretary, Fern Hartz, and field assistants Francisca Muriente, Rafael Rodríguez Casteñeda, Olivia Hernández de Rodríguez, and Professor Elizabeth Hegeman. Muriente and Rodríguez Casteñeda were exceptionally helpful in updating information on Puerto Rican and Cuban informants. For discussing with me various aspects of the Puerto Rican and Cuban projects I want to thank the late Douglas Butterworth, a former student of Lewis's who later joined the faculty of the Department of Anthropology at the University of Illinois. I also learned a good deal, especially about the chronology of the Mexican fieldwork, from Dr. Gene L. Lewis, who spent many years in the field with his parents.

For comments on various drafts of the manuscript I am grateful to Ruth M. Lewis, Elizabeth G. Dulany, Judith Lewis, and Professors Lisa R. Peattie and Herbert Gans. To Ruth Lewis and Professor Gans I owe a special debt for their many constructive suggestions. I also want to thank Theresa L. Sears for editing the final manuscript.

I am very grateful to Dr. Carolina Luján for permission to quote from her correspondence with Oscar Lewis; the letters were among my most important research sources, and had I not been able to present Luján's position in her own words, chapters 3 and 5 would have been much more difficult to write. I also want to thank Professor Conrad Arensberg for permission to quote from his letters to Oscar Lewis and Carmen and Margarita Rosado Muñoz for permission to quote from letters written by Muna Muñoz Lee. For making available all of the letters written to and by Oscar Lewis, and for permission to quote from her letters and those of her husband, I am very grateful to Ruth Lewis.

It is to Ruth Lewis that I owe the greatest debt for aiding and facilitating the research for this book. Clearly I could not have undertaken a study such as this if she had not given me unrestricted access to all field materials. However, it is necessary to say that she did not do so to enable me to write a book about her husband; access was an inevitable part of our research collaboration, as well as of our joint project to prepare the materials for archival use. She was extraordinarily generous with her time and answered thousands of questions about the conduct of the research and the editing of field materials. Nevertheless, this book should not be regarded as authorized, and the conclusions are mine alone.

Finally, I want to thank Fred and Diane L. Gottheil for introducing me to Oscar Lewis and for arranging the meeting with Ruth Lewis that led to my collaboration with her on the Cuba project.

THE CULTURE FACADE

INTRODUCTION

Oscar Lewis sometimes practiced anthropology as if it were a plastic art. In a thirty-year career (1940–70) that encompassed field research in Mexico, Cuba, Spain, India, Puerto Rico, Canada, and the United States, he gradually learned to use the tools of his profession to shape works that were a fortuitous blend of social science and art. Throughout his career Lewis was convinced that he could successfully employ academic approaches to pursue humanistic concerns and combine science in method with art in reporting. He acknowledged that his work ran the risk of becoming uncategorizable, of "falling between the cracks," but maintained that this did not bother him because he found exact categories artificial: "I think that to understand life we cannot apply rigid norms or rules. Life is fluid and crosses over all classifications and divisions, without respecting those barriers we humans have invented. The truth is that I see no conflict between social science and literature."[1]

Everyone in the social sciences comes quickly to understand, if not to accept, how jealously disciplinary borders are guarded. One might stray occasionally, or enter into a collaborative relationship with someone in another field, but to continuously and unapologetically transgress these boundaries at will is professionally dangerous unless one is already well established in one's discipline or has alternate means of support. Oscar Lewis not only ranged across several disciplines in the social sciences but committed the more egregious error of crossing over their outer limits and into the arts, so far that he was accused of overthrowing science for art.

It is no easy task to list precisely all of Lewis's research interests; it is harder still to identify the people and work that helped define those interests. Lewis was a man who seemed to take something for later use from everyone he studied or worked with and from everything he read. He never studied one problem at a time except when required to in graduate school or in his early work in applied anthropology. In the fieldwork *he* initiated he had multiple objectives and tried to achieve them all. Some of the many broad problems motivating Lewis's research were: cultural change in transitional peasant societies; the effects of urbanization and technological change on culture and mental health; the impact of revolution on culture and family life; the requisites for and obstacles to vertical mobility within and between classes; the "psychology of the poor"; the value structure and "total personality" of the individual; interpersonal relationships within the family and the role of the family in personality formation. Lewis used the "traditional techniques of sociology, anthropology, and psychology" to do, sometimes simultaneously, community and family studies and to collect individual life histories.[2] With his use of biography and the narrative technique he hoped to reach an audience who would not otherwise read academic tracts on poverty, peasant societies, or cultures in transition. He also wanted, as he often wrote, to let the poor speak for themselves.

Lewis called himself an "eclectic materialist."[3] While I have no clear idea of what he meant by the combined use of the two words, he was both eclectic and a materialist. He was eclectic in the sense that he belonged to no particular school of thought or group of theorists and borrowed approaches and analytic frameworks from a variety of disciplines. He took just what he wanted, sometimes altering an idea or concept by removing it from the original context or overall rationale. He was a materialist in the sense that he was narrowly empirical, accepting as evidence only what could be confirmed through his own observation or experience, believing in the primacy of material over spiritual well-being, and defining progress almost solely in terms of material conditions. In the study of culture he assigned seminal importance to understanding economic organization, level of technology, and material culture, and particularly to finding out who possessed what and how they had acquired it. His materialism was associated with a grounding in Marxism, but this he did not accept as political dogma and little more as theory, for in its pure form he found it crudely deterministic. As with his other borrowing, Lewis was highly selective in what he took.

Eclectic materialism does not define any identifiable approach or philosophy, and to use it as such suggests a level of integration in Lewis's work and thinking that, in my view, did not exist. Calling himself an eclectic materialist was Lewis's way of claiming an association with Marxism while at the same time dissociating himself from historical materialism and announcing that, in the study of cultural formation and culture change, he would not be locked into any one theory of causation.

Lewis never recognized the viability of truly discrete disciplines within the social sciences, and he was never satisfied with the methods or approaches of any one of them. He was certainly never content to rely on any one approach to the study of culture. For example, he

did not believe that a culture could be reconstructed from the testimony of a few informants, and he did not trust oral accounts of
life events that were not confirmed in repeated interviewing with the
same and other informants; he also was deeply suspicious of questionnaire data on attitudes and opinions and did not accept projective
test analyses if they were unsupported by life histories and direct observation. He was skeptical of all problems too narrowly defined and,
ironically, given his culture of poverty thesis, of answers too neatly
stated. He saw himself as employing a holistic approach and assumed
there was no such thing as too much information.

Lewis objected to what he saw as a trend in the social sciences to
make science a "sacred cow."[4] He did not denigrate scientific methods as such, and certainly not the need for system and controls in
social science research, but he disliked intensely what he considered
mechanical borrowing from the physical and biological sciences. On
this issue he had a long-standing disagreement with his friend Jules
Henry, who characterized as "anti-intellectual" Lewis's opposition to
his borrowing from communication and learning theories.[5] Lewis responded: "I am all in favor of theory but I want theory that throws
light on the major problems I am concerned with. Theories from other
fields which can only help 'metaphorically,' as you yourself seem to
imply, are nothing to get excited about."[6]

Lewis saw his generation as breaking away from the poetic and
intuitive approaches of first- and second-generation American anthropologists and in 1953 wrote that "the increased use of quantification
has been one of the most significant developments in anthropological
field work in recent years."[7] Yet he was contemptuous of the claim
that *only* scientific method, narrowly defined, could produce hard,
accurate, verifiable data of significance for theory building. He believed that certain kinds of information—in particular, that essential
to understanding the problems closest to his concerns—were inac-
cessible through such a method. Lewis argued that a prerequisite to
judging the reliability of information on family and cultural practices
was a deep knowledge of the source. To him the detached stance
of the scientist made it impossible to develop the relationship between researcher and respondent necessary for his research. "The
most effective tools of the anthropologist," he wrote, "are sympathy
and compassion for the people he studies."[8] These tools would not
only help the anthropologist obtain, for scientific purposes, the most
reliable information on culture but would also serve the underlying
humanistic objectives of anthropological inquiry.

Nevertheless, Lewis was serious about conforming to *his* conception of scientific method and said that he had spent a good deal of

his early career trying to make anthropological methods "more scientific."[9] He meant that he had tried to collect data in a more thorough and intensive manner, with greater emphasis on the precise, detailed, exhaustive recording of material conditions and with less dependence on the spoken testimony of a few informants. He believed that anthropologists had spent a disproportionate amount of time interpreting myth, religion, and ritual at the expense of providing fuller descriptions of technology, material culture, economic organization, wealth distribution, and stratification, as well as searching archival records to support or complement data derived from oral testimony.

If one were careful about how data were collected, Lewis believed, one should be allowed some freedom in deciding how that information would be presented to readers, especially if it were the content and not the method that one wanted to communicate. Thus he saw no real conflict between social science and literature. Information gathered systematically, with great care for its accuracy, could be communicated through literary forms.

It was the potential that Lewis saw in anthropological investigation and reporting for combining several approaches and pursuing multiple objectives that led him to abandon history as his field of study. Anthropology, he wrote, had "scientific and humanistic and artistic aspects."[10]

> Throughout my career as an anthropologist I have sought to integrate approaches to the study of man and society which too often have been viewed as contradictory, but which always seemed to me to be complementary. For example, I have tried to combine both the scientific and humanistic approaches in my work as well as the historical or diachronic and the functional or synchronic. Indeed, a good deal of the discussion . . . as to the difference between the approaches of science and history strikes me as trivial. As far as I'm concerned, any science of society worth its name must be a historical science.[11]

A man who did not like restrictions of any kind, Lewis was frustrated and boxed in by the limitations of writing for a social science audience. He resented having to make the choices academic research forced on him. Many alternatives were, he believed, artificially and unnecessarily juxtaposed, when a constructive synthesis would serve better than choosing one option or another. Nevertheless, for the first half of his career he was a traditional academic; he played by the rules, observed the disciplinary boundaries, and spoke the language. Then the popular and critical successes of *Five Families* (1959) and *The Children of Sánchez* (1961), anthropological reporting that employed literary formats, released Lewis from some of the constraints of writing only for academic audiences. He called this new form—which he developed with his wife and collaborator, Ruth Maslow Lewis—"ethnographic realism," and he believed it would provide him the range and license he needed to be scientist and artist, participant and observer, objective and subjective, detached and involved, all the while serving the people he studied as friend and patron, mediator and messenger to the outside world.

In trying to generalize about his research he felt less responsibility to social science qua science than he did to social science as handmaiden to policy. Therefore, he wanted his work to have a practical application; and just as he felt it unfair that he should have to choose between science and art, he did not believe he could engage in pure research only at the expense of applied anthropology. Lewis considered the relationship between theoretical and applied anthropology to be a dynamic one, and he conducted his field research with this in mind. From his Tepoztlán project he concluded that "the combination of research and service programs might be an excellent way of integrating the fields of applied and theoretical anthropology. I realize this may sound heretical to the purists."[12]

To bolster this position Lewis cited Bronislaw Malinowski, one of the most famous and prodigious fieldworkers of the early twentieth century:

> The pose of academic detachment and persistent blindness to the fact that theoretical anthropology can learn quite as much from practical issues as it can teach in return, have considerably handicapped modern developments in the Science of Man. . . . In my opinion there is no doubt that the whole-hearted concern with practical matters will more directly lead the theoretical student into the understanding of the dynamic aspect of culture change than any other avenue of research. What is practically urgent to man, whether it be desirable or detestable, whether inspiring or galling, soon becomes a collective drive, that is, a relevant social force.[13]

Working in the postwar era of rapid political and economic change called for, Lewis wrote, "a re-evaluation of the relationship between the anthropologist and the people he studies, most of whom are desperately poor."[14] Anthropologists, "particularly those active in applied anthropology, must find ways to ease the strains in peasant communities during this period of transition to new social forms."[15]

Lewis went so far as to say that he thought all modern anthropologists were anticolonial and that they identified with the poor of the world. "We believe that all people have a right to be independent. . . ." When asked by the newspaper reporter interviewing him if this was not "almost messianism," Lewis answered: "It might be, but if one does not do his research with love, in an almost religious way, it will be impossible for him to reach people [no se puede llegar al corazón de la gente]. The cold application of the most highly perfected scientific techniques will not yield anything [worthwhile]." [16]

Despite his partially successful attempts to break with them, Lewis still belonged more to that first wave of American anthropologists, with their historicism and qualitative methods of analysis, than he did to the postwar generations. "History," Lévi-Strauss wrote, "organizes its data in relation to conscious expressions of social life, while anthropology proceeds by examining its unconscious foundations." [17] Against this standard Lewis's approach clearly belonged more to history than to anthropology. He was never much interested, for example, in the collective unconscious as expressed in myth and ritual; this was too great an abstraction for him and not sufficiently vulnerable to verification by his own observation and experience. In any case, because Lewis saw the larger part of any society's ideas and values as reflections of material conditions (yes, he was more of a historical materialist than he admitted), he was more interested in understanding the conditions themselves. Even after his Tepoztlán research, when he spent so much time trying to delve into the "inner lives" of his informants, he was intent on explaining them in terms of a cause-and-effect relationship with economic conditions. That is, he was not so much interested in explaining the unconscious motivations for individual or collective behavior as he was in documenting what was, in his view, the psychological damage caused by poverty.

Although Lewis was trained as a historian and regarded anthropology as above all else a historical science, he found historical research, as it was conducted in the 1930s, too little concerned, both in its process and focus, with the individual. [18] Of all the social sciences, except for psychology, anthropology was to him the one most committed to the study of the individual. But from his perspective psychology employed too clinical an approach, regarding the individual as an object of research, leaving too little room for interaction or personal involvement. It was because of his love for working with people and his preference for being in the field rather than in the library that Lewis fit more easily into the company of anthropologists than of historians. Yet it was his love of people and his insatiable fascination with their variety that caused him problems away from the field. He said that in reacting against the absence of people and the overgeneralizations in Robert Redfield's ideal types and Ruth Benedict's cultural configurations he had "developed methods which sought [to identify] the range of phenomena rather than the common core." [19]

But as his career progressed, Lewis became so adept at documenting this variety, so caught up in it, that he rendered himself unable to effectively generalize about a common core. In any case, he said that he did "not like dichotomies or analytical models" and thought that theories and jargon too often reduced people to the mechanical level.[20] But if he disliked the absence of people in the theoretical constructs of Redfield and Benedict, he should have admitted that in his own theorizing people kept getting in the way. When he wrote a statement on a common core among his informants (i.e., the culture of poverty thesis) to introduce his family studies and biographies, he put thesis and antithesis side by side, unsynthesized, unresolved.

The more successful Lewis became, the more defiant he was of the demands made on him by his profession. Perhaps no other social scientist of his generation so fully and dangerously liberated himself as did he in the last years of his career, from definitions, technical jargon, precision of language, and disciplinary boundaries, while still remaining in academic life. But Lewis chose not to leave his university position because he had developed a research habit that could be supported only by the kind of large grants that require the sponsorship of governmental or academic institutions. And, regardless of how well his books sold, he remained essentially a researcher, not a writer.

The professional habits Lewis developed were those of a workaholic; he typically wrote up one project while researching a second or third and planning a fourth. He read widely but not casually; most of what he read had some relationship to his research. Along the way he did not develop much of a sense of humor about himself or his work. But he was utterly devoted to studying the poor, and he believed completely in what he was doing.

NOTES

1. "Oscar Lewis: Los Hijos de la Pobreza," an interview with Lewis by Lorenzo Batallan that appeared in the newspaper *El Nacional* (Caracas, Venezuela) on November 6, 1967 (translated from the Spanish by the author).

2. Oscar Lewis, "The Culture of Poverty," *Scientific American*, October 1966, p. 4.

3. Oscar Lewis, *Anthropological Essays* (New York: Random House, 1970), p. viii.

4. Letter to Fernando Cámara, March 9, 1962 (no. 73 in the Appendix).

5. Letter to Jules Henry, May 7, 1957.

6. Letter to Jules Henry, June 1, 1957.

7. Oscar Lewis, "Controls and Experiments in Anthropological Field Work," in *Anthropology Today*, ed. A. L. Kroeber (Chicago: University of

Chicago Press, 1953), pp. 452–75 (reprinted in Lewis, *Anthropological Essays;* see p. 6). On this Lewis took issue with his teacher Ruth Benedict, who told him shortly before her death that "just as soon as you begin to quantify, you are no longer studying culture" (ibid.).

8. Oscar Lewis, *The Children of Sánchez: Autobiography of a Mexican Family* (New York: Random House, 1961), p. xx.

9. Tape-recorded comments made by Lewis to a symposium at Stephens College in Columbia, Missouri, on January 17, 1968 (he participated via a phone hookup from Urbana, Ill.).

10. Letter to Carlos Fuentes, January 26, 1962 (no. 72 in the Appendix).

11. Lewis, *Anthropological Essays,* p. viii.

12. Oscar Lewis, *Life in a Mexican Village: Tepoztlán Revisited* (Urbana: University of Illinois Press, 1951), p. xv, n14.

13. Quoted in ibid.

14. Oscar Lewis, *Five Families: Mexican Case Studies in the Culture of Poverty* (New York: Basic Books, 1959), p. 2.

15. Lewis, *Anthropological Essays,* p. 254.

16. *El Nacional* interview.

17. Claude Lévi-Strauss, *Structural Anthropology,* vol. 1 (New York: Basic Books, 1963), p. 18.

18. In a letter to James Wilke, on December 23, 1964, Lewis wrote: "I tend to agree with [the] dictum that anthropology shall be history or nothing."

19. Letter to Berenice Hoffman, February 13, 1969.

20. Letter to Jules Henry, May 7, 1957.

CHAPTER ONE

BACKGROUND

There is little doubt that Oscar Lewis's interest in documenting the lives of poor people grew in part out of his own childhood in poverty, his perception of himself as an outsider, and his early exposure to socialist writings.[1] He began life at Manhattan's Jewish Maternity Hospital on December 25, 1914, as Yehezkiel Lefkowitz[2] (his parents also gave him the Anglicized first name Oscar). His father, Chaim Leb Lefkowitz, had come alone from Poland about six years earlier to establish himself and make a home for his wife, Broche Biblowitz Lefkowitz. She and their four children had stayed behind at the small mill owned and operated by the Biblowitz family near the village of Sopotskin (just north of Grodno and now in the Soviet Union). Jews living in this area were subject to recurring pogroms, so Mrs. Lefkowitz and her children were fairly insecure during the five years it took them to make the necessary arrangements to leave for the United States.

In Poland, Mr. Lefkowitz had been a rabbinical student, supported in large part after marriage by his wife's family, who had arranged the union. In the United States he tried to earn a living as a rabbi, presiding over marriages and funerals and teaching Hebrew. He also worked as a sexton at a synagogue on East 13th Street on Manhattan's Lower East Side, just a few blocks from where the family settled. When he developed symptoms of heart disease a doctor recommended that he move to the countryside. Somehow, by the time Oscar was five or six years old, the family had saved or borrowed enough to make a down payment on a small farm near Liberty, New York. While working it as a farm they gradually converted its buildings into a summer boardinghouse and then into a family hotel. Mr. Lefkowitz named it The Balfour, for Lord Balfour and the commission that had recom-

9

mended the creation of a homeland for Jews in Palestine. The business just managed to support the family—although poorly by American standards—and was always in imminent danger of failure.

While Lewis was in school the family lived year-round at The Balfour, but later they spent winters in the city. He grew up, then, in the countryside, hunting, fishing, ice-skating, boxing, doing farm chores, and working in the hotel during the summers. (Lewis said he was once the featherweight boxing champion of Sullivan County.) In biographical notes he left among his personal papers, he described these years as rather unhappy and said he had only vague recollections of them. He was often ill, having suffered from life-threatening attacks of gastroenteritis in early childhood and from typhoid fever at age ten. Lewis had three older sisters (not counting one who had died in infancy in Poland) and a brother, fourteen or fifteen years older, who had enlisted during the First World War and was away from home when Lewis was very young. Lewis remembered his as a lonely childhood; he was much younger than his siblings, and his only playmates were a few Gentile boys on adjacent farms from whom he grew apart as he reached adolescence.

As the son of poor immigrants and a Jew in a Gentile world, Lewis clearly felt like an outsider. In some ways—being U.S.-born, without an accent (although he grew up speaking Yiddish), not formed by an old-world perspective, and not a religious Jew—he became an outsider in his own family. Of the five children he was the scholar, and his father harbored some hope that Lewis would take up religious studies. As he grew older, in the years after his Bar Mitzvah, he had increasing conflict with his father over his shortcomings as an observant Jew, but this was never serious enough to threaten what was a very close relationship.

Lewis received his elementary education in a one-room, white frame schoolhouse in nearby Ferndale. At age twelve he entered Liberty High School and became interested in history and philosophy, particularly in socialism. He was introduced to Marxism through his friendship with a Communist party organizer who, with his family, spent summers near Liberty and occasionally came to work at The Balfour. He shared with Lewis an interest in music and chess, as well as politics, and provided stimulating companionship in a community where people were primarily concerned with farming and the resort industry. With his friend's encouragement Lewis began reading Marx and Lenin.

Education

Bored with his schooling, Lewis hurried through, graduating from high school at age fifteen, "hoping," he wrote in his notes, "to be happier in college." He entered the College of the City of New York (CCNY) in 1930, several months before his sixteenth birthday, the first in his family to attend college. Tuition was free, but with no money for his own apartment, he lived with his married sisters and their families. To earn money for books and supplies, and to give his sisters something toward his board, he worked in the maternity ward of a Brooklyn hospital, as a box boy in a grocery store, and, in the summers, as head waiter at his parents' hotel.

At CCNY, Lewis pursued his political interests through his course work, concentrating on the histories of trade unionism and of black slavery in the United States. The teacher of these courses was the Marxist historian Philip Foner, one of the principal intellectual figures of Lewis's undergraduate years. It was a revelation to Lewis to learn that many African-Americans had revolted against their enslavers, and it was a source of great excitement to discover the potential historical studies held for investigating the lives and contributions of oppressed peoples. His interests were catholic, and he took a wide variety of courses, but none interested him as much as history and philosophy. The latter field he studied with two of the most popular teachers at CCNY in the 1930s—Morris R. Cohen and Abraham Edel.

In 1936 Lewis earned a bachelor's degree in social science, with a concentration in history, and immediately entered Columbia Teachers College to study the teaching of history. There he found a more traditional and conservative department than at CCNY; he soon became discontented and decided to switch fields. On the recommendation of his future brother-in-law, Abraham Maslow, who was then doing postdoctoral research in psychology at Columbia University, Lewis went to the anthropology department to speak with Ruth Benedict.[3] He was drawn immediately to her and to the discipline as she described it, and shortly thereafter he transferred to the anthropology department at Columbia.

Although he studied with Benedict and with Ralph Linton, and he knew others who were or were to become central figures in the new subfield of culture and personality (e.g., Margaret Mead and Jules Henry), Lewis did not develop a strong interest in this area while in graduate school.[4] He was not a student of Freudian thought or criticism, nor a believer in the utility of psychological testing for studying culture. Like Benedict he did not accept the need for anthropologists in this specialization to undergo psychoanalysis or any kind

of therapy. Only four of the twenty-three courses he took in graduate school can be placed firmly within the culture and personality
subfield; two were taught by Benedict (from whom he took a total
of nine courses), one by the social psychologist Otto Klineberg, and
one was the famous culture and personality seminar taught jointly
in 1937–38 by Linton and Abram Kardiner, a psychiatrist from the
New York Psycholanalytic Institute. These seminars had as guest lec-
turers senior anthropologists like Franz Boas and outstanding new
researchers like Cora DuBois.[5] As culture and personality became a
leading research area in anthropology, Lewis tried to rectify his lack
of academic preparation for it by shifting his minor area of focus from
history to psychology and by doing a great deal of independent reading. In this respect he benefited from his friendship with Solomon
Asch, the social psychologist who had been Ruth Maslow's teacher at
Brooklyn College.

In general Lewis's interests in graduate school paralleled those he
had developed in his undergraduate studies; that is, they were centered upon issues of economic stratification and class distinctions, as
well as the relationship between economic conditions and cultural
institutions and processes. In addition to his work with Benedict, Linton, and Kardiner, Lewis studied archaeology with William Duncan
Strong, Native American cultures with Alexander Lesser, technology
and culture with Gene Weltfish, and economic organization and field
techniques with Ruth Bunzel. These people represented not only a
variety of topical specializations but also different approaches to the
study of anthropology. Lewis was not won over to any single concentration or approach, nor was he a disciple of any of his teachers.
Because he wanted to study with both Benedict and Linton, he did not
want to take sides in their so-called feud.[6] Between the two, Lewis
had far greater admiration for Benedict as a person, but he probably
had equal respect for their intellectual abilities.

Benedict was as helpful to Lewis as, by all accounts, she was to
all her students. He was not as personally close to her as were other
students of that era, such as Jules Henry, but he did consult her on all
aspects of his graduate education, as well as about personal and career
matters. The existing letters from Benedict to Ruth and Oscar Lewis
show the concern for personal circumstance, details of research, and
furtherance of career that endeared her to so many students. Benedict
arranged the funding that made possible Lewis's first field trip—to
the Blackfoot reservations in Montana and Alberta—and provided
his transportation as well, letting him and his wife drive her car to
the field site. Later she found a small amount of money to help him
write up part of his field notes for publication. (In the usual manner

of Columbia's anthropology department at the time, the money was transferred to Lewis via a personal check from Benedict.)

One could easily overstate the influence on Lewis of any one of his teachers. He was impressed by the broad sweep of and poetic license in the writings of Benedict, by the importance she placed on kinship studies, and by her great skill in interpreting them. He also admired the work on racism that she did late in her life, because he believed it was important to find a way to express in one's professional life a personal commitment to larger social issues. This set him apart from Benedict, who apparently only reluctantly undertook the work on racism and viewed any active political involvement by her colleagues as detrimental to their research and professional obligations.[7] For all his adulation of Benedict, Lewis was little like her. He was as visceral as she was cerebral; he would become as annoyed by professional duties as she was dedicated to them. For Benedict, field trips seem to have been brief interludes in a career centered on urban universities; she devoted as much time to reflection on the field work of others as on her own and to the active support of Columbia's graduate students. An interest in studying society through the individual came late in her career, and her "passionate detachment," as Mead described it, including her aloofness from the cultures she studied and the people she worked with, were not at all compatible with Lewis's own personality and research orientation.

Ralph Linton's focus on the individual and his reputation as a prodigious fieldworker appealed to Lewis, while William Duncan Strong helped him overcome his bias against archaeology and was at least partly responsible for his lifelong interest in material culture studies. The work of Abram Kardiner, because of its emphasis on personality and the dynamics of family life—especially the study of family neuroses—made an important contribution to the development of Lewis's later focus on the family and individual personality.

Lewis claimed—although this is the kind of statement most of us are likely to make about our graduate education—that he really learned anthropology from a group of faculty and graduate students who met for lunch at a restaurant on Amsterdam Avenue, near the Columbia campus. The group varied in composition, but during the years Lewis attended it included (according to Ruth Lewis and Zunia Henry) faculty members Al Lesser and Gene Weltfish and fellow graduate students Morris Siegel, Jack Harris, Joe Bram, Natalie Joffee, Irving Goldman, and Jules Henry. From this group Lewis made some of his closest collegial friendships, including Goldman and also Jules Henry, with whom Lewis later worked at Washington University.[8]

Lewis's research experience during this period was largely confined to library studies that were historical in approach. His only field experience was the trip to the Blackfoot reservations during the summer of 1939. The expedition was organized and led by Benedict and included a group of her students and some of their spouses, none of whom had had any prior field experience.[9] The trip was not designed just as a training exercise, however; Benedict wanted to build on prior work done with the Blackfoot by Clark Wissler (the Southern Piegan) and by Lucien (June) Hanks and Jane Richardson (the Northern Blackfoot).[10] As Lewis described it, Benedict designed the project "to test the effect of differences in government administration and policy upon a people of a common cultural background."[11] The students were divided into four groups and assigned to work on the reservations of four different tribes. Oscar and Ruth Lewis were sent to Brocton, a reservation of the Northern Piegan, and there set up their army cots and established residence in an abandoned house.

Because the students were scattered across a wide territory from Montana to Alberta, they came together for group instruction only a few times during their four-month stay. Benedict traveled between sites but the Lewises saw little of her. As a student of Boas she was a great believer in the need for primary research, but neither she nor Boas offered their students very concrete guidance in how to design and carry out a field project.[12] The students were left on their own to organize and direct their individual studies of the four reservations, and there was not much coordination of research at the various sites.

The following year, 1940, Benedict did organize a project to produce a monograph on the Blackfoot tribes that would integrate the 1939 research with that done earlier by Richardson and Hanks. Lewis was to have written an introduction providing historical background and a chapter on the Northern Piegan. But the various collaborators ended up publishing their work separately, with Lewis producing one article (see below) and using the historical research as the basis of his doctoral thesis: "The Effects of White Contact upon Blackfoot Culture, with Special Reference to the Role of the Fur Trade." Because of the importance Boas and Benedict attached to basing dissertations on original field studies, Lewis had trouble finding a thesis advisor. He maintained that Benedict herself, who was on sabbatical in California the year he was writing, was not interested in his choice of topic. But she did ask him to send her drafts of the thesis and also arranged for financial support from the Buell Quain Fund.

When completed, the thesis was good enough to be selected for publication in a competition sponsored by the American Ethnological Society.[13] It remains—ironically, because it was based on analysis of secondary materials and Lewis became famous for his field technique—one of his more well regarded works. In it Lewis analyzed the impact of contact with European fur traders on Blackfoot culture, approach to war, and development of their social and economic institutions. It contained his first discussion of intracommunity wealth differences and opportunities for vertical mobility, an issue he was to examine in some way in every succeeding project he undertook.

Politics and Religion

Just as it would be easy to overstate the influence of any one of his teachers on Lewis's work, so could one make too much of the impact of the Great Depression on his political beliefs or academic interests. Because he was so poor prior to this period, the depression did not appreciably change his economic position for the worse; in fact, Lewis was able to work his way through undergraduate and graduate school during its peak years. But his introduction to Marxism did coincide with the depression, and the conditions it produced in the United States probably reinforced his belief in the need for socialist solutions to the problems of unemployment and inequitable distribution of wealth. His political activities, with the exception of general support for trade unionism, were focused more on foreign than domestic policy. He joined the League Against War and Fascism and participated in related activities: raising funds for the Republican side in the Spanish Civil War, boycotting Japanese products in protest of the invasion of China, and supporting an Allied pact with the Soviet Union to fight a two-front war against Germany. As a Jew, Lewis had a personal stake in stopping the rise of nazism-fascism, but at that period in his life it is possible that he was also motivated by the threat presented to international socialism and to the Soviet Union itself. It is difficult to sort out the association between his Jewish identity and his leftist allegiances, but like many on the left in the 1930s Lewis saw an alliance with Russia as the best hope for stopping Hitler and Franco.

The rise of Hitler and the subsequent Holocaust were, I believe, more significant in their impact on Lewis's political thinking than was the depression. (Fifty-five of his known relatives perished in the Holocaust.) He had an abiding fear of anti-Semitism that, while it appears not to have had a profound effect on his style or behavior, was sufficient to make him wary and put him on guard in certain situations. When he entered Columbia University he began using Lewis—the name taken by relatives who had settled in England—as a surname, and in 1940, the year of his graduation, he legally changed his name from Lefkowitz (the only one in his immediate family to do so).

Later, when he was in the field, Lewis avoided the subject of his religion and ethnicity whenever he thought it might impede his ability to establish rapport with his informants. In fact he seems to have faced this problem rarely, since most of his informants were not particularly interested in his religion after finding out that he was neither a Roman Catholic nor an *evangelista* who had come to convert them. It did matter to some reporters, however, and after Lewis became well known in Mexico they found convoluted ways to work into their articles the fact that he and his wife were Jews.[14]

In the United States, while he may have been on guard with certain individuals, he certainly did not disguise his Jewishness; he sang at temple services and at Jewish Federation fund-raisers and had a repertoire of Yiddish folk songs that he frequently sang in public or at social gatherings. He had enormous feeling for his tradition, but he simply had no religion. Lewis rebelled against orthodoxy, not because he rejected Judaism or his ethnic tradition, but because of a generalized distaste for anything he believed constricted his thought or movement. Until the last decade of his life he tended to be far less open about his politics than about his ethnicity, never more so than during the McCarthy era, when the atmosphere at his own university and in the country at large made him decidedly edgy.

Lewis's affiliation with leftist groups at CCNY and Columbia, and his occasional participation in their activities, could not have taken much of his time because he had a heavy academic program and held part-time jobs. Nevertheless, these were the years when he was most politically active. A radical in his beliefs but not in his actions, he tried to find expression for his political values in his work. After graduate school—during the war and immediately afterward—he worked for the U.S. government, which (under the Hatch Act) prohibits its employees from partisan political activities. Once he began his academic and field career, Lewis devoted himself completely to that work, leaving little time for political activity or any other kind of outside interest. The one exception was his lifelong study of operatic voice; wherever he stayed for longer than a month, he took lessons and either rented a piano or hired an accompanist.

Throughout his life Lewis remained a socialist by orientation and outlook, but he was not a joiner and he had neither the intellectual makeup nor the particular kind of discipline (or subservience) that it takes to sustain dogma. His political conceptions were not very complex or well thought-out, and for that reason, I think, he never had to undergo much revision in his political thinking. He did not use socialism to chart his course, only to specify its general direction, and this he never changed.

Chaim Leb Lefkowitz and his son Oscar, circa 1922. All photographs used courtesy of Ruth M. Lewis.

Oscar Lewis on his first field trip, June 1939, at a roadside stop somewhere between Montana and the Brocton Reservation in Alberta, Canada. (Photograph by Ruth Lewis)

Marriage

In its meaning for his later career, the most significant event of Lewis's graduate school years was his marriage in November 1937. During his first year at Columbia, Lewis got a job on a WPA project investigating the contributions of African cultures and traditions to U.S. culture. The twenty-five dollar weekly salary made it possible for Lewis to marry Ruth Maslow, whom he had met at a party five years earlier when he was seventeen and she was sixteen.[15] Maslow, who had just graduated from Brooklyn College, put aside her plans for graduate study in psychology and switched to a field that offered a better opportunity for employment. She took a master's degree in special education at Columbia Teachers College and spent the years 1938–40, when Lewis was completing his Ph.D., teaching physically and mentally handicapped children, first at Philadelphia's Overbrook School for the Blind and later at Harlem's P.S. 96.

It was during a summer vacation from teaching that Ruth Lewis accompanied her husband to the Brocton Reservation. She located the informant, Widow Grassy Water, who told her of the "manly-hearted" women among the Northern Piegan. Both Lewises worked on the subsequent interviewing, organization, and write-up of field notes that resulted in Oscar Lewis's first publication. It marked the beginning of a thirty-year collaboration.[16] Although Ruth Lewis's role changed somewhat from one project to another, she participated in all of the subsequent research, except for that in India, where neither of the Lewises knew the local language.

Oscar Lewis was convinced of the importance of husband-wife field teams, particularly for family studies. He believed that having his own family with him in the field put potential informants at ease, decreased suspiciousness, and thereby helped to develop rapport. In addition, he believed it was good to have both male and female interviewers to compensate, when necessary, for one another's inability to develop a working relationship with informants of the opposite sex. He wrote that if the two had different backgrounds, training, and values, perhaps they could provide complementary interpretations of the data as well.[17]

No one could review Oscar Lewis's field papers without noting that Ruth Lewis left some mark on most of the work her husband published. Although Lewis rarely wrote a research proposal without explicitly assigning work to his wife, he usually did not request an official position or salary for her. In 1944, however, Ruth Lewis did serve as assistant coordinator of the Tepoztlán project and twenty years later as assistant director of the Puerto Rican project. She held a similar position for the Cuban research and succeeded her husband as project director after his death. There were only a few years, near the beginning and at the end of their collaboration, when she drew even a token salary.

Lewis usually identified his wife as his "major collaborator," but during his lifetime he submitted for publication only one book-length manuscript and published just one article under joint authorship with her. Ruth Lewis has said that she always took it for granted that they would have only one career between them, and in the context of the times that was not unusual. It is difficult to make a definitive statement about her influence because in many ways she and her husband worked and thought alike, and the original drafts of some early manuscripts were written in both hands. In general, Lewis was the initiator, implementor, and driving force behind the fieldwork, and he was the main interpreter of it. Ruth Lewis helped develop their family study method and was an important fieldworker in Tepoztlán, Mexico City, Spain, and Cuba, but not in Puerto Rico or India. She also helped to coordinate the work of the large field staffs in Tepoztlán, Mexico City, and Cuba. While Oscar Lewis was the key figure in the conduct of the fieldwork, Ruth Lewis played a greater creative role than he did in the preparation of the raw field materials for publication. (By comparison, her editing of her husband's scholarly articles did not have a great impact on their content.) Her contributions to *The Children of Sánchez, Five Families,* and *La Vida* perhaps, but to *Pedro Martínez* for certain, entitled her to joint authorship had she wanted to claim it. (Note that the shifting reference in the text from "Lewis" to "the Lewises" is intentional and indicates the differences in their roles, as discussed above.)

Early Work History

When Lewis finished graduate school in 1940, the country was still recovering from the depression. Jobs, especially academic positions, were scarce. Most colleges and universities had not established independent anthropology departments; if they recruited anthropologists at all, it was to supplement existing sociology faculties. Lewis does not seem to have had very well defined career goals or research plans, but he was hoping to find a job that would permit him to do fieldwork among the rural or urban poor. However, he spent his first year after graduation preparing his dissertation for publication, driving a taxi, and teaching night school at Brooklyn College. That year Ruth Lewis quit teaching to have their first child, and Oscar, having completed his monograph on the Blackfoot, began to look for a permanent position.

By this time the United States had entered the Second World War and jobs were opening up everywhere. Because he fit into the War Manpower Commission's "pre–Pearl Harbor father" classification (i.e., he had become a father before December 7, 1941), he was not in danger of being drafted during the early years following American entry into the war. In 1942 Lewis accepted a position with the Strategic Index for Latin America (SILA), a subdivision of the Human Relations Area Files at Yale University. (He also taught rural sociology at nearby Connecticut State College.) He had been recommended to its director, George Murdock, by Ralph Linton, who at the same time suggested to Lewis that he enroll in an intensive Spanish-language training program. With Linton's assistance Lewis got a grant from the American Council of Learned Societies to spend the summer of 1942 in Philadelphia, studying at a government-run language school for servicemen and diplomats. With this training and the following year's work with the SILA, Lewis was able to develop an area specialization in Latin America. (In graduate school he had taken only two courses on this region, one in archaeology and one in ethnology.) He spent his first three months in New Haven translating material from Spanish and German and doing bibliographic research. Then he was promoted to the position of field supervisor and given the responsibility for "organizing interviews with Latin American experts, travelling to make contacts with Latin Americans in this country, including members of various South American embassies and legations, analyzing and organizing information obtained from interviews, . . . organizing and preparing reports from government agencies, and similar activities."[18]

Lewis's experience with the SILA led to two government appointments involving research on Latin America. For seven months in 1943 he worked in the Organization and Propaganda Analysis Section of the Justice Department's Special War Policies Unit. This is how he described what his assignment would be:

> . . . I would analyze the activities and ideologies of various organizations in this country of Spanish and Latin American origin to determine whether they are a danger to the internal security of the United States. . . . I would be asked to write up recommendations for action on specific cases. For example, I might be asked by the Post Office Censorship Division to [give] an opinion on the nature of a Spanish magazine that was being sent through the mails. . . . I was told that they would put me in charge of their files on Falangist organizations so that I would soon become an expert on the Falangist movement. . . . I would be doing work of

interest which would be directly part of the war effort, and with tie ups
with the Latin American field, Mexico, and Puerto Rico, in particular.[19]

In August 1943 Lewis was named field representative for Latin
America for the National Indian Institute, Department of the Interior.
In this position he acted as a liaison between the U.S. Office of Indian Affairs and other members of the Interamerican Indian Institute,
interpreted "U.S. government policy on Indian affairs to interested
Mexican government agencies," and prepared "studies of existing
government services being rendered to Indians."[20] Lewis was also
assigned to coordinate a research project under the sponsorship of
the Interamerican Indian Institute, headquartered in Mexico City, to
study "the effects of government administration policies upon the
democratic sentiment and personality of the Mexican Indian."[21] While
fulfilling these duties he developed his first major field project, a study
of the village of Tepoztlán (discussed in chapter 2).

Lewis was little interested at the time in the personality research he
was assigned to undertake; he wanted the opportunity to work in a
Latin American country and to develop a field project of his own. He
was interested, however, in research that might have a chance to influence government policy. In fact, early in his career he seemed to have
almost as much interest in working in some area of applied anthropology as in finding an academic appointment. In 1941 he became
a charter member of the Society for Applied Anthropology and was
still optimistic that detailed culture studies would reach, and have an
impact on, high-level policymakers.

In the fall of 1944, after completing the Mexican assignment for the
Office of Indian Affairs, Lewis unsuccessfully sought an academic appointment. The government apparently was considering transferring
him from the Interior Department to the State Department to work as
a cultural attache in South America, but it could not do so because
he was potentially draftable.[22] Instead, Lewis was transferred to the
Department of Agriculture, where he accepted a position as social
scientist in the Bureau of Agricultural Economics (BAE). As part of a
reevaluation of certain federal farm policies, and of the rural county
agent system in particular, Lewis was assigned to review work being
sponsored by the BAE in rural communities across the country. During the early months of 1945 he traveled by train, bus, and pick-up
truck, first through the rural counties of Texas and Mississippi and
then through the wheat-farming counties of the Northwest and the
lower plains states, ending up in Emporia, Kansas, just as the war in
Europe came to an end.

In the course of these travels Lewis attended many Farm Bureau and Grange meetings as well as community social events such as dances and "pie parties." This was an area of the country little known to him, and he was surprised to find, in Iowa and Kansas, people reading Thomas Mann and farmers who were well informed about the war and who talked as if Washington were a nearby city. He had not expected to be able to communicate so easily with people of whom he knew so little and for whom at some level he held a certain degree of suspicion (as they probably did for all outsiders). As he interviewed dozens of farmers he discovered a truth about his work preferences that presaged some of the problems to come: ". . . if I can get hold of myself, I'll get started organizing my data. You see, it's rather easy and pleasant for me to work with people. I just never run out of questions. . . . I amaze myself sometimes on that score. But getting to work on my notes is a very different matter."[23]

Lewis wrote up his field notes in the form of letters home, but the observations have no great depth because he covered an enormous amount of territory and spent only a few days in each place. They do, however, reveal his intrinsically comparative approach, as he described every place he visited in relation to where he had just been, comparing the working conditions, attitudes, and dress of white and black, Mexican and Native American farm laborers, as well as farming methods, and wealth, religious, ethnic, and political differences from county to county and from North to South.[24]

In early 1946, when the reconnaissance phase of the study was complete, Lewis chose Bell County, Texas, one of the first places he had visited, for intensive study, and he and his family moved to Belton for several months of fieldwork. Out of this came Lewis's second monograph, *On the Edge of the Black Waxy: A Cultural Survey of Bell County, Texas.*

As he was completing the Bell County study, Lewis was notified by the BAE that he had to be released by order of the Civil Service Commission; all junior people were being dismissed to make room for servicemen returning to their old positions. Although he did not like being let go while his research was in progress, he was very happy with his experience at the BAE. He had great respect for the work of rural sociologists (if not for all the county agents he worked with) and had developed a very good working relationship with his supervisor, Carl C. Taylor, with whom he maintained a correspondence for many years.

In the fall of 1946 Lewis accepted his first full-time academic position as an associate professor in the Department of Sociology and Anthropology at Washington University in St. Louis. He stayed there only two years before accepting a similar position at the University of Illinois at

Urbana-Champaign. Having established himself in an academic post, Lewis only once more accepted work in applied anthropology—in 1952, when he heard that the Ford Foundation needed a consultant on its rural development projects in India. While he knew little of that country, its languages or cultures, the demands of the position—supervising fieldworkers and reviewing field projects—were similar to those he had undertaken for the BAE. Furthermore, Douglas Ensminger, the director of Ford's India projects, was a former BAE employee and a friend of Carl Taylor, who recommended Lewis for the position.

Thus, in 1952, with a committment to stay for two years, the Lewises left for India, by ship via England, with their son and daughter. Once there, Lewis was "to help develop a scheme for objective evaluation of the rural reconstruction program which was going on in fifty-five pilot community projects."[25] In carrying out these duties, Lewis said he tried to impress upon the evaluation officers "the relevancy of the intimate understanding of village life and organization to the design of rural development projects."[26] As an example of how to do this, he organized, with a grant he had received from Ford for independent research, a study of a village near Delhi. (The study itself was apart from and in addition to his official duties.) It was not intended to be the kind of community study he had done in Tepoztlán; rather, the investigation was to concentrate on those aspects of village life that Lewis thought were most relevant to agricultural development planning: land tenure, social and political relationships within the village, and local decision making, for example. His range of inquiry was also restricted because he did not know the local language. The project was carried out with the assistance of a group of Indian students in anthropology, psychology, and social work from the University of Delhi.

Lewis used the project to write a guide for Ford staff on how to undertake community studies. From the beginning of his stay in India he had trouble with some members of the staff over the relevance of anthropological research to the planning and evaluation of Ford-funded projects. In a personal evaluation (unpublished notes) of his work for Ford, Lewis wrote that he was assigned to work with a man who insisted that they limit their research "to the development of methodology. I was just as insistent that we needed to learn more about the nature of village social organization, value systems, needs, etc., and that only by getting to study the content could we develop better methods of study. This difference in approach continued to the end." When Lewis completed his study of village factionalism, he could not get Ford's permission to publish it. However, he had already submitted the article and it was subsequently published without permission. This angered Douglas Ensminger, who seemed to regard Lewis as a rather undisciplined subordinate.[27]

A large part of Lewis's problems on Ford's India project stemmed from a clash of personalities and working styles. Lewis was highly independent and not well socialized into the mores of the Ford staff. Given his basic self-definition as a permanent outsider, he never was able to feel like one of "the boys"—as Ensminger called his staff— perhaps never less so than when he worked for Ford in India. Both of the Lewises were somewhat uncomfortable with the rather grand style in which they lived as Ford employees, and most of the friendships they made were with the Indian students who worked in the village or with Delhi University faculty rather than with Ford staff. Near the end of his first year of traveling around India visiting sites of Ford-sponsored projects, Lewis became very ill and, in reaction to medication prescribed to control his illness, developed intestinal sprue. He was hospitalized first in Rome and then in New York City. He did not return to India but spent the second year of his appointment working in the foundation's New York headquarters. Summing up the Ford experience in his notes Lewis wrote: "One of the objectives of the evaluation program was to study the effects of the program on the culture of the people. To do this one had to have some understanding of the culture. For months I did what I could to emphasize that we must do more than count manure pits in the evaluation program. I trust this emphasis had some beneficial effects."

Lewis's association with Ford, if not always a happy one, was a very valuable one. His writing on factionalism and group dynamics in the village of Rampur holds up very well and is quite unlike anything he was to do later. The experience helped him to understand that, despite his interest in policy-related research, he could work more effectively as an academic than as a government or foundation employee. Lewis was not an organization man; he could not function at his best as a subordinate and had no natural gift for accommodation.

In 1954 he returned to his position at the University of Illinois. This was to be his academic base for the remainder of his career, although for at least nine of his twenty-two years there he was on full leave doing fieldwork. Lewis estimated in 1970 that he had spent twelve of his thirty years in anthropology in the field.[28] He and his wife spent their lives living out of boxes, moving more than thirty times during their first fifteen years of marriage. They did not own a house until after nearly twenty years of marriage, and even then they were not often in it. For a stay of any duration, the entire family moved to the field site.

Not quite comfortable in the Midwest, Lewis still hoped in the 1950s to leave Illinois for the East Coast. Over the years, however, the university was generous in supporting his research, awarding supplemental grants, released teaching time, and full leaves. During the last decade of his career, when he did not have much interest in teaching, except for on-site instruction in field methods, this freedom to come and go from the field was very important. Lewis developed a certain loyalty to the institution for its support of his work, and he also realized that another school might not allow him an equal amount of independence. Later, when he could have moved, the only offer he seriously considered was from New York University, but at the last minute he decided to stay at Illinois.

Although he spent the remainder of his career in a university post, Lewis was never socially comfortable in the academic milieu nor in middle-class Gentile society in general. The vicious and arbitrary anti-leftism of the McCarthy era compounded his fear of anti-Semitism so that he came to speak frankly to almost no one outside his family. An ambitious man, Lewis tried to blend in by changing his name and suppressing Yiddish-influenced syntax and a New York accent to the point that his public speaking voice came to sound constrained and affected. In Lewis's not unrealistic view, these attempts at assimilation permitted him to work and travel more freely, as just one more middle-class North American professor. His insecurity and social discomfort help to explain why he was happier in the field than in the classroom and also to account for part of the reputation he developed as a difficult and conflictive personality.

NOTES

1. The sources for this chapter include biographical notes written by Lewis, his personal records and documents, including resumes, and information provided by Ruth Lewis, some of which was given to her by Lewis's eldest sister, Mrs. Anna Goldsmith.

2. Lewis's birth certificate records his name as "Clara Lefkowitz"; no one in the family knows why, since he was never called this and it is clearly a girl's name. The guess is that the Lefkowitzes intended to name him Charles and the recordkeeper could not understand their broken English.

3. At the time Maslow was interested in culture and personality studies and was in contact with Benedict, Mead, and others at Columbia. He wrote at least one article on this topic, called "Personality and Patterns of Culture," in Ross Stagner, *Psychology of Personality* (New York: McGraw-Hill, 1937),

pp. 408–28. The recommendation of Benedict to Lewis is the only influence I know of that Maslow had on Lewis's work; neither Lewis nor Maslow had any particular interest in the other's work.

4. Benedict published her classic *Patterns of Culture* in 1934. The culture and personality subfield was still very new, having been launched by Edward Sapir and John Dollard at Yale in the early 1930s. A review of the major research and publications in the field can be found in Weston La Barre, "The Influence of Freud on Anthropology," in *American Imago* 15 (1958): 275–328.

5. Lewis never studied with Boas, who retired from the department chairmanship and regular teaching the year Lewis entered graduate school.

6. The "feud" had its origins in the choice of a new department chair to replace the retiring Boas. Benedict was apparantly the choice of Boas and a number of others in the department, but the Graduate College brought in Ralph Linton from the University of Wisconsin. Benedict and Linton had different approaches to the study of anthropology, as well as incompatible personalities. This period has been discussed by Margaret Mead in *An Anthropologist at Work: Writings of Ruth Benedict* (New York: Atherton, 1959) and *Blackberry Winter: My Earlier Years* (New York: William Morrow, 1972) and by Adelin Linton and Charles Wagley in *Ralph Linton* (New York: Columbia University Press, 1971).

7. See Mead, *Anthropologist at Work*, pp. 348–50, for a discussion of Benedict's attitude toward political involvement; see also Esther S. Goldfrank, *Notes on an Undirected Life: As One Anthropologist Tells It* (Flushing, N.Y.: Queens College Press, 1978), pp. 123–24. Ruth Benedict's principal work in this area was *Race: Science and Politics* (New York: Modern Age Books, 1940) and a condensed version (written with Gene Weltfish) called *Races of Mankind* (Public Affairs Pamphlet, No. 85; New York: Public Affairs Committee, 1943).

8. Lewis helped recruit Henry for a position at Washington University. They were not only colleagues but neighbors as well, living in an apartment complex where other residents included the playwright William Inge, German émigré artist Max Beckmann and his wife Matilde, and the biologist (later environmental activist and presidential candidate) Barry Commoner and his family. All of the men were on the faculty of Washington University.

9. Others on the trip were Gitel Poznanski and her husband, Robert Goldfield (later Steed); Rae Wolowitz and her husband, Max Geltman; Harry Biele; Marjorie Lismer; and Esther Schiff Goldfrank, who wrote about her experiences on the Blood Reservation (in *Notes on an Undirected Life*, pp. 127–50). Like Ruth Lewis, Goldfield, Geltman, and Goldfrank were not students.

10. When Hanks and Richardson went to study the Northern Blackfoot in the summer of 1938, Ruth Lewis's brother, Abe Maslow, went with them to do research of his own. According to Ruth Benedict (as told to Ruth and Oscar Lewis and others on the 1939 trip), Maslow had created problems by asking the Blackfoot questions about "intercourse." It is not clear whether the objections originated with the Blackfoot or with the government agent on their reservation. Benedict said that in negotiating the arrangements for the 1939 fieldwork, she had smoothed things over by explaining to the agent that

Maslow had probably been asking about verbal interchange rather than about sexual relationships.

11. Lewis, *Anthropological Essays*, pp. 21–22.

12. See Margaret Mead on this subject; she has written that before going to Samoa, "I had a half-hour's instruction" from Boas (in *Blackberry Winter*, pp. 137–38). She also wrote that Benedict had little patience with her suggestions that students be better prepared for the field (in *Ruth Benedict* [New York: Columbia University Press, 1974], p. 34).

13. Oscar Lewis, *The Effects of White Contact upon Blackfoot Culture, with Special Reference to the Fur Trade* (Monographs of the American Ethnological Society, No. 6; Seattle: University of Washington Press, 1942).

14. An example of how this was done would be a reporter pointing out, when referring to Lewis's wife and daughter, that Ruth and Judith were "Jewish" names.

15. Ruth Maslow, the fifth of seven children, was also the child of immigrants, her parents having come from Kiev, several hundred miles from the Grodno region the Lefkowitzes left. Like her husband she was born in Jewish Maternity Hospital and began life on Manhattan's Lower East Side, although she grew up in Brooklyn.

16. Oscar Lewis, "Manly-Hearted Women among the Northern Piegan," *American Anthropologist* 3 (1941): 173–87 (reprinted in Lewis, *Anthropological Essays*, pp. 213–28).

17. Oscar Lewis, "Controls and Experiments in Field Work," p. 458 (reprinted in Lewis, *Anthropological Essays*, pp. 11–12).

18. Resumé prepared by Lewis in 1946.

19. Letter to Ruth Lewis from Washington, D.C., n.d. (February or March 1943).

20. Resumé prepared by Lewis in 1946.

21. Oscar Lewis, "The Tepoztlán Project: Report on Administration and Field Problems" (prepared for the National Indian Institute, U.S. Department of the Interior, 1944), p. 1.

22. Letter to Ruth Lewis from Washington, D.C., n.d. (August or September 1944).

23. Letter to Ruth Lewis from Pasco, Wash., May 23, 1945.

24. Lewis published two articles from his field notes: "Bumper Crops in the Desert," *Harper's Magazine*, December 1946, pp. 525–28; and "Rural Cross Section," *Scientific Monthly*, April 1948, pp. 327–34. Both are reprinted in Lewis, *Anthropological Essays*, pp. 231–48.

25. Oscar Lewis, *Village Life in Northern India* (Urbana: University of Illinois Press, 1958), p. viii.

26. Ibid.

27. The differences between Ensminger and Lewis are detailed in their correspondence, much of which can be found in the Oscar Lewis Papers.

28. Letter to Berenice Hoffman, February 13, 1969. Hoffman, now a literary agent, was at the time of the letter an editor at Random House and had worked on *La Vida*.

CHAPTER TWO

TEPOZTLÁN:
FINDING A METHOD

Lewis's first opportunity to organize a large-scale field investigation came when he was sent to Mexico as U.S. representative to the Interamerican Indian Institute.[1] In making this appointment, John Collier, U.S. commissioner of Indian Affairs, was looking for someone who, according to Lewis, could "organize and get underway a study of Indian personality and education which will . . . parallel the study . . . carried out in the States. . . ."[2] The U.S. project on Indian personality was undertaken jointly by the Office of Indian Affairs and the University of Chicago's Committee on Human Development and was sponsored by the National Indian Institute.[3] By 1942 investigations were underway in twelve communities on five Indian reservations in the United States. The coordinator of this research was Laura Thompson, an anthropologist affiliated with the Committee on Human Development; she was also married to John Collier.

The purpose of the Indian Personality Project, as stated in the research design, was "to determine the degree to which the personality of the Indian child is able to develop fully, and the factors in the physical and social environment, including the influences of governmental programs, which affect this development."[4] Fundamental to the inquiry was the administration of a battery of psychological tests that had been assembled by Thompson and her collaborators. Therefore, to carry out the work in Mexico, Collier and Thompson were looking for specialists in culture and personality research. They decided on the husband-wife team of Benjamin and Lois Paul, but before arrangements could be finalized, Ben Paul was drafted.[5] When the offer was made to Oscar Lewis, who had worked under Paul on the SILA Index

27

in New Haven, it was with the understanding that he and his wife also could work as a team in the field investigation. Lewis had none of the necessary training for psychological testing and evaluation, but his wife had taken every psychology course Brooklyn College had offered when she was an undergraduate. She therefore was to handle the psychological aspects of the research, while her husband was to serve as project coordinator. Ruth Lewis began preparing for this role before leaving New York City by taking instruction in the administration of Rorshach tests from a student of Bruno Klopfer, a friend of Ruth Benedict and the author of one of the most widely used texts on Rorshach testing.[6]

En route to Mexico by car with their son, Gene, the Lewises stopped over at the University of Chicago to receive additional training and instructions from Collier, Thompson, and other members of the Committee on Human Development. They were given cursory instruction in the administration of the Thematic Apperception Test (TAT) by William Henry, an associate of Henry Murray, who had developed the TAT. (Henry analyzed the TATs administered to Hopi children as part of the U.S. side of the project.) Ruth Lewis was also given training in the other tests she would have to administer in Mexico. Meanwhile, she and her husband took advantage of being at the University of Chicago to meet with Robert Redfield and discuss his research and writing on Mexican culture.

Arriving in Mexico in October 1943, the Lewises settled in Mexico City, where Oscar assumed his administrative and editorial duties with the Interamerican Indian Institute. The field investigation he was to organize would be carried out with the cooperation and sponsorship of the Institute and its director, the distinguished Mexican archaeologist Manuel Gamio. By the end of October the Lewises, with the help of Gamio and Julio de la Fuente, an anthropologist who had worked with Bronislaw Malinowski in Oaxaca, were busy scouting research sites for the personality study. Thompson's provisional plan called for the research to be conducted simultaneously at as many as four sites, with a coordinator directing and tying together the work at all locations. A number of towns and villages were considered, including Teotihuacan, which had been studied earlier by Gamio. De la Fuente, who was about to leave for the University of Chicago to study with Sol Tax and Robert Redfield, suggested that Lewis choose Tepoztlán, where Redfield had worked in 1926. He accompanied the Lewises on their first trip to the village, and from there the three traveled by horseback to the outlying villages of the *municipio* (also named Tepoztlán).

Tepoztlán, the *cabacera*, or seat of *municipio* government, and the largest of the villages, was chosen as the place to begin the research because it met all of the project's criteria: it had a Spanish-speaking Indian population; it had been the subject of a major ethnographic study by Redfield on which the project could build;[7] and it was in the radius of a Mexican government health center. The latter condition was essential for getting doctors from the Department of Health and Welfare to participate in the research. In addition, Tepoztlán was not far from Mexico City, where Lewis's other duties with the Institute kept him much of the time. To provide comparison, Lewis selected the outlying village of Ocotitlán, one of the smallest and poorest in the *municipio*. He also decided, due to the shortage of qualified personnel, to study the villages in succession rather than to have two investigations underway simultaneously. In this way he could serve not as project coordinator but as the principal investigator at each site.

Before Lewis was ever hired by the National Indian Institute there had been an understanding between Thompson, Collier, and their Mexican colleagues that various agencies of the Mexican government and the National School of Anthropology and History would contribute personnel to the project. It was Lewis's job to collect on this promise by visiting the relevant agencies and recruiting the appropriate people and arranging their work schedules. As project director he also had to plan and direct the work they would do in the village.

By December, Lewis was planning to field a staff of twenty (including himself and his wife), fifteen of whom eventually did work in the village. All but two of them, Ruth Lewis and Alejandro Marroquín, a Salvadoran lawyer living in exile in Mexico, were provided through government auspices.[8] From the Department of Health and Welfare, Lewis was able to recruit two social workers and two doctors to examine project informants and help establish a clinic; from the Department of Agriculture, agronomists to help map out the village, study cultivation patterns, and give expert advice on agricultural problems; from the National School of Anthropology and History, four graduate students to assist in the fieldwork; and from the Department of Indian Affairs, an additional fieldworker and the artist and illustrator Alberto Beltrán. In all, Lewis received personnel and research assistance from at least eight different agencies. Matching the skills of these individuals with the needs of the research, training the students (most of whom had no background in cultural anthropology), laying out and reviewing their weekly assignments, juggling their work schedules and resolving the administrative problems entailed in "borrowing" them from the government, all consumed much of Lewis's time throughout the first seven months of work in the village.

Before the fieldwork was ever underway, Lewis knew that the

project he was shaping was going to be quite different from Redfield's research and also "much more than a personality study."[9] When it became clear that he would be able to recruit a sizable field staff from government agencies (and at virtually no cost to the project), and that he would actually be planning and directing their work in the field, he saw that he could put together a major ethnographic study of the village. In this way he could design an independent project that would allow him to work in areas much closer to his research interests than did the personality study, which in any case was put under Ruth Lewis's supervision.

The research got underway in December 1943 when Ruth Lewis moved with their son to the village. She began instructing her assistants in the administration of the personality tests and supervised the work of the field staff. Her husband remained in the city during the week, living in a fifth-floor walk-up they had rented from the Mexican anthropologist Alfonso Villa Rojas. On weekends Lewis drove to the village to train his student assistants and supervise the collection of basic demographic and economic data. This is how he described his daily routine for the first months of the project:

> I arrive at the office at nine to pick up the mail and make necessary phone calls. I then leave for some government office, either to arrange for getting personnel or to do research. I'm back at the office by eleven or twelve to talk over matters with Gamio. . . . In the afternoon I answer necessary correspondence, see various visitors on business concerned with the project, etc., and do translating for the bulletin [El Boletín Indigenista, a publication of the Institute] when that is necessary. Otherwise I do research for the project in government offices until closing time by 4 p.m. For the past month I have been spending my evenings organizing the material obtained from this research work. I leave for Tepoztlán late Friday afternoon. Saturday and all day Sunday is spent reviewing the work of each of the workers, writing new instructions, etc. . . .
>
> I have found that there is very useful material on Tepoztlán scattered in government archives. The first job is to locate [it]. . . . The data . . . gives me excellent leads for directing the research in the field. Furthermore I am learning a lot about the nature and quantity of government services rendered in Tepoztlán. Most of the material has come from the files of Agrario, and Forestry. There is still Salubridad, Gobernacion, Hacienda and Ganaderia to do. This data will make it much easier for me to write up the section on government administration.
>
> I have also been working in the archives of Cuernavaca where I have gotten data on income derived from Tepoztlán by the State of Morelos in taxes for the last fifteen years and the amount spent by the state during each of these years. The story is one of unashamed exploitation.[10]

Gene, Oscar, and Ruth Lewis enroute to Tepoztlán, October 1943. (Photograph by Esther Goldsmith)

The main street leading to the plaza in Tepoztlán, 1943. (Photograph by Oscar Lewis)

A street in Tepoztlán, 1940s. (Photograph by Oscar Lewis)

The home of Pedro Martínez as it looked in the 1950s. Although still occupied by family members, the house looks completely different today as the result of remodeling. (Photograph by Oscar Lewis)

On his first weekends in the village Lewis formulated his work plan through a sequence of steps that he would adhere to on all of his later projects. He began with a survey, then moved into an intensive phase in which the territorial scope was restricted but the inquiry was more intensive.[11] During the survey phase Lewis visited all eight villages in the *municipio* and each of Tepoztlán's seven barrios in order to map out the territory and identify the problems on which the research would focus. He sometimes described the early stages of his investigations as a "buckshot" approach because he tried to scatter his efforts across as broad a site and over as many topical areas as possible in order to identify the areas of inquiry crucial to understanding the general problem he would be studying. It also helped him to determine how much information he could get from which sources so he knew where to concentrate his efforts.

In his official capacity as a representative of the Interamerican Indian Institute, Lewis carried with him letters of introduction to village leaders from several state and national government officials. The government connections that were supposed to open doors instead made villagers suspicious that he was an agent who had come to conduct investigations related to taxation and conscription. To try to allay these fears, Lewis asked the heads of families from each barrio to come to meetings where he explained his work and asked them to discuss their village and its problems. He found that specifically asking Tepoztecans about their needs and problems provided him with a fuller understanding of how they viewed their community and the overall quality of life there. Even though later he would be criticized for designing his research to elicit negative material, Lewis wrote: "The difference between asking people about their history and customs and asking about their problems may be very significant in the total view of the culture a field worker gets." In fact, he found villagers' responses so "instructive" that on all subsequent projects he used some version of a "felt needs" questionnaire.[12]

What Lewis learned from these early group meetings was that if the villagers were to help him with his research he would have to help them solve their most pressing problems. Whereas he had expected the research findings to be used later by government officials in formulating Indian policy, he found that he would have to do something much more immediate and tangible if he were really serious about undertaking a thorough investigation of village life. Lewis wrote that the barrio meetings "led quite unexpectedly to the organization of a program of services as a corollary to the research project."[13]

Setting up an action program turned out to be important for securing the cooperation of government workers as well. For example, the Department of Health and Welfare was not very eager to participate in research devoted to theoretical concerns and claimed that it could not spare a doctor to assist in the personality study. However, it was more than willing to contribute to a program of community services, to help set up a medical cooperative, or to treat the sick. In the end, "the experience with service programs," Lewis wrote, "led to some of our best insights into the culture and personality of the Tepoztecans."[14]

From an informational standpoint this combination of service with research was very fruitful, but it was rife with the potential for undermining Lewis's neutral stance as a researcher. Villagers began to trust project workers more than local officials and came to them with some of their most difficult and politically sensitive problems. Lewis had to be very careful how, and on what matters, he intervened in order not to alter the research situation or to alienate himself from any group within the village. As a general rule he tried to assist only in those matters that would benefit the village as a whole and not specific individuals or any one faction. For example, when a group of *tlacololeros* (landless cultivators of the communal hillside lands) sought his assistance in a boundary dispute with a nearby village over access to wooded lands in the national reserve, Lewis declined to help them in his official capacity. However, he felt free to help them as a friend because this was not a dispute pitting Tepoztecans against one another. In addition some of the families cooperating in his research stood to benefit from a favorable resolution of the dispute, and Lewis did not want to turn away from an opportunity to help them. But it was his assistant Alejandro Marroquín, the former lawyer and political activist, who helped most by providing legal advice and other practical assistance.

The Tepoztlán project was an unusual, and sometimes uncomfortable, combination of applied anthropology and independent research. However, Lewis always defined his responsibilities in the village as fundamentally those of a representative of a government agency committed to public service. Thus, in comparing the focus of his research to Redfield's, he wrote:

> The awareness that the results of our study were . . . intended primarily to serve as a basis for drawing up proposals for the improvement of conditions in Tepoztlán, set the tone for the entire investigation. It determined both the subject matter that was to receive special attention as well as the techniques used. So for example, the study of land tenure, agricultural techniques, soil fertility, health conditions, etc., received more attention than the study of religious ritual, ceremonial dress, etc. Also, we placed greater emphasis upon obtaining quantitative data, for the

administrator concerned with organizing services for a community must have not only a descriptive knowledge of how institutions function but also detailed quantitative data."[15]

Such an approach, Lewis believed, conformed to the mandate he had received from the National Indian Institute, even though his conception of what information was necessary to fulfill his responsibilities differed considerably from the original research plan conceived by Laura Thompson and her collaborators. Lewis had no thought of slighting the personality study, but he found it both necessary and desirable to add on to it a whole new set of objectives. He wanted "to broaden the scope of the project to include a study of the social, economic, and political life" of Tepoztlán and to do "a more rounded study [that] would make it possible better to understand . . . the relationship between culture and personality."[16]

Lewis understated considerably the actual reach of the project he was putting together in the early months of 1944. One of his preliminary work schedules was comprised of twenty-six objectives, many of which stemmed from his planned evaluation of the economic base of the village: studies of landownership, access to and use of communal lands, cultivation practices and productivity, economic and social stratification (based on a wealth assessment of every household in the village). The breadth of this inquiry, as presented to the National Indian Institute, prompted its director, Ernest Maes, to warn Lewis that what he was trying to do was "an impossible task."[17] Maes thought that Lewis had no workable methodology for implementing his plan, and he could not see how, even if Lewis were successful in gathering all of the information he sought, he would be able to integrate it into the write-up of what was intended to be a culture and personality study.

Lewis was surprised but undaunted by Maes's criticism. He was not one to worry about establishing analytic relationships between various aspects of the research while he was still in the field; with his holistic approach he accepted a priori that the relationships existed and that, if not immediately apparent, they would become so during the evaluation and write-up of the material. In the meantime he would take the research where opportunity, circumstance, and his interests led him. He was careful at the outset of the project, however, to establish a common organizational focus for the collection of data, one that would serve as an operational link between his ethnography and the Indian personality study. Lewis decided to use the family as the basic unit of research for both investigations. In explaining this decision he wrote:

The traditional anthropological reliance upon a few informants to obtain a picture of the culture and the people, though perhaps feasible in a small, primitive, tribal society, was inadequate in this situation. . . . But how could we best study the individual and understand his relationship to the culture? How might we reveal the great variety of practices and the range of individual differences in such a complex village? How might we understand Tepoztecans in all their individuality. . . . It was in response to my sense of the inadequacy of the usual techniques that I turned to the study of the family. It seemed to me that the intensive study of representative families, in which the entire family would be studied as a functioning unit, might give us greater insight into both the culture and the people.[18]

Lewis selected as a representative group three families with different income levels from each of the village's seven barrios. Testing for the personality study was done on the 112 adults and children in these twenty-one families, and the adults also served as the principal informants for the investigation into village culture and economy. The Lewises, with the help of Marroquín, began a comparative study of two of these families while student assistants were assigned to observe the remaining nineteen and, wherever possible, to live with them. Lewis gave the students instructions in the fairly concrete task of collecting the income and budget data he needed for his study of the village economy, but writing observations of family life was another matter. To facilitate this work, Ruth Lewis wrote a fifty-nine-page guide containing eighty-four multiple-part questions, some with more than twenty-five separate items. The guide was too difficult to implement for students who had been trained in physical anthropology and archaeology, so the Lewises consolidated the most important questions into ten themes and then asked their informants to write essays on these topics.

To supplement data collected in this way, the Lewises prepared three other lengthy questionnaires: on pregnancy and birth (forty-six items); on child deportment (thirty-one items); and on illnesses, symptoms, and cures (fifty-one items). Ruth Lewis's guide for taking family histories easily equaled in its range and specificity the questionnaires her husband wrote for collecting the ethnographic data. Together they prepared *100 pages* of questions to ask Tepoztecans about themselves, their families, and their village. From mapping the *ejido* to exploring the mind, from plotting house sites to the analysis of dreams, the work plan for studying Tepoztlán gave new meaning to "holistic approach."

By February 1944, with about half of his projected staff in the field, Lewis sent this progress report to the National Indian Institute:

On the whole the project is going along well. . . . In accord with my instructions and field guides the first six weeks were spent gathering data on demography, economics, and composition by barrios (family income and expenses) and political organization of the community. We have done little on religious and ceremonial matters for it seemed to me that Redfield's material was adequate on that score. . . .

On about February 1st the workers were asked to begin a study of the case histories of each of the selected families. Unfortunately the case history material is coming in very slowly and the work is poor. This is indeed a serious problem for we consider the case history material fundamental for the psychological part of the study. Of course, anyone who has done field work in Latin America knows that it is very difficult to get intimate life history material. But in addition to this there is the fact that the students are untrained and terribly slow. Mrs. Lewis wrote a guide for them but to date they are using it very mechanically and with little originality or imagination. Frankly we are puzzled as to how to solve this problem. I may have to spend a few weeks in the field doing some work on case histories.

Another difficulty in the field is the matter of getting informants. The people of Tepoztlán are a very busy hard working lot, and it is next to impossible to get an informant to work for more than an hour or two at a time, that is, on the basis of friendship and gifts. On the other hand, we cannot afford to pay all of our informants because of our limited budget. In my field work in Canada I used to put in ten and twelve hours a day with an informant. Nothing of the kind is possible down here. And incidentally, if there is one conclusion that can be made at this stage of the research it is that the picture of Tepoztlán as written by Redfield and Stuart Chase has been highly romanticized.[19] Actually their lot is a hard one and more important, they are aware of it. . . . At this rate we plan to begin the study of the other village . . . by early May . . . and [it] should take about five months. . . .[20]

With all phases of the research underway, Lewis continued to press for the cooperation of government agencies, both with the research and the service programs he had promised to bring to the village. In March, the Department of Health and Welfare provided a doctor to give medical examinations to project informants and to help establish a small clinic in the village. As soon as it was functioning, Lewis called a town meeting to instruct villagers in how they could form a medical cooperative to maintain the clinic after the research project was completed. In taking this and other actions to improve the quality of life in the village, Lewis risked encroachment on the vested interests of those who benefited from whatever aspect of the status quo he was trying to change. Setting up a medical cooperative, for example, led to opposition from native healers (curanderos) who stood to lose both status and income by the presence of doctors in the community. They were able to make common cause with others of various political inclinations, including a few local politicians running for office, to try to stop both Lewis's service programs and his research project.

Village politics during those war years presented a real opportunity for disaster because there was a small but influential group of pro-Nazi Sinarquists in the *municipio* who were opposed to Lewis's research and in particular to psychological testing. Allying themselves with others opposed to the Lewises' presence in the village, they managed to close down the cooperative and stop the psychological testing while local officials investigated their complaints and summoned the Lewises to the town hall to explain the purpose of their research. After a month of organizing politicians and sympathetic villagers in support of the project, and defending it before a town meeting (with the help of an eloquent speech from the former lawyer Marroquín), the Lewises were able to resume their work.[21]

By late spring, when Lewis was preparing to begin work in Ocotit-lán, he found that the $3,200 Viking Fund grant the Interamerican Indian Institute was using to pay for the research was almost depleted. The U.S. National Indian Institute had committed $600 to the project but that money had already been allocated. With months of work still ahead, Lewis found himself not only without funds but without a job. In June, a cost-conscious Congress, trying to find ways to pay for the war, reported out of conference committee a Department of the Interior appropriation bill that cut off funds for the National Indian Institute. Although the Institute began looking for private funding, Maes advised Lewis that he would have to complete his work on whatever funds were left in his account. In July, when the full Congress gave its approval to the appropriation bill, the Institute was left without operating funds.[22] In any case it had been living on borrowed time, as the draft had already picked it clean of almost every able-bodied man. As the war dragged on, Lewis too had been moving ever closer to draft-eligible status. Protesting about having to leave work in progress, he was ordered to return to Washington no later than August 15, whereupon, if not drafted, he would be reassigned to another government agency.

When they left Mexico the Lewises had not yet begun the work in Ocotitlán. In Tepoztlán they had completed the psychological testing of subjects in the twenty-one families, had done most of the background research, and had well underway the two family case histories that they had chosen as their own personal project. Although part of the ethnographic data had been written up for *América Indígena*, most of it was still unanalyzed.[23] Thus they left for Washington with the intention of returning to the village as soon as possible.

From Community to Family Studies

For the duration of the war Lewis was assigned to the BAE, and it was not until after he joined the faculty of Washington University that he was able to return to Tepoztlán. With support from the university and the American Philosophical Society, the Lewises, along with their friend Alejandro Marroquín, spent the summers of 1947 and 1948 in the village. It was during this period, with most of the background work done and without a large staff to supervise, that the Lewises were able to concentrate on collecting life histories and developing a family study method. They turned their efforts to household observations and intensive interviewing with the Rojas and Martínez families. As the two-family study progressed, Lewis became convinced that the family study approach "revealed a much wider range of custom and personality types" than he would have uncovered if he had simply tried to describe culture patterns. Anthropologists, he wrote, had been working too swiftly and taking the easy way out in settling for the identification of patterns in a culture. The family study method required much more time but offered "an excellent way to build up inductively a picture of the total culture."[24]

Lewis was so impressed by the possibilities of this approach that he gave greater priority to the preparation of the family case studies than he did to the write-up of the village study. While he was occupied with the latter task, Ruth Lewis took responsibility for preparing "Two Family Portraits," which was submitted for publication before the write-up of the village study was completed. The book was based on analyses of household economies, personality tests, interviews, and day studies that examined time use, division of labor, and intra-family relationships. The two families lived in different barrios and had markedly different standards of living; their stories were intended to illustrate variation within the culture, the differential effects of the Mexican Revolution on families of different economic backgrounds, and the opportunities for and obstacles to vertical mobility in the village. This, the first of the Lewises' many family studies, was the only one submitted for publication under joint authorship, the only one prepared as an analysis of field materials rather than edited into a first-person narrative format, and, not coincidentally, the only one not to find a publisher.

Despite his growing interest in family and personality study, Lewis was far from abandoning the more traditional concerns of ethnology. In the summer of 1949, in pursuit of an adequate historical context for the village study, Lewis took his research to Extremadura, Spain, from where so many conquistadores had emigrated to Mesoamerica. By studying a rural community in that province, Lewis hoped to be able to better distinguish between what was Spanish and what was Indian in the cultural heritage of Tepoztecans.[25]

After selecting the region around the town of Guadalupe for study, Lewis began gathering census data while his wife interviewed townspeople on family practices and life-cycle events. While making his survey Lewis soon noticed and began to inquire about the low ratio of men to women in one village near Guadalupe. The answers he received suggested that the government had executed a number of local men it suspected of involvement in antigovernment activities. Shortly after Lewis made his inquiries, the provincial governor asked him to leave the area. Instead the Lewises left the country and never again attempted to work in Franco's Spain.

During the following year Lewis worked with his wife and with Alejandro Marroquín in preparing the Tepoztecan materials for publication. He had planned to leave the write-up of the personality study almost entirely in his wife's hands, but Ruth Lewis felt she did not have the expertise to write full-scale analyses of the Rorshach test results. The two-family study consumed a good deal of her time and she was about to have their second child. So the Lewises took on as a collaborator the clinical psychologist Theodora Abel, president of the Rorshach Institute and a former associate of Ruth Benedict. (Abel in turn brought in her colleague Renata Calabresi.)

Lewis found himself drawn into this work and developing for the first time a genuine interest in the field of culture and personality. As early as 1944, when working with Ruth Lewis's preliminary analyses and personality profiles of test subjects, Lewis conceded that he and his wife were "amazed at the diagnostic value of the Rorshach."[26] Although he was not convinced of the value of the Rorshach as an independent tool of analysis, as he analyzed the field data he was impressed by how the combination of psychological testing, interviewing, and household observation had produced mutually reinforcing or validating sets of information. He concluded that in doing their family studies they were developing a method that could bridge the gap between the study of the individual and the culture by illuminating both the "public and private personalities" of informants.

Addressing himself to the concerns of Benedict and others in the culture and personality school who were trying to find a way to understand what they called "total personality," Lewis offered the family study approach as a contribution.[27] He argued that historically in anthropology life histories had been used almost exclusively to obtain information about customs and culture and therefore rarely got beyond issues of public personality. But with an approach that combined psychological testing, physical examinations, and household observations with intensive interviewing of all members of a family, it would be possible, he believed, to explore areas of personality, in particular what he called private personality, heretofore neglected in the literature.

While working on the Tepoztlán book in 1949–50, Lewis wrote a paper in which he defined public and private personality and tried to establish the importance of this distinction to the study of culture.

> The underlying principle in this distinction is of a functional nature. The public personality of an individual includes all those aspects of the total personality which are directly and appreciably influenced by the social norms and which, in turn, directly and appreciably influence or determine the social behavior of an individual. The private personality of an individual includes all those aspects which are not sensitive to social norms and which do not directly affect social behavior.[28]

Using his method of focusing on the individual within the family context, he argued, the researcher could sort out the relative influence of family, culture, and "bio-physical . . . states and processes" on the formation of culture.[29]

> It is in the context of the family that the interrelationships between cultural and individual factors in the formation of personality can best be seen. Family case studies can therefore enable us to better distinguish between and give proper weight to those factors which are cultural and those which are situational or the result of individual idiosyncrasies. Even psychological tests become more meaningful when done on a family basis. For example, on the basis of our family Rorschach tests we can study the extent to which personality differences run along family lines and the range within families, as well as what seems to be common among all families and can therefore be attributed to broader cultural conditioning.[30]

Establishing such patterns would require studying a large number of families in any culture group; it was a "cumulative process," Lewis wrote, and "especially important for understanding the covert aspects of culture."[31]

Lewis was more successful in working out his statement on the family study approach than he was in defining a method for the study of total personality. Colleagues were quick to point out the difficulties of operationalizing a dichotomy between public and private personality for research purposes. Lewis was unable to carry his idea further, and although he never submitted the paper for publication, he inserted the core of it into the last chapter of the Tepoztlán book. He never mentioned the paper again, but its inclusion as a kind of afterthought at the end of the village study signaled the direction in which his research was headed: away from community studies and toward the study of the family and individual personality.

The Redfield-Lewis Controversy

When *Life in a Mexican Village* was published in 1951, it was not the Indian personality study that caught the attention of other anthropologists but Lewis's criticism of Robert Redfield's model of folk societies, which Redfield had based in part on his work in Tepoztlán. Lewis challenged Redfield's portrait of the village as a romanticization of peasant life that downplayed the negative aspects of underdevelopment and the conflicts in social relationships. He also characterized as simplistic Redfield's early view that cultural change occurred along a continuum from one ideal society (folk) to another (urban). In Lewis's view, Redfield was destined to find harmony in "folk" cultures as a result of conceptualizing them as the polar opposites of contentious, conflictive "urban" societies.

In criticizing Redfield, Lewis took on at the outset of his career one of the giants of the profession. He saw himself in the position of being viewed as the upstart "immigrant" from CCNY taking on the "Great Patrician" from Hyde Park. Lewis held Redfield in high esteem and truly admired his contributions to anthropology. But the results of his own fieldwork, in addition to the philosophic bent he brought to its interpretation, led him to unavoidable disagreement with Redfield. Because he did not want this disagreement to be taken as anything more than a professional difference, Lewis sought out Redfield's reactions to his findings before publishing them, and he even dedicated the book to Redfield. Whatever private opinions they had of one another, and despite some heated exchanges in their private conversations, their professional relationship, maintained primarily through a lengthy correspondence, was quite correct and even had a kind of restrained cordiality.

Redfield wrote a promotional blurb for the dust jacket of Lewis's book, commending social science research in general for its ability to improve upon itself; but at the same time he reminded readers that he had already revised many of his earlier findings. Lewis later acknowledged that he had come to a fuller understanding of Redfield's work and even to a limited acceptance of the heuristic value of models and ideal types. But his criticism of Redfield carried a legacy for his career.

Part of the legacy of the so-called Redfield-Lewis controversy was that the two men came to represent different research approaches, personal styles, and predispositions, with Lewis's outlook and temperament categorized as the polar opposite of Redfield's. What came to be a fairly common comparison of the two men was summarized by Margaret Mead in 1974:

> In comparison it [*Life in a Mexican Village*] provides a most interesting example of the difference in perception and selection of materials between the two ethnographers. Redfield was interested in harmony; he was interested in what made things go well. Oscar, *as everybody knows*, was interested in what made things go badly. As a result, those two studies which are very interesting and very informative, are excellent statements about the temperaments of those two men [emphasis added].[32]

Mead implied that Lewis pored over newspapers "to discover how many murders had been committed," making it sound as if his primary purpose was to uncover the darker side of life in Tepoztlán rather than to give a more accurate and complete picture of the village.[33] She made a direct connection between Lewis's temperament and his search for "why things go badly," saying in essence that he was a conflictive personality who therefore looked for conflict in the people and communities he studied. This is a very reductionist interpretation of a broad range of differences between Redfield and Lewis and their work—differences that encompass their socioeconomic backgrounds, places and dates of professional training, timing and foci of their research on Tepoztlán, and philosophical orientations. Lewis's temperament, perhaps, but maybe just his common sense, told him to suspect the pastoral portrait Redfield had painted of village life.

From its inception Lewis's project differed profoundly from Redfield's in it scope, emphasis on personality study, and commitment to combining research with service programs. The latter fact made it inevitable that Lewis's personal contact with villagers would be different from Redfield's. In his aid-related work Lewis ended up wading unawares into an ugly, reactionary undercurrent in village politics. He several times had to face in town meetings small groups of people hurling accusations at him and his research, and even a few who threatened him and his staff with physical violence. Furthermore, he set out to explore issues—virtually ignored by Redfield—that were almost certain to lead him to conflict among villagers, as did, for example, his investigation into the impact of the revolution on wealth and status differences. From his first days in the village he heard accounts of violent incidents traceable to the postrevolutionary struggle for access to land and the attempts by *cacique* families to reestablish their dominance. Also, unlike Redfield, Lewis worked in Tepoztlán after the highway was built connecting it to Mexico City. As the village became increasingly popular with tourists, as well as for summer residence, it experienced a period of land speculation. Lewis followed this development closely over a number of years and was aware that it caused conflict and, on ocassion, even violence. In fact an informant's son was murdered because of his involvement in land speculation, so Lewis did not have to dig very deeply to come across such information.

Some of the darker view of village life that comes across in the 1951 book stemmed from Lewis's reporting on Tepoztecans' personalities and personal life. Through the family studies and the battery of psychological tests Lewis probed more deeply into this area than Redfield had. (In fact Redfield's research was done before the culture and personality school had developed within anthropology.) The personality profile of Tepoztecans as rather dour, ungiving, and constricted people was constructed by test interpreters Ruth Lewis, Theodora Abel, and Renata Calabresi, although Lewis did believe that it corroborated his own impressions as drawn from the interview material and from personal contact.[34] In any case, psychological testing had not been included in Lewis's investigation by his design; it was among the duties assigned to him.

Having stated these qualifications, it is nevertheless true that Lewis, as he readily admitted, went to Tepoztlán more disposed than Redfield to find conflict. He considered it inevitable that there would be some degree of conflict in all social organization and human relationships. This was probably not so much a function of his temperament as of his philosophical orientation. Of course one could argue that Marxism attracted him because its message of inevitable struggle was compatible with his temperament. But I think that few would argue that all people who find Marxism analytically useful or philosophically congenial have a common temperament. It is tempting to speculate that because Lewis was born into a family that had lived for years in a (to greatly understate the situation) conflictive environment—of offically condoned or tolerated violence against Jews—he came, by way of reality, to a negative and hostile view of the world. In fact Lewis appears from all evidence to have been upbeat and optimistic in his outlook, not because of a sanguine view of the contemporary world, but because of his belief in the inevitability of "progress." This, I think, along with the fact that it encouraged the examination of questions often neglected in other theoretical approaches in use at that time, was exactly what appealed to him in Marxism.

Because of the few basic assumptions he accepted from Marxism, or which Marxism confirmed for him, Lewis did not see conflict as necessarily, or even essentially, negative. He saw change in terms of the dialectical process: out of conflict—as out of the Hegelian juxtaposition of opposites—comes synthesis and advancement to a higher level. A completely peaceful society would be a static one, and Lewis believed in change. Change was usually, but not always, for the better. He had no romance for folk societies or for poverty in general and did not much fear what urbanization, industrialization, and technology might do to traditional societies. He worried too little, perhaps, about the impact of "progress" on traditional relationships and values because he thought more in terms of the transformation of material conditions. He was therefore less concerned about modernization than about resistance to change and the persistence of superstition, high infant mortality, short life expectancy, low productivity, unhygienic conditions, illiteracy, and bad housing. He was no friend of tradition for tradition's sake; nothing was successful, he wrote, just because it persisted: "The success of a social form must also be evaluated in terms of its human costs." [35] It was in this sense, in his belief in the potential for an ever-improving quality of life through technological change, that he was more optimistic than the folk-urban societies model revealed Redfield to be.

In *Anthropological Essays,* the last of his works published during his lifetime, Lewis tried to explain his view of conflict. Commenting on Redfield's observation that the difference between the two was that Redfield had asked "What do people enjoy?" while he had asked "What do these people suffer from?" Lewis wrote:

> There is . . . a more weighty and philosophical issue involved. . . . It seems to me that concern with what people suffer from is much more important than the study of enjoyment because it lends itself to more productive insight into the human condition, the dynamics of conflict, and the forces for change. A focus upon enjoyment generally leads to a static picture of a society. To stress the enjoyment in peasant life is to argue for its preservation. . . . The romantic view of the peasantry still held by a few anthropologists is, at best, a form of escapism from the problems of urban life and, at worst, a kind of inverse snobbism. To stress the problems of suffering of peasantry is to envisage the possibility of fundamental changes in technology, means of communication, and general fund of knowledge, which would alter the very meaning of peasant life. . . .

In my opinion one of the basic differences in our approach has to do with the question of what is a good society as an ideal type, against which I would measure both the urban life of Chicago and the peasant life of Tepoztlán and find them both wanting, for quite different reasons.[36]

The Lessons of Tepoztlán

If there was any aspect of the Tepoztlán research that was especially suited to Lewis's temperament it was his observation of family life and the use of open-ended interviewing to record life histories. This kind of direct, prolonged, one-on-one contact gave Lewis a good deal of personal satisfaction and made use of many of his best skills. Family study became his preferred method, and personality testing was an integral and essential aspect of that method. The day studies, material culture inventories, and income and expenditure analyses that were to figure so prominently in the later family studies all had their roots in the village study. The only tool important to the success of the later work that did not play a role in the original Tepoztlán research was the tape recorder.

Lewis did experiment with wire and disc model recorders while doing research for the 1951 book. They were unreliable and very cumbersome to use in the field, but he did manage to record on disc a number of interviews on village history and politics with one of his key informants. These would have been the first electronically recorded interviews Lewis used for publication had they not been stolen from his car while it was parked in Mexico City. It was only when he returned in 1956 to do a follow-up study of the village that he began making extensive use of the tape recorder.

The Tepoztlán project set another precedent for Lewis's later research in that it convinced him that "the days of the anthropologist as a one-man expedition must be over. . . ."[37] The village study established what Ruth Lewis has called his "entrepreneurial" approach. By this she meant that Lewis had a good, implicit understanding of what his strengths and weaknesses would be on a given project, of what work he could do himself and what he would have to recruit others to do. He excelled in finding good personnel and in delegating to them and supervising that work he was unable to do. His search for contacts and personnel was tireless and cut a broad swath through governmental agencies and university, professional, literary, and exile communities. The reason for recruiting large staffs lay originally in Lewis's sweeping approach. It was so broad that it inevitably encompassed areas of inquiry in which he had no competence. He could not, for example, do crop studies, give physical examinations, or analyze personality tests; he either had to scale down his objectives or add to his staff.

Lewis, it would turn out, had no aptitude for scaling down objectives or recognizing constraints in the field. Always he was looking for what other researchers had missed and trying to delve into areas they had ignored or shied away from; pursuit of the covert, private, or hidden was the common thread in both community and family studies. It was not that he was necessarily more interested in the covert than the overt, but information on the covert was essential to completing the whole. And Lewis was to spend the remainder of his career, whether studying community, family, or individual, in search of the total picture.

(Relevant correspondence can be found on pp. 185–218.)

NOTES

1. The Instituto Indigenista Interamericano was established by the First Interamerican Indian Congress in 1940. Its official founding came in March 1942 with a formal agreement between El Salvador, Ecuador, Honduras, Mexico, and the United States. It now has seventeen member nations. The Institute's purpose is to serve "as a clearinghouse for information on Indians and on methods of improving their social and economic conditions," and to initiate, direct, and coordinate "studies applicable to the solution of Indian problems that contribute to a better knowledge of Indian life." Manuel Gamio, the Institute's first permanent director, served in that post until his death in 1960. A history of the Institute's first forty years and a bibliography of its publications can be found in *América Indígena, 40 Años Indice General* (Serie Sedial 1; Mexico: Instituto Indígenista Interamericano, 1980).

2. Letter from Oscar Lewis to Howard Cline, October 25, 1943.

3. The Indian personality project was overseen by a subgroup for Research on Indian Education within the the Committee on Human Development. Its members included Laura Thompson, W. Lloyd Warner, Robert Havighurst, and Ralph Tyler. Their advisers in the Office of Indian Affairs, besides Collier, included Willard Beatty, Joseph McCaskell, Lucy Wilcox Adams, and Rene d'Harnoncourt. For a discussion of the project see Lawrence C. Kelly, "Anthropology and Anthropologists in the New Deal," *Journal of the History of the Behavioral Sciences* 16 (1980): 6–24.

4. Lewis, "The Tepoztlán Report," p.2.

5. I learned this from an undated report to the project coordinating committee written by Manuel Gamio.

6. B. Klopfer and D. M. Kelly, *The Rorshach Technique* (Yonkers, N.Y.: World Book Co., 1942).

7. Robert Redfield, *Tepoztlán: A Mexican Village* (Chicago: University of Chicago Press, 1930).

8. Alejandro Marroquín had been instrumental in the founding of El Sal-

vador's National Union of Workers and he had left the country under threat of political retribution. Lewis met him through mutual friends and took him on as a field assistant because Marroquín was having difficulty supporting his family in Mexico, where he was not qualified to practice law. Marroquín did much of the background work on village government and politics when working for Lewis in 1943–44, 1947, and 1948. He went on to retrain as an anthropologist in Mexico and had a distinguished career there. He joined the Interamerican Indian Institute in 1971 and was director of anthropological investigations at the time of his death in 1977.

9. Letter from Oscar Lewis to Ernest Maes, November 29, 1943.

10. Letter from Oscar Lewis to Ernest Maes, February 22, 1944.

11. This general approach parallels that pioneered by W. H. R. Rivers, but I believe it is coincidental. Like Rivers, Lewis also placed great emphasis on collecting large numbers of very detailed genealogies, although Lewis did not make much use of them.

12. Lewis, *Life in a Mexican Village*, p. xv, n12.

13. Ibid., p. xv.

14. Lewis, "The Tepoztlán Report," p. 5.

15. Ibid., pp. 6–7.

16. Ibid., p. 3.

17. Letter from Ernest Maes to Oscar Lewis, March 3, 1944.

18. Oscar Lewis, "Family Case Studies: A Technique for the Study of Culture and Personality" (paper delivered to the Midwest Sociological Society, April 29, 1949). An edited version of this paper was published as "An Anthropological Approach to Family Studies," in *American Journal of Sociology*, March 1950, pp. 468–75, and was reprinted in Lewis, *Anthropological Essays*, pp. 81–89.

19. Stuart Chase, *Mexico—A Study of Two Americas* (New York: Macmillan Co., 1931).

20. Letter from Oscar Lewis to Ernest Maes, February 22, 1944.

21. I have based this account on Lewis's "Tepoztlán Report," pp. 12–18. Lewis was denied permission to publish an account of this incident at the time, but he later wrote about it in "Medicine and Politics in a Mexican Village," in *Health, Culture, and Community*, ed. Benjamin Paul (New York: Russel Sage Foundation, 1955), pp. 403–35. This article was reprinted in Lewis, *Anthropological Essays*, pp. 291–313.

22. Lewis was warned of the possibility of budgetary cutbacks by Commissioner Collier in a letter dated May 3, 1944. The National Indian Institute had been created by executive order and had never operated on funds appropriated by Congress specifically for its functioning. A few members on the House Appropriations Committee, according to Collier's letter, believed that the commissioner was more interested in the Indians of Central and South American than he was in those of the United States. The budget issue was a frequent topic in Lewis's correspondence with the Institute between May and July 1944.

23. Oscar Lewis, "Social and Economic Change in a Mexican Village: Tepoztlán 1926–44", *América Indígena* 4 (1944): 281–314.

24. Letter from Oscar Lewis to Carl C. Taylor, April 20, 1948 (no. 22 in the Appendix).

25. The title of this project was "The Study of Culture and Personality in Rural Spain Through the Use of the Family Case Study."

26. Letter from Oscar Lewis to Ruth Benedict, April 26, 1944.

27. See, for example, Ruth Benedict, "Configurations of Culture in North America," *American Anthropologist* 34:1–27, esp. p. 24.

28. Oscar Lewis, "Public and Private Personality—Concepts for the Culture-Personality Problem" (unpublished ms.); see also *Life in a Mexican Village*, p. 422. The public-private distinction is clearly related to that made between overt and covert behavior in the culture and personality literature, which in turn draws heavily on the writings of Freud and the whole body of psychoanalytic literature. Bert Kaplan suggested that Lewis drew on O. Hobart Mowrer's two-stage learning theory to develop his idea, but this is not so. ("Personality and Social Structure," in *Review of Sociology*, Joseph B. Gittler, ed. [New York: Wiley, 1957], p. 105.) Mowrer was a psychologist at the University of Illinois who knew Lewis well; they often discussed related aspects of their work. But Lewis believed that the learning theory literature was gimmicky. He was much more influenced by the writings of Ralph Linton on differences between overt and covert behavior (see especially *The Cultural Background of Personality* [New York: Appleton-Century Crofts, 1945]).

29. Lewis, *Life in a Mexican Village*, p. 422.

30. Lewis, "An Anthropological Approach to Family Studies," p. 471.

31. Ibid., p. 472.

32. In *American Anthropology: The Early Years*, ed. John Murra. Proceedings of the American Ethnological Society (St. Paul, Minn.: West Publishing Co., 1974), p. 144.

33. Ibid.

34. Lewis, *Life in a Mexican Village*, pp. 306–18.

35. Lewis, *Anthropological Essays*, p. 254.

36. Ibid., p. 252.

37. Letter from Oscar Lewis to Ruth Benedict, April 26, 1944.

CHAPTER THREE

MEXICO CITY:
STATING THE THESIS

In 1951, the year *Life in a Mexican Village* was published, Lewis returned to Mexico to complete a project on Tepoztecan migrants that he had begun in 1944 as part of the village study. At that time he had compiled a list of villagers living in Mexico City for the purpose of studying the impact of an urban environment on their way of life and also to see if their return visits, or money sent home, had any impact on the village. With an eye to his applied work, Lewis hoped, in addition, to find out how the more educated among them might be recruited back to the village to work for their people.

Lewis kept only the first of these objectives for his 1951 project, which he characterized as a "Socio-psychological Study of Mexican Families of Rural Backgrounds in Mexico City."[1] He deployed a staff of student assistants, seven of whom he had brought with him from the University of Illinois, to administer a battery of questionnaires to 100 families scattered throughout the city. Essentially Lewis was motivated by the same line of thought that had produced his differences with Redfield. He believed that rural life had been idealized and that the dangers of urbanization, especially to social and psychological well-being, had been overstated. Indeed, in his analysis of the adaptation to urban life made by these Tepoztecans, he concluded that there could be "Urbanization without Breakdown":

> . . . this study provides further evidence that urbanization is not a simple, unitary, universally similar process, but that it assumes different forms and meanings, depending upon the prevailing historic, economic, social and cultural conditions. . . . I find that peasants in Mexico adapt to city life with far greater ease than do American farm families. There is little

evidence of disorganization and breakdown, of cultural conflict, or of irreconcilable differences between generations. . . . Family life remains strong in Mexico City. Family cohesiveness and extended family ties increase in the city, fewer cases of separation and divorce occur, no cases of abandoned mothers and children, no cases of persons living alone or of unrelated families living together. . . . There is a general rise in the standard of living in the city, but dietary patterns do not change greatly. Religious life . . . becomes more Catholic and disciplined. . . .[2]

In that same year, in an article on the impact of technological change on mental health, he made an argument parallel to that on urbanization: technological change does not *inevitably* lead to alienation or mental breakdown.[3]

Up to this point Lewis's work in Mexico City had a continuity with—in fact was simply an extension of—the research he had done in Tepoztlán. But in the summer of 1956, when he returned to Mexico after two years with the Ford Foundation, his work took a new course. This was the year he began using the tape recorder; and it was also the year he met the Sánchez family. Not coincidentally, 1956 marked the beginning of the second phase of Lewis's career.

From Ethnography to Biography

Lewis spent the better part of the next four years living and working in Mexico, beginning with fifteen months as a Guggenheim Fellow in 1956–57. Basing themselves in Mexico City, the Lewises spent the summer in Tepoztlán, again accompanied by a group of anthropology graduate students, doing a follow-up study of social, economic, and technological change.[4] This time Lewis took with him a reel-to-reel Tandberg tape recorder and began to redo interviews with informants for the two-family study, concentrating on Pedro Martínez.

Taping liberated Lewis from a preoccupation with writing down all information accurately and allowed him to move beyond simply asking questions to carrying on a conversation and establishing rapport. Tape recording also gave him a better method of getting at language and style and therefore of dealing not only with what was said but with how it was said.

Because the quality of the interviews improved and because he was able to gather more information from a greater number of people and to record oral testimony more accurately than under the old note-taking system, Lewis gradually came to depend on the tape-recorded interview for the collection of much of his data. This would eventually lead him to alter the direction of his research in that it brought him to rely more heavily on informants for his data than he ever thought he would when he was criticizing earlier anthropologists for their dependence on oral testimony from a few key informants and for failing to do sufficient historical research. Still, Lewis would manage to distance himself from this tradition by interviewing far more people (something the tape recorder helped make possible) within a culture group than virtually any other anthropologist of his or earlier generations. Although he relied far less on the recorded word than his use of biography suggests, he never again did quite as much historical research nor as thorough an ethnography as he had done in Tepoztlán.

The tape-recorded interview also encouraged the Lewises to take a new approach to the presentation of their material. Unsuccessful in their decade-long attempt to publish their two-family study, they gave up its academic analysis and concentrated on building a first-person narrative from the transcriptions of Lewis's newly redone interviews with members of the Martínez family. Lewis had a special fondness for Martínez as his first major informant and as a man who had participated in the Mexican Revolution, but he believed that Martínez and all of the other Tepoztecan informants could not provide him with the kind of data he would need to make the breakthrough that he was hoping for with his family study approach. They were too inhibited, reserved, and suspicious to reveal much of their "private personalities." But in working on the Martínez biography Lewis did see the potential of this new format, provided he could find more suitable informants. This was about to happen as he moved his research back to Mexico City.

The Urban Setting

After 1956 Lewis spent the majority of his field time in cities and never again undertook major research in a rural setting (although both the Puerto Rican and Cuban projects were intended to have rural phases). Studying poor people in a modern urban context seemed to awaken Lewis politically and to change his perspective on who he was studying and why he was studying them. Of course, in Tepoztlán he had been concerned about the plight of Indian people and the lower standard of living in the countryside, and he believed the primary purpose of his research was to make contributions in these areas. But he did not have the same sense of urgency about change when working in the traditional and relatively stable environment of Tepoztlán as he had when working in Mexico City's poor neighborhoods. Nor did he have the same degree of personal identity with villagers as he had with the urban poor.

Occurring simultaneously with the change of setting was the shift in research focus from community to family study. The exhaustive and exhausting effort that went into the village study helped to convince Lewis that the family was a more manageable research unit for his holistic approach. And there is no doubt that his first foray into this area of research dampened his interest in ethnology. Furthermore, the first-person, biographical approach served perfectly Lewis's need for a means of effectively communicating to a broad segment of the public both the suffering and the humanity of the urban poor. However, once locked into this course, Lewis committed himself to areas of investigation—family dynamics and neuroses, individual personality, psychological characteristics of the poor—in which he was ill prepared to undertake research. Work in these areas also tied him to personality tests as analytic tools for interpreting life histories and for explaining the consequences of urban poverty.

During the 1950s and 1960s these changes—in research setting, focus, and method—drew Lewis into two entanglements from which he was never able to free himself and which eventually caused him to lose control over interpretation of his field data. These entanglements, one with the culture of poverty thesis and the other with projective test analyses, were themselves deeply intertwined.

The First Entanglement: The Culture of Poverty Thesis

In September 1956, when Lewis returned to the city from Tepoztlán, it was to conduct an investigation into "Lower Class Culture Patterns and the Process of Urbanization."[5] He chose two housing settlements (or *vecindades*): the Casa Grande, where he and his staff administered questionnaires in 71 of its 157 households, and the Panaderos, where they studied all 13 households. By this time Lewis had a standard battery of questionnaires covering family size (and all related vital statistics), genealogy, residence and work histories, friendship and *compadrazgo* patterns, marital status, education, income, material culture, and health and religious practices. Lewis selected these two *vecindades* because they represented several socioeconomic levels within the lower class, a condition essential to this investigation into intra- and interclass wealth and status distinctions and the requisites for upward mobility.

From the project's title and objective it is clear that Lewis expected to find pronounced, categorizable differences in class and culture patterns. Therefore his findings, first published in 1959, held few surprises: "Various socioeconomic levels must be distinguished within the lower class in Mexico City. It may be useful to develop a typology along the lines of Lloyd Warner, distinguishing between the lower-

lower, middle-lower, and upper-lower, in terms which are meaningful for the Mexican milieu. In such a scheme our smaller *vecindad*
would probably fall into the lower-lower and middle-lower, while
the Casa Grande shows all lower levels with the beginnings of a
lower-middle class."[6] Supporting this conclusion were the questionnaire data, which showed, for example, marked differences in literacy rates, family organization, *compadrazgo* patterns, and frequency of
free-union marriages.

Given these findings and Lewis's expectation that he would find a
wide variety of adaptations to poverty, it is remarkable that he chose
this particular article to discuss his idea that *some* of the world's poorest people share a common culture.

> . . . poverty in modern nations . . . becomes a dynamic factor which
> affects participation in the larger national culture and creates a subculture
> of its own. One can speak of the *culture* of the poor, for it has its own
> modalities and distinctive social and psychological consequences for its
> members. It seems to me that the culture of poverty cuts across regional,
> rural-urban, and even national boundaries. For example, I am impressed
> by the remarkable similarities in family structure, the nature of kinship
> ties, the quality of husband-wife and parent-child relations, time orien-
> tation, spending patterns, value systems, and the sense of community
> found in lower-class settlements in London . . . , in Puerto Rico . . . ,
> in Mexico City slums and Mexican villages . . . , and among lower class
> Negroes in the United States.[7]

Among the evidence Lewis cited for his thesis was his own work in
Mexico City and Tepoztlán, but in this he had written convincingly
about the existence of a range of variations within class and culture.
This was precisely his point in the article on *vecindad* culture; and while
the evidence he offered did not negate the argument that at some
level within the lower class there is a shared culture, it did nothing to
support it either. The hypothesis was simply misplaced in an article
devoted to making a separate if not contradictory point.

At this point Lewis was only hinting at the negative social and
psychological consequences of poverty that were later to resurface as
"culture traits" and be used to form the core of the culture of poverty
thesis. Yet there was nothing in his reporting on poor Mexicans to
convince us that they constituted a culture group with a distinctive
modal personality. Tepoztecans would never sound much like urban
members of a culture of poverty, for as Lewis described them they
demanded correct behavior at all times, repressed hostility, were not
openly aggressive, and from childhood on discouraged sexuality. He
noted, "The people . . . seem to have good mental control . . . and
show themselves capable of attending to tasks that have to be per-

formed in the world around them."[8] In "Urbanization without Break-down," Lewis all but ruled out as members of a culture of poverty the Tepoztecans who had moved to Mexico City. The structure of the *vecindades* in which they settled, he wrote, provided the supportive and integrative mechanisms necessary to offset the kind of social disintegration that gave rise to a culture of poverty. He repeated this entire argument in the article on *vecindad* culture, as he described the strong sense of community in the Casa Grande and the Panaderos. But within the same space he presented, in his culture of poverty thesis, the case for urbanization *with* breakdown. Lewis did not try to explain why things fell apart for some people in the lower class and not for others, nor did he even acknowledge until much later the incongruity of introducing the thesis in this article.[9]

To give perspective to the growing body of material he was collecting on the lower class, Lewis needed comparative data. To this end he sought funding for a study of the Mexican middle class, "with special reference to family structure and problems of upward mobility." His objective was "to determine the social, economic and psychological criteria for lower and middle class membership in terms of the distinctive characteristics of the Mexican cultural milieu" and "to delineate the significant levels or sub-groups within each class. . . ."[10]

As a research site Lewis chose a complex of nineteen apartment buildings, most of whose occupants were professionals or other white-collar employees. For assistants he had a group of anthropology students enrolled in seminars he taught at the National School of Anthropology and History.[11] During the summers of 1959 and 1960 the students put in a great deal of time, administering the usual round of questionnaires and taking fairly detailed genealogies, each of them submitting a report on one family. Lewis could not get interested in this research as anything other than a training project and set aside all of the work. He summed up his attitude in a letter to Oliver LaFarge: "This is a big and complicated project and it frightens me a bit. Anyway the middle class is so boring."[12]

Instead of studying the middle class, Lewis examined upward mobility within the lower class. He planned a volume comparing families whose lifeways and standards of living typified subgroups he had identified within the lower class. To represent the rural poor Lewis chose the Martínezes, whom he had continued to interview even while working in the city; from the Casa Grande he chose the Sánchez and Gómez families to represent the middle and upper brackets of the urban lower class; and from the Panaderos, the much poorer Gutiérrez family. To this group he added the Castro family, whom he had met through a government social worker; Mr. Castro had worked his way from the slums to the upper middle class. Lewis presented the comparison in the form of edited day studies, into which he and Ruth Lewis interwove material from interviews. He called the book, published in 1959, *Five Families: Mexican Case Studies in the Culture of Poverty.*

From the book's subtitle and its introduction, which repeated verbatim the 1958 statement on the culture of poverty, one must assume that Lewis intended these families to represent a range of variation within the subculture. Yet at that point he still had not provided a description of the culture of poverty, and he did not make clear what criteria he used to place these families within it. He was imprecise in his use of class and culture and vague about the significance for culture of membership in any one of the lower-class subgroups. The Gutiérrezes were the poorest of the families and came closest to the modal culture of poverty type Lewis was to sketch out a few years later.[13] The Martínezes were best characterized by the Tepoztecan personality profile: hardworking, correct in behavior, task-oriented, sexually inhibited. The Gómezes were, as described by Lewis, observers of traditional culture, religiously active, and a stable family unit with a rising aspiration level and an increasing standard of living.[14] The Sánchezes were "moving out of the subculture," and the father was described as exceptionally hardworking and responsible toward his wives and children.[15]

These four families, although different in attitudes, values, and behavior, *were* all members of a broad lower-income group, and it is clear that income was the criterion Lewis used to place them all in the culture of poverty. Yet the Castros, whom Lewis classified as "millionaires," were put in the subculture for a different reason. When Lewis wrote that Mr. Castro had been born in the slums but had "by no means lost all his lower-class traits," he was clearly using value structure and not income as the criterion for inclusion in the culture of poverty.[16] This leaves the reader to wonder what determined the category—was it income (poverty) or was it value structure (culture)? Even then, as Lewis described the variation in incomes and life-styles among the families, it was much easier to see them all as part of the "Mexican cultural milieu" than to understand why what they shared was sufficient to set them in a group that had more in common with a universal poverty culture than it did with Mexican culture. Because the criteria that determined inclusion in the subculture were so fluid that they placed some of its members closer to people on the outside than to those within the subculture, an intolerable dissonance was created. There was greater variation within the category than its fragile definition could withstand.

The Casa Grande *vecindad* in Mexico City as it looked in the 1950s. It was razed by the government in August 1986 after sustaining damage in the great earthquake that occurred earlier that year. A new *vecindad* built on the site was inaugurated by President Miguel de la Madrid in December 1986. (Photograph by Oscar Lewis)

A patio in the Casa Grande. (Photograph by Oscar Lewis)

The Panaderos *vecindad* in Mexico City as it looked circa 1956. Like the Casa Grande, it was damaged by the 1986 earthquake and demolished by the government. New apartments are being built on this and adjacent lots. (Photograph by Oscar Lewis)

The Pandaderos as viewed from the street before the government built a wall enclosing it. Ruth and Judith Lewis are in the foreground, talking with residents of the *vecindad*. (Photograph by Oscar Lewis)

Why then, when there was such a poor fit between theory and fact, did Lewis choose to use the culture of poverty as the conceptual format for *Five Families*? The worst-case explanation would be that he did it for commercial reasons, that is, to reach a wider audience, but a review of his correspondence about the book suggests the opposite. Lewis never made much of a secret of his desire to reach a broad audience, and he believed that *Five Families* had potential as a general interest book. He thought it might be marketed to tourists and to others seeking an introduction to Mexican culture, by presenting it as a series of family portraits that illustrated different aspects of Mexican life. In the draft introduction Lewis wrote that each of the families "represents a distinctive sector of [the] modern Mexican population." After contacting a literary agent and a few trade publishers, however, Lewis abandoned his idea because the publishers "would want it cut down and revised in a manner that would make it more popular" and he was "not ready to do that." [17] It was when he decided to aim the book at a social science audience that he turned to the culture of poverty concept, because it satisfied the obligation he still felt when addressing that group to generalize about the significance of his work. He changed the book's subtitle from "The Anthropology of Poverty" (which he later used as the title of the Spanish-language edition) to "Mexican Case Studies in the Culture of Poverty" and removed from the text his statement that each of the families represented a different sector of the Mexican population; instead he wrote that four of the five families were from the "lower income group." [18]

Regardless of how he cited the evidence in *Five Families*, Lewis did not intend the culture of poverty thesis to encompass all of his informants, and it certainly was not a hypothesis generated by analysis of his data. The idea behind this generalization was no more than an impression he had formed about the existence of similarities between a small number of his own informants and poor people he had read about in the work of others. [19] Of all his Panaderos and Casa Grande informants, Lewis privately identified only several as fitting the culture's modal personality and design for living: the Gutiérrezes, Guadalupe Vélez and her husband Ignacio (Sánchez relatives), and Marta Sánchez. Because he saw something in these people that set them apart from his other poor informants, and even from members of their own families, it seems quite clear that, from the very beginning, the significance of the distinctive "something" Lewis noted could not be explained in terms of a culture construct.

It was because he was an anthropologist writing mainly for other anthropologists that Lewis discussed poverty in terms of its significance for culture. This was ironic because of his ambivalence about the utility of the culture concept and because his research was moving steadily away from culture study. Lewis's doubts about the concept's usefulness were twofold and had their origin in the Tepoztlán research. His primary concern was that the use of "culture" to identify characteristic patterns or configurations obscured significant variations which gave individuality, and therefore personality and humanity, to the individuals studied. "The demonstration of a considerable range in personality and family life within relatively homogenous peasant societies suggests the possibility that we anthropologists have overplayed the importance of . . . culture . . . as an explanatory concept and [this may] lead to the search for more refined concepts than basic personality and culture."[20] Second, Lewis thought that the importance placed on culture in explaining behavior belied the capacity of the individual to act independently of these norms. "Individuals are always solving problems in new and original ways. The notion that culture gives us ready-made solutions to problems should not be pushed too far lest we reduce individuals to automatons. This in a nutshell is my criticism of the anthropological use of the culture concept. . . ."[21]

Believing that the culture concept had been overplayed while creating a culture construct of his own should have struck Lewis as a rather serious contradiction. That it did not was, I think, because he did not believe, initially, that the culture of poverty statement was of any theoretical importance. Only later, as he tried to elaborate on it and turn it into an idea of significance, did he use culture to explain the behavior of his informants. But in its first use, in 1958, the phrase was just a convenient way for him to link the two things he was studying: culture and poverty.

After Lewis began studying the poor of Mexico City he started referring to the research he was doing there as the anthropology of poverty. Although he was more interested in the condition of poverty and its causes and consequences than he was in the concept of culture, he was by training an anthropologist. Culture was what anthropologists studied, so what he observed he called a culture. In his case this was the culture of poor people, hence, in shortened form, the culture of the poor, or the culture of poverty. The phrase became a concise way to describe what he was studying and at the same time to capsulize the significance of his research.

The Sánchez Study: Fleshing Out the Thesis

After completing *Five Families*, Lewis intended to follow up with an intensive study of each of the families, but of these, only two—the Sánchez and Martínez studies—were carried out. The Castro family was the first to be dropped from this plan because they did not come from Lewis's own group of informants and he did not know them well. They had been referred to him by a social worker who also had done the fieldwork used to write the day study. Lewis was uncomfortable working with middle-class informants and concerned about the greater potential for conflict with them over the contents of published materials and the greater risks to their anonymity. They and the people who knew them, he believed, would be more likely to read the published work than his poorer, and in some cases barely literate, informants. Although the Lewises did continue to see the Gómez and Gutiérrez families for many years, they too were eventually dropped as subjects for independent study; this was more or less by default, as work with the Sánchez and Martínez families absorbed almost all of the Lewises' time. Lewis would continue to interview Pedro Martínez through 1963 (and visit him for years afterward), but it was not until after the unexpected success of the Sánchez book that he found a publisher for the Martínez materials he and his wife had been working on periodically for twenty years.

Lewis met the Sánchez family in the late summer of 1956, when he was laying the groundwork for the *vecindad* survey. By September he had hired Consuelo Sánchez for the field staff to help administer questionnaires; she was ideal for the two *vecindad* projects because members of her family were long-time residents of the Casa Grande and her aunt Guadalupe lived in the Panaderos. Lewis knew very soon after meeting the four children of Jesús Sánchez that they were exactly the kind of informants he had been searching for to help him develop his family study method. They proved willing and able, albeit in varying degrees, to provide him with the kind of detail about their private lives and thoughts that Tepoztecans had refused or been unable to provide. This was especially true of Consuelo and Manuel, who were not only willing to talk but who were gifted users of the language and accomplished raconteurs as well. However, their father, the rural-born Jesús Sánchez, was, in his reserve and aloofness, more like Tepoztecans than like his own city-born children.

With the Sánchezes, Lewis hoped to do more than document the life-style of one poor family; he wanted to provide some insight into the "psychology of the poor" and to see if his family study method could be used to gather the kind of information necessary to compare the relative roles of culture and family in personality development. "As I began to learn something about each member of the family, I became aware that the single family seemed to illuminate many of the social and psychological problems of lower-class Mexican life. At this point I decided to try a study in depth."[22] The verbal skills, the histrionics, the panache of the Sánchezes added greatly to the literary merit of *The Children of Sánchez,* but I believe that their extraordinary articulateness and high theatrics (especially coming as they did after the long contact with Tepoztecan reserve) led Lewis to overestimate how much could be understood about personality—let alone culture—through the presentation of private lives and thoughts. The Sánchezes revealed a very great deal about what they were like and about the dynamics of their particular family at a certain point in time. But what they revealed about personality development and its relationship to poverty, or to a culture of poverty, is far from evident.

Any independent objectives Lewis may have had when he began working with the Sánchez children were simply swallowed up by their personalities, their strengths as informants, and the dynamics of intra-family relationships. He found them interesting for their own sakes, irrespective of how their stories could be fitted into the larger study of Mexican culture or a culture of poverty. By the time he was ready to publish *The Children of Sánchez,* Lewis was still uncertain about what larger significance the study had, if any. In a letter to the psychologist Gordon Allport, to whom he had sent the "Manuel" section of the book, Lewis searched for explanations: "I am curious to know whether this autobiography will tell you much about Mexican culture or whether you will be more impressed by the common cross-cultural psychological processes which come through—the old psychic unity of mankind—but on a detailed level. I am so impressed by the latter that I may be in danger of being thrown out of the anthropological association after this volume is published."[23]

When Lewis did submit the manuscript for publication, he was prepared to let it stand alone and let readers make of it what they would. But his Random House editor, Jason Epstein, insisted that Lewis provide some kind of introduction or commentary to put the family study in perspective. Lewis suggested putting such an analysis at the end of the book to avoid tainting readers' reaction to the Sánchezes with his own interpretations. But in the end he wrote an introduction in which he described the family and his work with them; he incorporated much of what he had written earlier on *vecindad* culture as well as new material on economic conditions in Mexico. He also elaborated on the culture of poverty and claimed the Sánchez family was representative of it.

In fleshing out his thesis, Lewis offered readers a "provisional conceptual model" that was "based mainly upon" his research in Mexico. The culture of poverty, he wrote, is "in short . . . a way of life, remarkably stable and persistent, passed down from generation to generation along family lines." (This was the first time he explicitly said that the family was a main agent of transmission.) As for its origins, Lewis argued that the culture of poverty "most commonly" came into being "when a stratified social and economic system is breaking down or is being replaced by another, as in the case of the transition from feudalism to capitalism or during the industrial revolution"; it could also develop in response to "imperial conquest" or to the "process of detribalization," as was occurring in Africa. The culture of poverty had "universal characteristics which transcend regional, rural-urban, and even national differences,"[24] Lewis wrote, and he identified several dozen of these in such areas as family structure, interpersonal relations, time orientation, spending patterns, and sense of community. (A complete list of these characteristics or "traits" can be found on pp. 114–15.)

This culture, however, was not defined solely by the individual traits—most of the social and psychological traits could be found in any culture—but by the frequency of their occurrence and by their patterning or clustering. In addition, he wrote, some of the traits, such as alcoholism and machismo, took on a different social function within the culture of poverty than they did when expressed in other cultural contexts. The traits could be viewed "as attempts at local solutions for problems not met by existing institutions and agencies because the people are not eligible for them, cannot afford them, or are suspicious of them."[25] The culture of poverty was not to be taken as a synonym for the lower classes or the peasantry and did not include "primitive peoples whose backwardness is the result of their isolated and underdeveloped technology and whose society [sic] for the most part is not class stratified." It encompassed only those "who are at the very bottom of the socio-economic scale. . . ."[26] For Mexico this meant "at least the lower third of the rural and urban population."[27]

Lewis sent a draft of the introduction to his friend and former colleague Conrad Arensberg, who immediately pointed out the problem in Lewis's thinking:

> I think you are failing to distinguish between source conditions, culture traits and institutions, subcultures and culture areas, all phenomena we need to deal with, but need to keep separate. Hunger and coping with it, or bad housing and crowding . . . are not cultural phenomena, any more than are cold and coping with cold, and though they are part of the lives of people, of the places, societies experiencing these phenomena, the copings do not make culture until we show them to be patterned differently from one society to the next, sanctioned and transmitted as collected. . . .[28]

Lewis wrote an appreciative response to Arensberg, but he defended the thesis by claiming that he could *prove* generational continuity. Then in a postscript characteristic of his uncertain certainty, Lewis added: "I'd hate to spoil it [*The Children of Sánchez*] with questionable models like the culture of poverty, but I've found nothing better to explain the similarities." [29]

Despite the fact that Lewis finally decided to use the Sánchez study to introduce a fuller statement of the culture of poverty thesis, he was aware that this single-family study revealed more about the individuals portrayed than about how they and their personalities were shaped by culture. This is why he subtitled the book "Autobiography of a Mexican Family," rather than "A Mexican Family in the Culture of Poverty," one of the several possibilities he rejected. In consulting his Random House editor about this, Lewis wrote:

> I find it difficult to come up with a really good sub-title for THE CHILDREN OF SÁNCHEZ. Why do you want one? Is it to interest the social scientists? What occurs to me is "Studies in the Culture of Poverty" which I don't like especially. . . .
>
> Can you counter with some better suggestions? "The Culture of Poverty" is a catchy phrase . . . [but] the Sánchez family is not the best example. . . . The family of the maternal aunt Guadalupe would have been much better, but by the same token much less expressive. It is interesting that Jesús Sánchez, the father, has worked his way out of the culture of poverty, whereas his children are still in it, more or less. This is just the opposite of what one might have expected, since the father was born the very year of the Revolution—1910—and still reflects the pre-revolutionary values of authoritarianism, while the children are all post-revolutionary and reflect the greater emphasis upon social mobility and even equalitarianism.[30]

In his final selection of a subtitle Lewis was, in essence, having his cake and eating it too. By discussing the culture of poverty in the introduction he was clearly using the family as an illustrative case; yet as he described them he left readers to infer (just as he had done in *Five Families*) that this study was far from the best evidence he had to offer for his thesis.

Indeed, when Lewis said the Sánchezes were "moving out" of the culture he denied them the sine qua non for membership in it, that is, generational continuity. If the family had ever exhibited the clustering of traits Lewis used to define the subculture, they had been doing so for less than a generation. Lewis undermined his own position when he pointed out the sharp differences in values and life-styles between father and children, making it clear that he believed that the children of Jesús Sánchez had not been socialized into a culture of poverty by their family. To follow Lewis's argument and to accept the Sánchez study as support for it, we have to think of generational continuity in terms of society, not in terms of the family. The city and the *vecindad*, their institutions and practices, and the Sánchez children's peer group have to be seen as the main agents of acculturation and the perpetuators of the culture. This would allow the major responsibility for passing on a negative set of traits to be transferred from the family to the community and to the society at large. This is not what Lewis wrote, but it is consistent with his thesis that the culture came into being as an adaptation to systemically created and perpetuated economic conditions.

The family study approach, however, presents obstacles to generalizing about society precisely because it focuses reader attention on the family and what happens within the family. The format itself communicates to readers the overwhelming importance of the family as an agent of socialization. Between what Lewis wanted to study and what he wanted to generalize about—that is, between his basic unit of research and his conceptual level of generalization—there was a great contradiction and a great deal of empty space. He never fully acknowledged that his research had undergone a shift in focus, but he did recognize that a few family studies did not provide sufficient evidence for his theorizing. Countless times, both in print and in correspondence, Lewis wrote that what he had to say about the existence of a culture of poverty could be tested only through the gathering of hundreds of intensive family studies in countries around the world. When considered en masse, he believed they would reveal a pattern that could not be detected from a single study like *The Children of Sánchez*. But he never made concessions on the utility of the family study method and its potential for providing information whose significance went beyond illuminating family life and individual personality. He acknowledged that this evidence had to be evaluated along with that provided by researchers working at other levels. But he never suggested a methodology for doing this, and he never discussed how he had arrived at his own generalizations.

Much of the description of the culture of poverty—such as its origins and its "universal characteristics"—as presented in the introduction to *The Children of Sánchez* is transparently (and, in places, admittedly) speculative; indeed, there is nothing in the evidentiary base ("my Mexican materials") to support substantial parts of the thesis. But the heart of the introduction is not the theory; it is Lewis's description of the nature of poverty in a modern city and his warnings about the consequences for social stability of economic and political inequality. The discussion of culture is a kind of prelude to a statement on the need to eradicate poverty and the difficulties of doing so.

> It seems to me that the material in this book has important implications for our thinking and our policy in regard to the underdeveloped countries of the world and particularly Latin America. It highlights the social, economic, and psychological complexities which have to be faced in any effort to transform and eliminate the culture of poverty from the world. It suggests that basic changes in the attitudes and value systems of the poor must go hand in hand with improvements in the material conditions of living. . . . even the Mexican capacity for suffering has its limits, and unless ways are found to achieve a more equitable distribution of the growing national wealth and a greater equality of sacrifice during the difficult period of industrialization, we may expect social upheavals, sooner or later.[31]

The basic humanistic thrust of this message is clear, but the policy implications of the material are not, and Lewis made no attempt to clarify them. Yet in the culture of poverty thesis he was making a latently political statement about the role of urban anthropologists and about the potential of his particular research approach to contribute to the fight against poverty. To begin to understand this one has to read, in context, the first two paragraphs Lewis wrote about the existence of a culture of poverty. He was trying to distinguish his research from that of anthropologists who went to "remote corners of the world" to study "primitive and preliterate peoples." These anthropologists accepted their informants' poverty, he wrote, as "a natural and integral part of the whole way of life" and sometimes even took it upon themselves to defend this way of life from "the inroads of civilization." But, he continued, "poverty in modern nations is a very different matter. It suggests class antagonisms, social problems and the need for change; and it often is so interpreted by the subjects of the study."[32]

Because of its potential for social conflict and its toll on the physical and psychological well-being of the people who lived in it, Lewis argued that poverty in industrial nations should not be defended or idealized but attacked and eradicated. Toward this end the findings of urban anthropologists could have "practical significance";[33] or, as he wrote to his friend Maurice Halperin, "I believe that anthropology has a new historic task in reporting honestly and realistically the way of life of these people. I don't know how my colleagues will take to this idea but I am convinced that there is a job to be done as a social scientist and a humanist. Indeed, anthropology has always had these two aspects and family studies offers an ideal medium for their combination."[34]

Lewis wanted to use his work to attack poverty. He thought his ethnographic realism would allow him to do this by conveying to the reading public graphic depictions of poverty, implicit in which, he seemed to suggest, would be messages about its causes and consequences, and perhaps about its solutions as well. However, if his work was to have a practical application, it was necessary that he first produce some findings of significance and relevance to the problem. But it is not easy to make a coherent and dramatic statement about the effects of poverty when one is generalizing about the range of variation in material conditions and life-styles of the poor. In any case Lewis did not like to make the kind of typically academic statement that begins "On the one hand . . ." and proceeds to lay out the irreducible complexities of a problem. Therefore he stopped trying to generalize about all of his informants and reduced the complexities of their lives to a simple and poorly developed hypothesis that had been drawn from the experiences of the worst-case poor among them. As he developed this into a fuller statement, he warned readers of the need to distinguish between poverty and the culture of poverty and pointed out that not all people who live in poverty share a common subculture. But he was not consistent in his use of the phrase, and he failed to make clear that in his view many, if not most, of his own informants did not live in a culture of poverty.

Even when culture was only marginally at issue in his writing, the culture construct, as employed in the culture of poverty theory, was too convenient, too all-purpose a tool for Lewis to abandon, because it allowed him to address a controversial subject such as the causes of poverty from behind a facade. Having trapped himself, he was left in the position of using culture to explain what he believed to be true about poverty's long-term effects on the poor. In the process of working this out, Lewis concentrated on the relationship among extreme poverty, personality development, and mental health, which was not surprising since his research was becoming increasingly centered on issues of personality. As he tried to elaborate on the meaning of these relationships and to develop a list of psychological traits of the culture, he became increasingly dependent upon interpretations of Rorschach tests and TATs administered to his informants. This drew him into his second and more serious entanglement.

The Second Entanglement: Projective Test Analyses

After being dragged kicking into research on culture and personality in Tepoztlán, Lewis became engrossed in the subject. Once he fulfilled his obligations to the Collier-Thompson project on Indian personality, he continued this aspect of the work, gradually increasing the emphasis placed on personality study until it overshadowed his research on culture. Through the remainder of his life he was either actively collaborating, or trying to establish a collaboration with, one or more psychologists or psychiatrists to administer and interpret projective tests and to analyze the psychological content of the interviews.

After completing the village study, Lewis turned first to Erich Fromm, who in 1951 was working in Mexico and lived just a block away from the Lewises in Mexico City. Fromm agreed in 1952 to analyze 300 recountings of dreams that the Lewises had collected in Tepoztlán, a project that was given the working title "The Psycho-Cultural Content of Dreams."[35] This collaboration never materialized, however. Fromm kept the data for many years but, perhaps because of the pressures of his own fieldwork in Mexico, did not undertake the promised analysis.

During the mid-1950s Lewis established a working relationship with members of the Asociación Psicoanalítica Mexicana in Mexico City, a group with which Fromm had formerly been associated.[36] In 1957 Lewis gave a series of nine lectures to the Association on the two-family study he had written up with Ruth Lewis and which they were still trying to get published; in return, Association members gave their impressions of the psychological content of the materials. From this group of men and women Lewis was seeking a different kind of collaboration than he had had with Theodora Abel, who was interested in culture and personality research and therefore in defining modal personalities for specific culture groups. Abel's approach required analyzing as a set a fairly large number of tests administered in the community being studied. She was not interested in doing the "individual write-ups" on a small number of informants that Lewis needed for the family study method he was trying to develop.[37]

Through the Association Lewis met Carolina Luján, a clinical psychologist who served as the Association's chief tester and test interpreter. Luján possessed a forceful intellect, wrote with great clarity, and believed completely in the correctness of her analyses. She was strong in exactly those areas of research on personality in which Lewis was weak. For almost a dozen years (roughly 1957–69) Lewis relied on her interpretations of his informants' personalities. It was Luján who administered and interpreted the Rorschachs and TATs of

Pedro Martínez and the children of Jesús Sánchez, as well as many of his later informants. On these particular tests Luján did blind analyses, but she later read and interpreted the psychological content of the interviews as well. The interpretations were crucial to Lewis because in *Five Families, The Children of Sánchez,* and *Pedro Martínez* he tried to show the effects of severe deprivation on personality development and the interrelationship between culture and personality. The Sánchez study in particular, he hoped, would give readers "a deeper look into the culture of poverty, its psychological manifestations, its effects upon personality development and family life, as well as its political implications."[38]

In 1961, when he was constructing the trait list for the culture of poverty, Lewis sent Luján his "provisional model," complete with trait list, and asked her to identify those traits that could be categorized as "universal characteristics" of the culture of poverty. Luján replied that, although she did not "really know very much about the external manifestations of the culture of poverty as a universal phenomenon," she thought its universal characteristics were:

> emotional and intellectual immaturity. . . . Since emotional and intellectual immaturity can be equated to psychopathology, psychopathology is endemic among the drastically poor. On the emotional level, this immaturity would manifest itself as a lack of control, violent reactions including physical manifestations, and a tendency to immediate satisfaction of instinctive needs. On the intellectual level, it would manifest itself as a lack of foresight, a "present time" orientation with little capacity for long-time planning and objectives. Thinking tends to be concretistic with very limited conceptual abilities. . . .[39]

Luján stressed the "implications of subhuman living conditions for mental health." According to her, the Sánchezes were not "neurotic, but much closer to psychotics and psychopaths, and only very special conditions of the culture, and the tolerance of the environment, keeps them from being more so."[40]

Lewis could not bring himself to accept Luján's conclusions that even when seen in the very narrow context of the culture of poverty these effects constituted emotional or mental illness. But he did believe (or accepted Luján's argument up to this point) that many of his informants had been "damaged" to the extent that their abilities to integrate into the larger society had been destroyed. In the introduction to *The Children of Sánchez* he wrote: "Even the best-intentioned governments of the underdeveloped countries face difficult obstacles because of what poverty has done to the poor. Certainly most of the characters in this volume are badly damaged human beings."[41]

However, even while using Luján's interpretation, albeit a very weak version of it, Lewis continued to argue with her over her diagnoses of mental illness. This prompted Luján to write:

> I hope you are by now desensitized on this point which I know has been for a long time very difficult for you to accept, because you seem to feel there was something derogatory to these people in describing them as mentally sick. Which of course *there most definitely is not*. It might as well be considered derogatory to say there is a high incidence of avitaminosis. And this brings me back to psychological determinism. A psychological determinist believes that what people do and what people are do not depend, as we have been traditionally taught, on "will power" and "conscious effort," but that what they are depends on natural endowment and what they do and what they become depend on environmental conditions and ensuing dynamics, especially early patterns in terms of object relationships. Therefore there cannot possibly be any value judgment implied since there is actually very little personal responsibility attached to what a human being sickened by environmental conditions is or does. However this is not something to be proclaimed and propagated. It would only be taken up and used "carta blanca" to rationalize any and all aberrations. Psychopathology should be understood and combated but never overtolerated, because overtoleration foments it and breeds more pathology, even to collective psychoses.[42]

Lewis's disagreement with Luján over what he saw as a mechanistic application of psychoanalytic theory intensified during his later work on Puerto Rico, but he never stopped using her interpretations.

Perhaps the most fundamental sources of the disagreements between Lewis and Luján lay in their different personal orientations and research interests. As an anthropologist Lewis had to generalize on a level beyond the individual, but as a psychologist Luján was primarily interested in the individual psyche. Luján believed that "psychopathology is . . . bred in the family, but it is the culture that will perpetuate or modify, to a great extent, the psychological structure of the future, and it is the culture that will determine what direction and what expression it will take."[43] This explanation did not satisfy Lewis, who argued that Luján's assessment of the role of the family environment on personality formation underestimated "social, economic and technical factors" that were systemic in nature.[44] Although he was doing little in his research at the time to study the larger social environment, unlike Luján he always had his families placed within a larger setting. Even if there were inaccuracies in the setting as he described it, Lewis did not consider his families in a social or political vacuum and did not want the individual family to have to bear alone the onus for producing "deviant" personalities. But he did not know how these systemic factors, which he accused Luján of neglecting, operated to shape the cultures or personalities of his informants.

Luján could not be of much help to Lewis on this because she was not interested in it as an intellectual problem and she never made any pretense of doing more than analyzing projective test responses and individual life histories. Personally and professionally she was not interested in things political; she did not concern herself with the origins of poverty and, as an analyst, concentrated only on what poverty meant to individual development and how it was experienced in the family. When Lewis asked her to comment on these larger issues, such as the impact of economic deprivation on personality formation, she posited relationships with such great certainty that Lewis, in the absence of an explanation of his own, accepted the general direction of her argument. However, when publishing Luján's interpretations he removed most of the psychoanalytic terminology and greatly understated the relationship she drew between poverty and psychopathology.

By providing Lewis with an explanation of the negative consequences of poverty, Luján helped him, in turn, to explain the significance and uniqueness of poverty experienced in modern urban settings. Lewis used this interpretation, all the while rejecting as nonscientific the psychoanalytic principles on which it was based. While Luján wrote about individual personality, Lewis generalized about the universal social-psychological characteristics of the culture of poverty. Over the years Luján criticized him for misapplying her interpretations, but Lewis claimed he had a right to use them in his own way, to rephrase them to fit the context of his research. He believed he had an obligation to protect his informants from prejudgment by readers and to spare his readers the burden of wading through clinical diagnoses and trying to make sense of psychoanalytic jargon. In addition, Lewis had his own interpretation to present: he wanted to emphasize the suffering, exploitation, and damage wrought by extreme poverty, but he did not want to make his informants appear beyond help or, for that matter, even beyond self-redemption. Herein lay one of his most difficult and sensitive differences with Luján: whereas Luján feared political action by the poor, Lewis thought it would be their salvation.

Lewis and Luján did have common ground in their commitment to the eradication of poverty. Luján believed that if politicians could be made to see, through work like Lewis's, the damage done by poverty, "then perhaps [they] would dictate sane, well-planned measures to change these sad conditions." "Such damage," she wrote Lewis, "has to be made known." [45] Luján did not think that the poor themselves could effect significant reform because she was convinced that the

"infrahuman conditions" in which they lived destroyed their potential for mature moral judgment and responsible political action. Lewis
found this view repugnant and could not reconcile it with his own
deep belief in the need for grass-roots political organization. He often
argued the point with Luján but, perhaps out of his great affection and
respect for her, never made clear the depth of this disagreement.
Luján, for her part, considered it a surface difference, a misunderstanding.

Obligated professionally to provide an explanation of what he meant
by "the psychology of the poor" and "what poverty has done to the
poor," Lewis used what he could accept—actually somewhat more
than he could accept—of Luján's interpretations. He removed technical terms and references to latent homosexuality which he thought
would be misinterpreted by readers, and he wrote of psychological damage rather than mental illness. He conceded impediments to
political organization and action among the people he studied, but
he refused to preclude them. He identified orality and the inability to
delay gratification as traits of the subculture, but he would not say that
his adult informants were immature or childlike, as did Luján, nor
would he state unequivocally that they were incapable of independent
action and decision making.

Not only did Lewis not believe the extreme versions of these interpretations, but I think he could not have faced his informants if he
had published them. His relationship with them was, after all, one
of friendship, whereas Luján's was one of clinician to patient. Even
though Lewis modified and softened Luján's test analyses and discussed them in a context of his choosing, he was to find, as he became
involved in debate over his Puerto Rican research, that he had gone
too far in his use of the psychological damage explanation of the culture of poverty.

(Relevant correspondence can be found on pp. 219–44.)

NOTES

1. This was the title of Lewis's proposal to the Graduate Research Board
of the University of Illinois to study Tepoztecan migrants to Mexico City.

2. Oscar Lewis, "Urbanization without Breakdown: A Case Study," *Scientific Monthly* 75 (1952): 31–41 (reprinted in Lewis, *Anthropological Essays*, pp.
424–25).

3. Oscar Lewis, "The Effects of Technical Progress on Mental Health in
Rural Populations," *América Indígena* 12 (1952): 299–307. This was first delivered as a paper at the International Congress on Mental Health, December 17,
1951, in Mexico City.

4. Oscar Lewis, *Tepoztlán: Village in Mexico* (New York: Holt, Rinehart and Winston, 1960). This book, a condensation of the original village study published by the University of Illinois Press, was prepared for the Case Studies in Cultural Anthropology series edited by George and Louise Spindler. The last chapter of the book is based on the follow-up study done in the summer of 1956. Because the series was designed for classroom use, this condensed version is, unfortunately, the only exposure most students have to the Lewises' original project. It is a poor representation of the effort that went into the first volume.

5. This was the title of Lewis's research proposal to the Wenner-Gren Foundation for Anthropological Research in 1955. Both Wenner-Gren and the University of Illinois Graduate Research Board helped to fund the *vecindad* culture study, supplementing Lewis's Guggenheim award.

6. Oscar Lewis, "La Cultura de Vecindad en la Cuidad de Mexico," *Ciencias Politicas y Sociales* 5 (1959): 349–50. This was first delivered as a paper at the International Congress of Americanists in San José, Costa Rica, in July 1958; the English-language version quoted here was reprinted in Lewis, *Anthropological Essays*, p. 440. The work cited by Lewis in this quote is W. Lloyd Warner, Marcia Meeker, and Kenneth Eells, *Social Class in America: A Manual of Procedure for the Measurement of Social Status* (Chicago: Science Research Associates, 1949). Lewis frequently cited Warner's work on intraclass stratification, which was closely related to his own original research objectives.

7. Lewis, "La Cultura de Vecindad," pp. 349–50; the English translation quoted here is from Lewis, *Five Families*, p. 2.

8. Lewis, *Life in a Mexican Village*, p. 310.

9. When Lewis reprinted this article as "The Culture of the *Vecindad* in Mexico City: Two Case Studies," in *Anthropological Essays*, he deleted his discussion of the culture of poverty concept "to avoid reduplication" (p. 427).

10. This wording is from research proposals Lewis submitted to the Social Science Research Council (summer 1958 funding) and to the National Science Foundation (1959 funding).

11. These students came from all over Central and Latin America to study at the National School of Anthropology and History (located in downtown Mexico City) and to participate in a seminar sponsored by the Organization of American States. As part of that seminar, which Lewis taught during the summers of 1959 and 1960, the students were assigned field projects in the Casa Grande and the Panaderos, as well as in the apartment complex. Lewis frequently recruited field assistants through the National School, where he occasionally taught courses.

12. Letter from Oscar Lewis to Oliver LaFarge, March 31, 1959.

13. Although the Gutiérrezes were the poorest of the families and came closest to the culture of poverty "ideal," Lewis said that of the five families they showed "the best adjustment to life conditions" (*Five Families*, p. 15). They were eventually able to move "up" from the Panaderos to the nearby Casa Grande, where they were living in 1983 when I visited them with Ruth Lewis.

14. Ibid., pp. 13–14. More specifically, Lewis described the Gómezes by saying: *"pertenecen ahora a la clase trabajadora—grupo medio superior . . ."* (*La Gaceta*, El Fondo de Cultura Económica, September 1961).

15. Lewis, *Five Families*, p. 16. Many times in letters and public lectures Lewis made the point that the Sánchezes were moving out of the subculture and said that Marta was the only family member who fully manifested the values and behavior he associated with the subculture. See p. 60 and the letters to Hyman Rodman (no. 90 in the Appendix) and Lloyd Ohlin (no. 106 in the Appendix).

16. Lewis, *Five Families*, p. 16.

17. Letter from Oscar Lewis to Virginia Rice, September 14, 1958.

18. Lewis, *Five Families*, p. 1.

19. At the time he first stated the thesis Lewis had been most influenced by American and British anthropologists and sociologists who studied lower- and working-class communities (see ibid., p. 2). Equal in importance to Lloyd Warner's work (see note 6) in its impact on Lewis's thinking was Allison Davis's research on kinship networks among blue-collar workers. In a letter to William Foote Whyte on March 4, 1961, Lewis wrote that he had been especially impressed by Davis's chapter on "The Motivation of the Under-privileged Worker," in Whyte's *Industry and Society* (New York: McGraw-Hill, 1946), pp. 84–106. After publishing the culture of poverty thesis, Lewis also began collecting "evidence" from novels about the poor in American and European cities. (At one time he planned to do a study on representations of the poor in popular fiction.) In addition to all of these sources, Lewis was also very taken with Henry Mayhew's *London Labour and the London Poor*, which he read around 1960. The similarities in their descriptions of the lifeways of the urban poor are striking. I read Lewis's copy of Mayhew's book, a condensed version edited by Peter Quennell (London: Spring Book, n.d.), in which he had made margin notes pointing out the similarities.

20. Lewis and Lewis, "Two Family Portraits," p. 4.

21. Letter from Oscar Lewis to Kimball Young, March 21, 1950 (see no. 29 in the Appendix).

22. Lewis, *Children of Sánchez*, p. xix.

23. Letter from Oscar Lewis to Gordon Allport, September 11, 1958.

24. Quotes in this paragraph are from Lewis, *Children of Sánchez*, pp. xxiv–xxv.

25. Ibid., p. xxvii.

26. Ibid., p. xxv.

27. Ibid., p. xxvi.

28. Letter from Conrad Arensberg to Oscar Lewis, May 10, 1960.

29. Letter from Oscar Lewis to Conrad Arensberg, November 3, 1960.

30. Draft of letter from Oscar Lewis to Jason Epstein, December 9, 1960. When Lewis rewrote the letter he omitted the second paragraph of this quotation.

31. Lewis, *Children of Sánchez*, pp. xxx–xxxi.

32. Lewis, *Five Families*, pp. 1–2.

33. Ibid., p. 2.

34. Letter from Oscar Lewis to Maurice Halperin, April 11, 1958 (see no. 48 in the Appendix).

35. Letter to Oscar Lewis from Erich Fromm, July 31, 1952. Lewis cited the project and its title as work in progress in his annual departmental report on professional activities for 1951--52.

36. Lewis was introduced to members of the Psychoanalytic Association by the Mexican psychologist Dr. Sara Mekler, who had received training at the institute established by the Association. Lewis and Mekler shared an interest in family studies and met at a symposium in Texas on family therapy. Some of the young physicians who founded the Association had received part or all of their training at Columbia University Medical School and/or its Department of Psychiatry, including a few who had studied with Lewis's former teacher, Abram Kardiner. These young doctors sought an affiliation with Erich Fromm's group when they were establishing the Association but later became quite antagonistic toward him and his approach. Lewis did not share the Association's view of Fromm and tried to keep open the possibility of future collaboration with him.

37. Letter to Oscar Lewis from Theodora Abel, October 30, 1949.

38. Letter from Oscar Lewis to Jason Epstein, May 14, 1960.

39. Letter from Carolina Luján to Oscar Lewis, January 10, 1961.

40. Letter from Carolina Luján to Oscar Lewis, November 18, 1961.

41. Lewis, *Children of Sánchez*, p. xxx.

42. Letter from Carolina Luján to Oscar Lewis, November 18, 1961.

43. Letter from Carolina Luján to Oscar Lewis, October 14, 1960.

44. Letter from Oscar Lewis to Carolina Luján, November 15, 1961 (see no. 69 in the Appendix).

45. Letter from Carolina Luján to Oscar Lewis, November 18, 1961.

CHAPTER FOUR

PUERTO RICO: TESTING THE THESIS

Even before *The Children of Sánchez* was published, Lewis had set his sights on Cuba as the location of his next research project. He wanted to return to the study of revolutionary change, this time not after the fact, as in Mexico, but as it was happening, using family studies as the method of documentation. In 1961, shortly after the Bay of Pigs invasion, he was able to visit the island on a reporter's visa (for *Harper's*) and found Castro's government receptive to his proposals to do research there. However, he was not able to solve the problems of funding and visas during 1961, and in the meantime *The Children of Sánchez* had been published to great critical success. In addition, in 1962 Michael Harrington used a variation on the culture of poverty thesis in *The Other America* to describe and explain poverty in the United States, and the result was a very popular and influential book.[1] It drew particular attention from politicians interested in poverty as a political issue.

Lewis was impressed by this and by the attention it brought to his own work in the United States and abroad. It also reinforced his belief in the utility of the thesis to provide a conceptual framework for material about which he found it increasingly difficult to generalize. Such a framework might give his research better standing in the social sciences and help him to obtain the large grants necessary to carry on the kind of intensive family studies he wanted to do. With the new priority given by the Kennedy administration to social welfare policy in the early 1960s, research proposals to test the culture of poverty thesis were eminently fundable.

The U.S. government's new interest in studying the poor dove-

72

tailed with a small backlash in Mexico against the success of *The Children of Sánchez*. There, a few of Lewis's critics, angered by a North American criticizing Mexico, suggested that he study poverty in his own country. Responding in part to both of these groups, and with hope dimming that he could work in Cuba for any extended period of time, Lewis put together two proposals for studying poverty in U.S. settings—one on Tepoztecan migrants in Chicago and a second on Puerto Rican migrants in New York City. The Tepoztlán-Chicago plan was not pursued beyond initial contacts due to problems with accessibility of informants. But Lewis did receive a large grant from the Social Security Administration (Department of Health, Education, and Welfare) to fund three years of research on families "living in the subculture of poverty" in Puerto Rico and New York City.[2]

After more than twenty years in the field, this was the first large research grant Lewis received. In the next half dozen years he would receive two more grants of similar size (from $100,000 to $200,000), and they would change the way he worked. Until the Puerto Rican project, all of Lewis's fieldwork had been carried out on shoestring budgets, usually by a series of very small grants (from 500 to several thousand dollars) that were awarded to cover just one or two aspects of the work, such as travel, typing, or translation. Although he was able to recruit volunteers and students who worked for short periods on small stipends, Lewis did most of the basic research himself. The accessibility of money and staff for the Puerto Rican research made this the first of his projects on which he had to spend more time in organization, supervision, and administration than he did on interviewing and other fieldwork. He planned and directed the initial survey of informants but personally administered only a small number of questionnaires. Whereas he had done almost all of the interviews published in *The Children of Sánchez* and *Pedro Martínez,* he would do only about one-third of all interviewing in Puerto Rico and New York. Between 1963 and 1970, more than fifty people worked on the Puerto Rican project (although probably no more than a dozen at any one time) as fieldworkers, transcribers, translators, and editors.

The major objectives of the Puerto Rican project as listed in the proposal were to:

compare family life, the quality of interpersonal relations, and . . . value systems . . . ;

test the hypothesis that the culture of poverty in the modern world has some social and psychological characteristics which transcend regional, rural-urban and national differences;

test the hypothesis that urbanization is accompanied by secularization, disorganization, increased individualism and a greater incidence of mental illness;

. . . determine the . . . stability . . . of the basic traits of the culture of poverty . . . ;

delineate the significant levels or sub-groups within the culture of poverty, providing data on the structure and psychodynamics of family life and the range and variety of family types associated with each level, with attention to . . . the relationship between income, standard of living, educational level, and social and religious participation.[3]

The breadth of these objectives reveals the lack of specificity of problem in Lewis's research design and also illustrates the kind of layered effect one can see in all the research proposals he wrote during the 1950s and 1960s. Lewis never put aside an old problem to study a new one; he simply added to his list. His research increasingly focused more on approach than on problem. As broad as his initial goals were, he added to them when he applied for a large renewal grant in 1966. He included no less than seven new objectives, among them to study the worldviews of schoolchildren, rural relatives of selected informants, second-generation families in New York, and a small number of North American black families; in addition he planned to compare "successful" with "unsuccessful" families, and the families of prostitutes with those of nonprostitutes.

The Fieldwork

Lewis went to San Juan in June 1963 and remained on the island through the following summer. Ruth Lewis joined him there in the winter, but she was occupied with the final work on *Pedro Martínez* and did not join the field team. To assist him Lewis brought along three anthropology graduate students from the University of Illinois (Douglas Butterworth, Vera Green, and Judy Hellawell), a senior from Radcliffe (Elizabeth Hegeman), and three friends from Mexico (Lourdes Marín and Consuelo and Manuel Sánchez).[4] Puerto Rican field staff were selected from recommendations made by Rosa Celeste Marín, head of the University of Puerto Rico's School of Social Work. This is how Lewis met Francisca Muriente, who became his principal field assistant and who, over the next six years, would account for nearly half of all interviewing done in San Juan and New York. More than a half dozen others worked for very short periods, but the only people who did any extended interviewing besides Lewis and Muriente were Butterworth; Anadel Lynton, Lewis's long-time assistant from Mexico, who joined the project in 1966; and Aida Torres de

Estepan, a Dominican exile Lewis hired in San Juan and kept on for the New York phase of the project.

Employing Manuel and Consuelo Sánchez as part of the field team was in Lewis's official work plan. He wanted to observe their inter-action with poor Puerto Ricans and see if their sense of identification would be greater than their felt differences. Consuelo and Manuel worked in the barrio of La Esmeralda in overlapping periods during the second half of 1963 and the beginning of 1964. They were assigned to different families to record household observations rather than to interview. Consuelo was more experienced in this work than was her brother, and she made far more detailed observations.[5] However, their field notes were never used in published work.

Lewis began the research, as he always did, with a survey. He chose four poor neighborhoods of metropolitan San Juan, each of which represented a different type of housing settlement.[6] After introduc-tions had been made through the barrios' *comisarios*, or presidents, he and his staff administered the usual basic questionnaires on house-hold composition, "luxury" household possessions, and residence and employment history.[7] To these Lewis added a new schedule on migration to the U.S. mainland. With the help of his assistants he wrote fifteen additional questionnaires, but these were intended for application only in the second, more intensive stage of the research, which would be devoted to family case studies.

Despite having deliberately chosen to conduct his survey in four dis-tinct neighborhoods, Lewis selected all five of his family case studies from one barrio, the oceanfront shantytown of La Esmeralda. In the summer of 1964, when the work in San Juan was well underway, Lewis moved the project to New York City, and during the following year he, Muriente, Butterworth, Torres de Estepan, and a few tem-porary workers began a survey of fifty families. All of the New York informants were related to people interviewed in San Juan and were chosen to provide a comparison between life on the island and on the mainland. The only New York households in which work continued beyond the survey stage were those of relatives or principals in the five case studies begun in San Juan.

Evaluating the Material

Between 1963 and 1969 Lewis and his staff collected more material than had been gathered on all of his earlier projects combined. In bulk and complexity it was formidable and its receptivity to manage-ment further diminished by the fact that in the field Lewis himself never kept records, logs, or diaries. With incomplete records of the fieldwork and no breakdown of data by individual or topic (except for that distilled from the four basic questionnaires and material culture studies), Lewis essentially processed all the data in his head.[8] (He and Ruth Lewis were the only people to read all of the material as it was sent into a central office.) No attempt was made to do a content analysis of the interviews—more than 30,000 transcribed pages—even though they contained the great bulk of the data. Working in this manner there was virtually no way to produce generalizations about the material that were anything more than impressions or intuitions.

From the Puerto Rican research Lewis planned to prepare, with the assistance of Ruth Lewis, eight separate manuscripts: an analysis of questionnaire data, five family studies, and two life histories of women in prostitution. As if this were not enough, during various stages of the research Lewis was involved in several other projects as well, such as the interviewing for and write-up of *A Death in the Sánchez Family* and planning the Cuba project.[9] During the first year of fieldwork in San Juan, *Pedro Martínez* was completed and published.[10]

In the midst of all this, Lewis was in failing health. He had been diagnosed as having heart disease (which had taken the life of his father and his older brother at age fifty-one) and was told that without a change in diet and work load he might live no longer than five years. A lifetime of chronic illness was also catching up with him; from childhood he had suffered from allergies, gastroenteritis, and migraines, and these had been aggravated by the many illnesses contracted in the fields, such as amoebic dysentery, food poisoning, intestinal sprue, and typhus. In the years after India, Lewis was rather heavily medicated and perhaps could not have functioned in the field otherwise. He was warned not to live in precisely those areas where he spent a good deal of time: the high altitude of Mexico City and the hot and humid climates of Puerto Rico and Cuba. He made virtually no concessions in diet, place of work, or work load, however, and by the mid-1960s some of the people closest to him noted the impact his health problems were beginning to have on his memory and critical faculties.

It is not surprising that under these circumstances Lewis had difficulty grasping the meaning of the Puerto Rican materials. Furthermore, he lacked confidence in his own hastily acquired knowledge of the island. When compared to his knowledge of Mexican history and culture, and of Spanish and Aztecan contributions to them, Lewis knew relatively little about Puerto Rico's history or culture, or the mix of native, Spanish, and African traditions. Lewis had done a great deal of historical research on Mexico, including substantial work with primary source materials, but most of what he knew of Puerto Rican

La Esmeralda, San Juan, 1964. (Photograph by Oscar Lewis)

A street in La Esmeralda, San Juan, 1964. (Photograph by Oscar Lewis)

history came from reading a fairly small number of secondary sources. He also had limited firsthand experience in the culture when compared to Mexico, where he had mingled for years with people from all but the highest levels of society and had established many close and enduring friendships. In Puerto Rico, too, Lewis had his usual wide circle of contacts in government and in the academic and intellectual communities, but the relationships were not of the same quality as those in Mexico. (The major exceptions were friendships with his collaborators Francisca Muriente and Muna Muñoz Lee.) As an avid student of Mexico, Lewis could communicate on an equal footing with his Mexican colleagues; but he did not enjoy the same give-and-take with Puerto Rican colleagues.

When compared with the time he lived in Mexico, the total time Lewis spent in Puerto Rico was relatively short; however, when compared with the field trips of other anthropologists, it was not at all insubstantial. After his first fourteen months on the island Lewis's project headquarters shifted between New York City and Urbana, Illinois; but in those years between 1964 and 1968, when Lewis had to divide his field time between the New York and San Juan phases of the project, he spent about three months of each year on the island.[11] However, in neither city did he live in his informants' neighborhoods, nor did he spend a great deal of time in their homes (although his assistant, Francisca Muriente, certainly did). He often found it necessary to conduct his interviews in the project's Manhattan office because of the noise and the lack of privacy in informants' homes.

Lewis was unable to establish relationships with his major Puerto Rican informants that went as deep as those he had with the Sánchezes and the Martínezes. This was not only due to their greater numbers and the smaller amount of time he spent with them, or to his lesser knowledge of Puerto Rico; it was because many of his major informants (and I refer *only* to these informants, not to all individuals interviewed, and most certainly not to Puerto Ricans in general) were unlike anyone else he had ever interviewed or had ever met. His contact with some La Esmeralda residents seems at first to have shocked him, then to have left him nonplussed. They were much more open and uninhibited in what they were willing to discuss and to allow fieldworkers to observe, protecting from direct observation only the most intimate acts of their private lives. About the Ríos family, for example, Lewis wrote that they came "closer to the expression of an unbridled id than any other people I have studied." It was to this he referred when he wrote that the Sánchezes, by comparison, were "almost middle class."[12]

Lewis had no apparent problems in establishing rapport with these individuals for interviewing purposes, but he does not seem to have been able to go much beyond this, perhaps because he could not identify with them. This was true even for the Ríos family, with whom he enjoyed an especially congenial relationship. Yet he did not form the "warm and lasting friendships," or the family relationship, he experienced with the Sánchezes.[13] Beyond the working rapport and the congeniality there was, in effect, a wall that Lewis could not penetrate—not because of resistance on the informants' part, but because he did not know the direction or have any conveyance for transporting himself into their world. He literally could not chart this territory. He could describe it, but he could not explain it.

Nevertheless, midway through the research Lewis published the first of the family studies (La Vida, 1966). In its introduction he had to describe the Ríoses and discuss them in relation to his other informants. Although he believed he knew the Ríos family well, he was not at all certain that he knew Puerto Rico or Puerto Ricans. Consequently, he had difficulty determining where the Ríoses fit in, both within his own subculture construct and within the larger context of Puerto Rican culture.

Lewis wrote about this problem to Elizabeth Herzog, an old friend from Columbia University, who was then with the Department of Health, Education, and Welfare, one of several funding agencies for the Puerto Rican project. He described his struggle to resolve the question of how representative the Ríos family was of a universal culture of poverty as compared with something "distinctively Puerto Rican. I have no doubt there are both elements here but it is difficult to say which is the predominant one. . . ."[14] In the same letter he also noted that he had been unable to determine whether the practice of prostitution by some of the Ríos women might not put them outside the subculture. In any case, as he had written Herzog earlier, he did "not want theory to get too far ahead of the facts."[15] This was somewhat disingenuous, since all the data were not even collected, let alone analyzed.

Lewis was unable to resolve the problem to his satisfaction and in La Vida presented the Ríoses "not . . . as a typical Puerto Rican family but rather as representative of one style of life in a Puerto Rican slum. The frequency distribution of this style of life cannot be determined until we have many comparable studies from other slums in Puerto Rico and elsewhere" (emphasis added).[16] He took the heart out of this qualification, however, by saying that the Ríoses "reflect many of the characteristics of the subculture" and by presenting them, through the book's subtitle, as "A Puerto Rican Family in the Culture of Poverty."[17] But the study's general utility, he argued, was the insight it offered, not into culture, but into "individual psychology and family dynamics."[18] By the end of the introduction the reader cannot be certain if Lewis meant the Ríoses to represent the culture of poverty or if he meant to present them as just one family who happened to be poor and Puerto Rican.

The Culture of Poverty after Puerto Rico

As it is stated in the introduction to *La Vida*, the culture of poverty thesis is a longer but not greatly changed version of what Lewis had written in the introduction to *The Children of Sánchez*. The significant elaborations and additions are these:

1. While reiterating his hypothesis that the culture of poverty had its origins in highly stratified, rapidly developing capitalist societies and among colonial peoples following their conquest by imperial forces, Lewis added: "The most likely candidates for the culture of poverty are the people who come from the lower strata of a rapidly changing society and are already partially alienated from it." This was defined to encompass "landless rural workers who migrate to the cities," which was the category into which most of Lewis's Puerto Rican informants fell.[19]

2. Lewis stated in much more definite and mechanistic terms the way in which the culture perpetuated itself: "By the time *slum children* are age six or seven they have usually absorbed the basic values and attitudes of their *subculture* and are not *psychologically* geared to take full advantage of changing conditions or increased opportunities which may occur in their lifetime" (emphasis added).[20] Here, again, he identified the culture with a place, that is, a slum, something he just as often claimed to be a misapplication of the concept. In his use of "slum children" he suggested, as he did earlier with the Sánchezes, that youngsters in these poor communities were being socialized into a culture that was "an adaptation to a set of objective conditions of the larger society" and not into "one style of life" particular to their family (as he speculated might be true of the Ríoses).[21] By stating that the community's shared values and attitudes, once internalized, rendered children unable to improve their lives, Lewis moved his generalizations into conceptual areas he had long tried to avoid—ideal types and modal personality. This violated the basic premise of his research that careful and prolonged study of any culture would reveal a significant range of variation in family type and in individual personality and behavior. In the process he was positing relationships among economic conditions, culture, and personality that he did not explicitly examine in his work. In essence the implied relationships

were these: certain economic and social conditions in capitalist societies induce a distinctive cultural response which creates an individual
and collective psychology that dooms its possessors to lives of impov-
erishment. In the longer version of the thesis, I think readers can see
that what Lewis was really talking about was not a culture of poverty
but a psychology of oppression.

3. Having established the centrality of the psychological traits to
the subculture construct, Lewis paradoxically made a half-hearted effort to modify his position on the consequences of extreme economic
deprivation for emotional and mental health. For a half dozen years
he had been quietly, but heatedly, disagreeing with Luján's continual
diagnoses of mental illness in his informants, and in the Ríos study he
finally stated this in print: "It has been my experience over many years
that the psychiatrists, clinical psychologists and social workers who
have read the autobiographies and psychological tests of the people
I have studied, have often found more negative elements than I am
willing to grant. This has also been the case with the present volume.
Their findings may reflect some bias inherent in the tests themselves,
but perhaps more important, it seems to me, is the failure to see these
people within the context of the culture of poverty."[22] This was all
part of Lewis's attempt to offset the negative aspects of his informants'
lives and to emphasize their individual and collective good points, as
well as the positive, adaptive mechanisms of the culture of poverty.
In spite of this, he retained in his model as a culture trait the high
incidence of psychopathology (a direct contribution from Luján's test
analyses).

4. Lewis took a much clearer position on what he thought were the
prerequisites for eliminating the culture of poverty: "basic structural
changes in society," "redistributing wealth," and political action by
the poor. "When the poor become class conscious or active members
of trade-union organizations, or when they adopt an internationalist
outlook on the world, they are no longer part of the culture of poverty,
although they may still be desperately poor. Any movement, be it
religious, pacifist or revolutionary, which organizes and gives hope to
the poor and effectively promotes solidarity and a sense of identification with larger groups, destroys the psychological and social core of
the culture of poverty."[23]

In using the culture of poverty to speculate about the systemic
causes of and solutions to poverty, as well as to explain the Ríos
family's behavior, psychology, character structure, and culture, Lewis
made clear his intention to use his thesis to generalize on several different conceptual levels and to link in causal relationships the various
phenomena he studied: the family, individual personality and charac-

ter structure, and community life and institutions. However, the part of his data that he did publish, and the form in which he chose to publish it, never proved adequate to the task of integrating the information produced from the several levels of investigation. The use of the culture of poverty theory to force an integration was not only artificial but led Lewis to postulate relationships he did not demonstrate, let alone prove, with his own data. Therefore his generalizations—on the family and socialization, personality and poverty, and capitalism and culture—remained parallel, no matter how hard he tried to make them converge.

The family study approach, which was so compatible with Lewis's skills and interests, was too limited conceptually for all that he wanted to write about, as he himself admitted in *La Vida:* "after having worked for a number of years on the level of family analysis, I find it helpful to return again to the higher conceptual level of history and culture." In an attempt to make his parallel lines of argument converge, and perhaps also to justify the family as a unit of study, Lewis claimed: "The intensive study of the life of even a single extended family . . . tells us something . . . about the history and culture of the larger society in which these people live. It may also reflect something of national character, although this would be difficult to prove."[24] Although he admitted that such statements went against his earlier views, and in particular his rejection of abstractions such as national character, he now found it "helpful" (if not necessarily warranted by the evidence) to generalize on this level, in order to link history and culture to family organization and personality formation.

To make these linkages and to explain differences in personality and life-style of his Mexican and Puerto Rican informants, Lewis offered his interpretation of the differential impact on personality formation of Mexican and Puerto Rican cultures and political histories. The version that appears in print is substantially less harsh than his draft versions, due in large part to criticism of the earlier version by his translator, Muna Muñoz Lee. Muñoz Lee was the granddaughter and daughter of two of the leading political figures of twentieth-century Puerto Rico, Luis Muñoz Rivera and his son Luis Muñoz Marín (governor of Puerto Rico at the time Lewis was working there). Muñoz Lee, whose mother was from Mississippi, had lived and studied in the United States, but she was first and foremost a Puerto Rican and a student of its history and culture. Throughout the course of the project Lewis found himself in continuous debate with her on his interpretation of Puerto Rico and Puerto Ricans.

Muñoz Lee felt that Lewis's greater attachment to and knowledge of Mexico led him to slight Puerto Rico's history and culture. There was truth in this, of course; Lewis had been in love with Mexico and Mexicans, and (especially) their revolutionary past, since he first went there in 1943. In his eyes Puerto Rico and Puerto Ricans always suffered by comparison; theirs was "an unusually sad history, a history of isolation and abandonment, a history with few glorious moments." Mexicans achieved "a much higher pre-Hispanic civilization" and had "a sense of a great past, a sense of historic continuity. . . ." But one of the greatest differences between the two countries, Lewis said, lay in "their very different reaction to oppression and exploitation. The Mexicans were fighters and revolutionaries"; their wars were "bloody, prolonged and heroic." The Puerto Rican people "were more broken by the Conquest and the colonial period" than were Mexicans, and "somehow this has left a distinctive mark on the family and personal lives of many of its people. . . ."[25] The differences that emerged between the Mexican and Puerto Rican families he studied, Lewis wrote in *La Vida*, were "undoubtedly related to the different histories of Mexico and Puerto Rico."[26]

Muñoz Lee rejected this interpretation and the importance Lewis assigned to revolutionary struggle. The Mexican Revolution seemed to her bloody but not heroic, and its effects "do not seem to have been far-reaching."[27] She thought Lewis understated the level of colonial resistance by Puerto Ricans and overstated the importance of their Indian past, when it really was their African heritage that was essential to understand. But mostly Muñoz Lee did not accept the logic that allowed Lewis to jump from historical events to personality traits. (See the complete exchange between Muñoz Lee and Lewis in the Appendix, nos. 93–101, 113, 115, 118, 120.)

In a letter to family therapist Nathan Ackerman, Lewis carried this logic to its outer limits and in the process stretched the culture of poverty concept beyond recognition: "Most of the people that I am writing about are a hurt people, and if a lack of a sense of history and a lack of identification with a great tradition are to be taken as crucial elements of the culture of poverty, then one might argue that all of Puerto Rico has a culture of poverty."[28] These comments have to be taken as casual remarks. Yet they do not misrepresent the central importance Lewis assigned to political history in the evolution of both culture and personality. Nor, I think, do they misrepresent his tendency to view Puerto Rico and its people as suffering from a psychology of oppression, a fatalistic outlook resulting from a prolonged period of victimization and insufficient resistance. I believe that this attitude colored all of Lewis's attempts to interpret the Puerto Rican material and was reinforced by his overconcentration on the poorest and most deviant of his informants.

Another factor influencing Lewis's thinking on the Puerto Rican work was his degree of dependence, due in large part to the size of the project, on collaborators and assistants. For his most detailed and intimate view of daily life in the households of the five "sample" families Lewis had to rely on Muriente, who was able to tred where Lewis could not. She had an uncanny ability to be accepted into the households as a peer, while at the same time performing as the compleat observer.[29] No matter how fine her work, no matter that Lewis planned and directed it, the observations made were not his own. The perspective on these families provided in the day studies, such as those published in *La Vida*, is Muriente's, not Lewis's.

In addition to relying on Muriente's contributions in the field, Lewis also depended upon Luján for analysis of the psychological content of the material and for projective test interpretations, Muñoz Lee for translation and guidance on Puerto Rican history and culture, and Ruth Lewis for organizing and editing the field materials. Among these collaborators Lewis could find no analytic consensus that might resolve his own uncertainties. Muriente was a trained sociologist but was mainly interested in practical applications of the work, which she approached with a missionary zeal.[30] She wanted to report the facts of poverty and was little interested in academic interpretations of these facts. Muñoz Lee, like Muriente, brought deep feelings of compassion and nationalism to the work, as well as a great intellect that she consistently used to challenge Lewis's views of her country. By contrast, Luján had no particular interest in Puerto Rico and no political agenda; her orientation was relentlessly clinical. In this sense she had little or nothing in common with Muriente and Muñoz Lee. Ruth Lewis was perhaps the only one who came close to sharing her husband's view of Puerto Rico, but she was never fully at ease with the project or the materials gathered because of how dependent she and her husband were on the fieldwork of others. For her, it was too great a departure from their prior twenty years of research.[31]

Of the eight manuscripts Lewis planned to develop, he published only two. Two life histories of women in prostitution were incompletely drawn and did not warrant publication (one of the principal informants left town while interviewing was in progress and Lewis could not relocate her). Three of the family studies were in the editing stage before work on them was suspended. A fourth, written up as a comparison of three generations of women in one family, prompted Lewis to rethink his whole culture of poverty construct.

(Relevant correspondence can be found on pp. 245–63.)

NOTES

1. Michael Harrington, *The Other America* (New York: Macmillan, 1961).

2. Grant application (#127-3-058) submitted to the Social Security and Welfare Administration, Department of Health, Education, and Welfare, in October 1962. With extension grants Lewis received a total of $136,497 between June 1, 1963, and May 30, 1965. He had supplemental support from a Guggenheim Fellowship ($6,000), the Wenner-Gren Foundation for Anthropological Research ($5,000), and the Institute for the Study of Man ($5,000). The proposal submitted to the Social Security and Welfare Administration had been turned down by the National Science Foundation in 1962.

3. Grant application (#6-2846) submitted to the Office of Education, Department of Health, Education, and Welfare. Lewis was to have received about $150,000 for the period 1967–70, but he terminated the project early in order to begin work in Cuba.

4. Butterworth and Green, both now deceased, and Hellawell all went on to become professors of anthropology. Hegeman studied anthropology at Columbia, then took a Ph.D in clinical psychology from New York University. Others who took part in the interviewing, but only for very short periods, were Richard Pieternella (Puerto Rico), Lourdes Marín (Mexico), Viviana Muñoz Borden (Puerto Rico), and Susan Holper (United States); the latter two worked only in New York.

5. As mentioned in chapter 3, Consuelo Sánchez did day studies for Lewis in Mexico. She had an extraordinary eye for detail and a unique writing style. Her brother Manuel was basically a storyteller and better at recording conversations and writing his own impressions than he was at objectively recording details. He had never been part of the paid staff in Mexico, as Consuelo had, but he had interviewed friends and relatives with Lewis's encouragement. From time to time, beginning in Tepoztlán, Lewis used informants as fieldworkers or turned fieldworkers into informants. He also liked informants to meet one another and to observe their interaction. For this purpose he arranged a meeting, for example, between Jesús Sánchez and Pedro Martínez in Mexico City.

The most interesting aspect of Consuelo and Manuel's fieldwork in San Juan was their interaction with informants. Manuel, who is much more congenial and outgoing than his sister, had little trouble striking up relationships in La Esmeralda, but he clearly did not feel any natural affinity with the people he was studying. He became homesick very early in the study and returned to Mexico. Consuelo, despite her gifts of observation and description, is not especially good at getting along with people. She felt out of place in La Esmeralda and, as evidenced by her word choice in the day studies, took a very judgmental stance toward some of the residents.

6. A description of the four neighborhoods covered in the survey can be found in the write-up of questionnaire data, *A Study of Slum Culture: Backgrounds for La Vida* (New York: Random House, 1968), pp. 33–38.

7. Lewis received assistance in his choice of informants from Dr. Marín

of the School of Social Work, who was studying 225 "low income, multiple-problem families" (see Lewis, *La Vida*, p. xxv). Lewis said he agreed to study 10 of the 225, among whom was the Ríos family of *La Vida*. But Muriente had already met and begun interviewing the Ríoses independently in the process of administering survey questionnaires in La Esmeralda. Lewis made contact through their social workers with the other "multiproblem" families who lived in different barrios around the city. He even considered using the social workers to do fieldwork, but their reporting was too clinical for him, and he did not continue working with any of the families he met through them.

8. Lewis saved everything, including notes written on the backs of envelopes, but he always regarded filing and organizing as wastes of time. Even the tapes he and his assistants recorded were often identified by no more than the first name of an informant, the date, the initials of the interviewer, and the tape speed—and sometimes by only the first and last of these items. Fern Hartz, Lewis's secretary from the time of the Puerto Rican project until his death, began to bring some order to his office files, but Lewis rarely had all the material on any one informant in the same place at the same time, so Mrs. Hartz could not have kept a complete record.

9. Although *A Death in the Sánchez Family* was not published until 1969, the interviewing on which it was based was done by Lewis in late 1962 and during 1963.

10. In late 1963, when Ruth Lewis was reading the galleys for *Pedro Martínez* (she had done almost all of the editing of the field materials used in preparing it), she pointed out to her husband certain informational gaps or ambiguities in the final version. He flew from Puerto Rico to Mexico to interview Martínez, collecting new material for insertion in the galleys.

11. While working out of New York City, Lewis maintained project headquarters in the offices of the Institute for the Study of Man. Vera Rubin, a Caribbeanist who founded and headed the Institute until her death in 1985, was a friend of Lewis and a long-time supporter of his research.

12. Lewis, *La Vida*, p. xxvi.

13. Lewis, *Children of Sánchez*, p. xx.

14. Letter from Oscar Lewis to Elizabeth Herzog, March 29, 1966 (see no. 117 in the Appendix).

15. Letter from Oscar Lewis to Elizabeth Herzog, March 10, 1966 (see no. 111 in the Appendix).

16. Lewis, *La Vida*, pp. xxv.

17. Ibid.

18. Ibid., p. xxi.

19. Ibid., p. xlv.

20. Ibid. This position is very different from the view of early socialization Lewis held when working in Tepoztlán. Then he thought "adult life experiences" had an impact on character and behavior. Letter from Oscar Lewis to Theodora Abel, January 18, 1950.

21. Lewis, *La Vida*, p. xlv.

22. Ibid., p. xxviii.

23. Ibid., p. xlviii.

24. Ibid., p. xv.

25. Letter from Oscar Lewis to Muna Muñoz Lee, May 24, 1965 (see no. 93 in the Appendix).

26. Lewis, *La Vida*, p. xv.

27. Letter from Muna Muñoz Lee to Oscar Lewis, May 25, 1965 (see no. 97 in the Appendix).

28. Letter from Oscar Lewis to Nathan Ackerman, January 4, 1966. Ackerman was one of the psychiatrists Lewis asked to interpret projective tests and psychological content of life histories for publication in companion volumes to his family studies. Lewis also used Ackerman's book, *The Psychodynamics of Family Life*, in his graduate seminar on family studies.

29. This can be seen in a reading of any of the day studies done by Muriente. An appearance by Lewis to check on the work (duly recorded by Muriente in the running notes she kept) interrupted regular activities and the conversation took on a more formal tone, whereas Muriente blended in with family members, joined in household chores, and was addressed as a peer. Her notes, however, sound as if they were written by someone standing outside and completely detached from what was happening. I have never observed Muriente at work, but I have visited La Esmeralda with her and have seen the ease with which she moved through the community.

30. I asked Muriente how she went about making initial contact with the La Esmeralda informants. She said she just knocked on doors and began chatting with people. She told them she had come from a poor Puerto Rican family and had been able to pull herself up and go to college and that they could do the same thing, if they would try.

31. Each of these four people—Muriente, Luján, Muñoz Lee, and Ruth Lewis—influenced *La Vida* in very tangible ways, and each of the four was strikingly different in background, academic training, and philosophical orientation. Certainly Lewis did not make sufficiently clear the influence of others on his work, but he did always mention his indebtedness. These contributions were invariably ignored by critics who complained that his books presented the views of the poor only as they had been filtered through the perspective of one "middle-class North American professor." As I have tried to make clear in this study, that phrase does not even describe Lewis very well and certainly cannot be applied to his closest collaborators. It is also important to call attention to the enormous amount of criticism he received and tolerated from the people he worked with most closely because he gained a not undeserved reputation for being intolerant of *public* criticism, particularly during the last decade of his life. Despite his differences with them, Lewis held Luján and Muñoz Lee in high esteem and maintained his friendships with them until his death. Muñoz Lee continued to work with Ruth Lewis, as translator on the Cuba project.

CHAPTER FIVE

REASSESSING

Following the success of *The Children of Sánchez* and *La Vida* (which won the National Book Award for nonfiction in 1967), Lewis traveled around the United States lecturing and attending seminars on the culture of poverty. A great deal had changed in the political atmosphere between the publication of these two books; by the mid-1960s poverty and what to do about it were the subjects of a national debate. Lewis's work received its greatest attention in this country during the peak years of the Johnson administration's War on Poverty. If he had published his argument on the existence of a subculture among the poor in the 1940s or the 1950s, perhaps it would not have received the attention it did and he would not have continued to use it. But in the 1960s the eradication of poverty was a central political issue and the culture of poverty was a dramatic yet conveniently vague phrase that helped to call attention to the problems of the poor—or, from another perspective, to the *problem* of the poor. The convenience of the phrase is that it contains something for everyone; in using it to describe the life-style of the poor, one can attach to it the causation of one's choice.

Several broad interpretations of the poverty problem received most of the attention in the United States. To the left of center were variations on the position that the causes of poverty lay in the structure of the economic system and that the solution therefore lay in changing that system. Occupying the broad middle ground, from left to just right of center, were those who argued that the problem lay not in the structure of the economic system itself but in certain weaknesses in it that could be overcome by compensatory and support programs initiated by the national government. Well to the right of center were those who maintained that there was nothing wrong with the system and that any glitches in it were caused, not cured, by government policies. They argued that much of the poverty in this country was no more than a temporary condition that people with sufficient industry could work their way out of in an unfettered market system. Poverty that persisted from one generation to another within the same family was probably due to the unwillingness or inability of the poor to work and take advantage of the system's many opportunities. There was disagreement within this group over what if anything should be done for the poor, but most agreed that it was a concern for private charity.

Oscar Lewis walked right into this cross fire with his culture of poverty thesis, unwittingly carrying ammunition for all sides. On the one hand he argued that poverty was *caused* by systemic conditions (murkily defined) that prevailed in capitalist systems (something for both the left and the center). On the other hand he said that poverty was *perpetuated* in *some* families not only by governments' refusals to eliminate its causes but also by the complicity of the poor themselves, as they passed on to their children the adaptations they had made to their poverty (something for the right). In saying this Lewis meant to dramatize the consequences of extreme poverty experienced in class-stratified societies and to demonstrate that it could damage people in permanent, irreversible ways.

Believing he was making an argument against poverty and the roles of government and society in causing and sustaining it, Lewis was stunned to find himself being attacked from the left for aiding and abetting the right in blaming the poor themselves for their poverty. He knew he had not spent two decades documenting the lives of poor people in order to point an accusatory finger at *them*. But his vague and unformulated thesis invited misunderstanding, because his choice of words established a cause-and-effect relationship between poverty and culture, not between poverty and capitalism. And his use of life histories and family studies focused attention (with the exception of *Pedro Martínez*) on the family and the individual, not on the system or even on the local community. In addition, until the mid-1960s Lewis was far from frank about the political implications of his argument, partly due to his public cautiousness about his own political inclinations and partly to the unformed nature of his political ideas. These were superficial in content but they *were* deeply held. As for the causes of poverty, "any intelligent ten-year-old already knows the answer to that," he wrote to a colleague.[1] His job was to provide the evidence; he already had the general answer, if not the specific solutions.

Lewis had tried, with his family studies, to deromanticize both poverty and the poor, showing all of the bad along with the good, but he had done little to mediate between his informants and potentially unsympathetic readers. To conceal the bad would have been to distort the lives and to defeat the purpose of portraying poverty's consequences as graphically as possible. But in the trendy leftism of the 1960s, romancing the poor was back in fashion. In the overheated political atmosphere in which the poverty debate took place, there was on the left a kind of competition within the competition to prove who was the best friend of the poor.

In earlier years, when Lewis had criticized the idealizers of "primitive and preliterate" people, he thought he was challenging researchers who were squarely in the Establishment's mainstream and who were generically different from him, both politically and professionally. Even then the differences had been stated, at least publicly, within the prevailing norms of professional etiquette. But in the 1960s Lewis found himself attacked by leftists and social scientists as dedicated as he was to eradicating poverty; and they attacked not only his methods but his motivations, character, and integrity.

Defending the Thesis

In this atmosphere Lewis found it increasingly difficult to hold his own in defending the culture of poverty thesis. By having lumped the Sánchezes and Ríoses under the same cultural rubric he had emphasized their similarities and downplayed their differences. He also had avoided discussion of what was particularly Mexican or Puerto Rican in their attitudes and behavior, as distinct from that which could be labeled a shared response to poverty. These were very sensitive distinctions and very controversial in the context of the times. (Fernanda Ríos was black, Puerto Rican, and poor.) Lewis had understood too late the political difficulties of claiming cause-and-effect relationships between class and negatively viewed culture traits. He did not want to add to this problem by associating the same traits with race, ethnicity, or nationality.

The most obvious action Lewis could have taken to resolve this confusion was to have withdrawn his premature conclusions until he had time to sort out the meaning of all of his field material. He seemed to have little trouble doing this in his personal correspondence or when speaking privately to people. There was never any doubt that he was ambivalent about the culture of poverty thesis and very unclear about what he actually was saying with it. The reasons he did not publicly renounce it were, I think, several. The first and most obvious was that the thesis had a utility to him as a social scientist; it served as a kind of hook on which to hang all of his poverty-related research, especially when writing grant proposals. He seemed to believe that he could use it for its labeling and descriptive value (i.e., studying poor people) while containing its theoretical portent. Second, some of his reluctance to give up the thesis was simply proprietary; he had an advanced case of that condition common to so many anthropologists who speak of *their* people and *their* villages. Michael Harrington may have popularized the culture of poverty concept in the United States, but Lewis had invented it and so laid claim to it. Another manifestation of this proprietary instinct was that he never completely put aside an old idea or piece of work; his cumulative approach to research did not allow for subtractions, only additions. Finally, Lewis believed, and never stopped believing, that the core of his theory was correct, namely, that among some poor people there was a distinctive way of life that set them apart from other poor people. By the late 1960s, however, he was reevaluating the roles of poverty and culture in creating and perpetuating this life-style.

Before he reached this point, Lewis tried two different tacks in dealing with his critics. Instead of renouncing the thesis he would say, when discussing it in public lectures, that it was simply an idea that needed to be tested and that he did not take it nearly so seriously as his critics did. (Actually it was not his critics who took the concept seriously but people who believed in its utility to explain long-term poverty.) Basically he was asserting that the culture of poverty was his idea but that it was not a very good idea and certainly not anything he regarded as a central contribution. For example, in 1967, he told an audience, "I'm afraid some people take certain constructs or models like the subculture of poverty more seriously than I do. My whole thrust is to try to show that no matter what generalization social science comes up with, be it the folk society or the subculture of poverty, or what have you, my own personal interest is to show the range of variation of human conditions and family life within what we generally present as a general construct."[2] In this remark Lewis shows how conscious he was of having made the same fundamental error he had accused Robert Redfield of making, that is, obscuring the complexity of real lives through the use of ideal types.

The second tack Lewis took in trying to rescue his thesis from its critics was to counter the accusation that it negatively stereotyped his informants. To do this he emphasized that the subculture itself was an adaptation; and, therefore, even if the adaptation was to bad socioeconomic conditions, it was still, by definition, positive because it enhanced the ability to survive in a given environment. This approach was quite different from the one Lewis had used in the previous half dozen years to defend his informants. He had been worried from the time of *Five Families* about the possibility that readers might be left with a negative image of poor Mexicans. To counter this he had called readers' attention to positive personal qualities, such as family loyalty, generosity and sharing, spontaneity, gaiety, courage, and the ability to love. In his new approach he tried to portray not only the people but the subculture itself as something positive, a position he had broached very tentatively in *La Vida*. For example, he said that while culture of poverty people might be alienated from the larger society, they were better off than most urban Westerners because they were not alienated from their own communities. He said that their sense of community and sharing was a repudiation of impersonal society, just as were their work habits. They *"will not* sell their souls or freedom for a paycheck"; they *"refuse"* to become "mechanical robots" and *"resist"* alienation by not falling into line and submissively punching a time clock every day." They *"avoid* promotion," "prefer unskilled jobs," and *"want* kindly, paternalistic employers who are not too demanding" (emphasis added).[3] According to Lewis, these otherwise negative traits had a positive function within the subculture, in that they personalized relationships within the community and reduced alienation. But his selection of verbs suggests preference and conscious choice on the part of the informants and tends to support the interpretation that the poor, not the system, perpetuate their poverty.

Lewis made a parallel argument for the positive role of machismo in the subculture. He said that when viewed on a social level this trait was maladaptive; it was "cruel and destructive" and led to the abandonment of women and children. But on a personal level it was a "way of fighting alienation" and "a type of self-realization."[4] He tried to make similar cases for a number of other social-psychological traits, arguing that they served a different function for people living in the subculture than for people living outside of it. He made a more concerted effort to distance himself from the conclusions of projective test analyzers—including those of Luján, who was consistently diagnosing paranoid and schizoid tendencies in his Puerto Rican informants. Lewis argued that these interpretations were instances in which mental health standards were incorrectly applied across culture and class lines. He maintained—in what was a near 180-degree turn from his public position in 1961—that most people living in the culture of poverty were essentially happy, mentally healthy individuals who had adapted well to their environments. To support his position Lewis singled out points from test analyses, such as Luján's interpretation that a personality trait like resignation had a "positive adaptive aspect in that it helps to maintain a psychic equilibrium. . . ."[5] In 1965 Luján registered sharp disagreement with Lewis's selective use of her findings. "Adaptations may be excellent for survival in a difficult world, and may or may not indicate some degree of ego strength, but it is hardly an indication of mental health if the adaptation is to a sick environment. . . . the fact that it is cultural does not convert psychopathology into mental health."[6]

Lewis may have been on solid ground in his complaints about the mechanical applications of mental health indicators, but he was the one who chose to have the tests administered and interpreted. And he continued to publish the analyses even while criticizing them, because he knew he was not qualified to diagnose mental health or illness in his informants. This did not prevent Lewis from trying to influence the findings, however, and there were several cases in which he had test responses analyzed by three or four psychiatrists and psychologists in an effort to find confirmation for his view that mental illness or personality deviation had been overstated.[7] However, no other test consultant ever won Lewis's confidence to the extent that Luján did, and throughout most of the 1960s he pursued the fruitless task of trying to influence her test interpretations.

> . . . I certainly agree that I did not describe the pathology of the Ríos family in the introduction. I simply mentioned that I knew there was pathology and I will try now to briefly summarize it. On the other hand, my statements about the tendency of psychologists and particularly testers to stress pathology in their findings is well documented from many sources including Eric Fromm who specifically made this point to me in connection with his analysis of Rorshach tests of some of his Mexican village subjects. . . .
>
> . . . this whole subject matter is not an easy one for me to handle. While it is true that I have used the insights of psychologists and social workers, I have used them in my own way so that the total effect of the statements that I've used is quite different in my context than in their original context.
>
> In reading your analyses of the Ríos family one would never dream that the positive things that I have said about them are even remotely possible or true and, mind you, you wrote some of your analyses after long discussions with me in which I tried to influence you toward a more positive view. You may be perfectly right in your appraisal; it's just that it seemed to me that it was one-sided and in my effort to correct the balance I may have gone too far.[8]

Despite resistance from Luján, Lewis continued for several years to argue the positive aspects of the poverty subculture. It was a position more congenial to his early skepticism about the reliability of projective tests, and at the same time it brought him closer to the prevailing political view on the left that while poverty was bad, the poor were good and in general more sane and whole than the people who oppressed them. By arguing that a subculture, negative in its contribution to the larger society, had positive consequences for the people living in it, Lewis seemed to set at least some of the poor on a collision course with the needs and demands of the larger society, should true reform ever come.

As the public debate wore on, Lewis went on the offensive against the critics who accused him of blaming the victim. He wrote that *La Vida* was "an indictment not of the poor, but of the social system that produces the way of life of the Ríos family with its pathos and suffering. It is also an indictment of some members of the middle class, government officials, and others who try to cover up the unpleasant and ugly facts of the culture of poverty."[9]

Lewis also tried to be more frank about the political implications of his thesis, insisting that it was the structure of class society itself that bore greatest responsibility for the perpetuation of the subculture. "Indeed, the subculture of poverty is part of the larger culture of capitalism, whose social and economic system channels wealth into the hands of a relatively small group and thereby makes for the growth of sharp class distinctions."[10] But however large the roles played by exploitation, neglect, and social stratification, he continued, class structure itself was *"not the only reason"* for the perpetuation of the culture of poverty.[11] Any policy that was aimed only at reducing stratification and redistributing wealth would fail to eliminate the mechanisms that the culture invented for its own survival. This is why Lewis took the position in 1967 that income and job-training policies could not eliminate the subculture unless complemented by long-term psychiatric social work assistance at the family level. But he had a hard time arguing this while also claiming that members of the subculture were mentally healthy.

Backing Away

By 1968–69, just prior to going to Cuba, Lewis had pretty well given up on these defenses of his culture of poverty thesis. He wrote more and more frequently to friends and colleagues about the inadequacy of the subculture construct. In a letter to Manuel Maldonado-Denis he said: "As you know, I have tried to develop some sociological generalizations about the culture of poverty. However, the more I study the poor, the more impressed I am by the wide range of variation and the subtle differences from family to family. No generalizations can really encompass the richness and variety of the lives which I am attempting to portray in the words of the poor. . . ."[12]

Lewis stated his dissatisfaction even more bluntly to Todd Gitlin:

The more urban slum families I study, the more I am convinced of the wide range of adaptations, reaction patterns, values, etc. that are found. I am sure that if we had a sufficient number of detailed studies . . . we could classify this range. However, to condense it all within a single abstract model like the subculture of poverty is inevitably to distort the lives of these people. Incidentally, I never intended the model of a subculture of poverty as a summary of the substantive data presented in my recent books. If only commentators would go to the trouble of doing their own homework and analyzing the biographies instead of relying upon my theoretical model, a great deal of misunderstanding would be avoided and a great deal of light would be shed.[13]

There is something bordering on both the cynical and the outrageous in Lewis's claim that he never meant his data to support his theory. Surely it was his obligation to make this clear, just as it was his responsibility and not that of others to analyze his own data. But in the Gitlin letter there is also a plea for others to give up on what he himself was still publicly embracing and to help him find a better explanation.

During this period, Lewis was trying to write an introduction to "Six Women," the second of his Puerto Rican family studies. The material, Lewis said, "cries out for analysis beyond that of my sub-culture of poverty concept, which may turn out to be much too conglomerate a concept for analytic purposes."[14] He sent dozens of letters to colleagues for assistance with the analysis and even organized a seminar at the Center for Advanced Study at the University of Illinois to gather the impressions of its Fellows to parts of his manuscript. It was this particular family study that finally forced Lewis to consider other than economic causes to explain the lives of those informants (a minority to be sure) who manifested the characteristic clustering of culture of poverty traits.

The study encompassed fifty-one members and relatives of the Arriaga family but focused on six women from three generations of that family. The two eldest were sisters, raised in rural Puerto Rico, near Vega Baja. One of them, Santa, had an uneventful, ordinary life in the country, farming with her sons (she had no daughters). The other sister, Carmen, following her grown daughters (she had no sons), migrated to San Juan and eventually to La Esmeralda, the most notorious of the city's slums. Several of the daughters became prostitutes and took a series of pimp-husbands; they had brushes with the law and one served time in prison. Gloria, Carmen's granddaughter, had been given up for adoption early in her childhood and had been reared in Puerto Rico by working-class foster parents. When interviewed, she was living in New York City, where she was a working-class housewife.

Because this study was organized as an examination of three generations within one family, Lewis had to try to explain both intra- and intergenerational similarities and differences. As he compared the different fortunes of Santa and her sons and Carmen and her daughters, he came to this conclusion:

> I believe that I can identify a number of selective factors operative in the rural areas which encourage individuals from families with an incipient culture of poverty, deviants from the traditional culture patterns, to migrate to urban slums. The urban slum environment therefore only develops a potential that was already present in the rural area. Indeed, it is my hypothesis that only individuals from such families will develop the symptoms of the subculture of poverty in the urban slum.[15]

But Santa and Carmen had grown up in the same family, so this presented Lewis with the question of whether Santa and her sons would have adopted the same life-style as had Carmen and her daughters when they moved to the city. He decided that they would *not* have because home environment and socialization within the family were not the only factors at work in reproducing the subculture life-style.

> In essence I am arguing that there are selective psychological factors among migrants which predispose them toward the deviation of the traits of the subculture of poverty in urban slums, because they come from rural families where traditional forms of control were already weakening or breaking down in the country. I would have to argue, therefore, that had the children of Santa ended up in [La Esmeralda], they would have retained the more stable family patterns of their mother than did the children of Carmen.[16]

The "deviant" psychological factor manifested by Carmen, but not by Santa, was her "spirit of independence and autonomy, and an ability to stand up against men and not to take it in the submissive way that the tradition required. Children raised by such mothers as Carmen had a model which inclined them towards a further development of female dominance. . . ."[17] (To avoid digression, I am deliberately avoiding all of the gender-related issues here, including the fact that Lewis did not seem to give much weight to the fact that Carmen's daughters had significantly fewer economic opportunities than did Santa's sons.) Lewis did not try to account for why Carmen's psychological makeup was so different from Santa's, but he did go on, in a related point, to speculate on the similarities between Carmen and her daughters and granddaughter. For the first time since the Tepoztlán work, he conceded the importance of trying to understand the role of heredity: "to my great surprise, Gloria turned out to be much more like her mother [who gave her up for adoption] than I had anticipated. It makes me wonder whether we social scientists haven't been neglecting the genetic factor."[18]

In addition, Lewis decided it was necessary to look in much greater detail at the subtleties of the socialization process.

> One of the theoretical objectives of some of my recent studies of families is to try to show how individuals who come from the same family and from the same social and economic stratum turn out quite differently because of a combination of factors which may include order of birth, parental favoritism, identification with one parent or another, being a shade or two lighter than one's sibling, and accidental factors of one's life history. In other words, single family studies by definition hold social and economic variables constant, and therefore can't tell you very much about these variables. Such studies are important because of the light they throw on psychological factors.[19]

In the end Lewis could not come to any solid conclusions about the meaning of the Arriaga family study; he died with the book in press and the introduction unwritten.[20] He did publish excerpts from the study, however, and in the introduction to one of these he attributed the family's fortunes to a combination of factors, but he placed primary blame on precisely those systemic conditions he himself had admitted were seldom discussed in his books.

> The story of *dona* Carmen and her relatives is in large measure the story of the degradation and deformation of a family, which despite its hard work, could not overcome the heritage of colonialism and was never able to rise very much beyond the bare subsistence level. Because this process occurred during the period when Puerto Rico was practically a colony of the United States, we must bear a large part of the responsibility. The fact that conditions in Puerto Rico were not any better under Spain prior to the United States occupation is little cause for celebration, especially in view of the great wealth and power of the United States. It is also a sad commentary on the Catholic Church of Puerto Rico that it has done so little for these people.[21]

Lewis went on to chide Carmen for not recognizing the systemic source of her problems and for failing her daughters by letting them believe the cause lay elsewhere. (This is one of the few passages in Lewis's writing where he really seemed not to like an informant.) "It is part of the tragedy that *dona* Carmen self-righteously places the blame for her daughters descent into Hell upon their character rather than upon the social system which failed to provide them with skills, education, and decent jobs. Unfortunately Carmen also fails to recognize her own responsibility in their fate."[22]

Even if one sympathizes with the point of view, one knows that Lewis was simply postulating; the study contains no exploration of the "interplay" of broad social and economic with personal and psycho-logical factors that he claimed led the family into the subculture. Making distinctions among members of the same family and among members of different families from the same socioeconomic stratum was crucial to a more adequate explanation of Lewis's research. Among his Puerto Rican informants in particular were a number of people whose behavior was, in the context of their own communities, deviant and even bizarre. This was due in no small part to Lewis's choice of a research site. As he moved from Tepoztlán to the Casa Grande to La Esmeralda, he studied communities that were fundamentally different from one another. Tepoztlán was an ancient rural village; the Casa Grande, one of many poor *vecindades* in Mexico City; but La Esmeralda was a community of outcasts. Located in a state more prosperous than Mexico, it had at the time virtually no safety nets for the landless poor, the unemployed, or the mentally and physically disabled.[23]

La Esmeralda was a community for the most down-and-out of Puerto Rico's poor: alcoholics, drug addicts, and some mentally ill and emotionally disturbed people who, for lack of money or social welfare programs, had nowhere else to go. (There was also a disproportionately high number of prostitutes in the barrio because of its proximity to a United States army base.) As early as 1965, Lewis had written that "urban slums attract people with deep psychopathology."[24] Expanding on this idea in a letter to Muna Muñoz Lee that same year, he wrote: "It would seem that the slum provides a very therapeutic environment for disturbed people because of the great tolerance for pathology and the permissiveness for acting out. In a middle class environment, people with such pathologies would get much sicker and eventually be institutionalized."[25]

If such people had migrated to La Esmeralda—and almost none of Lewis's adult informants had been born there—with their personalities and patterns of behavior already well formed, it seems likely that they had shaped the slum environment far more than they had been shaped by it. Evidence to support this conclusion was provided in an interview with one of La Esmeralda's first residents, who told fieldworkers that beginning in the 1930s, a different (and unwanted) class of people—he implied a criminal element—moved into the barrio; and with their coming the community was gradually transformed from a poor working-class settlement into a notorious slum.[26] What percentage of La Esmeralda's population could have been classified as criminal, as "disturbed," or as having "deep psychopathology" at the time Lewis was working in the barrio in the 1960s, I do not know. He was still able to identify a range of life-styles among the people he studied, although it was a smaller range than could be found in

Tepoztlán, the Casa Grande, or Panaderos. The five families Lewis selected for intensive study represented a range of behavior from the bizarre (people seemingly detached from reality), to the criminally deviant, to the fairly ordinary working poor.

What, then, was the relationship between the "high incidence of psychopathology" in La Esmeralda (assuming this were true in the 1960s) and the culture of its residents, or for that matter between psychopathology and extreme poverty in general? Did the slums attract people with incipient or deep psychopathologies (causes unknown) who, once in their new, more tolerant—even supportive—environment were free to feed their own and to breed new psychopathology? Or did poor, landless people who migrated to barrios like La Esmeralda only then begin their "descent into Hell," developing psychopathology and a supportive life-style in response to the forces of extreme deprivation and social and political isolation?

At some point while he was still working on the Puerto Rican materials, but after *La Vida* had been published, Lewis realized his research would provide no concise answer to those questions. He saw that the variation in the ability to cope with extreme poverty among his informants, both on the individual and family levels, defied simple generalization. He knew it was no longer plausible to use his research findings to causally link, in a few sweeping sentences, poverty, personality, culture, and capitalism. His theory was done in by his own obsession with documenting intracultural variation and by his attention to the detail of individual lives. His ever-improving technique for doing family studies and for gathering life histories that could draw out "total personality" took him deeper and deeper inside the family and the individual. There he got lost in a sea of particulars, trapped by his own technique.

In trying to shore up the culture of poverty thesis Lewis had talked himself into a cul-de-sac. Demoralized by his inability to provide a better explanation of the Puerto Rican material, he turned his thoughts to other projects. He wrote about completing a follow-up study of the grandchildren of Jesús Sánchez that he had begun in the summer of 1962. Then, with a full year of funding left for the Puerto Rican research, Lewis was invited by the Cuban Academy of Sciences to attend a conference in Havana in February 1968. During his two-and-a-half-week visit he was able to meet with Fidel Castro and other officials and to secure an invitation to undertake three years of research on the island.[27] Successful this time in his request to the Ford Foundation for funds and to the U.S. State Department for visa approval, he suspended the Puerto Rican project.[28]

Lewis had been trying for eight years to arrange for such an invitation, so one could not conclude that the Cuba project was engineered as an escape from the Puerto Rican quagmire. Nevertheless, it did serve this function: it opened a door and, momentarily at least, let in a rush of fresh air. Ruth Lewis encouraged her husband to take this opportunity because she was as eager to go to Cuba as she was to stop the work in Puerto Rico, where they had already collected more material than they could ever process. By 1968 both of the Lewises were suffocating, intellectually and emotionally, in the interior lives of their informants. Lewis himself expressed this pretty clearly in explaining to colleagues his reasons for going to Cuba. To Carolina Luján he wrote:

> In spending so much of my time in the study of the humble lives of these people, I feel that I myself am rapidly becoming illiterate, isolated and out of touch with the pressing events of our time. This distresses me. But it seems to be part of the price that I have to pay for having decided to specialize in the sub-culture of poverty. Perhaps my future study in Cuba will once again bring me into touch with more complex, more advanced, and more developed human beings—human beings whose lives have presumably been touched or influenced by the magic of revolutionary, socialist ideals, by conceptions of international solidarity and the brotherhood of man.[29]

More simply and directly he wrote to Howard Cline, "I feel that I have spent too much time in the slums, and this may be a good opportunity to get out.[30]

Cuba

Lewis went to Cuba in February 1969 to get back on his intellectual and political feet. He thought this research, by comparison with the work on Puerto Rico, would produce clean, uncomplicated material and be "much broader than the culture of poverty in its sociological context."[31] In his proposal to the Ford Foundation he outlined a three-year project that was to have an urban and a rural phase and would be subdivided into six separate studies.[32] Only one of these was designed specifically to test the culture of poverty thesis.

Since his 1961 trip to Cuba, Lewis had been speculating that the culture of poverty did not exist in socialist countries. The idea had been inspired by his return to Las Yaguas slum, where he had worked briefly in 1946; there he found all of its residents awaiting relocation to new housing developments, a marked improvement in the availability of goods and services, and a veneer of political organization, with offices of the revolutionary government's mass organizations visible on every street. His expectation that these and other changes would lead to the eradication of the culture of poverty was based on his conviction that the culture could exist only in class-stratified societies where the poor experienced not only great material deprivation but also near total social and political isolation. In a socialist system such as that developing in Cuba, income differences would be greatly reduced, although not eliminated, and a centrally regulated system of distribution would eliminate absolute poverty. Class, as defined in strictly economic terms, would disappear; class, as defined by values, would be diminished as the government propagated a standardized value structure through control of educational institutions, mass communications, and the institutional flow of information. The government would not tolerate social or political isolation and would provide the organizational infrastructure to force integration. Under these circumstances, Lewis believed, the conditions that gave rise to the culture of poverty would be eliminated. In addition, neither the freedom nor the necessity would exist to act out the old design for living. When basic revolutionary change occurred, he said, "the members of the culture of poverty undergo a spiritual change and show a great sense of loyalty to the new social system and its rulers, even though there may be no rapid change in the standard of living."[33]

To examine this problem Lewis proposed a comparison of two groups of residents resettled from Las Yaguas to two of the new housing settlements. From among seven settlements surveyed he chose one group (Buena Ventura) that in his view represented an unsuccessful adjustment to postrevolutionary life and another (Bolívar) that represented a successful adjustment. The guiding hypothesis—to use a rather elevated phrase for what was just a loose idea—was that the culture of poverty would be in the process of disappearing, or gone altogether, due to the elimination of absolute poverty, the weakening of class stratification, and the inability of any sector of society to choose nonintegration as a way of life. Exactly how the comparison was to be handled is unclear, but this became irrelevant when staffing problems and the government's curtailing of the research left the Bolívar study incomplete.

To carry out the research Lewis had arranged to bring into Cuba a half dozen people from Mexico and the United States, but for the work in Buena Ventura and Bolívar he trained ten Cuban students assigned to him by prior agreement with the government. Under his supervision they rewrote the basic Puerto Rican questionnaires to fit the Cuban context and vocabulary, and they created six new questionnaires as well. In contrast to Puerto Rico, where Lewis had expected to find low levels of political interest and involvement, in Cuba a great deal of effort was spent in determining levels of political and social participation. (The shortest questionnaire administered in Puerto Rico was that on politics.) From the survey questionnaire stage the work progressed just as it had in Puerto Rico; complete material inventories were taken and budget studies done in selected households, and a handful of families were chosen for intensive study.

Lewis had a great deal of difficulty getting this research off the ground. The students had no prior training and were highly politicized members of the Young Communists given to lecturing informants on their bad habits and lack of gratitude to the Revolution for all it had done. Their first round of work had to be thrown out and re-done. There was some resentment against Lewis as a North American granted personal and professional privileges that almost no Cuban had, including unrestricted permission to examine the less flattering aspects of the society. When Lewis began concentrating on developing the skills of a few of the best students, resentment toward him increased, and his demanding, workaholic ways did nothing to smooth over these differences.

The Cuban students worked for about a year in Buena Ventura under his direction before Lewis brought in Douglas Butterworth, his colleague from the University of Illinois, to supervise the fieldwork. Lewis wanted time for the other studies already in progress as well as time to initiate the rural phase of the research. It was Butterworth who wrote up the Buena Ventura materials after Lewis's death, but he did not address himself to Lewis's hypothesis on socialism and the culture of poverty. Butterworth did not have at his disposal data from the last three months of fieldwork, because these were confiscated by the Cuban government when it closed down the project in June 1970. All of the first year's transcribed interviews, some tapes, and many of the fieldworkers' notes had been brought into the United States by the Lewises during 1969 and early 1970, but the completed questionnaires, of which there were no duplicates, remained in Cuba and were confiscated.

While working in Buena Ventura with his students, Lewis concluded that few of its residents had been "touched by the magic of revolutionary socialist ideals," as he had hoped they would have been. Their lives were not transformed by the very substantial improvement in their material conditions nor by the attempts to forcibly integrate them into the new Cuba. He found more than a residue of the old life: unstable employment patterns; high levels of absenteeism, alcoholism, and truancy; some gambling, marijuana use, theft and black market activity; and nominal participation—if any at all—in mass organizations. He wrote to Muna Muñoz Lee: ". . . it is clear that many of the traits of the culture of poverty persist in this housing project. I believe I was overly optimistic in some of my earlier evaluations about the disappearance of the culture of poverty under socialism. However, there seems to me to be no doubt that the Cuban Revolution has abolished the conditions which gave rise to the culture of poverty."[34]

Following the internal logic of Lewis's original thesis, one could not expect much more to have happened in the ten years during which revolutionary programs had been in effect. If this design for living were in fact a culture, there was no reason to believe that a deeply embedded value structure would disintegrate in such a short period of time. Lewis believed too much in the transforming powers of political affiliation and integration, too much in one form of belonging over another. He believed so firmly that political integration alone could eliminate the subculture that he did not consider the possibility that the quality of integration—whether voluntary or coerced—could make a difference in his argument.

In Buena Ventura there were people who resisted the attempts of revolutionary activists to transform them and their community on the same grounds that La Esmeralda residents in Puerto Rico objected to social workers who meddled in their private lives. The source and intent of the interference did not make much difference in levels of receptivity. If either group could have material benefits without government interference, all to the good; if not, they would just as soon be left alone. Las Yaguas and La Esmeralda were the two most similar communities that Lewis studied; they were not simply settlements of poor people but communities of social outcasts. However, within these communities were still some people who would have jumped at the chance to move on to something better; others were not merely content to stay but organized against government efforts to eliminate their communities. (This happened several times in both places.) Of those who preferred to remain as they were, some were justifiably suspicious of government promises and thought they would be left with nothing. Others actually preferred the "freedom" and protection from the outside world offered by these "off-limits" shantytowns, and they were dependent upon, or unwilling to give up, the social networks that existed inside the settlements.

What made people with these attitudes so different from the great majority of the poor who work so hard to improve their lives and who are willing to take advantage of any new opportunity offered by outside agencies? Are they misfits who end up in communities like La Esmeralda and Las Yaguas because they have no place else to go? Do they share a culture; or are they merely bound by their common orientation to the institutions and practices of the dominant

La Esmeralda, San Juan, a community built between the oceanfront and a long, massive stone wall that separates it from the rest of San Juan. (Photograph by Oscar Lewis)

The main street in Las Yaguas, Havana, Cuba, 1961, one year before the community was torn down by the Castro government and its residents relocated to new housing. This photo illustrates how the slum was set apart physically from the capital city. (Photograph by Oscar Lewis)

culture and by their need for the freedom and security from the demands of the larger society offered in the slums? What accounts for the intracommunity—and even intrafamily—variation in response to, or ability to cope with, poverty that Lewis's collective family studies illustrate so well? Can any adequate answer be given without going beyond the environmental- or socialization-based theory of orthodox socialism?

In Cuba, Lewis gave this problem even less attention than before, because clarifying the culture of poverty thesis was less important to him than bringing his research back to the questions he had posed in Tepoztlán. There he had done his first family studies to examine the differential effects of the Mexican Revolution on the vertical mobility of the villagers. His biography of Pedro Martínez, in particular, was an attempt to get a firsthand account of a revolution from someone who had participated in it. In all of the life history material recorded by the eighteen fieldworkers in Cuba, the central focus was on the Revolution and its impact. The data were gathered primarily to set up comparisons with life after 1959 and to direct attention to revolutionary change rather than to the idiosyncratic characteristics of particular individuals or families.

During his first year in Cuba, Lewis did spend a good deal of time on the Buena Ventura project, due to the demands of training and supervising the Cuban students. But he spent the majority of his own interviewing time with middle- and working-class informants, not with those from the lowest income groups. He also directed an investigation into mass organizations, interviewed a number of officials and political activists, and sought out political dissenters as well. In contrast to this work, early in the second year of research Lewis undertook as a personal project a family study much like his earlier studies in that it focused on the personalities and attitudes of the individual informants and on family dynamics and family neuroses. The fact that these people lived in Cuba during the Revolution placed their story in a highly specific context and gave a very distinctive character to their problems. However, as the study progressed, the Revolution seemed to become more the setting for, rather than the subject of, the study. This was the same problem in method that he had fallen into in Puerto Rico, when he tried to delve so deeply into the "psychology of the poor" that their poverty (and the reasons for it) seemed in danger of fading into a secondary consideration. That Lewis was returning to these concerns in Cuba was a bad omen for the prospects of getting his research back on track.

Lewis's family study presented other problems as well because his informants had ties to a revolutionary hero whose life after the triumph had been something less than exemplary. This connection was unknown to Lewis when he undertook the work and was marginal, at most, to the study. However, the possibility that some of this information might find its way into print was probably one of the factors that led to the government's decision to close down the project. Shortly after the Lewises left Cuba in June 1970, one of the informant's for the family study was arrested and sent to prison.[35]

In the six months between his return from Cuba and his death, Lewis was preoccupied with the safety of his informants and with arranging a return to the island to complete his work and recover confiscated materials. Just two days before he died, in December 1970, he phoned the wife of the imprisoned informant to tell her he would be returning soon. Lewis never believed that Castro himself, who had negotiated the terms under which he was allowed to do research in Cuba, had made the decision to close down the project. As did so many Cubans during that period, Lewis tended to blame Cuba's problems (or in this case his own) on officials other than Castro. He believed that if he could speak directly with Castro and tell him what had happened, then Castro would live up to the terms of the agreement by releasing the imprisoned informant and allowing Lewis to complete his research.[36] But there is no evidence whatsoever that Lewis would have been allowed to return to Cuba as anything other than a tourist and no reason to believe that his project could have been terminated without Castro's knowledge and authorization.

Not long after returning to the United States, Lewis submitted "Six Women" for publication, but without analysis or an introduction. It is impossible to say whether he would have written any more on the culture of poverty had he lived longer. He was too shattered by the Cuban experience and the imprisonment of an informant, and too preoccupied with his ostracism by the ideological Left, to think much about anything else. Certainly reformulating the thesis was not a high priority.

With his publications on Cuba, Lewis hoped he would be able to communicate what he had previously been unable to make clear in his writings on the culture of poverty: ". . . it occurs to me that in my earlier writing on the culture of poverty I have not stressed sufficiently the factor of exploitation and of the imposition of the way of life by the institutional setup of the larger society—by the social, economic, and class discrimination which is an important factor."[37] If his Cuba research could demonstrate that the culture of poverty did not exist in one socialist system, it would lend support to his claim that the subculture was unique to capitalist systems. But Lewis left Cuba more confused than ever. His critics in the social sciences had undermined his academic explanations, and Castro and the Cuban Revolution had taken away at least part of his political rationale. Intellectually he was too disoriented to think his way out of this dilemma; physically he was too tired and too ill to work his way out of it.

Lewis had been warned not to subject himself to the heat and humidity of Havana or to such a potentially stressful political environment. Just as he had ignored earlier warnings, he went to Cuba working full tilt: training the ten Cuban students, supervising six other fieldworkers and a clerical staff, interviewing for and directing several separate studies. As usual, he and his wife were occupied with other things as well, correcting the galleys of *Anthropological Essays* and, whenever possible, editing "Six Women." The combined effects of the difficult climate, long hours, the stress of supervising an unprepared and sometimes resentful team of fieldworkers, and the large doses of medication weighed Lewis down and perhaps also impaired his judgment. But he did not slow down until he had an angina attack in the office of Raul Roa, the Cuban foreign minister, while listening to Roa read the charges against him (among them, that Lewis was a C.I.A. agent) and learning of the decision to close down his project.[38]

Lewis never used his work for overt political purposes, and it is unlikely that, had he lived, he could have brought himself to use the Cuba material in this way. But he did want to communicate what was good about the Revolution, and to do that he had to reveal what was bad about it as well. He did not expect anyone to look at the Cuban Revolution uncritically, but, at the same time, as he had written earlier about the Mexican Revolution, he thought it was important for North Americans to understand, or at least not to fear, revolution.[39] In like manner, in his uncompromising depiction of poverty he wanted readers neither to despise nor to idealize the poor but to understand their condition so that they might respond more intelligently and compassionately. It was one of the great disappointments of his life that in doing this he was attacked from the left as a stereotyper of the poor and later as an enemy of the Cuban Revolution.

Given his health profile, there is no reason to be melodramatic about the role of the Cuba project in Lewis's death. Yet I do think that the back-to-back experiences of Puerto Rico and Cuba left him spiritually depleted. He had worked for many years among the poor and had always gained energy and strength of purpose from his research. This was due in part to the life-enhancing quality of personal contact with the people he studied. But Lewis's powerful sense of personal efficacy and general optimism also acted to insulate him from the despair that could easily have overtaken him. La Esmeralda was and is a great cavern of deprivation and defeat that can rather quickly and easily deplete one's entire reservoir of hope. By the late 1960s Lewis felt in danger of this happening to him. Cuba was supposed to restore his optimism but instead broke another part of his faith. I cannot say whether what was shattered was his sense of efficacy alone or whether it was his faith in revolutionary change and socialist ideals as well. If it was the latter, he never admitted it.

(Relevant correspondence can be found on pp. 264–83.)

NOTES

1. Letter from Oscar Lewis to Fernando Cámara, March 9, 1962 (see no. 73 in the Appendix).

2. I have taken this quote directly from the tape of a talk Lewis gave to the Latin American Institute at the University of Wisconsin-Oshkosh in May or June 1967.

3. Ibid. Lewis made the same comments in a letter to Elia Kazan, March 1, 1967.

4. From the talk at Oshkosh. Lewis went on to say that women could achieve this kind of self-realization, too, but that they "need to beat men down to do it."

5. Letter from Carolina Luján to Oscar Lewis, January 10, 1961.

6. Letter from Carolina Luján to Oscar Lewis, July 1, 1965.

7. This was true of his handling of the test responses of Gabi, son of Felícita Ríos (*La Vida*). Lewis was convinced that Gabi was much healthier mentally than Luján's diagnoses showed him to be. It was his open disagreement with Luján's conclusions at a mental health conference in Boston (she was not present and did not know he was going to attack her findings) that brought their differences to a head, with Luján accusing him of misrepresenting her conclusions and of being disloyal to her. As with all their differences, this one was soon smoothed over. For a transcript of similar comments Lewis made at another conference, see Joseph C. Finney, ed., *Culture Change, Mental Health and Poverty* (Lexington: University of Kentucky Press, 1969), pp. 149–72. The remarks illustrate very well Lewis's conflicted view of the utility of projective tests. See also nos. 122–27 in the Appendix.

8. Letter from Oscar Lewis to Carolina Luján, May 5, 1966.

9. *Current Anthropology*, December 1967, p. 497. This issue contains twenty reviews of *Pedro Martínez, The Children of Sánchez*, and *La Vida*, as well as Lewis's reply to those reviews.

10. Ibid., p. 499.

11. Ibid.

12. Letter from Oscar Lewis to Manuel Maldonado-Denis, September 3, 1968.

13. Letter from Oscar Lewis to Todd Gitlin, August 8, 1968.

14. Letter from Oscar Lewis to Morris Opler, November 8, 1968.

15. Letter from Oscar Lewis to Eric Wolf, December 12, 1968.

16. Letter from Oscar Lewis to Carolina Luján, November 12, 1968 (see no. 134 in the Appendix).

17. Ibid. Lewis made the same point about Fernanda and her daughters, when he wrote about "the bizarre ways in which they express their independence." This view of Puerto Rican women was a source of disagreement with Muñoz Lee (see nos. 97, 118 in the Appendix).

18. Letter from Oscar Lewis to Carolina Luján, October 3, 1968 (see no. 132 in the Appendix).

19. Letter from Oscar Lewis to Marvin Harris, September 12, 1969.

20. Ruth Lewis withdrew "Six Women" from publication in 1972 because she was directing the Cuba project and did not have time to make the necessary revisions; it remains unpublished. Four excerpts from the manuscript were published in 1969 and 1970: "One Can Suffer Anywhere," *Harper's Magazine* 238 (1969): 54–60; "The Death of Dolores," *Trans-action* 6 (1969): 10–19; "Gloria and Spiritism," *New York Magazine* 3 (1970): 32–39; "La Esmeralda: Self-Portrait of Life in a San Juan Slum," *The Critic* 5 (1969): 12–23.

21. "La Esmeralda," p. 13.

22. Ibid., p. 14.

23. At the time of Lewis's fieldwork, Puerto Rico had only minimal relief assistance; Magda, of the Arriaga family, for example, received $7.50 per month per child. Island residents did not become fully eligible for the major federal transfer payment programs such as food stamps and aid to dependent children until the 1970s.

24. Letter from Oscar Lewis to Hyman Rodman, July 26, 1965 (see no. 90 in the Appendix).

25. Letter from Oscar Lewis to Muna Muñoz Lee, June 5, 1965.

26. Interview by Francisca Muriente and Elizabeth Hegeman, August 20, 1963, with Wenceslao Morales Ayala, who moved to La Esmeralda in 1908. Señor Morales, who died shortly after the interview, said the barrio had its beginnings as a settlement of workers who were employed at a nearby slaughterhouse. The community was stable and crime-free until the depression years, when land ownership fell into dispute and a different group of people built shanties and took up residency there. This new group included a large number of unemployed, unmarried women with small children; the women came to La Esmeralda at a much younger age than the workers who had settled there almost twenty-five years earlier.

27. Ruth Lewis describes these arrangements and the project's fate in Lewis, Lewis, and Rigdon, *Four Men*, pp. viii–xxv. Readers who want to know in greater detail about Lewis's attempts to do research in Cuba may want to read the correspondence on this subject before reading the remainder of chapter 5 (see nos. 136–53 in the Appendix).

28. Although the Puerto Rican project officially ended when Lewis went to Cuba, some work continued in 1969-70. On trips back to the United States from Cuba, and after the project's demise, he did interviews for his family studies in New York City. At the time of his death he was preparing to leave New York for San Juan.

29. Letter from Oscar Lewis to Carolina Luján, October 3, 1968 (see no. 132 in the Appendix).

30. Letter from Oscar Lewis to Howard Cline, July 19, 1968.

31. Draft of letter from Oscar Lewis to Howard Cline, July 19, 1968.

32. The complete proposal, minus budget, can be found in no. 145 in the Appendix.

33. Letter from Oscar Lewis to Bernard Shiffman, April 16, 1961 (see no. 66 in the Appendix).

34. Letter from Oscar Lewis to Muna Muñoz Lee, September 2, 1969 (see no. 147 in the Appendix).

35. This subject is discussed in greater detail in chapter 8.

36. Lewis made several attempts to reach Castro, but to no avail. He wrote first to Castro's friend (and until her death the minister to the presidency) Celia Sánchez, but the letter was intercepted. After being denied a meeting and having left the country, Lewis wrote directly to Castro and sent the letter to Cuba with photojournalist Lee Lockwood, who was on friendly terms with Cuban officials. Lockwood met with Rolando Rodríguez, then head of the Book Institute and now in the Ministry of Culture, but he never saw Castro.

37. Letter from Oscar Lewis to Muna Muñoz Lee, March 23, 1966 (see no. 115 in the Appendix).

38. See Lewis, Lewis, and Rigdon, *Four Men*, pp. xviii-xix, for a complete list of the charges.

39. Lewis, *Pedro Martínez*, p. x.

CHAPTER SIX

THEORY AND METHOD: AN EVALUATION

The Puerto Rican project was the only research Lewis specifically designed to test the culture of poverty thesis, and the introductions to the two books he published based on that research contain his longest statements on the theory. The methodological problems of testing the thesis were quite different from those Lewis faced when doing community and family studies in Mexico. In Tepoztlán he had studied culture and personality change in an ancient Aztecan village, populated by Nahuatal-speaking Mexicans. He had spent weeks reading the archival records of the state and *municipio;* he had studied cultural artifacts, local music, and folklore, and had traveled to Spain to trace the origins of cultural practices in the village. But these techniques could not be applied in trying to determine the existence of the culture of poverty because, by definition, it had no geographic location—no single national, regional, or community setting—where one could go and be certain of finding it. It had no archival record, distinct music, folk art, or artifacts. There was nothing from which Lewis could extract the traits said to characterize the culture of poverty except from his interviews and projective test analyses. But by the time he set up his research project in Puerto Rico, he was already more comfortable abstracting personality traits from life histories and family studies than he was abstracting culture constructs from ethnographic data.

From the standpoint of testing his thesis, Lewis's methods suffered from at least six problems of a fundamental nature:

1. The selection of informants was not made from a sample of low-income families but from a group Lewis thought was most likely to manifest subculture traits.

2. The subculture was defined by a trait list, but Lewis had no working definition of "trait" or of the functional relationship between traits and culture.

3. Lewis worked with no fixed definitions for specific traits (e.g., authoritarianism) and no set of indicators for establishing the presence of the traits in the subculture. He offered no evidence on the frequency of their occurrence in Puerto Rican culture, so there was no standard against which to judge the extent to which subculture traits represented a deviance from the dominant culture.

4. Lewis's definition of culture was rooted in the conception of a way of life handed down from generation to generation, but it was not supported by longitudinal research. Generational change was studied by interviewing at the same point in time members of several generations within a family, with little attention paid to identification of the agencies of cultural transmission and only token follow-up work done with the younger generation.

5. The validity of the culture of poverty thesis depended on establishing cause-and-effect relationships between economic, cultural, and personality processes. But Lewis's research was not designed to explore these relationships, and the family study method as he employed it was inadequate to explain them.

6. Lewis was attracted to the exceptional cases among his informants and had a tendency to be overly influenced by visual impressions or by that which could be concretely observed.

Selection of Informants

Lewis selected his 100 San Juan families (a total of 605 adults and children) "from slums that represented significant ecological, racial, socioeconomic, and religious variables. . . . The principal criteria used in the selection of families . . . were low income, relatives in New York, and willingness to cooperate."[1] After the staff administered the four basic questionnaires, Lewis chose a small number of individuals from the bottom income quartile ($1,200 or less a year, or $20 per month per capita) for further study. The selection criteria were clearly dictated by practicalities and the needs of the project rather than by any of the usual procedures for drawing a sample. The cut-off point for income was arbitrary in the sense that it was not meant to define a dollar threshold for poverty; Lewis simply selected those people in the lowest income category because it was among them that he expected to find the culture of poverty. By choosing families who knew the names and addresses of New York relatives, he excluded those who had relatives in the city but who did not keep in touch with them. This tended to lead him to the more closely knit families and perhaps reinforced his belief in the importance of kinship ties and the extended family to the culture of poverty. By relying on individuals who were the most accessible and willing to cooperate, Lewis selected out many people who were fully employed and hard working, as well as those with a strong sense of personal privacy. He had no choice in this matter, however; the only alternative was to do a very different kind of research. His approach was so exhaustive and the intrusion into lives was so great that the informants' motivation to participate had to be fairly high.[2]

The selection criteria are not very useful for identifying all those who were eventually incorporated into the research because the criteria were applied only to the first household chosen for study in any given family. As each family study progressed, it encompassed all major related households, such as those of married children or siblings. Among the six principal *La Vida* households, for example, only one had an annual income under the $1,200 ceiling Lewis had set for inclusion in the original study; Simplicio Ríos's annual income was four times higher.

The main criteria for selection of families living in New York were their relationship to and active communication with the families being studied in San Juan. Except for an expanded migration questionnaire, which covered life on the mainland, the battery of questionnaires administered to the New York City families was the same as that used in San Juan.

Those New York and San Juan households remaining in the study after the survey stage was completed were asked to cooperate in budget and genealogical studies and to allow inventories to be made of all their household possessions, including clothing. In addition, individuals who were part of one of the five family studies were asked to participate in psychological testing and to allow multiple, day-long observations to be made of their household activities. Life histories were also collected from these individuals. For this latter group of informants the amount of information collected was, of course, far greater and vastly more complex than that gathered on first-round informants. In numbers of interviews the differences ranged from the two to four done with individuals included in the survey to from ten to fifty-four done with principals in the family studies. At this intensive level of work the number of informants dropped drastically, from the original 803 included in the survey to the 25 major and 134 minor informants for the five family studies.

To guide this round of interviewing Lewis had fifteen additional questionnaire schedules prepared, but he did not insist upon or even attempt to achieve uniformity in their application. They were used more as interviewing aids than as instruments for collecting data readily subject to quantification. He did try to obtain comparable information on each major informant, but he never required that the full battery of questionnaires be systematically administered *as a set*. Because the questions from these fifteen schedules were asked in taped interviews, answers were usually not written on the forms, making it extremely difficult to tabulate answers to any one question. One would have to sift through thousands of pages of transcribed interviews to find a complete set of responses to any one question. Treating the data in a vertical, segmented manner, that is, as raw material for separate family studies, made it almost impossible to keep discrete all information collected on a specific personality or culture trait. Therefore any analysis for the purpose of testing the culture of poverty thesis was made extraordinarily difficult.

After two years of research Lewis was able to compare all of his Puerto Rican informants on income and educational levels, family size, residence and job histories, and luxury possessions. This information was recorded by hand directly on questionnaire forms and was fairly easy to summarize. In addition, Lewis was able to compare the second-round informants on their expenditure patterns and material possessions. Collecting this data and summarizing it was a very laborious task, but it did lend itself quite easily to comparison. Douglas Butterworth tabulated and analyzed all of this material, and it was published in 1968 as *A Study in Slum Culture*. However detailed and valuable this information may be about specific individuals and families, it is fairly meaningless in terms of providing support for the culture of poverty thesis. There is considerable variation in economic circumstance among these informants and very little evidence of a distinctive set of shared values. Lewis did not begin to get at value structure until he went beyond the collection of economic data and into open-ended interviewing and household observation. But this is exactly the stage at which the method of data collection made analysis so cumbersome a task.

Defining Culture by Its Traits

Once he had committed to print his intuition about the existence of a universal poverty subculture, Lewis was left in a position of having to flesh out his statement. To define the subculture he resorted to the construction of a trait list, even though up to that time he had been in complete agreement with Ruth Benedict's caveat that cultures "are more than the sum of their traits."[3] Although the subculture came to depend for its definition on this list, nowhere in his discussion of it did Lewis establish exactly how he was using the word "trait." In fact it was on just this point that the culture of poverty thesis received its first criticism from Conrad Arensberg.

The list of traits had its origin in Lewis's first discussion of the sub-culture, wherein he identified eight overlapping areas of similarity in the lives of poor people: family structure, husband-wife and parent-child relationships, kinship patterns, notions of time, spending patterns, system of values, and sense of community.[4] The similarities were restated in *Five Families*, but two years later, in *The Children of Sánchez*, Lewis had broken down these categories into—depending upon how one parses the sentences—thirty-six traits. The final list (prepared in 1965 but not published until 1969; see Table 1) identifies sixty-two traits, but it is, in fact, identical to the one published in *The Children of Sánchez*, except that some of the traits are subdivided or listed more than once. Over the years, for no apparent reason, Lewis variously claimed there were thirty-six, fifty, sixty-two, seventy, seventy-two, or eighty different traits.[5]

Insofar as I can tell, Lewis adopted the final list from an itemization in a term paper written by one of his students. The student culled the additional twenty-six traits from the prefatory and summary remarks Lewis had written in discussing the list in *The Children of Sánchez*, simply by counting some traits more than once, and, in a mechanical reading, must have misunderstood that in a paragraph identifying psychosocial traits, the word "other" referred to other psychosocial traits, not a separate category.[6] Hence the incomprehensible categorization of traits such as resignation, fatalism, present-time orientation, and high tolerance for psychopathology under "other" instead of under "social and psychological."[7] Similarly unreasonable divisions were created by identifying unemployment as an "economic" trait but a "higher proportion of gainfully employed" as an "other" trait. It is indicative of Lewis's ambivalence toward the concept and, in particular, its definition by a trait list, that he so carelessly—or better said, cavalierly—adopted this itemization without any apparent concern for its internal logic.

The Social and Psychological Traits

It was the psychosocial traits that Lewis said were the key characteristics of the culture of poverty. To help construct and support this list he relied heavily on the analyses of Thematic Apperception and Rorschach tests.[8] These analyses consistently pointed to feelings of mother-deprivation and inferiority, weak ego structure, orality, de-

Table 1. List of Traits of the Culture of Poverty

Economic
Unemployment and underemployment
Low wages
Miscellany of unskilled occupations
Child labor
Absence of savings
Chronic shortage of cash
Absence of food reserves in the home
Frequent daily food purchases in small quantities
Pawning
Borrowing from local money lenders at usurious rates of interest
Spontaneous informal credit devices
Use of secondhand clothing and furniture
Constant struggle for survival
Social & Psychological
Crowded quarters
Lack of privacy
Gregariousness
High incidence of alcoholism
Violence
Violence in training of children
Wife beating
Early initiation into sex
Free unions
Abandonment of mothers and children
Mother-centered families
Predominance of nuclear family
Authoritarianism
Emphasis upon family solidarity (only rarely achieved)
Local residence a kind of small community
Stable residence
Lifetime friendships
Daily face-to-face relations with same people
Extended family ties quite strong

Local community acts as a shock absorber for rural migrants to city
Use of herbs for curing
Raising of animals
Political apathy
Belief in sorcery and spiritualism
Cynicism about government
Hatred of police
Limited membership and participation in both formal and informal associations
Critical attitude toward some of beliefs and values of dominant classes
Mistrust of government and those in high position
Cynicism which extends even to the church
Members attempt to utilize and integrate into a workable way of life the remnants of beliefs and customs of diverse origins
Strong feeling of marginality
Strong feeling of helplessness
Strong feeling of dependency
Feeling of inferiority and personal unworthiness
Little sense of history
Not class-conscious
Others
Strong present-time orientation with little ability to defer gratification
Resignation and fatalism
Male superiority (machismo)
Corresponding martyr complex among women
High tolerance for psychological pathology
Provincial and locally oriented
Marginal to national institutions (social security, labor unions, banks, etc.)
Low level of education and literacy

Relative higher death rate	Higher proportion of gainfully
Lower life expectancy	employed (because of working
Higher proportion of individuals in	women and child labor)
the younger age groups	

Source: Oscar Lewis, "A Puerto Rican Boy," in *Culture Change, Mental Health and Poverty*, ed. Joseph Finney (Lexington: University of Kentucky Press, 1969), p. 150.

pendency, fatalism, resignation, and confusion of sexual identity. The Rorschach in particular is widely considered by its critics to point to psychic deprivation and emotional or mental disturbances while ignoring other aspects of personality. In any case, the psychological testing Lewis did in Puerto Rico was not comparable to that done in Mexico and could not have been used in the same way to establish a composite profile or modal personality. In Tepoztlán, Ruth Lewis had administered 112 Rorschachs to adults and children from the "sample" families; test analyzer Theodora Abel set 100 as the minimum number she was willing to work with for the purpose of establishing a modal personality. In Puerto Rico only a few dozen Rorschachs were administered, and these were never analyzed as a set; instead they were used primarily to assist in the interpretation of biographical material. While I am not qualified to contest the validity of individual test analyses, I can state emphatically that, even if one accepts their validity, given the number administered, the tests do not provide sufficient evidence to establish the above-listed characteristics as culture traits.

Aggravating the paucity of psychological test data was the fact that Lewis did not include in his design any provision for medical examinations of his informants. Yet their physiological well-being (not to mention their natural endowments) must have had some bearing on the behavior and personality characteristics that Lewis labeled "psychosocial." In his early writing he referred to the importance of understanding the "bio-physical state" of informants, and he did administer two related questionnaires in Mexico and Puerto Rico: one on health, which took a short medical history and dealt with symptoms of illness, and a second on treatment of illnesses, which sought information on traditional curing practices and attitudes toward physicians, clinics, and hospitals.[9] But no expert diagnoses of informants' physical conditions were sought, except in cases where the presence of disease was apparent and Lewis or his assistants intervened to obtain medical care.

There were practical reasons why physical examinations were not included—such as the added cost to the research project and the difficulties of getting people to agree to them. But thorough physicals and expert diagnoses could have made a significant contribution to testing the thesis. There were a host of problems that may have accounted for some aspects of his informants' behavior; for example, poor prenatal care and dietary habits of pregnant women and new mothers; poor childhood nutrition; parasites and gastroenteritis; tuberculosis; the effects of home curing practices; and the excessive consumption of caffeine, nicotine, and alcohol.

A high incidence of alcoholism was listed as a trait of the subculture, but poverty was certainly not the causal factor since the great majority of Lewis's poor informants were not alcoholics. In fact Lewis offered no hard evidence that the incidence of alcohol abuse *was* higher among the people he studied than it was among all Mexicans or Puerto Ricans. He did not view alcoholism as a disease, nor did he consider the tendency toward alcoholism as an inherited characteristic, as researchers are inclined to regard it today. Instead he interpreted its incidence among his informants as a response to poverty, indeed, as an adaptation to it.

Two of the Mexican informants Lewis cited as archetypes of the culture of poverty, Guadalupe Vélez and her husband, Ignacio, were very heavy drinkers. Vélez, the maternal aunt of the Sánchez children, suffered from cirrhosis of the liver, and it was at least a contributing factor in her death (see *A Death in the Sánchez Family*). She came from a family with a history of alcohol abuse, including that by her sister Lenore, the mother of the Sánchez children. Vélez was born into poverty, and there was little chance, given the nature of Mexico's political and economic system, that she could have escaped it, even if she had been a nondrinker. But her abuse of alcohol may have had a direct effect on her level of poverty and the way in which she organized her life. Some of the extremes in her "design for living" that made such an impression on Lewis perhaps could be traced more fairly to her drinking than to her poverty per se.

What Lewis labeled "psychological" traits of a culture might be categorized more accurately as personality traits of individual informants. In fact he worked with a conception of personality that was dangerously close to his definition of culture as a design for living, as in Gordon Allport's statement that "personality . . . represents the mode of survival that the individual has consciously worked out for himself."[10] To Alex Inkeles's dictum, "The adjustment of any person to his objective class situation is clearly a problem in psychology," Lewis could add that it was a problem in culture study as well, as long as that mode of adjustment was passed from one generation to another.[11]

While Lewis skirted discussions of the functional relationship between culture and personality, he implied a relationship that was consistent with viewing culture as "the individual psychology thrown large upon the screen, given gigantic proportion and a long time span."[12] In his one serious effort to define personality Lewis said that any useful definition had to encompass both behavior and value structure.[13] In the aggregate, these were also the two central components in his definition of culture. Values were "one of the most important determinants of behavior," Lewis wrote, but also the "most difficult thing to get at" in research. He "equate[d] values with motivation" and believed that motivation, in turn, largely determined behavior.[14] From this position it was easy to work backward from observing behavior to imputing both personality and culture traits.

In Lewis's work distinctions between personality traits, culture traits, attitudes, habits, and behavior do not exist. His trait list obscures distinctions made by leading researchers of the time, such as Allport, who created separate categories for what he called authentic traits of personality, present activities (temporary states), and evaluative terms.[15] Whereas Lewis listed cynicism toward government and the church, and mistrust of the police and government officials, for example, as four different traits of the poverty subculture, according to Allport's scheme these would be better seen as four different attitudinal aspects of a single personality trait.

Carolina Luján cautioned Lewis on his trait scheme when he asked her to read the draft introduction to *The Children of Sánchez*. She objected both to how he categorized the traits and to the significance he assigned to the individual traits. As an alternative to Lewis's "somewhat haphazard" grouping of characteristics into economic and psychosocial traits, Luján preferred creating categories that would distinguish among: socioeconomic conditions; social or cultural factors; home environmental factors; conduct representing attempts at solving economic problems; conduct that was the external manifestation of psychopathology; and psychic states. She wrote to Lewis that "the greater part of the characteristics which you refer to as 'psychological' are merely on the level of conduct.' "[16] Because Lewis was essentially an observer, it is not too surprising that he relied heavily for his conclusions on what he saw. Even his particular use of the "design for living" definition of culture implies a greater reliance on a pattern of conduct he could observe than on an internalized pattern of values he would have to abstract from the interviews.

The Economic Traits

The methods used to identify the psychosocial traits of the culture of poverty seem especially inadequate when compared with the very sound and exhaustive research that produced the economic trait list. It is hard to think of any American anthropologist of Lewis's era who was more interested in material culture or who developed better methods for studying household economics. While he was best known for the flashier aspects of his work, such as the vivid and sometimes controversial interview material, over the years he and his assistants spent thousands of hours in the laborious process of taking inventories of household possessions and clothing and in doing income and budget studies. They recorded every piece of furniture and clothing, every ornament, photograph, and religious artifact. Separate inventories were made of kitchen items and of "luxury" possessions. Places, dates, sources of gifts and purchases, as well as purchase prices, were recorded. This, combined with the study of income and expenditures, gave Lewis an extraordinary grasp of the material lives of his informants, especially when compared to his understanding of their inner lives and personalities. In addition, the basic economic data were collected from a much larger group of households than were included in the family studies, which meant that Lewis often got (except in Tepoztlán) a fuller understanding of a community's overall economic condition than he did of its culture.

The questionnaire data used to establish the economic traits provided evidence only of poverty, and poverty was a necessary, but far from sufficient, condition for the subculture to exist. The economic traits were no more, nor less, than a description of the material conditions in the homes he studied at that point in time. His data show generational continuity only in the poverty itself, not in the exact conditions of the poverty. They show that within a single generation differences existed in the degree of poverty, income, expenditure patterns, and material culture. For example, 83 percent of all his Puerto Rican informants had migrated from the countryside to San Juan. Reconstructions of their lives in the country and interviews with their rural relatives indicated changes in means of livelihood; in source, amount, and use of income; in design and materials used for housing; and in amount and type of household furnishings. For those who went to New York from San Juan, still another set of microeconomic conditions were recorded. These changes were mandated by poverty experienced in different settings and were solutions to immediate problems (or what Arensberg called "coping"). They were, however, equated by Lewis with adaptation and elevated to the status of culture traits.

Weighting the Traits

As late as 1968 Lewis wrote, "I have not yet worked out a system for weighting each of the traits, but this could be done and a scale could be set up for many. . . ."[17] The traits were never assigned any objective values, and the frequency of their occurrence was left unquantified. Instead, Lewis expressed their relationship to traits of Mexican or Puerto Rican cultures in a vague and tentative manner, such as "higher incidence of," "higher tolerance for," "little sense of," "higher proportion of," or "strong feeling of," and so forth. On the few occasions that he deviated from this pattern—for example, by giving the literacy rates, numbers of two-parent families, and numbers of free unions for the Casa Grande and Panaderos *vecindades*—the figures did not support his thesis.[18] (The literacy rate he gave for the Casa Grande, for example, was way above the national average for Mexico.) Lewis's whole subculture argument was greatly impaired by the fact that he provided no comparable list of, or weightings for, traits of the dominant cultures. Yet, to support his argument that what he was describing really was a subculture (let alone one that transcended national boundaries), he had to establish how it was different from the larger part. It was not only necessary to abstract common traits from the life histories and projective tests but also to locate their origins in the socialization processes of the family and the community (which in turn required a description of the distinctive institutions, customs, and practices of the subculture) and then to demonstrate the extent to which the resulting design for living deviated from that of the national culture.

Lewis provided a good example of the lack of distinction between culture and subculture in his introduction to *La Vida*, where he wrote, "The remarkable stability in some of the behavior patterns of the Ríos family over four generations . . . suggests we are dealing with a tenacious cultural pattern."[19] The specific behavior singled out as examples—high incidence of early marriages, free unions, multiple spouses, and birth of children out of wedlock—he also cited as generally common in Puerto Rico as a whole.

Had Lewis devised standards of measurement or sets of indicators for the presence of the social and psychological traits—what ratio of inhabitants per room constituted crowding; how many moves constituted an unstable residence pattern; at what point of disinterest a person was classified as "politically apathetic"—he could have brought some system to his analysis of the work. Even if the standards had been inadequate, they would have provided him with a yardstick against which to make consistent comparisons of his informants and to contrast his informants with those outside the subculture. The standards would also have let readers know how he made his decisions on who belonged inside and who outside the culture of poverty. In addition, Lewis should have established a hierarchy of traits in order to clarify the patterning or "clustering" that he said was indicative of the culture.

In comparing subculture and culture Lewis often used as a norm, or point of reference, an idealization of middle-class life rather than a construct of the Mexican or Puerto Rican culture. Because of his tendency to think in terms of social stratification and class, it was natural for him to see cross-national similarities among the middle classes, just as he did among the lower classes. His reliance on a class construct magnified the differences he saw between the lower and middle classes in the social-psychological traits, while many of their similarities went unnoted. This is because the very poor make a lesser effort or have less success in covering up negatively viewed behavior. The poor can afford neither the privacy nor the disguises the middle class can buy.

Lewis never studied the middle class, and there were, at the time, few available studies of the middle class that focused on concerns similar to his own. The great avalanche of published studies on the middle class in the United States, for example, came after Lewis's death. He would have benefited enormously from findings that suggested that income and class are far less significant factors than he had assumed in the incidence of domestic violence, child abuse, incest, alcoholism, and drug abuse, as well as by the more recent sociological and political studies pointing to fairly widespread early initiation into sex, the frequency of free unions, and a growing cynicism toward government and authority. Some of these findings are due to better reporting on the middle class, but others, perhaps, would not have obtained twenty or thirty years ago. However, if middle-class culture, through social change, is moving closer to the clustering of social and psychological traits that defined Lewis's subculture, then one might ask what kind of change the subculture itself is undergoing. It is impossible to answer this question because the culture of poverty is not a real culture but an ideal type. Real people change and in the process reshape their cultures, but ideal types are impervious to historical forces. When Lewis conceptualized his subculture as lying at the zero point on a continuum, he fixed it in time and removed all need to deal with questions of change.[20]

Possibly, Lewis was able to observe so much unflattering behavior among his informants because such behavior did not conflict with their values and, therefore, they had no interest in concealing it. If this were true, then Lewis might have been correct when he said that his informants adhered to a distinct set of values. However, his trait list does not directly address the question of values, only the comparative frequency of certain kinds of behavior.

Generational Continuity in the Expression of the Traits

When Lewis first began doing family studies he believed that they could be completed in from two to three months (i.e., over the summer school break).[21] At the time, however, he was treating the family as a mirror of local culture. He associated the culture group with a given geographic location and assumed a certain degree of generational continuity. But after committing himself to the study of the family and its psychodynamics, he needed time to probe more deeply into individual personality. And after proposing the culture of poverty thesis he had to demonstrate continuity in values and behavior to support his claim that he had identified a distinct culture group. Therefore near the end of his career he was arguing that family studies would require minimal periods of from five to ten *years* of research.[22]

Lewis did study six families for periods of from six to twenty years, long enough to make judgments that their "behavior was clearly patterned and reasonably predictable."[23] But he did not study any "slum children" long enough to support his contention that they were locked into a self-defeating life-style by the time they were six or seven years old. Most of his adult informants who actually lived in what we would call slums—and this does not include the Casa Grande—had migrated to them after being raised in the countryside. From his own materials the only evidentiary base Lewis had to support his fatalistic predictions were the interpretations of projective tests administered to about a half dozen children from La Esmeralda.

Lewis twice undertook special observations of the children of his informants. The first was a study of the grandchildren of Jesús Sánchez, which he worked on throughout the 1960s with the help of Consuelo Sánchez.[24] The second study, on the children of five La Esmeralda families, was assigned to Francisca Muriente. Lewis's plan for the Sánchez children was to monitor their progress over a period of many years, but the Puerto Rican children were to be studied during a relatively short period of time, through intensive observation of their lives both inside and outside the home. The latter plan proved very difficult to implement, because, whereas the trained observer might develop sufficient rapport to blend into household life, it was almost impossible for an adult to integrate into a child's outside activities with a similarly low degree of disruption. The study of Puerto Rican children was never completed, and Lewis did not live long enough to undertake on his own the kind of follow-up work he had done on the Sánchez grandchildren.

Francisca Muriente has kept track of some of the Puerto Rican children, as Ruth Lewis has of the Sánchezes, but what is known gives a mixed message rather than unqualified support for Lewis's claims for generational continuities. Some children have made rather sharp breaks with their backgrounds and are economically better off than their parents; others live lives fairly similar to their parents'.[25]

Even though he lacked the methodical and patient temperament to do longitudinal studies, Lewis did have a system for the collection of data on generational continuity in culture traits. It depended on the use of three separate approaches to the subject area: taking life histories from several generations within a family at the same point in time, charting family genealogies, and—the most indirect of the three—making household observations.

Taking life histories from several generations in a family is not a substitute for longitudinal studies since so much of the information is reconstructed from personal recollections and not directly observed. Furthermore, the content of the life histories often pointed to substantial discontinuities in life-styles between generations, particularly between those individuals raised in the countryside and the children or grandchildren raised in the cities, as Lewis himself often noted. Although he did not actually analyze his material along these lines, Lewis thought he demonstrated some of the continuities and discontinuities by including more than one generation of voices in a single study. The last family study he worked on before his death, for example covered three generations from a single family.

In charting genealogies Lewis was interested in more than constructing a family tree, discovering how many relatives an informant could identify, or what their sense of family history was. He wanted to trace back as far as he could the occupational histories of ancestors and, in particular, their relationship to the land. Informants were also asked to discuss generational differences or similarities in child-rearing and to describe the dress, behavior, and personalities of older relatives they had known.[26] Because Lewis was so dependent upon personal recollections for the reconstruction of the past, he relied on multiple accounts of the same events for validation of information.

The household observations, or day studies, were used to collect information on several different topics, including division of labor and patterns of time use, but the role of the family as an agent of socialization was also a fundamental concern.[27] The underlying assumption was that children were internalizing cultural patterns as manifested by others in the household and that they were destined to reflect the attitudes and behavior to which they were exposed. Lewis's research did not ignore the mediating impact of exposure to the community environment, the larger culture, the school, peer groups, rural relatives, television, or movies, for example, but it was difficult to incorporate all of this information into a family biography. The format itself emphasized the primacy of the family as a social and cultural unit without directly addressing the questions of how effectively the family functioned in this respect and how much was transmitted from one generation to the next. Inferences can be drawn from reading the day studies, but without long-term observation of a family, one cannot be certain just how much the children absorbed and integrated.

Lewis's claim that his informants' behavior was clearly patterned and reasonably predictable might hold true for the individual, but it seems to me it would not obtain in the aggregate as an expression of culture. In other words, each of Lewis's informants might be reasonably consistent in behavior if we look at each as an independent actor in his or her own life story. But the collective behavior of informants did not conform to the pattern he identified as a culture of poverty, and it was not reasonably predictable using that pattern as a guide. Even on an individual level Lewis's informants show more consistency in values and personality than in behavior. Based on their published life histories or on his culture construct, I would not have successfully predicted, for example, the way the Sánchez children have lived their lives in the twenty-five years since their story was published. Yet, when I met Manuel, Roberto, and Marta they were, as personalities, exactly as I expected them to be.[28] As circumstances have changed, or opportunities presented themselves, these particular individuals have been able to change certain aspects of their behavior. Thus it seems that the rigid, interlocking relationship between values, behavior, and personality that Lewis explicitly or implicitly suggested in the culture of poverty theory was substantially overstated. Had he looked more closely at the evidence for generational discontinuities within his own material, or had he undertaken longitudinal studies, I think he would have revised his deterministic language about early psychological conditioning and how it influenced behavior.

Culture, Personality, and the Family Study Approach

Lewis was committed to family studies as "probably the best method to establish the presence or absence of the more than 70 traits which I have suggested in defining the culture of poverty."[29] The unusual aspect of this conclusion was that while he found the family intrinsically interesting as an agent of socialization and a transmitter of culture, as a shaper of personality and a unit for studying interpersonal relationships, he worked with no more than broad assumptions about the family's role in any one of these areas.

Lewis chose the family study approach because it provided an interesting and manageable unit for his holistic method, not because the family itself had any special theoretical or analytic importance in his thinking on cultural and personality processes. His commitment to the holistic method gave him an aversion to breaking down the whole of his data into units suitable for analysis. To him everything was related, and the whole could be broken into its parts only through the use of artificial constructs. The family study provided a way to divide his material vertically into descriptive segments without having to break it down analytically.

Lewis was always torn between treating the family as a representative unit of culture or, in Jules Henry's conception, "as a little world unto itself, with its own laws . . . in many of its traits a sub-culture."[30] In his Tepoztlán research, Lewis clearly regarded family life as culture writ small; but the longer he worked, the closer he came to Henry's conception of the family. This should have led Lewis to stop claiming that his individual family studies were representative of a culture construct, or to withhold that claim until he had accumulated a sufficiently large number of studies to separate the unique from the typical. Collecting so many family studies was clearly beyond the lifework of any one researcher like Lewis who was trying to establish the existence of a subculture that was universal in scope. Making a definitive statement on culture in fact did become a long-term goal for Lewis, while in the near term he tried to provide the best possible description of a single family and its individual members.

The family was an ideal level on which to focus, Lewis wrote, if one were interested in the relationship between culture and personality processes because it was the great mediator between the two. "One cannot study personality formation against the background of generalized culture patterns. It is not culture patterns as a whole that influence the child. It is culture patterns as mediated by a particular family situation."[31] His research, however, always paid less attention to demonstrating how the family functioned as a mediator of cultural influences than it did to describing the individual personalities that comprised the family and how they interacted with one another.

If an interest in establishing the uniqueness of each family pushed culture study to the background in Lewis's later Mexican research, his interest in individual personality removed it to the far horizon in the Puerto Rican research. As early as the Tepoztlán project he wrote that he hoped to develop a technique for the study of private personality, or that aspect of personality "largely determined by many non-cultural factors such as constitution, condition of health, and unique life experiences. . . ."[32] Lewis intended to combine this with the study of culturally determined aspects (i.e., the public personality) in order to describe total personality. But this would still leave him on the levels of the individual and the family. How would he get from there back to culture?—especially if his teacher Ralph Linton had been right in saying that "cultural processes, and indeed culture as a whole seem to have little effect upon the processes involved in the development and operation of the personality."[33]

In fact Lewis got back to culture only on the theoretical level, by postulating that his informants shared a culturally shaped personality configuration. Where did the family as a shaper of personality and a mediator of culture fit into Lewis's scheme? There is no way to tell, because in the culture of poverty theory the family appears as no more than an assumed agent of cultural and personality processes.

The Origins of the Culture of Poverty Prototype

In relying heavily on his impressions to make and support his generalizations, Lewis gave full vent to personal characteristics that actually worked to distort his data: he was more influenced by visual stimuli than by reasoned analysis; he was fascinated by extremes in personality and behavior; and he tended toward hyperbole in his speaking and writing. The most extreme cases of poverty and the most extreme responses to it overshadowed the more typical or ordinary, and it was often these exceptional cases that Lewis singled out for publication. If anthropologists, as he claimed, often had "omitted their most vivid and dynamic" cases in order to identify a general pattern, he himself ignored the general pattern in favor of concentrating on his most vivid and dynamic material.[34]

Lewis wanted to convey to readers precisely those observable aspects of his informants' lives that had so influenced him. During the last ten years of his career, this objective affected both his choice of informants—those who could most graphically present their lives to readers—and of format. The underlying message sent to readers was no longer, "This is what I have come to understand about how poor people live their lives," but rather, "This is what I have seen; don't you see the same things too?" The weakness of this approach was well summarized by Barrington Moore in his review of *La Vida*, when he reminded Lewis that "vivid impressions by themselves are no substitute for knowledge."[35]

At least two kinds of problems arose from Lewis's overemphasis on exceptional cases. One, of course, was that because they were not representative, they distorted the meaning of the material as a whole. This is one reason why readers might have trouble seeing what Lewis saw as he represented it in the culture of poverty construct. The archetypes of the subculture were often not the individuals whose lives he captured in his books. Those who most closely fit the subculture syndrome were the most difficult to understand; the most lethargic in speech; and the most unreliable as informants because of low information content, poor memory, poverty of language, and, at times, physical incapacitation due to alcohol abuse. Others who *were* more representative of all informants often had little information to give, no interest in participation, or no ability to express in an interesting way the information they did have. To use the format of autobiography or multiple biographies, and to hold reader interest, Lewis was dependent upon people who had an exceptional ability to express themselves or who had lived unusually interesting lives, the events of which could compensate for any shortcomings in verbal skills.

As Lewis cropped the larger picture to manageable size, readers were asked to take him at his word on what he had omitted. He acknowledged that, in this sense, his method had a "few loopholes" and people had to "trust in my integrity and commitment."[36] Of course, Lewis intended eventually to round out the picture presented in *La Vida* by publishing all of the family studies he had done in La Esmeralda. It is not easy, however, to interest a publisher, especially a trade publisher, in releasing five successive studies of families from a single neighborhood.

A second problem created by Lewis's attraction to exceptional cases was a confusion in the attribution of cause and effect in his theorizing about the relationships between poverty, culture, and personality. This point occurred to me while examining his photographic collection on research sites and informants. The several published informants he singled out as archetypes of the culture of poverty had something singularly different about their person or dress that immediately caught the eye. In physical type these individuals were under- or overweight, had slightly stooped postures and rather dull gazes that suggested mental or physical lethargy; they often had hollowed cheeks from missing teeth and sometimes striking physical features like scars or tattoos as well.[37] There was often something extraordinary about their housing and possessions as well, such as a unique use of salvage materials in the construction of their homes or an extreme disorganization of their possessions.

It was that minority who fit this extreme-case type who attracted

Lewis's attention; and even though his sample families always represented a range of life-styles, it was the much more "vivid" material that he published first. At least part of the reason for this decision was that, from Lewis's perspective, this material would more quickly capture readers' attention and make a stronger, more urgent case for economic and social welfare reform.

The Arriaga family of "Six Women" provides a good illustration of this point. They were the most eccentric people Lewis ever worked with and the central household in the study was characterized by extraordinary confusion and disorganization. The mother, Carmen, roughly fit the physical description of a culture of poverty "type," but she suffered from diabetes and a number of ailments that might have affected her physical appearance. Her daughter Magda was a younger, heavier version of her mother and was married to an alcoholic. Magda's sister, Lola, was underweight, badly scarred from razor fights, abused alcohol and other drugs, suffered from attacks of paralyzing hysteria, and was ravaged by tuberculosis. (She died early in the study after refusing the hospitalization arranged by Muriente and Lewis.) To Lewis these three women were examples of the effects of gross economic deprivation; he did not sort out the differential impact upon them of heredity and environment, nor did he distinguish between disease-related and culturally influenced behavior.

What happened in Lewis's reasoning here, I believe, was similar to the confusion, discussed years earlier by Kurt Lewin and Gordon Allport, between genotype and phenotype, the former being a causal category and the latter a physically descriptive one.[38] Allport wrote that when people have a common phenotype, what appears to be effect may be due to radically different causes; one effect may be due to heredity, another to environmental conditions. In not generalizing from a statistical (or otherwise systematically arrived at) norm, and in not distinguishing between cause, effect, and associational relationships, Lewis came closer to the construction of a personality typology in the subculture concept than to the identification of a culture pattern.

In Allport's definition of typology:

> . . . the reference point is always some attribute, a cluster of correlating attributes abstracted from various personalities, a biosocial reference, defined by the interest of the particular investigator. . . .
>
> Whatever the kind, a typology is always a device for exalting its author's special interest at the expense of the individuality of the life which he ruthlessly dismembers. Every typology is based on the abstraction of some segment of the total personality, and the forcing of this segment to unnatural prominence. All typologies place boundaries where boundaries do not belong.[39]

This is far too harsh a characterization of Lewis's work if one is referring to anything other than the culture of poverty thesis, because the
published interviews do stress individuality and therefore do not lend
support to any typology. When looking at informants as individuals
and as members of families, as readers are asked to do in *The Children
of Sánchez* and *La Vida*, it is precisely their individuality and the detail
of their lives that impress and inform. The format tends to emphasize the idiosyncrasies of the particular individual or family. The only
connections between individual, family, and the culture, besides those
inferred by the reader, are the weak links provided by Lewis in the
culture of poverty thesis.

Lewis tried to account for discrepancies by saying that "it is point-
less to seek a one-to-one correspondence between the model and all
of the characters" in *The Children of Sánchez* and *La Vida*.[40] It would be
more useful, he continued, to think of their lives as falling along a
continuum between the subculture of poverty and the working and
middle classes. In any case Lewis did not publish works such as these
to give support to the culture of poverty thesis so much as to give
memorable witness to the effects of economic deprivation on specific
individuals and to present people whose life stories—with or without
historical or theoretical perspective—were interesting in themselves.

While having as a focal point of his research the documentation
of diversity in social organization, material culture, and individual
behavior and personality, Lewis let himself become associated with
a concept that obscured individual differences and emphasized the
common denominator of poverty. This was the greatest paradox of a
career filled with contradiction; it undercut the very purpose of his
research and violated some of the basic standards he used to separate
his work and that of his contemporaries from the work of first- and
second-generation anthropologists.

> Most anthropologists would be making great strides ahead if they would
> employ the simple arithmetic process of addition or if they would con-
> sistently ask the question of their field data, "Out of how many cases is
> this true?" or if they were more careful in selecting informants and in
> using sampling procedures.
>   . . . when Linton writes ". . . the total culture pattern construct is de-
> veloped by combining all the culture construct patterns which have been
> developed." . . . what happens is that we are adding up our guesses and
> arrive at a total guess, namely the total pattern construct. That anthro-
> pologists often guess brilliantly is to their everlasting credit, but this
> can hardly be equated with a scientific methodology. (It is no wonder
> then that some persons think of cultural anthropology as a branch of the
> humanities rather than of the sciences.)[41]

Had Lewis been able to live up to these standards in the analysis and presentation of his materials, as he did in the conduct of his field research, he would have been able to make a more credible statement about poverty than he achieved in the culture of poverty thesis.

NOTES

1. Lewis, *Study of Slum Culture*, p. 21.

2. In Puerto Rico an almost equal number of men and women were interviewed, but women became the principal informants for most families because they were more accessible. Almost all of the informants came from households where at least one adult had some kind of employment, but the men worked outside the home more frequently than did the women. Women who worked for wages often did so in their homes, for example, as laundresses, seamstresses, or operators of mini-stores; so even if they were no less busy than the men, they were more available to fieldworkers. It is also possible that women were more willing to take advantage of the interview situation to air their views and discuss their private lives. In any case women did not become the primary informants more often than men because there were no men in the homes or because Lewis had better rapport with women. The majority of the interviews with Puerto Rican women were conducted by women.

3. Ruth Benedict, *Patterns of Culture* (1934; Boston: Houghton, Mifflin, 1959), p. 47.

4. Lewis, "La Cultura de la Vecindad," p. 350.

5. When Lewis was organizing quantifiable data into summary charts, or when he was drawing conclusions from them, he was very exacting; but in other circumstances, for whatever reason, he used numbers in a very inexact way, as he did in numbering the traits. Lewis would never have treated anything he took seriously in such an offhand manner.

6. Lewis, *Children of Sánchez*, pp. xxvi–xxvii.

7. The categorization of these traits as "other" came about, I believe, because Lewis added on to what he had already written a list of traits provided by Luján (see the last sentence on p. xxvi in ibid.). All of the "other"-listed traits were identified by Luján as universal characteristics of the culture of poverty after she read a draft version of the introduction to *The Children of Sánchez* (letter from Carolina Luján to Oscar Lewis, January 10, 1961). I deduced this from the Luján–Lewis correspondence, but I cannot prove my point because I could not locate the draft introduction to *The Children of Sánchez*.

8. For a discussion of the personality tests available to fieldworkers in the 1950s and 1960s, see Alex Inkeles, "Sociology and Psychology," in *Psychology: Study of a Science*, ed. Sigmund Koch, vol. 6 (New York: McGraw Hill, 1963), pp. 342ff.

9. Lewis, *Life in a Mexican Village*, p. 422.

10. Gordon Allport, *Personality: A Psychological Interpretation* (New York: Henry Holt and Co., 1937), p. 119. Lewis met Allport through his friend and former teacher Otto Klineberg at the International Psychological Society meetings in Mexico City in December 1957. Lewis later asked Allport to read parts of the Sánchez manuscript.

11. Alex Inkeles, "Sociology and Psychology," p. 373.

12. Ruth Benedict, "Configurations of Culture in North America," *American Anthropologist* 34 (1932): 24. Although this is the definition of culture most closely associated with Benedict, it is only one of the possible ways she suggested for viewing culture.

13. Lewis, *Life in a Mexican Village*, p. 421.

14. Ibid., p. 422; see also the letter from Oscar Lewis to Irving Goldman, November 28, 1954 (no. 42 in the Appendix).

15. Allport, *Personality*, pp. 290–95; Gordon Allport and Henry Odbert, "Trait-Names: A Psycho-lexical Study," *Psychological Monographs* 47 (1936): v–37.

16. Letter from Carolina Luján to Oscar Lewis, October 9, 1961.

17. Lewis, *Study of Slum Culture*, p. 12.

18. Because Lewis relied so heavily on his impressions, it would not be surprising if another reader of his material, one with a different perspective, came to somewhat different conclusions. For example, reading the Puerto Rican materials with the orientation of a political scientist, I found the political content substantial, rather than very low, as Lewis reported. I was not impressed by the informants' "feelings of inferiority" but by their contempt for the middle class and its general life-style. I saw less evidence than he did of "authoritarianism" (although I am using the term just as loosely). Compared to his Mexican informants, who were generally stern, very strict, and intolerant of disobedience in child-rearing, for example, the Puerto Rican informants were unusually permissive. Similarly, I was not convinced that his informants had "little sense of history." In using this phrase Lewis meant that his informants had little knowledge of historical figures, places, events, and dates of the kind sought on a grade or high school history test. A student who memorized the answers might do very well on a test yet not have a very good understanding of history. Lewis's informants *did* have some historical perspective and at least some understanding of political and economic change and its impact on their lives. They were more likely than not to know the economic status of their ancestors—for example, if they had been landowners or tenants; if they had lost their land and the conditions under which they had lost it. I would not be the first to point out that if they had not been able to look back and remember fairly well, Lewis could not have collected so many life histories. However, it must also be noted that Lewis's edited versions of life histories camouflaged the difficulty he and his assistants had in drawing out and piecing together this information.

19. Lewis, *La Vida*, p. xxvii.

20. Lewis, *Anthropological Essays*, p. x. The static, ahistorical nature of the culture of poverty concept was pointed out to Lewis in 1960 by Conrad

Arensberg (letters of May 10 and November 11) and later by Herbert Gans at the Race and Poverty Seminar (see also Gans's "Culture and Class in the Study of Poverty," in *On Understanding Poverty*, ed. Daniel Moynihan (New York: Basic Books, 1969), pp. 209ff.

21. Lewis, "An Anthropological Approach to Family Studies," p. 474.

22. Letter from Oscar Lewis to Corrine Shelling (from the Race and Poverty Seminar), February 5, 1968 (see no. 170 in the Appendix).

23. This conception of what constitutes culturally determined behavior is drawn from Ruth Benedict: "A culture, like an individual, is more or less a consistent pattern of thought and action" (*Patterns of Culture*, p. 46).

24. In 1961 Lewis applied for and received a grant (#M-5556) from the Department of Health, Education, and Welfare to carry out an "Analysis of Three Generations in Mexican Families." He intended to study the progress of children and grandchildren in three Mexico City and three Tepoztecan families. Most of the work accomplished during the summer of 1962 focused on the grandchildren of Jesús Sánchez and remains unpublished.

25. In general it can be said that the grandchildren of Jesús Sánchez have done better than the children of Puerto Rican informants, all of whom, of course, are U.S. citizens. It appears, or at least it seemed so before the oil bust of 1984–85, the 1985 earthquake, and other internal problems in Mexico, that a number of the Sánchez grandchildren would achieve standards of living considerably higher than those of their parents and their grandfather Jesús. Of Manuel's four children by his second wife (his first wife died in childbirth), the two youngest are still in school; a third child graduated from a business college, and the fourth dropped out of preparatory school and married a man who works for the government. Of the older four (those born before *The Children of Sánchez* was published), the eldest spent some time in the United States as an undocumented worker, but he returned home because he missed his wife and two children. He now sells in the market where his father works and lives in a nearby modern apartment building in a unit he and his wife have bought. The other son also lives near the market and works as a hairdresser. Of the two daughters, one dropped out of school in the third grade and became the only one not to surpass her father in education. She lived with her husband in the Casa Grande, until it was torn down in 1986, and sells clothing in the market. The other daughter is married to a man with a good job in business; they have two children.

Roberto's only child, a son, dropped out of preparatory school for the priesthood and began studying bookkeeping and accounting at a business school. He now lives with his parents and works at whatever job he can find. Consuelo's two teenage sons were still in school in 1986. Marta had eleven children by two husbands and has brought them up alone. Of her five eldest daughters, three are married and raising families. A fourth has been living and working in the United States for over a decade and is married to an American citizen. The fifth daughter was stabbed to death in 1983 by her husband, a soldier, shortly after she left him. Marta's eldest son is a graduate of a state medical school and is now serving his residency. Two other sons completed basic secondary schools but were unsuccessful in attempts to get scholarships to attend a merchant marine and fishery school; they have been working on construction jobs and living with a married sister in northern Mexico near the U.S. border. Of the youngest three children, two daughters are in school and a seventeen-year-old son, who is retarded and severely epileptic, lives at home and has never attended school.

I have only very sketchy information on the children from La Esmeralda families, but what I have learned leads me to be very pessimistic about their futures. By the early 1980s, according to Francisca Muriente, who has kept track of eight of the children, only one had gone beyond the eighth grade. This young woman found a good clerical job after graduating from high school and moved out of the barrio. The son of a different family was fatally shot by police in the barrio after he had escaped from prison; he was seventeen at the time. Of six children from the Arriaga study, two were chronically in trouble with the law after moving to New York, and one has been in prison off and on since 1968. A third child joined a hippie commune in the late 1960s and reportedly was a drug abuser. The other three children, who were barely literate, were irregularly employed at low-skill jobs, one in New York and two in San Juan.

26. Lewis had one field assistant, Anadel Lynton, who specialized in genealogical studies.

27. Lewis's method of executing day studies became progressively more exhaustive. In the first studies done in Tepoztlán in the 1940s, he had a fieldworker sit in an inconspicuous place and take handwritten notes on activities, conversations, and interactions among family members. Primary attention was paid to the division of labor and the duration of activities, because Lewis was interested in time use within the household. Later, after he began taping interviews, he had informants reconstruct their activities of the previous day or week and used these to complement the household observations. For the Puerto Rican project Lewis instructed fieldworkers to describe activities within time blocks of fifteen minutes in order to improve observations on time use. For some of the studies Lewis assigned a second observer to record conversations, thus freeing Muriente to concentrate on recording activity. To assist her Lewis hired Frank Franco, a Puerto Rican familiar with La Esmeralda who was by training and profession a court stenographer. On other occasions Lewis assigned two fieldworkers to the same day study in order to see what kind of variance there would be in recording and interpreting activities and conversation.

28. Manuel, who in the published study was the most irresponsible, became a stable family man (he has been married for over twenty years to the same woman), a kind of father figure, the one the others turn to for help as they had once turned to their father. Manuel and his wife have raised their children with great emphasis on education and achievement. Marta, who Lewis said was the only true culture of poverty type in the family, has had the most difficult time of the four. A convert to an evangelical sect, she is a deeply religious woman of simple skills but enormous emotional resources who has

kept her large family together without benefit of assistance from her former husband. In her fifties she became a neighborhood activist and a delegate for the PRI's Women's Federation.

Consuelo, with her labile temperament and all her theatrical ambitions, settled down (albeit rockily) with one man and raised their two sons under the strict conventions of Seventh Day Adventism. (Her conversion was influenced by Pedro Martínez, after Lewis took her to Tepoztlán as a fieldworker.) Roberto's behavior has perhaps been the most predictable because his alcoholism has never permitted him to maintain stable employment. About twenty-five years ago he married a working woman, better educated than he, who owned a home, where they still live. Although Roberto made his wife quit working after their marriage, she is an exceptional manager of the resources they do have, and their standard of living is considerably higher than his was in the Casa Grande.

In the lives of the Sánchezes there is no departure from the past that rivals the shift in behavior of Felícita Ríos. A few years after *La Vida* was published she became involved with a prosperous grocer, moved into a well-ordered apartment in a tenement on Manhattan's Lower East Side, enrolled her children in school, and joined the P.T.A.! Even if only a temporary departure, as I believe it was, I would argue that it was not "reasonably predictable" behavior. In addition, the behavior of Felícita Ríos and the Sánchezes lends no support to Lewis's characterization of culture of poverty people as "resigned" or "fatalistic."

29. *Current Anthropology*, December 1967, p. 480.

30. Lewis quoting from an unidentified manuscript by Jules Henry. Similar descriptions of the family can be found in Jules Henry, "Family Structure and the Transmission of Neurotic Behavior," *American Journal of Orthopsychiatry* 21 (1951): 800–818; and in Henry, *Culture against Man* (New York: Random House, 1963), p. 323.

31. Taken from handwritten notes for the introduction to *Five Families*.

32. Lewis, *Life in a Mexican Village*, p. 425.

33. Linton, *Cultural Background of Personality*, p. 121. Anthony F. C. Wallace has made a different but related point (and perhaps one even more relevant to Lewis's methodological problem) in writing that "it is culture which is shared . . . rather than personality, and culture may be conceived as an invention which makes possible the maximal organization of motivational diversity" (*Culture and Personality* [New York: Random House, 1961], p. 41).

34. Oscar Lewis, "Family Case Studies: A Technique for the Study of Culture and Personality" (paper read at the Midwest Sociological Society meetings, April 29, 1949), p. 8. In the published version ("An Anthropological Approach to Family Studies") Lewis deleted the following two sentences: "We have become prisoners of our categories. In our desire to reduce our materials to their lowest common denominator we have left out some of our most vivid and dynamic materials."

35. Barrington Moore, "In the Life," *New York Review of Books*, June 15, 1967, p. 3.

36. From taped remarks delivered via telephone hookup to a Stephens College conference, January 17, 1968.

37. See Lewis's comments on Gregory Bateson's and Margaret Mead's photographic study of Balinese character, which he singled out as a "major innovation" for providing " 'objective' data . . . for the description of psychological phenomona" (*Anthropological Essays*, p. 17).

38. Allport, *Personality*, pp. 16ff.; and Kurt Lewin, *A Dynamic Theory of Personality: Selected Papers*, trans. Donald K. Adams and Karl E. Zener (New York: McGraw-Hill, 1935).

39. Allport, *Personality*, pp. 295–96.

40. Lewis, *Anthropological Essays*, p. x.

41. From remarks made at the Allerton Conference on Social Psychology, sponsored by the Department of Sociology and Anthropology and the Department of Psychology at the University of Illinois at Urbana-Champaign, December 1950. The proceedings were published as *Problems in Social Psychology*, ed. J. E. Hulett, Jr., and Ross Stagner (University of Illinois, 1952), see pp. 224–25. The parenthetical remark at the end of the quotation was omitted from the published remarks.

CHAPTER SEVEN

ART AND METHOD

In the early 1950s Lewis began writing notes for an autobiography, not in order to leave a record of his life but to try his hand at writing for a nonacademic audience. In these notes he expressed the hope that when writing about his own life he would feel freer than he did when writing about his informants: "In trying to gather life stories from informants in Mexico or Spain or India I was always so impressed by the fact that I was getting the most superficial aspects of their lives. This was frustrating and led me constantly to probe and probe and probe. . . . it would be satisfying, I imagine, to be able to produce a work of art in contrast to the dead sort of stuff I write in anthropology."

At this time Lewis was already searching for a publication format that was "half way between a novel and an anthropological report."[1] By 1959 he referred to his informants as "characters in my book." *Five Families* is introduced with a "setting" and a "cast of characters" and seems almost tailored for adaptation to stage or screen. (In fact the Gutíerrez day study was adapted almost immediately after publication for presentation on television's *Camera Three*.)[2] Lewis wrote about "capturing" his informants and their daily lives as if framing them in a picture or, more accurately, a series of photographs. The Beltrán drawings used to illustrate Lewis's books on Mexico are, I believe, at least in part compatible with the material because they enhance the Lewises' scenic-centered or scenic-inspired editing. These drawings, with their accuracy in detail, are both instructive and evocative and help establish mood and a powerful sense of place, just as a good stage set might. The development of these properties in the published work is related to Lewis's belief in the greater communicative power of the tactile and the visual—in short, the sensate—over the abstract and intellectual message.

Lewis always hoped to reach a broad audience with his writing and had a long-standing interest in the arts, especially the performing arts. Sometimes when he told people of his youthful ambition to sing opera professionally, it was taken as an indication that he was a frustrated performer. For them this helped explain his interest in literary formats and the turn his career took in the 1960s. There is some element of truth in this. Lewis did not want to be chained to academic forms and jargon because they restricted the audience and had a leveling effect on language and style. And he did want fame and recognition. Yet one cannot easily jump to the conclusion that these were the driving forces in his work; to do so is to ignore the fact that he always intended to go to college and find a place in or near academic life. Lewis did not actively pursue collaboration in the arts until the last decade of his life, and even then it was a minor preoccupation in terms of time spent. Furthermore, he was never so much driven by the need to perform as he was by what he wanted to communicate. He needed social science to support his research and gather the evidence, and he needed the arts to deliver his message.

It was the use of edited interviews and day studies that some critics said transported Lewis from the social sciences to the arts. There were even accusations that his informants were fictional and that he had written their stories himself. These were so transparently without foundation that Lewis could afford to be amused by them; and it gave him some satisfaction that there were people who thought he could write as well as his informants spoke. His usual reply to such charges was that if he were capable of becoming a writer he would stop working as an anthropologist. An awareness that he was "without any special literary talents," Lewis wrote in his biographical notes, was sometimes "painful" to him.

Interviewing

The two aspects of method about which Lewis was most often asked, and the areas in which his social science colleagues seemed most concerned that he might have overthrown science for art, were his interviewing technique and the editing of field materials for publication. Each of these is very difficult to describe precisely because of how much art *was* involved in their doing. At the outset of a project Lewis did lay out the information he was seeking in questionnaire formats; but as has been noted, he did not pay much attention to the internal logic of individual schedules, nor even to the clarity or sensitivity of wording. No attempt was made to maintain a strictly professional relationship between informant and interviewer after the basic questionnaires were applied. The distance that was beneficial to structured interviewing was detrimental to open-ended interviewing and to household observation. This is less serious than it may seem to someone who thinks of questionnaires as scientific instruments. Lewis never had any intention of trying to tabulate responses to questions on attitudes and opinions. Therefore getting responses to questions that had been asked in exactly the same way of each informant was not a high priority. In any case Lewis did not trust answers to these kinds of questions and thought that responses had greater validity when read in the context of life histories than when used to construct a statistical profile of informants as a group.

The work of all interviewers was monitored by Oscar and Ruth Lewis, both of whom read transcriptions of taped interviews and wrote new lists of supplemental questions to be asked in follow-up interviews. These were written separately for individual informants and were usually designed to elicit information needed for a fuller, more complete life history rather than to collect information that would be suitable, in the first instance, for comparison and generalization. The burden of this work fell more heavily on Ruth Lewis because she edited and organized the material and therefore had a good sense of what was missing.

Most people who are interested in Lewis's interviewing technique are less concerned with how he administered questionnaires than they are with how he established rapport. Of course the essence of this process is impossible to describe because it rests so much on the chemistries of the parties involved and the interlocking of their personalities. The level of success Lewis had in establishing so many productive relationships was, I think, due to his ability to communicate some mix of conviction in his work with compassion for and interest in his informants. Lewis did have his failures in the field, occasions when he could not strike up a working relationship with someone he thought was important to the research. He did not spend a lot of time trying to make these relationships work because he knew rapport could not be forced and he would not have trusted the information he might have been able to get under such circumstances. In these instances he found assistants—sometimes his wife—who were capable of establishing a more productive relationship and turned the work over to them.

Ruth Lewis has told me she believes that the quality of relationship her husband was able to establish with his informants was his greatest overall contribution to the research. According to her, Lewis had his greatest success in establishing rapport with "more dependent people who needed a father figure . . . and affection." From this perspective, rapport was the successful union of interlocking personalities. Ruth Lewis has compared her husband's interviewing technique to her own more ordinary style by saying she had a "cooler, more distant approach" and never "imposed herself as a personality"; she said there was "a limitation to what I got and what I wanted to get." She told me that she never shared her husband's feeling that the informants were lucky to be participating in the research or that she was necessarily helping them by interviewing them. In addition, she said, her husband had a "special gift for inspiring confidence in certain people."

One important way in which Lewis showed his interest in informants was by being flexible in his direction and not expecting them to accommodate to his research needs. He was capable of changing his line of questioning, and even the problem he was focusing on, in order to maximize an individual's strength as an informant. However, his attempts at establishing relationships did not include trying to fit into informants' lives; he was always more an observer than a participant. Instead of trying to be accepted as a peer in the worlds of his informants so *he* could report on their lives, he tried to get inside his informants' minds so *they* could report on their own lives. Lewis never changed his appearance or tried to hide his white-collar identity, but he changed his vocabulary and inflection to fit an informant's or made some adjustments in body language or conspicuous forms of behavior to fit in better.

Although Lewis often wrote of the need to live among the poor to understand them and suggested that he did in fact live *with* them, this cannot be taken literally. Tepoztlán was the only field location in which the Lewises lived very much (in terms of material conditions) the way their informants lived. With this proximity and daily contact, relationships with villagers were cordial but still formal. The Lewises attended barrio festivals and important family celebrations, exchanged courtesy visits, helped in medical emergencies, and entered into *compadrazgo* relationships with members of several families they were studying. Oscar Lewis attended political and religious (Seventh Day Adventist) meetings in the Martínez home and went to the fields with the *tlacololeros*, but never as a worker. In Mexico City, Lewis accompanied Jesús, Manuel, and Roberto Sánchez to their work places, but again it was only to observe.

Lewis sometimes became entangled in his informants' lives, but essentially he maintained a life apart. He did this instinctively, not by design; but overall, I think, it helped him develop rapport because a good one-to-one relationship cannot develop if there is uncertainty about the identity or objectives of either party. By being himself and not trying to blend in, Lewis established himself as a distinct persona each informant could accept or reject. Even though his physical appearance did set him apart, he seems to have had little difficulty in establishing a commonality of interests with his informants.

Because establishing rapport is so dependent upon the personalities involved, a good working relationship does not take a single form. For example, Lewis got some of his best material from Pedro Martínez, whose limitations as an informant he often noted. There was a formality and a certain distance between the two men, because that is what Martínez expected, but by interviewing slowly over a twenty-year period, Lewis managed to collect what I think was his best published account of a life lived in a specific cultural setting. A large part of this was due to Lewis accepting what Martínez could give him and seeing how it could be used in a valuable way. When he complained about Martínez's limitations, what he meant was that Martínez would not permit him to do what *he* preferred to do, that is, a real family study, with a good deal of probing into the personalities and private lives of the individual family members. But if Martínez was not all that Lewis wanted him to be as an informant on himself, Lewis did accept him for what he was—an outstanding informant on the village and on himself as a Tepoztecan. The relationship that evolved between the two men was not bilateral but rather triangular, involving Lewis, Martínez, and the village. When Lewis wrote about Martínez, he wrote about the village. He never had another informant who represented a place in the same way that Martínez represented Tepoztlán.

Another of Lewis's best informant relationships was with Manuel Sánchez. Again, it produced wonderful material, but for completely different reasons. Lewis's relationship with Manuel was open, direct, gregarious, and one-to-one. It did not require the patience, distance, finesse, or nuancing of questions needed to interview Pedro Martínez. More than representing the residents of his *vecindad*, or the poor, or other Mexicans, Manuel was best at representing himself as an individual and as a member of his family. Unlike Martínez, all of the Sánchezes were more interesting for what they told Lewis about themselves than for what they told him about their country or city. Although Mexico City functions as more than a setting for their story, its presence is not felt in *The Children of Sánchez* in the same way Tepoztlán is felt in *Pedro Martínez*. I do not mean to say, of course, that the Sánchezes were somehow less Mexican or less representative of some aspect of Mexico's culture than was Martínez. The point is that they functioned differently as informants. Lewis recognized what they had to offer and put it to good use.

Editing

The most common criticism Lewis received from social scientists about his family studies was that he did not adequately explain how he had used the raw materials to create them. Anthropologists in particular wanted Lewis to discuss how extensively the interviews had been edited so they could judge whether they had been altered to the point of manipulation. In short, they wanted to know how accurately Lewis's informants were being represented. They wanted to see the questions and the responses exactly as they were given, or at least to have Lewis explain his system of editing.

Before discussing the editing process, the basic point must be made again that following the publication of *Five Families* Lewis was no longer the principal editor of his material. Throughout most of his career he counted on his wife to edit his writing; but organizing interviews and household observations into what were essentially literary formats took a special skill, and neither of the Lewises had any experience in this prior to *Five Families*. In their first attempt at editing raw field materials for publication, the Lewises had the assistance of Helen Kuypers, a gifted editor with a background in literature and poetry (and from whom Ruth Lewis said she learned many of the skills she used to edit *The Children of Sánchez* and later works).[3] While Ruth Lewis undertook with her husband the organization and editing of raw materials, Kuypers specialized in refining the writing style. In the former task Lewis involved himself mainly in the process of arriving at the organizational plan and then in supervising editing work in progress. The only notable exception to this division of labor was his decision to take on the (rough) editing of the interviews of Jesús Sánchez for a prologue and epilogue for *The Children of Sánchez*.

About learning to edit, Ruth Lewis told me that "necessity was the mother of invention in this case. I was handed a pile of material and I had to work on it . . . and I figured out ways of doing it." She said she brought to the work "a feel for story line" and great "devotion to detail." She worked like a sculptor, "building up this and cutting away that . . . building a three-dimensional figure. . . . Gradually you get the feeling that you're dealing with a whole person." Her overriding consideration was always to be true to the informant, but in "thinking out the construction of a book" she also had to consider what the readers could handle. While editing the interviews she put herself in their place and asked if they would be able to follow a sequence of ideas exactly as presented by an informant. If the answer was no, she usually felt free to change the sequence. An awareness of the potential for distortion in cutting and editing, however, placed limits on how much freedom she could exercise and "imposed a discipline" on her work. Although even "little things" like moving "two or three words on a page" would offend purists, she said, it did not bother her; and she added, "I was the one with the pencil making the decisions; there was no committee to consult."

Throughout the 1960s the Lewises had dozens of assistant editors— some working in Spanish, others in English. Some did routine work such as removing questions, while others had a freer hand to experiment with organization, but always with a small part (e.g., interviews with a single informant) of a large study. Much of the trial editing was done on material that remains unpublished.

The process began with transcriptions, and here Lewis attempted to prepare as accurate a record as possible of what each informant said on tape. Transcribers were directed to make literal renderings of responses, retaining mispronunciations, dropped syllables, ellipses, asides, and so on. Judgment, of course, came into play in punctuating the transcriptions, and a few transcribers chose not to punctuate at all rather than make those decisions. There was a sequence of steps, but no rigidly adhered to system, for preparing the materials for publication. Even for the most banal procedures, such as removal of questions and the splicing together of responses, one cannot make a comprehensive statement. An example of an original transcript in its first stages of editing, taken from the work with any single informant, would not be representative. Some informants made complete responses to questions, while the answers given by others were incoherent or fragmentary. Sometimes a question had to be asked several times, or stated in a number of different ways, or broken down into parts, in order to get a complete response. These interviews, of course, were more heavily edited than those of the more articulate informants. Some would speak on a given subject for the length of time it would take to fill several manuscript pages, but not in the long, organized monologues that appear in print. In fact all information on a given subject might have been spliced together from three, four, five, or even ten different interviews. In the process there would almost certainly be cases where a missing but implied fragment of a sentence would be added to complete a thought. There is a kind of inevitable leveling that takes place in editing several fragmentary responses into one complete coherent sentence, as less articulate and responsive informants are made to sound as if they usually rendered whole thoughts in complete sentences. This kind of distortion is inherent in the use of edited materials to build a first-person narrative format.

The editing process also required moving some material from its original context, and a purist might want to argue about how this could affect the original intent of the words. In this respect there are two important points to make. One is that the informant was not speaking spontaneously to begin with but was being interviewed. The interview situation itself is an artificial construct in which the context for many of the informants' responses are created by the interviewer. Second, the editor moving material from place to place would have read all of the original material and would have had a very good idea of who the speaker was—and would therefore be in a position to make an informed judgment about whether the speaker's intent was being violated. The validity of the process depends in great part on the integrity of the editor and on his or her knowledge of the informant. No purist would work in the way the Lewises did, but their objective was not to offer material for linguistic or literary analysis, for textual deconstruction; they simply wanted to convey the overall worldview, character, and value structure of the individual. Realizing that the raw material has a research utility beyond their purposes, they did preserve the original tapes and transcriptions.

The real art in the editing process lay in finding a way of organizing a variety of raw materials into formats compatible with their content. The different kinds of information and combinations of material on which *Five Families, The Children of Sánchez, Pedro Martínez,* and *La Vida* were based demanded individual tailoring in order to bring out their best aspects. For *Five Families* the raw material consisted of interviews done by Lewis, some recorded by hand and others on tape, and the household observations and conversations that field assistants took down by hand, as well as questionnaire data. Putting this material together required more writing than editing. For *The Children of Sánchez* the Lewises integrated edited interviews transcribed from tape with material written by Manuel and Consuelo in response to specific questions or on assigned topics. A large part of the "Consuelo" segment of the book was edited from these little essays rather than from interview transcriptions. *Pedro Martínez,* by comparison, was constructed almost completely from edited interview transcriptions, while *La Vida's* organization intersperses edited interview transcriptions with five day studies. The days were constructed from Muriente's hand-recorded dialogue and observations, into which were woven descriptions of the setting and "characters."

The content of the raw materials varied so much from study to study that a common organizational approach to them would not have been appropriate. In editing the Sánchez materials, for instance, the Lewises gave equal weight to each of the four children, using not Mexican culture or *vecindad* life but their father's life—as told in a prologue and epilogue—as the point of departure. Implicit in this presentation was a measurement of the children against their father's life and values. Since the children's interviews revealed that a large part of their interior lives was absorbed in their attempts to live up to their father's expectations of them, this format was a perfect complement to the content and substance of the materials.

With the Ríos family study, the mother, Fernanda, could not have been used as the center of the book, as Jesús Sánchez had been, because her relationship with her children was completely different. There was enormous affection between parent and siblings, but Fernanda was almost as much a peer as an authority figure.

La Vida was organized, therefore, with Fernanda treated as an equal member of the family, not as a standard against which to measure her children. For chronological considerations the book begins with her voice, but it would not have been appropriate to end with it too, thereby using her life (as Jesús Sánchez's had been used) to frame her children's stories.

A second major organizational difference between the Ríos and the Sánchez studies was that with the former the Lewises felt a much greater need to communicate the organization of household life. The Sánchez story was essentially a psychological drama in which the most interesting things that happened took place in the minds of the informants. (This, I believe, is why it has been so difficult for the book to be translated successfully to the visual media, despite many attempts.) The book would not have been as interesting, and probably not as informative, if it had been organized around edited day studies; the daily routine in the Sánchez household was quite unexceptional, especially when compared with their intellectual and emotional lives. In addition, family members could verbalize so effectively that anything interesting about the household arrangement could be communicated by them.

With the Ríoses, by comparison, understanding how the five separate households functioned was essential to any adequate characterization of the family. They were not involved in intrafamily personality struggles to the same extent the Sánchezes were—or if they were they could not describe them. In any case they were far less articulate than the Sánchezes, and more of their lives had to be "pictured" through the day studies. This was an important consideration because their family dynamics and household organization were quite different from those of any of the other families the Lewises interviewed. In fact this was one of the primary reasons the Ríos study was the first of the Puerto Rican work to be published.

Ruth Lewis has told me that over the years she has worried little about criticism of the editing process because what liberties were taken were "justified" by the objective of trying to get readers "to understand what is going on in the world" and "to respond in a positive way to remove injustice." Reading and editing the interviews with informants, Ruth Lewis said, left her "with a sense of awe about people" and "a tremendous respect for the human individual." To pass this on to readers and to give them "some insight . . . into the lives these people led" was a more important aspect of the work than the study of culture. Both she and her husband believed that art was more effective than social science in eliciting a response from people; therefore, when they hit on a format for *Five Families* that was closer to literature than social science reporting, they both understood immediately and without ever having to discuss it that "it was powerful." Ruth Lewis said, "we felt it would reach a large audience [and] would give them a grasp of . . . Mexican urban life . . . in a way that social science reporting could not do—it wouldn't reach them; they wouldn't read it, or if they did, they either wouldn't understand it or respond to it in any way." By contrast, she said, their work (especially in Mexico) had "aroused social conscience, and that's all we ever hoped to do."

Translation

The translation process, too, inevitably involves some distortion because it is extremely difficult to achieve equivalency in quality of language. In the case of the Mexican material, there were criticisms that the language of the Sánchezes in particular had been translated "up" by someone with great literary flair. In fact the Sánchezes sound even better in Spanish, just as one would expect writers to sound better in their native languages. The skill of translator Asa Zatz was in retaining their style; he had no need (and was certainly given no instructions) to improve upon it. (Zatz translated almost all of the Mexican material, including that in *Pedro Martínez*.) By comparison, the Ríoses were less articulate, had smaller vocabularies, and had fewer ideas to express. Their material was translated a little more freely by Muna Muñoz Lee. (She also translated many of the unpublished Puerto Rican interviews and almost all of the Cuban material.) Muñoz Lee was the most highly skilled, scholarly, and literary of any translator Lewis used. It was hard to contain all of this ability, and to the extent that any of Lewis's informants do sound better in print than on tape, it is in Muñoz Lee's translations of some of the less articulate Puerto Rican informants. To give one small example, there is a lack of variety in common profanities in the Spanish used by these informants. To make the English less repetitive, Muñoz Lee chose to translate a single word (e.g., *coño*) several different ways if it appeared a number of times within a few sentences. But she tried to find words of equal intensity and wrote into her copy long editorial comments on the equivalency of various words. With these fairly minor exceptions, considerable effort was made not to magnify any improvement of language that occurred in the editing with further refinements in the translating process. Although some book reviewers lamented that translations of the Puerto Rican and Cuban interviews were not equal to those of the Sánchezes, the simple truth is that none of the informants before or after equaled the Sánchezes in verbal skills.

Translation of Work to Stage and Film

Lewis's interest in reaching a wider audience led him to think seriously about the possibility of having his works adapted for stage and screen. In 1958, while preparing the Sánchez materials, he wrote: "I sometime think a movie on this stuff would be a natural—but that may come later." [4]

After the appearance of *Five Families* and *The Children of Sánchez*, Lewis did occasionally receive inquiries about full or partial adaptations of these works. He knew Luis Buñuel, the Spanish film director who lived in exile in Mexico and France, to be interested in *Five Families*, and Lewis arranged to meet him through their mutual friend, Carlos Fuentes. Lewis regarded Buñuel as a man of great artistic and political integrity, someone he could trust to convey the basic message in his books. But Buñuel was also a realist who understood that it would be politically impossible to make an honest movie about Mexican poverty in Mexico.

In 1961 Lewis sold the screen rights for *The Children of Sánchez* to the award-winning screenwriter Abby Mann. Mann went to Mexico, met the Sánchez family, and worked sporadically on the project before giving it up in 1965. [5] When it appeared that Mann was not going to exercise his rights, Lewis tried again to persuade Buñuel, who by this time was more interested in *Pedro Martínez* than in *The Children of Sánchez*. But Buñuel wrote Lewis that he was as determined as ever not to try to film in Mexico.

Your book is admirable and in some respects superior, if that is possible, to *The Children of Sánchez*. But as to making a film of it in Mexico, it is as impossible, or even more so than the other. I don't believe you should nourish any hopes about that. Of course, by limiting the film to the more positive aspects of the book—or those which would be so regarded by the gentlemen of the government—it would be easy enough to carry out this project. However, I am not willing . . . to make any kind of compromise. The film should reflect the same objective, complete, vital image as regards politics, society, etc., that is presented in the book. That is something we can't even dream about at present. Better to wait for a more favorable time . . . if it ever comes.[6]

Despite Buñuel's refusals, between 1966 and 1968 Lewis continued to try to convince the director to change his mind. But Buñuel did not waver, writing that it was at that time still "completely absurd to try to make this film in Mexico."[7] Lewis understood well the political problems of shooting in Mexico and never pressed Buñuel to overlook them; however, he did not care where in Central or Latin America the film was made, so long as it was Buñuel who directed it. In fact Abby Mann and his associates had had the same concerns about filming in Mexico and Lewis had made a trip for them through Guatamala and El Salvador scouting for alternative sites.[8]

In 1969, when the screen rights to *The Children of Sánchez* became available again, the independent filmmaker Hall Bartlett made a bid. Lewis did not know Bartlett's work, but his friend Albert Maltz, the novelist and screenwriter, was familiar with Bartlett's documentaries and recommended him. Lewis was eager to see his book on film and at the time no one else was interested in it, so through his agent he arranged for the rights to pass to Bartlett. Lewis did not live long enough to sign the contract—Ruth Lewis did that—or to see the film that was released seven years later.

Unlike Buñuel, Bartlett was apparently not worried about Mexican censorship. A reported 50 percent of the financial backing for the film was provided by the government-run film industry, which was headed by the brother of then president Luis Echeverría. Bartlett hired the Italian screenwriter Cesare Zavattini, who wrote a script that mixed rather freely Italian and Mexican traditions. Ruth Lewis objected to substantial parts of the script, especially to the portrayal of Consuelo as a prostitute and of Roberto as a *marijuanero*. She sent her objections to Bartlett but had no legal control over any aspect of the film's content or production.

Everything Buñuel feared, and worse, came to pass, although it would be difficult to identify which, if any, of the films many inaccuracies could be traced to direct or indirect government pressure. From the standpoint of depicting Mexico's poverty, its culture, or the Sánchezes themselves, the film was a disaster. The distortions, which began with an opening scene of the religious skeptic and anticleric Jesús Sánchez marching in a religious pilgrimage, were maintained throughout. The film family's standard of living was far higher than the Sánchez family's had been in real life. Of Lewis's ethnographic realism, nothing was left. The only compensation has been that the film has had a mercifully limited distribution.[9]

The film so offended Consuelo Sánchez that she sued Hall Bartlett, his production company, and a number of others, including Ruth
Lewis, who were directly or indirectly involved in the making and
showing of the film. This action was a shock to Ruth Lewis, who
had gone to Mexico in 1977 to urge the Sánchez family to join her in
protesting Zavattini's adaptation of the book. At that time, Consuelo
read (with Ruth Lewis's assistance, since it was written in English)
most if not all of the screenplay and refused, as did other members of
the family, to pressure Bartlett to make changes. One cannot blame
the family for not trying to interfere with the film's production, because they would have shared in the net profits if the film had been
successful. Consuelo also hoped to act in the film, if only as an extra. Nevertheless, after the film's release, she tried to persuade family
members to join her in the law suit, but they all refused.

Before the case went to trial, Ruth Lewis was dropped from the
suit on a jurisdictional technicality, but she was left in the unhappy
position of having to give a deposition and surrender confidential
materials on the Sánchez family that certainly contributed to Consuelo losing the suit. Given the film's many distortions, it is difficult
to understand why Consuelo chose to build a case by attacking the
veracity of events that documents could easily prove to be factual.
The suit further alienated her from her family and also broke, perhaps
permanently, her twenty-five-year relationship with the Lewis family.

A much more successful attempt to adapt *The Children of Sánchez*,
this time for the stage, was made by Mexican playwright Vicente
Leñero. His play had a fairly good run in Mexico City in 1972–73.[10]
Other attempts were made to adapt the book for the stage, either as a
drama or as a musical, but rights have never been granted.

In 1966 Lewis did sell the screen rights for *La Vida* to the writer
and director Elia Kazan, involving himself more directly in this project
than he had in the adaptations of the Mexican work. Both Oscar and
Ruth Lewis tried their hand at writing outlines for the screenplay, but
their efforts were fairly short-lived because they were soon involved
in the Cuban project. A screenplay was drafted by Budd Schulberg,
but Kazan never exercised his rights to film.

Art over Science?

Lewis flirted with the arts for many years, and at the end of his life
he was seduced by them. Selling the screen rights for *The Children of
Sánchez*, a responsibility shared by Ruth Lewis, was one of the worst
mistakes of his career—not because it produced bad art, or even bad

social science, for that matter, but because the film offended the people whose lives it pretended to represent. As interested as Lewis was in literary forms and the translation of his work to film, he never overthrew science for art in the conduct of his research. He carried out the Puerto Rican project no differently, in terms of basic method, than his earlier work in Mexico City. It is true that he never used random sampling techniques, never thought of a questionnaire schedule as a scientific instrument, never applied quantitative methods of analysis to his data, and never worried if the data were statistically meaningful. But he had a system for collecting his data, albeit one with shortcomings from the standpoint of science, and he adhered to it, even in the last years of his career, when he knew he would publish his field materials in a first-person narrative format with a minimum of analysis. Lewis never went into the field thinking that it did not matter how he did his research as long as what he published was interesting. Granted, late in his career he did less of the groundwork himself; yet he insisted that it be done, and his passion for thoroughness often drove his assistants to distraction. He lost interest in any discussion of method, however, as he came to believe that it detracted from what he was trying to communicate. Method was important to *him*, of course, but he did not see why it would be important to the general reader. And like the actor who does not want to be caught acting, Lewis did not want to be seen doing science.

The literary formats the Lewises worked out for *Five Families, The Children of Sánchez,* and *La Vida*, in particular, belied the research efforts that went into them. By comparison, I believe it is impossible to read the original Tepoztlán volume and not be impressed by what a prodigious effort went into producing it, even if one disagrees with the conclusions. It was a very comprehensive job of reporting, with Lewis leaving out little of his ethnographic materials. In *La Vida*, however, one is exposed to only a small part of the overall research effort in the community where the Ríos family lived. (Lewis sometimes used Margaret Mead's term "chunk ethnography" to describe this kind of reporting.) The format and readability of the book also intentionally disguise the traditional research methods that were used to produce the raw material. In fact, the Lewises' art made it look too easy. When *The Children of Sánchez* and *La Vida* appeared, it was a not uncommon view in academia—I heard it a number of times myself in the 1960s—that anyone could turn on a tape recorder and publish the transcripts but this hardly constituted social science research. Lewis promised companion volumes for *Five Families, The Children of Sánchez,* and *La Vida* that would deal with some of the supplementary research materials in a more analytic way, but he did this only for *La Vida*. In his desire to bring out the artistic aspects of the work, Lewis under-represented his work as a social scientist. He did, however, leave a valuable archive which has already been used by a number of scholars to further their research in linguistics, ethnology, and comparative literature.

On the difficulties of trying to make sense of his kind of research materials, Lewis wrote: "If one agrees with Henry James that life is all inclusion and confusion while art is all discrimination and selection, then these life histories have something of both art and life. I believe that this in no way reduces the authenticity of the data or their usefulness for science."[11] However valuable his edited life histories may be as art, or however accurate as representations of life, the usefulness of his research to science lies in the raw materials.

NOTES

1. Letter from Oscar Lewis to Oliver La Farge, November 21, 1950.

2. The program was produced for WCBS-TV by John McGiffert and shown on November 15, 1959. A kinescope is contained in the archival collection of Lewis's papers.

3. Oscar Lewis met Mrs. Kuypers through her husband, one of a number of friends Lewis made among the faculty of the School of Music at the University of Illinois. Kuypers worked with the Lewises up through the publication of *La Vida*, when she became ill and was unable to continue.

4. Letter from Oscar Lewis to Maurice Halperin, April 11, 1958.

5. In a letter to Luis Buñuel, dated March 25, 1966, Lewis said that Mann's project failed because Columbia Pictures was afraid to finance a film without prior approval from the Mexican government. Lewis thought that giving what constituted censorship rights to the Mexican government was "very bad and established a precedent that would work against the interests" of the film industry.

6. Cablegram from Luis Buñuel to Oscar Lewis, November 15, 1965.

7. Letter from Luis Buñuel to Oscar Lewis, February 6, 1966.

8. Mann had hoped to get Vittorio de Sica to direct his film, and it was with an associate of de Sica's that Lewis went to Central America in the fall of 1962 and located a site in El Salvador.

9. Neither Ruth Lewis nor I saw the film during its theatrical release. I am grateful to David Dolan, a graduate student at UCLA, for providing the opportunity to view it. While doing research on Lewis he came to Urbana to interview Ruth Lewis, bringing a videocassette of the film with him.

10. Lewis first met Leñero at the Writers' Center in Mexico City in 1961.

Leñero made informal arrangements with Lewis to adapt the book for the stage (according to Leñero it was at Lewis's suggestion), but he did not complete the play until after Lewis's death. Asa Zata, the translator of Lewis's Mexican field materials, has translated the Leñero play into English and hopes to get it produced in the United States.

11. Lewis, *Children of Sánchez*, p. xxi.

CHAPTER EIGHT

POLICY AND ETHICS

While visiting Caracas, Venezuela, a few years before his death, Oscar Lewis was asked by a newspaper reporter if with his published works he was trying "to expose, to convince [people of], or to solve" the problems of poverty. "To expose and to convince," Lewis said, "but not to solve. I don't think I have the solution, nor do I think that it is my task. My goal has been to acquaint the whole reading public—the middle class, and the upper class that wields the power—with how these people live. The first step toward revolution is to live with these poor people and to gain their confidence."[1]

According to Lewis, his objective in exposing poverty, especially worst-case poverty and its effects, was to convince people that it was a social and political problem requiring a public response. He said that by allowing the poor to speak for themselves his work could serve "to bridge the communications gap between the very poor and the middle-class personnel—teachers, social workers, doctors, priests, and others—who bear the major responsibility for carrying out anti-poverty programs" by providing "a deeper understanding of the poor, their individuality, and the great variety in their life styles so that all the poor are not lumped together in a similar, blurred homogenous mass."[2]

In trying to present the poor as individuals and to give as complete a picture as possible of their lives, Lewis chose a method that required exposing them to the varied judgments of readers. As the individuality of the informants met the individual perspectives of the readers, however, it was inevitable that diverse impressions and conclusions would be formed. Because they did not have a common view of their poverty, the informants could not bridge the communications gap with a unified message. It was left to Lewis, then, to mediate this diversity and to provide a unified statement on its meaning; or, more accurately, to address himself to its implications for poverty policy. Without making this effort he could not expect his books to give much direction to policymakers beyond offering compelling evidence of poverty's enormous potential for laying waste to human talent.

Despite what he said about it not being his responsibility to provide solutions, Lewis clearly had some hope of being able to effect policy. No one who spoke of his research as a stepping stone to revolution could have intended otherwise. The policy-making process, however, with its laborious dissection of problems, discussions of detail, and the arm-twisting, haggling, and compromise that are essential to it, did not interest him. Lewis rarely sought any face-to-face contact with policymakers, preferring to send them copies of his books without comment. The most notable exception was a 1967 conversation with Senator Robert Kennedy, arranged by *Redbook* magazine.[3] Lewis described this meeting as "dull and unrewarding" and said he found Kennedy "cagey" and "much to the right of Martin Luther King," open only to solutions to world poverty that involved private investment and the promotion of capitalism.[4]

Notwithstanding Lewis's lack of direct involvement, some observers assigned to him part of the credit—or blame—for the poverty program adopted by the Johnson administration, because of frequent use by some policy advisers of the culture of poverty explanation. One such argument was made by Charles Valentine, who wrote that the culture of poverty concept deserved part of the blame for the failure of the War on Poverty.[5] In his reply to this charge Lewis showed that he had no patience whatsoever for such criticism: "What a naive and absurd conception of the power of social science in our society! It is not the concept of a culture or subculture of poverty which is responsible for the lack of success of the anti-poverty program, but rather (1) the failure of the President and the Congress . . . to understand the degree of national commitment necessary to cope with the problems; and (2) the Vietnam war, which has been draining our economic and human resources."[6]

In fact Kennedy's and Johnson's advisers had picked up the concept *not* from Lewis, who had as yet written nothing on poverty in the United States, but from Michael Harrington's *The Other America*. Harrington, who had borrowed the term, without citation, from *Five Families*,[7] was once called in as consultant by Sargeant Shriver's office during the early stages of policy formulation. James Sundquist, a member of the task force that wrote the enabling legislation to create the Office of Economic Opportunity (OEO), wrote: "Perhaps it was Harrington's book that identified the target for Kennedy and supplied the coordinating concept; the bedrock problem, in a word, was 'poverty'. . . . That the word itself embodied various definitions, each leading logically to its own line of attack, only became apparent as the War on Poverty developed."[8]

The meaning of poverty, and distinctions between it and the culture of poverty, were so vague that John Wofford, former deputy director of the Community Action Program (CAP), wrote of the work mandated by the OEO bill:

> Little thought, if any, was given by those of us who helped administer CAP to a distinction between poverty (a lack of money) and the "culture of poverty" (the life style that goes with poverty). If we had been forced to say which of these concepts was a more central target of CAP, we probably would have responded that the emphasis (and it was only a matter of emphasis) was on attempting to deal with the life style of the poor, but primarily through qualities in the environment—particularly institutions—that effect the life style. Still, as soon as one emphasizes changing institutions and removing environmental barriers to opportunity, one is necessarily talking about attacking both poverty and the culture that goes with it.[9]

Despite this assessment of the overall goal, the 1964 enabling legislation for OEO did not deal with broad questions of life-style; more than anything else it was a job-training bill.[10] It was at least two years after the bill's passage before Lewis found himself in the position of being sought out by policymakers or advisers for his views on the antipoverty program. Up to this point he had nowhere put forward any concrete proposals for dealing with poverty in the United States, and it soon became clear that a job-training bill as a primary effort was not an approach he favored.

The one aspect of the OEO bill that did have something in common with Lewis's position was Section 202, the community action provision, which called for "maximum feasible participation" at the local level. (Attempts to implement this provision met with tremendous opposition from mayors and governors.)[11] Lewis frequently wrote that the one sure way to end the culture of poverty was for the poor to organize themselves to demand change, or for others seeking the same ends to organize the poor and to integrate them into political life. While Lewis's position was compatible with the community action provision, he had nothing to do, directly or indirectly, with its inclusion in the OEO bill. This was an idea to which several members of the task force reportedly had become committed through the example of action-oriented programs funded by the Ford Foundation.

The policy recommendations that Lewis did make were offered in academic fora rather than directly to policymakers. The most important of the meetings was a 1967 series of seminars on race and poverty sponsored by the American Academy of Arts and Sciences, to which Lewis was invited by Daniel P. Moynihan, former assistant secretary of labor for policy planning and research in the Johnson administration. Other participants included leading anthropologists and sociologists involved in the study of the lower class, as well as former policy advisers to the Johnson administration, most notably Adam Yarmolinsky and James Sundquist, both of whom had served on the OEO task force. To this group, according to Sundquist, Lewis recommended "mass socialized therapeutic measures" and an intensive case work approach, "undertaken by middle class people who have been trained 'to overcome the great sense of distance they felt toward the poor.'" After five years this would show, Lewis told the conference, "startling and remarkable results in human rehabilitation."[12] Without this complementary effort, he believed, a jobs and income strategy directed at those who lived in a subculture of poverty would not work.

What Lewis had in mind when he made these recommendations was assistance to the worst-case poor, those who he said lived in the culture of poverty. He did not intend his remarks to be prescriptions for aid to the poor in general. He did stress at conference sessions the importance of identifying subgroups among the poor so that different policy strategies could be devised for the separate groups, but he was no more successful than he had been in his publications in maintaining these distinctions.

Even though Lewis's books may have been the most widely read among works written by conference participants, his views and recommendations were no more influential than those of other participants such as Lee Rainwater, Walter Miller, S. M. Miller, or Herbert Gans, all of whom took issue with part or all of Lewis's argument. In fact, whereas Lewis focused on the psychological damage done to the individual by extreme poverty, the dominant view of the OEO task force several years earlier had been that the most appropriate point of focus was "the sick communities" in which the poor lived. They believed, in the words of James Sundquist, that previous solutions proposed by planners and social workers "were not working and were conceptually wrong" and that "if the Economic Opportunity Act was anything, it was a revolt againt 'a social work solution.'"[13] Sundquist also did not believe that separate strategies for eliminating poverty had to be tailored for distinctive subgroups among the poor.

Criticisms made by conference participants of his recommendations for psychiatric therapy for the drastically poor sensitized Lewis to the need to be much more precise in his language when discussing such a controversial issue. In his first publication after the seminar, Lewis implied—in a footnote apparently added in response to the criticism he received at the seminar—that he had changed his mind about the utility of the social work approach to the elimination of the culture of poverty in the United States.[14] The following year, however, he reaffirmed his belief in the need for intensive social assistance to cope with problems inherent in the subculture; but this time he made an effort to put his recommendations in context.

> The crucial question from both the scientific and political point of view is: How much weight is to be given to the internal, self-perpetuating factors in the subculture of poverty as compared to the external, societal factors? My own position is that in the long run the self-perpetuating factors are relatively minor and unimportant as compared to the basic structure of the larger society. However, to achieve rapid changes and improvement with the minimum amount of trauma one must work on both the "external" and "internal" conditions.[15]

Between 1967 and 1970 Lewis waffled on the question of whether radical or reformist solutions were necessary to eliminate the culture of poverty. There were reasons for this indecisiveness other than political caution, and Barrington Moore came close to guessing them in his 1967 review of *La Vida:* "Perhaps the main value of the introduction lies in the way it reveals the understandable tension between Lewis's meliorist outlook—his desire to be useful to the established order and its agents, the social workers—and his obvious feeling that nothing short of revolutionary change is likely to help these people, for whom he displays an admirable compassion completely free from condescension."[16]

Lewis faced a more fundamental conflict, however: that between his identity with his informants and respect for their individuality and freedom, and his identity with socialist goals and the desire to see them implemented. He did not think in terms of the "deserving" and "undeserving" poor; to him the existence of poverty in societies possessing the material means to eliminate it was morally and politically indefensible. Still, he was convinced that a *minority* of the very poor are incapable of changing the conduct of their lives without outside intervention. (In this I think Lewis was correct, even though I do not believe that the failure to change is due to cultural conditioning.) His position raised a question that he did not fully or honestly confront: what are the consequences for the poor when the environments to which they have adjusted so well (according to Lewis) are destroyed by benevolent government intervention?

Revolutionary governments certainly want, even demand, a change of conduct in return for the material support they provide. Philosophically, Lewis supported such an exchange, but on a practical level he saw the potentially ugly ramifications for the poor and for society in general. On the one hand he endorsed the attempts of revolutionary or reformist governments to integrate the poor into mainstream society; and on the other he admired and even envied the "spit-in their-eye" attitude some of his informants had toward the established order. He was caught between his self-imposed role as advocate and spokesman for the poor and his personal and political identity with the very groups most determined to reform them.

Lewis himself would never have had the will to make or enforce the kind of revolutionary policies he advocated when endorsing the Castro revolution, for example. His own policy recommendations called for only limited intervention in individual lives, and proposals for legislation that would require the involuntary participation of the poor often disturbed him. He was occasionally asked about such proposals when he served on the planning committee of the Federal Parent and Child Center Project, a unit of Project Head Start. Head Start was the only antipoverty program with which Lewis had direct involvement, and it was the one for which he reserved his greatest respect. He liked it because it offered assistance to disadvantaged children at a very early age, with a minimum of intrusion into the children's homes. Lewis objected when faced with the suggestion from Bruno Bettelheim that Head Start programs had to go much further and actually remove children from their homes to kibbutz-like child-rearing centers run by the government. Except in cases of physical abuse, children belonged with their parents, Lewis believed, because the proximity to mother and family was more important than the training they would receive in a communal arrangement. He said that such programs could not be effective unless they originated in the slum communities and were initiated by the residents.[17]

When discussing revolutionary change, Lewis tended to focus on the systemic level and to avoid issues of privacy and individual freedom. He said there was always the hope that a revolutionary government would not "fall into the errors of the regime that it has overthrown." In this matter, he said, "I am an eternal idealist."[18] If change was to come through revolution, then Lewis wanted a revolution that benefited both society and the individual, and one with minimum costs to all but the oppressors. It was as if he took all the naivete and sentimentality he refused to expend on the poor and invested it in his political ideals.

As the sixties wore on and the general political mood swung to the left, Lewis did speak more openly and more frankly about the need for structural reforms. "One way of abolishing the culture of poverty," he said, "is the abolition of capitalism—that's quite clear.

That involves a change of major institutions. Another way of doing it is by developing the welfare state. That doesn't do it in as radical a form, and *it perpetuates some of it,* but it does reduce it" (emphasis added).[19] Lewis agreed that the welfare approach could work in the United States if the nation were really committed to it and were willing to enact something much more sweeping than the "shot-in-the-arm" programs of the War on Poverty. However, when he discussed Central or Latin American poverty he called for stronger measures: "What I've learned about the way of life is that if you had strong leadership, if you had a kind of *personalismo,* with a good deal of authoritarianism in it, plus some benevolence, [with] this combination . . . I think you could create a revolution in the slums. . . . On the other hand, if you went at it in the typical American democratic way, I don't think you'd get much of a response."[20]

These remarks have overtones of paternalism and a double standard for democracy, but Lewis had little faith in the *spontaneous* revolutionary potential of the very poor. Yet the key to the demise of the culture of poverty, in his view, *was* political integration. (He referred to people who were politically unorganized as possessing a "primitive culture.") To eliminate the poverty subculture, he said,

> I think that . . . a society should begin by organizing itself in order to produce its own leaders; this for me is the authentic revolutionary process. . . . as they become more and more conscious of their conditions and better informed and aware of their needs, they are going to ask for more. With this will come a higher aspiration level which is implicit in the process. As I see it, poor people should organize so they themselves can express their needs to the institutions of their respective governments. I know that in each case the results will depend a great deal on the flexibility of the respective governments in listening to and paying attention to the demands presented by their citizens.[21]

Consciousness-raising among the poor was, according to Lewis, the first task for anyone who wanted to foment change. His assertion, "The first step toward revolution is to live with these poor people and to gain their confidence," could be taken to mean, and Lewis probably intended it to mean, that participation in his work contributed to consciousness-raising among the poor. This is not to say that he saw it as his job to educate informants about the conditions responsible for their economic circumstance. One would find no evidence in interview transcripts that he ever made political statements to informants or that he prodded them to draw specific conclusions. Lewis opposed all overt politicization of research and in the field was committed to maintaining, in terms of a doctrinal position, as neutral a stance as possible. In Cuba he was frustrated by the inability of his student trainees to grasp the fundamental importance of this. The only "political" view he ever thought essential to communicate to his informants was one of sympathy with their plight.

There were two ways in which Lewis believed his interviewing did contribute to consciousness-raising. The first was to create, through his line of questioning, a situation in which his informants were encouraged to reflect on their economic condition. For example, Lewis might ask them why they were poor, about who or what they thought was responsible, what they thought of government efforts to help them, or what they might do themselves to improve their situation. Lewis believed that in formulating answers to such questions his informants might become more aware of the need for change and more *receptive* to it, even if it was unlikely that they would ever organize themselves to work for political change.

A second path to consciousness-raising lay in the informants' potential to project their humanity and suffering through the published accounts of their lives. Their words might arouse the sympathies of readers to the point of organizing or agitating for reform on behalf of the poor. This is what I infer from Lewis's assessment of his work's significance: "Indeed, it seems that the proper and precise recording of the social facts of poverty and inequality in peasant villages and in the urban slums, and their destructive effects on human beings, is in itself a revolutionary act!"[22]

Making a Difference in Informants' Lives: Intangible Contributions

On the *individual* level Lewis believed he helped his informants just by showing an interest in them and listening to them. In 1965 he wrote: "I just got back from a quick trip to Mexico where I saw the Sánchez family. I was delighted to see that the book has helped give them a new sense of identity and self-confidence. I suspect that they got more out of five years of working with me than they might have gotten out of traditional therapy."[23] This is not a modest statement, yet it is not without foundation. Marta and Manuel Sánchez, for example, have spoken (once in my presence) of the importance of Lewis's friendship in providing personal and moral support. Marta called Lewis "my great friend, almost my father." Manuel, who read both *Five Families* and *The Children of Sánchez* in Spanish, told Lewis that he had learned a great deal about his family and gained a new respect for them. He admitted that reading the books had also made him take a long, hard look at himself.

It was not through friendship alone that Lewis believed he was building up the egos of his informants but by convincing them that their lives were of significance and that their participation in his research was a contribution to society. About the Sánchez family in general he said, "They have gotten a sense of their importance and the publication of the book has awakened a great interest in improving themselves and getting ahead."[24] This is perhaps somewhat overstated because most members of the Sánchez family, especially the father, were highly motivated individuals, but Lewis no doubt encouraged their ambitions. He was certainly successful—likely aided in large measure by the book's popularity—in passing on to them his conviction in the importance of the research. Jesús Sánchez told Lewis that by participating "my life has not been in vain because I . . . have added a grain of sand to history." Manuel said that he no longer felt "like a worm crawling across the earth." He also believed that the book about his family would lead to reform in Mexico: "When the world knows our way of life our government will feel a push and will have to see what is going on and act to improve the state of things."[25]

The Sánchez and Pedro Martínez families were exceptions among the hundreds of people Lewis interviewed in terms of the amount of time he spent and the interest he took in them. It is quite possible that others might not have felt as these two families did about the value of the work, or even have given it any thought. Lewis himself believed the research offered something intrinsically valuable to the informants as individuals in that, as they revealed their lives to him, they might discover themselves. This is perhaps why he associated the effects of taking life histories with the benefits of therapy. Reading interview transcripts one can sense that some of his informants had a great need to talk and to have someone to talk with. In some instances a simple question would prod a person to respond in a mini-monologue that, in its content, went way beyond what the question asked.

Reading these extended answers one can occasionally get the sense of a patient-therapist relationship and of there being a "talking cure" in progress. I do not mean to suggest that Lewis ever entertained the notion that he was solving personal problems specific to individual informants, only that the attention paid them was at least of some short-term use or comfort to them.

Making a Difference in Informants' Lives: Tangible Contributions

Like most anthropologists Lewis maintained that he had an obligation to give something back to the people he studied. He used a felt-needs questionnaire (as discussed in chapter 2) to guide him in deciding how he might help his informants solve one or more of their most pressing problems. In Tepoztlán this led to the establishment of a health clinic, introduction of a new crop, and provision of legal advice in a land dispute. In the Panaderos *vecindad* in Mexico City he was instrumental in getting the government to build a wall in front of the settlement, which residents had long wanted for protection from street traffic and passers-by. In the summers of 1959 and 1960 Lewis assigned his students to write reports on the housing and general living conditions in the Panaderos and Casa Grande, then used these reports as evidence to press the housing ministry to undertake basic improvements in the two *vecindades*.[26]

In Puerto Rico, Lewis had similar discussions with government officials about housing in La Esmeralda, but there the strongest commitment to helping informants came from Lewis's assistant, Francisca Muriente. After the research had ended, she became a volunteer community organizer and helped with many projects, including opening a small library-reading room and establishing a program of financial support for barrio youth attending university. In addition, while she was still interviewing there, and for many years afterward, she helped informants obtain medical assistance and jobs, find housing, and apply for welfare. She became a godmother to children of informants and in a few cases took children into her home and saw to their schooling. The Lewises assumed such extensive personal responsibilities only for the Sánchez family. Had they tried to do the same for all their informants, they would have been swallowed alive, as I believe Muriente nearly was in La Esmeralda. The collective neediness of these people is overwhelming.

The Lewises did, of course, try to help all informants with gifts and advice, and they aided or encouraged them to take advantage of opportunities (e.g., for jobs or schooling) that they would not, or could not, pursue on their own. Where relationships endured beyond the research, as was the case with the Sánchezes, the obligations became those of friendship. In fact, the Lewises were so often sought out for advice and assistance by the Sánchezes that it threatened to interfere with the research situation. Ruth Lewis has said that restraint had to be exercised not to provide information or assistance that might affect attitudes or personal circumstances while the interviewing was underway. This turned out to be an impossible line to maintain on an absolute basis.

Over the years the Sánchez family's involvement in the Lewises' work almost certainly changed their lives.[27] They met people from the arts and academia they would not otherwise have known. Consuelo traveled to Guatemala with the Lewises and lived with them in the United States. She was employed for many months as a field-worker on their projects in Mexico City, Tepoztlán, and Puerto Rico (as Manuel was in San Juan), and with the Lewises' help she tried to return to school, although she did not stay. Some would frown on such interaction because it "contaminates" the research and makes the informants unsuitable for long-term study. In the case of the Sánchez family, this is undoubtedly true.

The material needs of the Lewises' hundreds of informants were so enormous that the economic assistance they could provide to any one of them could not have had a long-term impact on their standard of living. Lewis did not make a practice of paying informant fees, but he did pay Tepoztecans like Pedro Martínez, who he believed had to be compensated for all the hours he kept them away from the fields. Consuelo and Manuel Sánchez were at times on project payrolls but as fieldworkers rather than informants. In Consuelo's case the line is somewhat blurred since she also was paid to keep a diary on her own life.

Questions about Lewis's personal responsibilities for, and financial obligations to, his informants were occasionally raised after his post-1960 publication successes. The central issue was whether a person who made money selling books about the poor had an obligation to share that money with them or to otherwise alleviate their poverty. In the narrow legal sense none of Lewis's informants was entitled to royalties since none was ever a party to a book contract. The Sánchezes, however, were designated, by other means, as recipients of royalties derived from adaptations of their family study.[28] They and the Ríoses and the other Puerto Rican informants whose work was to be published received a lump-sum payment—the amount varied with the number of individuals involved in a publication—upon signing a release form after completion of interviewing. But promises of such payments were not made during the course of the work.

The broader legal question of who is entitled to royalties is certainly not unique to Lewis's work, and it is usually resolved with reference to practical, not philosophical, considerations. If one were to pose this question in a moral context and discuss who is entitled to remuneration by virtue of contributing to a published work, then its resolution would be very problematic. For example, Consuelo and Manuel Sánchez played a far more creative role in Lewis's research than did other members of the family, while the four children gave much more of their time to the project than did their father or others involved. On the Puerto Rican project virtually all royalties were earned from the Ríos family study, but more than a hundred informants were involved in the five family studies and well over a dozen individuals gave more time to the project than did members of the Ríos family. Then, too, there were the very substantial contributions of Francisca Muriente. If every cent of *La Vida* royalties had been divided on a fair-share basis, however, the individual allotments would have been very small.

By suggesting how complicated the problem is when considered in the very unrealistic context of pure justice, I do not mean to excuse the failure to confront the basic moral dilemma. A simple, practical solution would be to agree that in each case where a family study results in a publication, the people on whose lives it is based would legally share in any decisions on how that material would be used in any medium and also would share in any compensation therefrom. An egalitarian—if any exist—would probably accept this. But Lewis was very proprietary about his work and did not recognize other people's contributions to it as equal to his own. The books may have been *about* his informants' lives, but they were, in his view, his creations, products of his energy and vision, and they were dedicated to his objectives. The idea of sharing legal control over their use was not, I think, a notion Lewis could have entertained. He did, however, obtain legal permission from informants to publish their stories, and he always consulted the Sánchezes about adaptations of their family's study to other media.

Since the Lewises were the sole recipients of book royalties, the fundamental question is, Were they obligated to use royalties to alleviate their informants' poverty? Pursuit of this issue is basically an academic diversion because the Lewises were far from being millionaires and did not have the resources to make drastic changes in informants' lives. They also had no right or authority to tell informants how to use the money they did receive. In a few instances the Lewises were able to create opportunities for the Sánchezes, but they could not be expected, and should not have been able to, keep someone in school who did not want to be there, for example, or convince others to have fewer children, or control drinking and spending habits. (A special case that confronted the Lewises many times was whether to continue giving money to someone who, refusing rehabilitation, was using the money to drink himself to death.) In all, members of the Sánchez family received a fairly large sum of money, but its economic impact was limited because it was divided five ways and distributed over a period of years.

Rather than parceling out royalties to dozens of individuals, the Lewises used a substantial portion of their money to carry out new research. On the Cuba project, for example, they were required, first by the Ford Foundation as a condition of its supporting grant and then by necessity after the grant expired, to personally underwrite 10 percent of the cost of the fieldwork. In the end the Lewises funded closer to one-third of the project's total costs.

The way in which critics raised the money issue in connection with the Lewises' work seems to me to have been exceptional. It may have been because the work depended upon a special relationship with informants, or it may have been simply a by-product of the political atmosphere of the 1960s, when there were circulating many highly romanticized notions about what it meant to be a defender of the poor. Such criticism took little notice that the Lewises spent most of their lives doing work for which there was little remuneration, or that they spent twenty years working on *Pedro Martínez*, a book whose royalties could not, and were not expected to, repay in money the time, effort, and care invested in it. Leaving the Sánchezes behind in the *vecindad* while they went off to North America to live in relative comfort was an emotional burden the Lewises carried with them. But how many anthropologists have done the same, and how many have been taken to task for it? Anthropologists and sociologists have been studying poor people and publishing life histories for generations, and some, such as Margaret Mead and Claude Lévi-Strauss, have surely sold far more books than Lewis ever did. But rarely do their colleagues, or outside observers, expect them to "fix" the lives of their informants.

Lewis never directly responded, as far as I know, to anyone who specifically criticized him for making money by writing about the poor. In 1969, however, he implied that it was unfair to hold social scientists accountable for anything more than the accuracy and reliability of their research. They should not be held responsible, he argued, for applications of their work as well: "To my knowledge, the many studies of tribal and peasant societies have rarely led to any marked improvement in the conditions under which these people live."[29] Still, Lewis should have addressed himself to the more reasonably stated questions about how he handled the ethical problems that arose when he received some financial reward and a good deal of fame from studying the poor from such a personal vantage point. What obligations do exist? What kinds of expectations are kindled? How can they be resolved to everyone's satisfaction? Were they in fact resolved to everyone's satisfaction? In the case of the Sánchezes these are very heady questions, because with no other family were there any equivalent emotional bonds and no other informants were ever so creatively involved in the writing of a family study.

Protecting Informants: Mexico

The family studies the Lewises did after 1956 were inherently controversial in content and format because they involved risks to the informants' privacy and personal relationships. If individual identities were discovered, the informants faced the possibility of their published statements being subjected to the scrutiny of friends and relatives and of relationships being damaged as a consequence. And if their stories attracted widespread public attention—something not anticipated by the Lewises in the late 1950s—the informants might face invasion of their privacy by the press. This did in fact happen to the Sánchez family in 1964.

The scandal that erupted in Mexico in 1964, some months after the publication of the Spanish-language edition of *The Children of Sánchez*, precipitated a national debate among journalists, academics, politicians, and government officials over Lewis's methods, motivation, and political tendencies. He was accused, in a complaint filed with Mexico's attorney general by members of the Mexican Society of Geography and Statistics, of publishing obscenity, manufacturing data, defaming Mexican institutions, and being an F.B.I. agent and an opponent of the Mexican Revolution.[30] (Lewis's account of the charges can be found in no. 160 in the Appendix.)

The scandal caught Lewis off-guard. *The Children of Sánchez* had been available in English for three years, and before that Lewis had written two other books on Mexico, one of which—*Antropología de la Pobreza* (*Five Families*)—had been published in Spanish in 1961. This book had been very well received, with negative reaction limited to exchanges between Lewis and a handful of academics and journalists. But there were several factors that separated *The Children of Sánchez* from Lewis's earlier work on Mexico. It dealt with urban residents who were much more knowledgeable about the city and the problems of life in modern Mexico. They were familiar with corruption in official circles, and they expressed themselves in language that was graphic, frank, critical, and nondeferential to those in authority. As informants on Mexico the Sánchezes, I believe, were taken much more seriously by some critics than were the rural informants, who could be dismissed as belonging to the still backward part of Mexico. When compared to the Sánchezes they also were more inhibited, less articulate, far more respectful of authority, and much more inclined to observe status distinctions.

The fact that Mexico was being held up to scrutiny in a work written by a North American added to the attack against the book and against Lewis personally. Just as important was the fact that the person most instrumental in the book's Spanish-language publication was also a foreigner—Arnaldo Orfila Reynal, an Argentinian who served as director of the government-owned press, the Fondo de Cultura Económica. Orfila was an important figure in Mexico's literary circles and had been responsible for publishing books by other left-leaning

North Americans, such as C. Wright Mills. According to Lewis the most important motive behind the attack on *The Children of Sánchez* and on him was the desire by rightist and centrist antiforeign elements in government and industry to remove Orfila as Fondo director and replace him with a Mexican. In this view the attack on Lewis as "anti-revolutionary" (read anti-Mexican) and an agent for the F.B.I. was not antirightist in nature but antileftist and antiforeign.

A number of Mexico's leading academics, writers, and journalists defended publication of the book; some specifically defended Lewis's integrity and the veracity of the work, while others stressed the right to freedom of expression under Mexican law.[31] In April 1965, two months after the charges were filed, the attorney general issued a finding of "no merit" in the complainants' charges and refused to take criminal action. Orfila was replaced as head of the Fondo and Lewis found a publisher in the private sector.[32] Although the furor over *The Children of Sánchez* was an outgrowth of an internal political struggle and had virtually nothing to do with the veracity of the work or with any substantive issue of ethical behavior, similar charges were to follow Lewis for the remaining six years of his life.

Lewis took steps to insulate the Sánchez family, but he could not protect them from the ravages of publicity because, in the end, the family did not want to be protected. The privacy issue took care of itself when Manuel Sánchez, in an attempt to defend Lewis and the authenticity of the book, identified himself. Later, three other family members, for their own reasons, made themselves known to members of the press. Since that time Consuelo and Jesús Sánchez have spoken to various reporters and she probably will again (Señor Sánchez died in January 1987). It is not hard to understand. They are chronically in difficult financial situations and have their reasons for using whatever contacts they can. The more serious question is, What was the motivation of those journalists who, having raised the issues of invasion of privacy and exploitation of informants, proceeded to make every effort to locate and identify the family, with no apparent concern for their privacy or welfare?

Protecting Informants: Puerto Rico

Coming on the heels of the Mexican scandal was the controversy surrounding the publication of *La Vida* in 1966. The Ríos family study produced the most sexually explicit material Lewis had ever published, and this led to charges that the book was a slur on Puerto Rican people and their culture.[33] But Lewis was not trying to depict Puerto Ricans in general or their culture. The Ríos family was, he said, representative of a subculture that by definition was a deviation from the cultural norm. Nevertheless, Lewis can be fairly criticized for how little effort he made to emphasize these distinctions, or those between the Ríoses and other Puerto Rican or Mexican informants he said shared this culture with them. The publication in a separate volume of the summary data on all the Puerto Rican informants also did not address itself to these distinctions and in any case, given its dry and pedestrian format, could not have offset the impact of *La Vida*.

Although one family study could not represent fairly all the Puerto Rican families interviewed, *La Vida* did not misrepresent the Ríos family as they were at the time of the study. But is the depiction of people as they really are always the right and fair thing to do? Might one not run the risk of hurting more than helping? The possibility of precipitating a backlash was given serious consideration by all people directly involved in the book's publication: the Lewises, Francisca Muriente, Muna Muñoz Lee, and Jason Epstein and Berenice Hoffman, the Random House editors. Decisions on the deletion or inclusion of the most potentially damaging—including the most sexually explicit—material were often made by consensus, as those working on the manuscript weighed the costs to the veracity of the work against the possibility of damage to the informants. One may disagree with the final judgments, but they were made in good faith by people who did take the Ríos family's welfare into consideration.

Lewis himself took a hard line on the issue of acting as mediator between informants and the reading public. This brought him into disagreement with anthropologists like Margaret Mead, for example, who took a more protective attitude toward the cultures they studied.[34] Like his colleagues, Lewis wanted readers to think well of the people he studied, but to make their lives more pretty than they were would be to put the lie both to social science research and to the underlying objective of his work, which was to expose poverty at its worst. This meant that he could not always maintain the stance taken by the great cultural relativists like Mead. He had to take a position, often to his own consternation, closer to that of those crusading missionaries in Asia and Africa who seemed to argue, "Love the people; change their culture."

Lewis was so committed to his position of no mediation that he would not compromise on this issue even after the controversy created by the publication of *La Vida*. He was asked by Random House editors to act as a kind of interpreter for his informants by interspersing commentary and analysis with the interview material included in "Six Women," but he refused to do so.[35] He continued along this path partly, I believe, out of commitment to his original purpose of giving the poor a public forum, and for this he is to be commended. But he was also influenced by his inability to decipher the complex message in his data and, more important, by the fact that his informants spoke with a frankness that both awed and eluded him in his own writing. In this sense he let the poor speak not only for themselves but for him as well. To the extent that he used this as an escape from professional responsibilities, he can be roundly criticized.

Protecting Informants: Cuba

The most serious of the charges ever leveled against Lewis about his relationship with his informants were those made in connection with the Cuba project. At this late date Lewis was well aware of the potential risks to privacy and anonymity faced by his informants. He also knew that Cuba had a secret police network that could further jeopardize every informant and that his field materials, which contained highly sensitive personal information, could fall into government hands. But he believed that if he could get Castro's personal assurance of protection from government interference, then his informants would be safe. After obtaining such promises, Lewis wrote them down and took them as a binding commitment. Apparently he was alone in this, because the Cuba project was terminated by the government at midpoint, in June 1970, and the Lewises' home and office were raided by the secret police. Copies of all field materials were confiscated. Shortly after the Lewises left the country, one of their informants was arrested and imprisoned.

The informant, Señor X, served two years and nine months of a seven-year sentence, most of it in labor camps. He suffered loss of liberty and career opportunities, separation from family, beatings by prison inmates, illnesses, and countless personal humiliations. His release was followed by seven years of restricted activity and no real choice in employment. He and his family were able to leave Cuba in 1980, under the 1977 political prisoner agreement between Presidents Carter and Castro and with the aid of letters written by Ruth Lewis on his behalf to the U.S. government.[36]

It is easy to claim that if the Lewises had not gone to Cuba, Señor X would not have gone to prison. But this sequence of events explains little about degrees of responsibility for the imprisonment. There can be no doubt about Oscar Lewis's role in the decision to interview Señor X and his family, and to continue with the family study in the face of a deteriorating situation within Cuba and a growing official coldness toward the project. But, unique among Lewis's informants in Cuba and elsewhere, Señor X and his wife were familiar with

Lewis's work and the attention it had received. They were certainly well acquainted—much more so than were the Lewises—with the nature of their government. Interviews with family members were conducted no differently than those with any other Cubans, with Lewis relying for informant protection on the official permission he had received to include in his research critics of the government. But early in the study, when he realized that Señor X was going to couple very frank criticism of the Revolution with open admiration for the United States and Castro's opponents, Lewis had to consider the possibility that, with these interviews, he might cross over the threshold of government tolerance of dissent. At that point he discussed with Señor X the wisdom of continuing the work. Lewis felt obligated to discuss dangers inherent in the situation and to give Señor X a chance to back out of the project. But he was happy when his informant agreed to proceed (Ruth Lewis said he "insisted") because he believed that this study illustrated better than anything else he had done in Cuba the impact on personal relationships of intrafamily differences over support for the Revolution.

Prior to beginning this family study, Lewis had interviewed a number of Cubans who were critical of government policies and of state and party officials, and no one had taken much note of it. However, most of these critics had been less educated, less well off, and without contacts among, or firsthand knowledge of, people in or around the higher circles. Lewis appears not to have conducted his research with a full understanding of Cuba's different standards of freedom of expression for the poor and middle classes, and he did not change his research plans to accommodate the more tenuous political situation prevailing in the spring of 1970 (i.e., following the failure of Castro's economic plan). But Lewis must have understood that if there were dangers in this to anyone, it would have been to Señor X and his family, not to himself and his family. The government could close down the project, but there was little chance that they would arrest, let alone imprison, a well-known North American who had been invited to Cuba by the government.

Señor X, in effect, lost ten years of his life, and after applying for exit visas he and his family suffered personal harrassment and even greater economic hardships. The trauma of the arrest and the project's demise may have been catalysts in Lewis's hospitalizations shortly after his return to the United States and in his death several months later. All of the principals in this episode, except Castro, suffered, and it was one of those more-common-than-not situations for which there was sufficient blame to go around—for the Lewises and their informants, and for Castro and his government. It was the one time in Lewis's field career when he really went too far in pursuing his research interests, not because he delved too deeply into the intimacies of family relationships or personality, but because he had a too shallow understanding of the most obvious features of an authoritarian government.

It would have been safer for everyone involved if the Lewises had not gone to Cuba. But would it have been wiser for no one to have seized the opportunity to do intensive, open-ended interviewing in a socialist country? Because people weigh differently the costs and benefits of social science research there is no one answer to that question. Given his sympathy for the Cuban Revolution, open admiration of Castro, aggressiveness in pursuing the opportunity to study the Revolution, and reputation for unsentimental depictions of poverty in capitalist systems, it is possible that, at the time, this kind of opportunity would not have come to anyone but Lewis. All these characteristics also made him less likely to be sensitive to the dangers in the research situation. Lewis gambled and lost in Cuba, but not so badly as did Señor X and his family.

By 1970 controversy was no stranger to Lewis. The success of his work had subjected him to every kind of critical evaluation and personal attack: that he exploited his informants; that he engaged in ethnic and cultural slander; that he was an F.B.I. or a C.I.A. agent; that he put personal ambition before the integrity of the work; and, in the overwrought words of one critic, that he was an "ethical-civic failure."[37] When charges such as these are levied against any white, middle-class North American who studies the poor in "third-world" countries, the benefit of the doubt is almost certainly not going to be given to the researcher. It is the poor as "victims" who co-opt our sympathy and whose position leads us to question the motives of anyone who profits (materially) from contact with them. Underlying many charges of this nature, including those directed specifically at Lewis, I would argue, is a paternalistic view of the poor as naive people bound to be used and exploited in all contacts with the middle class and incapable of independent, let alone self-serving, motivations. The Sánchezes in particular are strong-minded and strong-willed and act independently to pursue their own needs. Lewis did not lead on people like the Sánchezes, or Pedro Martínez, or Fernanda Ríos, or, for that matter, Señor X, and he could not have made them do things that they did not want to do or that did not have some utility for them. Lewis was no pied piper; he responded as much to the personalities of his informants as they did to his. It is patronizing to believe that most of the people he studied could not and did not hold their own with him. They had their own motivations for participation in his projects, and they were able to set limits that Lewis could not have crossed even if he had tried (as he did try and fail with Jesús Sánchez and Pedro Martínez). Each of them got something from their participation. Whether it was sufficient in return for what they gave is for only them to say.

(Relevant correspondence can be found on pp. 284–300.)

NOTES

1. *El Nacional* interview, November 6, 1967 (translated from the Spanish).

2. Remarks prepared for the National Book Awards ceremony in New York City, March 8, 1967.

3. "A Redbook Dialogue: Robert Kennedy and Oscar Lewis," *Redbook*, September 1967, pp. 73ff. Lewis did not take the initiative to meet with Robert Kennedy, but he did try to arrange an invitation to attend a session of President Kennedy's Scientific Advisory Committee to make suggestions for the "development of science in Latin America." In letters to Stephen P. Boggs, executive secretary of the American Anthropological Association, in May and June 1962, Lewis asked Boggs to send a copy of *The Children of Sánchez* to President Kennedy as part of this effort. At various times Lewis also asked his publishers to send copies of his books to officials in other countries, including to Fidel Castro and to Luis Muñoz Marín, then governor of Puerto Rico. Lewis met and spoke at length with both of these leaders, not about policy, but about problems related to his research.

4. Letters from Oscar Lewis to Muna Muñoz Lee, May 8, 1967, and Carolina Luján, May 9, 1967.

5. Charles Valentine, *Culture and Poverty: Critique and Counter-Proposals* (Chicago: University of Chicago Press, 1968), pp. 15–17, 48–77.

6. *Current Anthropology*, April–June 1969, p. 191. The quote is from Lewis's reply to Charles Valentine, whose *Culture and Poverty* was reviewed in this issue.

7. In the postscript to a February 1, 1966, letter to Lloyd Ohlin, Lewis wrote: "I have now had direct confirmation from Michael Harrington that he never heard of the concept of a culture or a subculture of poverty before reading my book in 1959."

8. James L. Sundquist, "Origins of the War on Poverty," in *On Fighting Poverty*, ed. James Sundquist (New York: Basic Books, 1969), p. 8.

9. John G. Wofford, "The Politics of Local Responsibility: Administration of the Community Action Program—1964–66," in ibid., p. 71.

10. Public Law 89-794, H.R. 15111 (War on Poverty), enacted November 8, 1964.

11. For a discussion of this clause see John C. Donovan, *The Politics of Poverty* (New York: Pegasus, 1967), pp. 33ff.

12. Sundquist, p. 247. These remarks also appear in minutes taken at seminar meetings, which were sent out to participants.

13. Letter from James L. Sundquist to Oscar Lewis, May 26, 1966.

14. Lewis, *Study of Slum Culture*, p. 19n.

15. *Current Anthropology*, April–June 1969, p. 192.

16. Moore, "In the Life," p. 3.

17. Lisa Hammel, "Can a Kibbutz, American Style, Save the Children of the Slums?" *New York Times*, November 5, 1969, p. 50.

18. *El Nacional* interview. Lewis added, "If we can go to the moon, why can't we invent a way to avoid the bureaucratization which invariably develops fifty years into a revolution" (translated from the Spanish).

19. From a talk at the Latin American Institute, University of Wisconsin at Oshkosh, 1967.

20. Ibid.

21. *El Nacional* interview.

22. Lewis, *Anthropological Essays*, p. xii.

23. Letter from Oscar Lewis to Alfred Kazin, September 20, 1965.

24. *El Nacional* interview.

25. Interview with Manuel Sánchez by Oscar Lewis, May 1962 (translated by Elena Flores).

26. The students' reports are part of the archival collection.

27. Manuel Sánchez has told Ruth Lewis several times (once when I was present) that identifying himself as *"un hijo de Sánchez"* has helped open doors and also provided him with some protection in his work, which *in the past* was not always technically within the law. He called his status as one of the children of Sánchez his *"seguro social."* Jesús Sánchez once revealed his identity in a letter to a newspaper in a successful effort to save the job he had held for three decades. And Consuelo, who at one time hoped to find work in the theater or film industry, used contacts made through Lewis to further this pursuit.

28. The five principal informants for *The Children of Sánchez* received, in equal shares, the Lewises' royalties from Vicente Leñero's adaptation of *The Children of Sánchez* for the stage, and they would have received the Lewises' share of royalties (2½ percent of the net profit) from the film version had it been successful.

29. Lewis's reply to Charles Valentine, in *Current Anthropology*, April–June 1969, p. 191.

30. The charges against Lewis and statements made in defense of his work can be found in *La Gaceta*, the monthly newspaper of the Fondo de Cultura Económica, March 1965. Although the charges were filed in the name of the Society's board of directors, some members claimed that no official vote was ever taken within the Society on whether the membership supported the charges made on its behalf.

31. *La Gaceta* printed many of these statements in its March 1965 issue.

32. Spanish-language editions of Lewis's family studies were published by the small firm Editorial Joaquín Mortiz, under the direction of Joaquín Diez-Canedo. That firm was bought out by Planeta of Spain in 1983, and the Spanish-language rights to Lewis's works are now owned by the huge

Barcelona-based Editorial Grijalbo. In 1983 Grijalbo began releasing new editions of Lewis's family studies and translating the unpublished work.

33. These charges against Lewis received a great deal of press coverage in the San Juan papers during 1966 because they were leveled by (among others) two prominent Puerto Rican officials: Samuel Quiñones, president of the Senate, and José Monserrat, head of the Migration Division of the Department of Labor.

34. I learned of this disagreement from Ruth Lewis, who witnessed part of a heated exchange between her husband and Mead at what she recalls was a Wenner-Gren Foundation conference in the late 1960s. Mead wrote about her views on this subject in "The Role of Science in Society," *Orthopsychiatry 1923–48: Retrospect and Prospect* (New York: American Orthopsychiatry Association, 1948), pp. 367–73. See also Mead, *An Anthropologist at Work*, p. xx.

35. Letter from Jason Epstein to Oscar Lewis, March 6, 1968.

36. When Ruth Lewis and I were writing up the Cuban material we did not know what Señor X's sentence was, the conditions under which he was held, nor those under which he was released. The only information we had, from telephone conversations between the Lewises and Señora X, was that he was incarcerated in a work camp. Ruth Lewis and I made no later attempts to contact the family because we believed it would put them at even greater risk; in fact, Señora X was taken in for questioning by state security agents at the time the books were published in the United States. In 1980, after the arrival of Señor X and his family in the United States, Ruth Lewis and I went to Miami to talk with them. There the formal charges were shown to us (namely, that he had given unfavorable information about Cuba to a North American), and for the first time we learned about the conditions of his imprisonment.

37. The various charges against Lewis have a number of sources, including the Cuban government (that he was a C.I.A. agent); Mexico's Society for Geography and Statistics (that he was an F.B.I. agent and had fabricated material); Samuel Quiñones and José Monserrat (see note 33; that he defamed Puerto Ricans and Puerto Rican culture). John Womack, in his review of *Four Men* in *The New York Review of Books*, August 4, 1977, was especially unflattering to Lewis personally and strongly suggested that Lewis might have been an agent for the C.I.A. Also unflattering on the personal level were Marvin Opler and Theodore Caplow in *Current Anthropology* 8 (1967): 485–86, 488–89, wherein they accused Lewis of rushing work into print (including *Pedro Martínez*, which the Lewises worked on for twenty years) and slurring Puerto Rican culture. The quotation in the text is from Anthony Leeds, "The Concept of the 'Culture of Poverty': Conceptual, Logical, and Empirical Problems, with Perspectives from Brazil and Peru," in *The Culture of Poverty: A Critique*, ed. Eleanor Burke Leacock (New York: Simon and Schuster, 1971), p. 281. Despite Leeds's self-righteous pronouncements about Lewis's character, his article is full of very sound criticisms of the culture of poverty thesis.

CONCLUSIONS

When viewed as a whole the field career of Oscar Lewis appears to have had a central focus: the study of poor people through ethnography and family studies. In fact, the work for which he is best known—that published between 1959 and 1969—did not result from investigation into clearly defined research problems. By the time he began interviewing the Sánchez family in 1956, it is fair to say that what he wanted to know about his informants was—quite simply—everything.

In its reliance on historical research and on amassing huge amounts of primary source material—and probably only in this respect—Lewis's approach drew on the Boasian tradition. He did not, however, have the patience of a Boas or a Benedict to organize, classify, and reflect on his data or to delay generalization or publication. With respect to life histories, Lewis had varying degrees of interest in, but little patience for, postcollection phases of data use, whether it was cataloging, distillation and analysis, or editing and annotation for publication. It was not an error of omission when, in outlining his nine steps for producing family studies, he included no step for analysis of data.[1] By contrast, he had much more patience for, and skill in, analysis of secondary sources, perhaps because the information contained in them was so much more receptive to organization and generalization than was the detail of biographical studies.[2]

Lewis was always at his best when in the field, but increasingly so as his career progressed, and he relished these experiences. His greatest strengths were his organizational and leadership skills, his ability to recruit and train good personnel, and the personal qualities that made it possible for him to establish rapport with so many informants. For all their shortcomings in yielding statistically meaningful data, Lewis's field methods were exceedingly good for obtaining certain kinds of information. The technique he developed for observing family relationships, individual behavior, and household routines made the day study an important complement to his interviewing. Due to the quality of rapport he was able to develop with so many informants, Lewis became adept at eliciting attitudes on sensitive issues and information on what he labeled "inner" lives and "private per-

173

sonalities." He and Ruth Lewis had superb understandings of what was necessary—beyond basic descriptions of major events in the life cycle—to the construction of a life history that would give insight into the individual's value structure and at the same time interest the reader in both the informant and his or her culture. The method, born of skepticism, that led Lewis to seek the same information more than once, and from as many different informants as possible, produced the interesting organizational format of multiple biographies and, more important, eliminated from published accounts many of the half-truths, evasions, or even lies told in early interviews.

Lewis's principal weakness lay in his inability, in his later years especially, to stick to clearly defined objectives and consequently to set limits on his projects. As a practical guide to data collection the study of total personality came to mean little more than trying to accumulate as much information as possible on each informant studied. With that as a general goal, it became very difficult to design limited, well-focused research. Time, funding, availability of informants, and pressures to publish—not the conviction that the necessary data had been collected—were what brought these studies to a close.

Lewis was an ambitious man, and this, too, made it difficult for him to limit his work and not try to take advantage of every field opportunity that presented itself. This was an asset in that it gave him a certain bravado in pursuing research opportunities, but it also led him to undertake work for which he was not fully prepared or that presented a threat to his health. Over the years, as his projects became all-encompassing, they also became all-consuming, and in working as intensively as he did, and driving those who worked with him in the same way, he burned himself out physically.

In the 1960s the dialectic did not function in Lewis's thinking; it was all juxtaposition and no synthesis. His analytic and critical abilities, which were strong in the 1930s and 1940s, leveled off in the 1950s and, in association with his health, began to decline in the 1960s. Lewis's creativity in the field stayed with him, however, for in this his responsiveness to Latin cultures, his entrepreneurial skills, and his intuition for choosing good informants combined to produce intensely detailed life histories and some good ethnographic data as well.

After 1961 Lewis began a slow intellectual retreat from academic life. He spent approximately half of the decade off-campus, either at field sites or directing the work from a central office nearby. Even though he published a great deal during this period, including most of his best-known books, he actually *wrote* very little that was new. His publications were drawn largely from interviews, edited by Ruth Lewis and a staff of assistants, and day studies that he wrote/edited with his wife and Helen Kuypers. The introductions to his books consisted in part of reworkings of material written and published earlier; only the introduction to *La Vida* required analysis of new data, and the thesis section was republished a number of times in article form and also was used to introduce *A Study of Slum Culture*. The remainder of the volume was drawn from data analysis written up by Douglas Butterworth and edited by Ruth Lewis. Ruth Lewis also wrote the new material for the introduction to *A Death in the Sánchez Family*. In fact, during the 1960s Lewis wrote (excluding articles comprised of interview excerpts) only one major article based on new data: "The Material Possessions of the Poor."[3] A great deal of his writing energies went into personal and professional correspondence. At the same time he was redirecting his focus from academia to the arts, as he explored the possibilities, with film directors such as Luis Buñuel and Elia Kazan, of adapting his works on Mexico and Puerto Rico for the screen.

The success of *The Children of Sánchez* and *La Vida* convinced Lewis, I believe, that the books in themselves were achievement enough and that he was not under any obligation to write for the social science community. He thought that publishing additional family studies, or making available to a wider audience works he had already published by adapting them for the screen, would be a greater contribution than anything he could write for social science journals. Furthermore he had strong objections to academic jargon and to the overinterpretation of the interviews.

Moving closer to the arts also suited Lewis's personal interests and needs. The artist, unlike the social scientist, is not expected to interpret his or her work; that job is left to critics and consumers. For Lewis, with his work increasing in quantity and complexity and his health and critical faculties declining, this difference was quite important. Although he had begun his career eagerly anticipating a life of scholarly research and analysis, after the first decade it became steadily less interesting, and hence less rewarding. He liked the physical activity of ferreting out information and of debating the big issues in anthropology, but he did not enjoy being or working alone. He had little capacity for long solitary hours of reflection or for the often dry and pedestrian or overly esoteric arguments common to academic writing. He liked to be on the move and to bring his work to completion, whether or not the fine points were resolved. He preferred getting on to the next project, accomplishing a new goal, and making the big point.

Lewis clearly believed that if he could continue to do research and to publish family studies his obligation to social science would eventually be fulfilled. The pattern that was undetectable in several family studies would, he thought, be revealed through the publication of a large number of them, or by the analysis of the raw materials on which they were based, if someone were enterprising enough to do that. I do not think he cared much if those answers supported his thesis or if, instead, they led to some new formulation that might defuse the whole culture of poverty controversy. In any case they would offer a better basis from which to generalize about the social and psychological consequences of poverty than had previously been available to cultural anthropologists.

With this objective in mind, I believe, Lewis began to see all of his work as of a single piece. Instead of looking at each project as discrete, he developed the habit of taking generalizations that may have held for one set of data and applying them as givens in subsequent research. Late in his career he was even capable of adding to a body of conclusions a set of sometimes competing or contradictory findings. For this reason almost everything he published in the 1960s is full of contradictions.

It was through this cumulative process that Lewis constructed a set of hypotheses and a trait list for the culture of poverty several years after he had coined the phrase. He drew heavily on his own earlier findings and on the work of others, such as that of the social historian Henry Mayhew on the poor of London, and from novels about the poor, particularly those set in the great cities of Western Europe.[4] These works Lewis frequently mentioned as influences on his thinking about lower-class cultures, but he also borrowed ideas from Allison Davis on the importance of kinship networks in the American working and lower classes and from W. Lloyd Warner on social distinctions and class stratification in American communities.

In less overt ways Lewis drew heavily on the intellectual legacy of his teachers: Foner, Klineberg, Kardiner, Linton, and Benedict. He believed that his approach, in its exhaustiveness, concern for economic factors, and focus on the individual, distanced itself from the poetic, abstractly intellectual qualities of Benedict's work. He opposed her Apollonian-Dionysian dichotomy and the use of the configurational concept to define culture. But in the end he took every bit as much poetic license as she had; and in his use of a trait cluster to define the culture of poverty he was not that far removed from her usage of "configuration."[5] Finally, Lewis drew on the Marxist tradition for the philosophical vantage point from which he viewed his research and the prism through which he filtered its meaning.

It is a paradox that a man so innovative in his field methods was so derivative in his conclusions. In reading Lewis on the culture of poverty one sees not the results of a reasonably systematic analysis of his data but a mosaic of shards culled from the literature of anthropology, psychology, psychiatry, sociology, and economic history, as well as from novels about the poor. In pasting together these odd bits and pieces, Lewis produced in the culture of poverty concept a kind of Watts Tower of ideas, dramatic in effect but structurally unsound.

The culture of poverty, as it is defined by the trait list, is in itself impossible to analyze because there is—as Gertrude Stein said of Oakland—no there, there. The words are all free-floating, unattached to definition or concrete values. There is no point in trying to make sense of the list because its ambiguities and internal contradictions are too great. One is left simply to admit that it is useless, or to wander forever in a circle that cannot be closed. The publication of the trait list was the nadir of a career filled with outstanding work.

Perhaps there is a culture that is shared by some, or even many, of the world's poorest people. I do not know. What I do believe is that what Lewis called a culture was not a way of life or an adaptation to a highly specific set of economic conditions handed down along family lines. That *small portion* of his informants who did share the characteristic clustering of traits did not, I am convinced, acquire it through the agencies of culture. Rather, I believe, these traits were the manifestations of a variety of problems—among them, emotional and mental disorders, alcohol and other drug addiction, and a variety of illnesses and diseases associated with poverty. The condition of extreme poverty shared by these people sometimes brought them together in communities "reserved for," or taken over by, social pariahs, as in the case of La Esmeralda, and this lent a similarity to the outer appearance, or the externalities, of their lives.

If Lewis were able to respond he would probably say that such an argument is the unconstructive nitpicking of an academic and that in the end the problem is still poverty, and its elimination is a necessary first step toward dealing with the other problems. From a political perspective I have no quarrel with this, but I cannot accept that the words and concepts used to explain a problem are of no real consequence. If we want to communicate with precision a message as urgent as the one Lewis was trying to deliver, some respect has to be paid to the integrity of words. Lewis realized this near the end of his life. Just as he admitted in La Vida that the family unit was not the appropriate level for his generalizations, he acknowledged that he had boxed himself in with his use of "culture." But he never seemed to fully grasp that he was trying to make a political statement by dressing it up in anthropological terminology.

The clearest, if not the most accurate, statements about the poor have been delivered by ideologues and romantics who have tended to homogenize the poor into a mass of heroic, virtuous, suffering victims, or alternatively into a mass of unmotivated and undeserving layabouts. In these terms the problems of poverty, if still not so easy to solve, at least become easy to explain. But as Lewis presents them in his books—in contrast to his theory—poverty and the poor are not at all easy to understand. Amid the particulars of so many lives, cause and effect appear to exchange places from one life to another, a problem Lewis recognized but could not deal with on a theoretical level: "In general terms poverty in our times is never caused by the poor themselves; it is the product of socio-economic systems. This is important [in people's thinking about the poor] and it creates a vicious circle that I very much want to break by showing what is cause and what is effect. For this reason one has to insist on the great difference between pure poverty and a so-called culture of poverty."[6]

Lewis failed to keep these distinctions front and center in his work, primarily because of the imprecision of his language (as in the use of the term "slum culture," for example) and the selective presentation of his data. One has to overlook his labels and catch phrases and remember that he consistently stressed the range of variation in behavior and values within each of the communities he studied. This was just another way of saying that the poor are as distinct from one another as are people who are not poor. What they have in common is an economic condition that sets them apart from the middle and upper classes. One can make a better case that this condition is perpetuated at least as much, and probably more so, by political and economic policies than by cultural processes. This is exactly the argument Lewis was trying to make, but whenever he had to deal with a controversial political issue, his writing took on an extraordinary opacity. As an anthropologist he apparently believed that to have credibility he had to explain his findings in terms of the culture concept. And as a leftist working in an academic environment hostile and even punitive toward leftists, he may have thought he had to hide behind it. Meanwhile, the culture of poverty phrase passed into the vernacular, virtually devoid of any specific meaning other than that assigned to it by the individual user.

Despite earning a level of success and fame achieved by relatively few academics, Lewis would probably not be pleased by his place in anthropology today. I judge this to be the isolated position of a maverick, one befitting Lewis's latter-day self-liberation from the conceptual and methodological confines of the discipline. His thirty-year career produced fifteen books and monographs and more than fifty articles, but it is a body of work accomplished so thoroughly in Lewis's own highly eclectic style that it is very difficult to build upon. He left no conceptual framework and few instructions for the conduct of field investigations or for the preparation and analysis of field materials. He directed the work of many students on projects in Mexico, India, Puerto Rico, and Cuba, and was anything but a loner in the field. But just as his personality was too strong and his ways too independent for him to have been anyone's disciple, these qualities in turn limited his attractiveness as a model for his students. His interests were too broad, his approach too highly personalized or idiosyncratic to be easily conveyed, the research too time-consuming and expensive, his personality too demanding, and his position within anthropology too controversial for him to attract many disciples. Lewis fashioned his own mini-discipline around an approach designed to employ his best skills and innate abilities, as well as those of his wife. This took years to develop and was fully deployed only after he was secure in his profession.

Within anthropology Lewis will probably continue to be most highly regarded, if not best remembered, for his earliest work, particularly for his critique of Redfield's model of the folk-urban continuum. His best-known work—*The Children of Sánchez*, *La Vida*, and *Five Families*— is seen, in my judgment, as a unique achievement but unduplicable, a contribution to the anthropological literature but not to method or theory.

From all his productivity subsequent to the Tepoztlán research, Lewis had hoped to leave some mark, at least on method if not on theory. However, he did little to help his own cause. He found it difficult to describe the highly personalized aspects of his work and too boring to write about its routine and systematic aspects. He enjoyed showing students how to work in the field but did not like to teach methods in the classroom and could not have imparted this in a textbook. He saw no "need for a tool kit on how to do the work," perhaps because much of what was best in his own field technique was instinctual.[7]

Lewis's reluctance to discuss his methods was almost certainly abetted by the fact that he was never very eager to reveal how dependent he was on the collaboration of others to produce his family studies. The research, editing, and translation essential to such studies are very labor-intensive and require a variety of skills rarely possessed by one person. Had Lewis had to translate and edit his materials, or to carry out the household observations and all of the interviewing in Mexico and Puerto Rico, he would not have had the time or opportunity to gather anywhere near the volume and quality of material he was able to collect with that assistance. Some of these contributions, such as Ruth Lewis's editing, Zatz's and Muñoz Lee's translations, Luján's personality assessments, and Muriente's Puerto Rican day studies, were truly creative, and Lewis was sometimes painfully aware of that. None of these contributions, however, alter the fact of his own central, creative role, and it is unfortunate that his acknowledgments of others were so nominal.

For his attitude of wanting to do it all, and consequently of not doing some things well, Lewis has had to pay in professional reputation in a discipline that is vastly different from the one he entered fifty years ago. He ignored the postwar trend toward specialization, scientism, and "objectivity" and maintained a commitment to the holistic approach and to the arts and humanities tradition. There is evidence that Lewis felt increasingly isolated and in danger of being left behind by the new social science. As early as 1961 he wrote to a friend about the scarcity of like-minded colleagues: "The anthropologists whom I most admired and whose evaluation of my work would have meant most to me, are now gone. I refer to Ruth Benedict and Ralph Linton (my teachers), Robert Redfield, Clyde Kluckhohn and Alfred Kroeber. These were the great humanists in anthropology and I'm afraid the humanistic focus has become a scarce commodity among the younger generation."[8]

Today it is unlikely that a young social scientist could adopt a research stance similar to Lewis's and survive to tenure in a university setting. I find this a sad development, despite all the gains that have accrued from deploying quantitative methods on social science questions. Although Lewis was responsible for one truly bad idea, his method produced four books of exceptional power (*Five Families, The Children of Sánchez, La Vida,* and *Pedro Martínez*) and one truly innovative and finely drawn work of ethnography (*Life in a Mexican Village*). Probably the best description of the method that produced these works is Jules Henry's characterization of it as "passionate ethnography."[9] The phrase is appropriate, not because it accurately identifies *what* Lewis did, but because it puts the right inflection on *how* he did it. Oscar Lewis saw his research as both mission and mitzvah. It was his way of keeping faith and making a contribution, even though the cynic can add that the work did not do Lewis any harm either. His research was not the revolutionary act he idealized it to be, nor was it even a catalyst for serious reform. It was, however, at the very least, a good work passionately pursued.

NOTES

1. Lewis, *Study of Slum Culture*, p. 30.

2. The Tepoztlán study was an example of this, but see also "Controls and Experiments in Field Work," in Kroeber, *Anthropology Today*, pp. 452–75 (reprinted in Lewis, *Anthropological Essays*, pp. 3–34); and "Comparisons in Cultural Anthropology," *Yearbook of Anthropology*, ed. William Thompson (New York: Wenner-Gren Foundation for Anthropological Research, 1955), pp. 259–92 (reprinted in Lewis, *Anthropological Essays*, pp. 90–134).

3. *Scientific American* 221 (1969): 114–24. I do not include "Mexico since Cárdenas," published in 1961, because Lewis wrote it in 1956.

4. In 1985, while revising the manuscript for this book, I read Gertrude Himmelfarb's chapter on Henry Mayhew, entitled "The 'Culture of Poverty'," in *The Idea of Poverty* (New York: Alfred Knopf, 1983), pp. 307–70. I was surprised by how similar some of her criticisms of Mayhew's reporting were to those I have made of Lewis's research, even though Himmelfarb favorably contrasts Lewis's work to Mayhew's. Himmelfarb writes, for example, "In making poverty a form of social pathology, a cultural rather than an economic condition, Mayhew and his flock of imitators gave yet another turn to the ideological history of poverty" (p. 366). According to Himmelfarb, Mayhew intended that *London Labour* would be the first in a series of volumes in which he promised "to do for 'all classes' what he had already done for a 'comparatively small and obscure portion of the community'. . . . Neither then nor later did he carry out his original intention . . ." (p. 323). I found the most striking similarities between Lewis and Mayhew in Himmelfarb's characterization of Mayhew's attitude toward the people he studied: "From [his] account of the 'moral physiognomy' of the street folk, one might assume that Mayhew himself was less than sympathetic, or even hostile, to them. And so it often must have appeared to his readers. Yet this was far from his intention. In fact, some of his most shocking and seemingly harsh revelations of immorality and brutality were accompanied by explanations that were meant to excuse by way of explaining. If they did not quite succeed in this purpose, it was because the descriptions were so much more vivid than the explanations that the latter could never undo the effect of the former" (p. 326). Himmelfarb writes later that even "where he was most intent upon humanizing and socializing the street-folk, restoring them to the civilized world, he was also brutalizing and degrading them—and this with the best intentions: to dramatize the need for society's help and to condemn the society that withheld that help" (pp. 331–32).

5. Benedict wrote that any given trait might be found in many cultures, but variations in the functions traits served, and in the different patterns or configurations woven from them by different groups of people, were what created distinct culture groups. Similarly Lewis wrote that culture of poverty traits could be found in every class, not just among the poor, but it was the "clustering" of traits that made the culture of poverty a distinctive way of life.

6. *El Nacional* interview, November 6, 1967 (translated from the Spanish).

7. Letter from Oscar Lewis to George and Louise Spindler, October 4,

1968. The Spindlers had written to Lewis asking him to write a book on methods for the ethnography series they edited. Lewis replied, "As a matter of research strategy, it seems to me that there is a much greater urgency in the world today for the finished product of my research than for a tool kit on how to do it."

8. Letter from Oscar Lewis to Gordon Ray of the Guggenheim Foundation, October 16, 1961.

9. Jules Henry quoted by Margaret Mead in her introduction to the 1975 edition of *Five Families*, p. viii.

APPENDIX: CORRESPONDENCE

Some may say that it is an act of Nemesis that Oscar Lewis is being allowed here to speak for himself in words edited by someone he did not know in a manner he did not foresee. But Lewis's professional correspondence is extremely useful, in fact essential, to any discussion of the evolution of his work and thinking. Almost everything he set in print he discussed first in letters to colleagues and friends. Other than the field materials themselves, these letters were the most important source I had for this study. Lewis held so many conflictive positions on his work and its meaning that it is difficult to summarize them in any way that really establishes the level of contradiction he was able to tolerate in his thinking. But the letters also illustrate the consistency in values and objectives that underlay his life's work.

The majority of the correspondence from which the following excerpts come are in the Oscar Lewis Papers, a restricted collection in the archives of the University of Illinois Library at Urbana-Champaign. The collection contains the greater part, but by no means all, of Lewis's professional correspondence. It does not include his letters to or from his principal assistants and collaborators, nor any personal correspondence. Ruth Lewis made available her husband's letters to her, as well as those written to and received from translators Asa Zatz and Muna Muñoz Lee, psychologist Carolina Luján, Random House editors, and all fieldworkers. Excerpts from letters that are not part of the archive collection are indicated by a cross preceding the entry. The numbered excerpts are organized by topic and are meant to support specific sections of the text.

Tepoztlán

1. Oscar Lewis to Ernest Maes, director of the National Indian Institute, October 27, 1943

I have begun work on getting the personality project going. I think we will be able to count on the cooperation of [Juan] Comas and he may even be able to go into the field for short periods of 10 to 15 days each to administer tests in fields of his interest. However, at the Chicago discussions with Collier and Thompson we had decided that most of the tests should be given by Mrs. Ruth Lewis, that is the Rorshach, Grace Arthur battery, the Thematic Apperception and the free drawing tests. Furthermore, [we] agreed not to limit the study to children but to include adults of all age levels. This broadens the scope of the study and at the same time should make more effective the original objective of evaluating the effects of Mexican educational policies on Indian or mestizo children. One can't understand children's needs except in terms of adult needs. It seemed to us that one of the limitations of the Chicago–U.S. study was the failure to study adult life as an integral part of the entire project.

The immediate problem is to select two communities. . . . I have consulted various people for suggestions and a choice will apparently have to be made from among the following: San Pedro, Joñex, Ixtlan, in Oaxaca, Mitla, Tepoztlán, Tarahumara, Huichol and Teotihuacan. Everyone approached for suggestions quite naturally recommended the group he or she had worked with. Thus Gamio prefers Teotihuancan, Caso prefers Oaxaca, etc.[1] This means that Mrs. Lewis and myself have to read all the available literature on the above communities in order to be sure that we make the best possible choice. I have almost completed the manuscript left by Malinowski on the market systems of Oaxaca and nearby towns. It is a straight economic [study] and a competent piece of work. However I got the impression that Malinowski was more interested in finding out how to create markets for Singer sewing machines and other products of western civilization than in improving the lot of the Indians. Fortunately these objectives are not mutually contradictory.

1. Alfonso Caso was the director of the National School of Anthropology and History.

2. Oscar Lewis to Ernest Maes, November 6, 1943

Since my last letter to you there has been considerable progress in regard to some of the preliminary aspects of the personality project.

It is certainly a job to translate into action what sounds like a simple matter on paper. Let me familiarize you with some of the difficulties I am running into. Probably the most important is the shortage of available personnel to go into the field. There are only a few students in the National School of Anthropology, about ten in all. . . . But there are a number of projects going which apparently are in much closer touch with the School than we have been and therefore have priority. For example Sol Tax has a project going in Chiapas and three students are already committed to go into the field for him in December. Then there is the new Institute organized by Julian Steward. Steward is sending George Foster down to teach anthropology and then to take a group into the field with him, to the Tarascan area. All in all there are few students left to cooperate with us. Furthermore when I spoke to [Ruben] Borbolla about our needs and Caso's commitment to help us, he suggested a counterproposal, namely that if we want the School to pay the expenses of a group of students in the field for six months that Mrs. Lewis and myself should give a course on modern ethno-psychology from March to June in order to prepare the students for the work involved.[1] Though I don't doubt that the students need such a course this suggestion was impossible for a number of reasons. First it would mean delaying the beginning of our study until next June. Second, I explained that I would probably have to go to Central America within a few months. However I am attempting to work out a compromise solution whereby I will pledge a minimum number of lectures in return for their cooperation. Mrs. Lewis will not take part, however, for I want her to get to work in the field.

. . . We visited Teotihuacan last Sunday in an attempt to do a rapid survey of conditions. This is essential in selecting a community. . . . We are going to Tepoztlán today with Julio de la Fuente, who is in my opinion by far the best trained and most capable person around here in . . . social science. Unfortunately for this project he is leaving for the States on a fellowship obtained for him by Redfield and Tax.

. . . we are still faced by the problem of choosing two communities. In this regard Comas insisted that the project would have no practical significance for the Institute at all if we didn't choose two communities which were of the same historical background, same geography, same language, but of different degrees of acculturation. Only in this way, he believes, will we be in a position to determine the effects of government policy upon the lives of the natives. This would indeed be a neat comparative set-up but it adds many difficulties. It would mean going a long way from Mexico City, and having to live in a more or less isolated area where the necessary doctors to examine the subjects would not be available. Furthermore if we chose a really unacculturated community for comparative [reasons] there would not be a large enough number of individuals who could speak Spanish thereby adding to the difficulties of administering the tests. Then there is the matter of health conditions. Mrs. Lewis will not take the baby to malaria country. Dysentery was bad enough. I have therefore suggested a compromise and I think we will choose Tepoztlán which is now on the main tourist highway and compare it with a village near Tepoztlán which is still three hours distance and only accessible by horse, has no lights, newspapers, radios, movies, etc.

Finally I am convinced, and [in] this Comas and Gamio agree entirely, that the project as written up passed much too lightly over the question of getting an adequate background picture of the communities. It was assumed that two communities could be found for which there was adequate background material. This is not the case. Redfield's book, for example, was written in 1926, long before the road and tourist and other influences were at work in Tepoztlán. Furthermore, Redfield's interest was very selective and his material of [the] most general sort. It will be necessary to devote more time to the background study. . . .

. . . Another matter concerns the item of the coordinator of the project. Since we will be doing one community at a time I am cutting out the job of the coordinator thereby saving 7,000 pesos according to the budget, but actually only 3,000, for again the commitment of the Mexican agencies on this score was ephemeral. However it will be essential to have someone guide, plan, and work with the group. Mrs. Lewis will therefore be in charge in the field and I will take over the job of coordinating the work. I will go to the field each weekend, review the data gathered and hold group sessions with the field workers. I find that I also have to do most of the planning as to the detailed information we want the workers to get. I plan to use some of the money saved by cutting out the coordinator's job to pay field workers who might not otherwise be available to us.

. . . It seems to me that the major part of the energies of the personnel here is devoted to getting out the two publications of the [Interamerican Indian] Institute. I too am now involved in this work and the translating to be done from Spanish to English is piling up. . . . I don't want to be merely a highly paid translator here.

1. Ruben Borbolla was professor of anthropology at the National School of Anthropology and History.

3. *Oscar Lewis to Robert Redfield, anthropologist, November 9, 1943*

You will be interested to know, I am sure, that after much discussion and a few rapid surveys of suggested communities we have decided upon Tepoztlán and the nearby village of Santo Domingo [1] [Ocotitlán] as the two communities for our personality study.

Mrs. Lewis and I, accompanied by Julio de la Fuente, visited Tepoztlán just the other day. We were impressed by the beauty of your "first love" and by the friendliness and warmth of the Tepoztecans. From there we went to [Ocotitlán] by horse. Though it was only a two hour trip, the contrast, at least superficially, between Tepoztlán and [Ocotitlán] was impressive. The most glaring differences were the lack of good lands, the poverty, the differences in house types and the layout of the village. [Ocotitlán] gave us the sad feeling of being years and years behind Tepoztlán, but, for this very reason, it is suitable for our purposes.

The Kirchoffs were our hosts in Tepoztlán and were of real assistance.[2] They have introduced us to one Vicente Campos a native and resident of Tepoztlán who is the senator for [the state of] Morelos and much beloved by the Tepoztecans. Campos is eager to have us work in Tepoztlán.

. . . there is no study of [Ocotitlán]. So . . . we will have to [do] the ethnography there from the ground up. I believe also, that it will be necessary to study the changes which may have occurred in Tepoztlán since you were there and to fill in whatever additional background material is necessary for our purposes. In this connection, have you any unpublished material that you could make available to us. I believe that you and Mrs. Redfield have published various articles on Tepoztlán, in addition to your book, which will be our primary source of information, but I am not familiar with the sources of publication.

I have run into the difficult problem of getting adequate personnel for our study. . . . Would it be possible for you to arrange for an advanced student to do field work here on a cooperative basis? Such a student could work either in Tepoztlán or [Ocotitlán]. . . .

I realize that a request for cooperative work of this type in anthropological field work is perhaps unusual. However, I believe it might work out very well in this case. . . . Should you seriously consider this suggestion let me say that anyone sent down here would have a wide choice of subject matter and would be free to publish independently, if this were desired.

. . . I should like very much to keep you posted on our progress and with your permission to discuss our problems with you as they arise. . . .

1. In all his early references to this village Lewis called it Santo Domingo, presumably its non-Indian name. I have substituted Ocotitlán to avoid confusion with the barrio of Santo Domingo, which formed part of the village of Tepoztlán.
2. Paul Kirchoff was a German anthropologist who taught in Mexico City and kept

a summer home in Tepoztlán. Kirchoff was divorced from the woman Lewis refers to here and later married the anthropologist Esperanza Domínguez Reina, Ruth Lewis's assistant in Tepoztlán.

4. *Ruth Lewis to Laura Thompson, anthropologist and coordinator of the Indian personality project, November 13, 1943*

The question of personnel has been a source of difficulty. Caso has granted us four students who will be free to work only during their vacation, which amounts to 45 working days. None of the students have had field experience and their preparation at the University is entirely inadequate for our project. Two of them, men, are physical anthropologists with no ethnological training at all. The other two, women, have had work in linguistics and demography, with only one poor course in ethnology. To make matters worse they all have examinations from the 15th to the 30th of November, which allows little or no time to prepare them. We are insisting that they read at least Redfield on Tepoztlán. This is not as simple as it sounds because there is no translation and the students do not read English. Dr. Lewis has found it necessary to read the book with them for one hour a day. He is also planning to give them 5 or 6 lectures between now and December 1. He is writing up a plan of work, containing specific instructions, outlines, etc. for each student and the burden of supervising them will also fall upon him. . . . He will also go to the field for two days each week to review the data obtained and to direct the research. I am preparing the material for the social workers and will supervise their work in the field. I will be in charge of all the psychological aspects of the study.

5. *Oscar Lewis to Ernest Maes, November 29, 1943*

Our project is turning out to be much more than a personality study. After much work I have succeeded in getting the cooperation of many government agencies, including some who had no previous knowledge of our project. Today I obtained the promise of getting two agronomists from the Department Agrario for a period of two or three months. They will study the soils of both communities, the flora and fauna, problems of water supply, agricultural techniques, etc. The Department of Statistics has given me two workers, full time, to copy the results of the 1940 census for our two communities. This will take at least two weeks. All in all I am delighted with the cooperation I have been getting from Mexican government agencies. My only fear is that the project may get too big in scope and will demand more time than I can possibly give it, what with my other work of translation, attending to correspondence, etc. . . .

We rented a house in Tepoztlán for Mrs. Lewis. She is leaving for the field on December 5th, only a few days hence, and I am busy with last minute preparations, buying the necessary furniture, getting equipment for the group, etc. I have been chasing around the government agencies trying to borrow field equipment, cots, lamps, stoves, etc. but no luck so far.

6. *Oscar Lewis to Ernest Maes, December 17, 1943*
. . . I am enclosing another copy of the budget, somewhat revised in form and one which I believe will take care of the difficulties you pointed out in the tentative version I had sent you. You were correct in surmising that the salaries for many of the workers were only supplementing and this explains the seeming discrepancy between the salary of Mrs. Lewis and the others. . . .

I do not understand what you mean by your reference to Mrs. Lewis as a part time worker. You should know that hers is a full time job. She has to give about 300 Rorschach tests and the same number of other tests. One person can give on the average of 3 to 4 Rorschachs daily and it takes about two hours to score each one. This does not include the interpretation of each test which is a much longer job and will have to wait for the write-up. So much for the Rorschach, but then there are all the other tests to score and interpret, not to mention case histories, etc. Mrs. Lewis is training two students to help out with the administration of the Thematic Apperception Test. In my absence during the week she is helping to direct the work. Our house is the meeting place for all the workers. They come each night from the various barrios to type up their field notes and to discuss their problems.

Forgive this somewhat lengthy discourse on Mrs. Lewis. Frankly, I find it very uncomfortable . . . being put into the position of justifying her work in any way. . . .

Another question you raise concerns my including write-up money in the budget. I thought I had made it clear in my past letters to you that I not only agreed to write up the social, economic, and political material as part of my job here, but also that I considered it a real privilege and that I am looking forward to this work with great enthusiasm. However, I am not a psychologist and if the project is to really be a personality study, a large part of the material, if not the bulk . . . must be psychological material. I thought, therefore, that Mrs. Lewis should write up her own materials which will include test results, case histories, and a general analysis of what it all means. Another consideration is the matter of time and a reasonable division of labor. It seems to me that I will have my hands full writing up the background material. I think Dr. Gamio is in complete agreement on this matter.

7. *Oscar Lewis to Ernest Maes, December 21, 1943*

It seems to me that on the whole my relationship with Gamio is excellent; with Comas just fair. There has been only one source of trouble and that began a long time ago. Shortly after I arrived in Mexico City, Gamio, Comas, Mrs. Lewis and myself got together to discuss the personality project. In the course of the conversation a number of theoretical and even academic subjects came up among which were the value of physical anthropology and bio-typology and the possible contribution of these . . . to our study. I said quite frankly that I did not see what contribution physical anthropology could make to this study, especially since we were getting the services of a doctor to check the general health and physical condition of our subjects. The subject then turned to the broader question of what contribution physical anthropology can make to the solution of Indian problems and whether or not the Institute should sponsor such studies. I see now that this discussion was a mistake on my part. I did not know at the time that Comas was essentially a specialist in physical anthropology. Comas took our differences of opinion very seriously and personally was offended. Following the discussion his attitude toward me became much cooler. Since then we have been getting along well enough in our work but I sense a lack of warmth which is regrettable. Gamio told me later that it was undiplomatic of me to have been so critical of physical anthropology. However, it did not occur to me at the time that Gamio too might have been offended for he identified with the position of Comas. I felt that Gamio was just on the verge of seeing the relative unimportance of cephalic indices, etc. in comparison to real cultural studies but he must have relapsed to the old Mexican tradition of which he has been a part for so many years. At any rate Gamio suggested that we include a study of physical anthropology as part of our personality study and when I asked for an explanation of the relationship of such data with the objectives of our study he just couldn't show one. When I repeated this two or three times on different occasions he finally got sore and reminded me that he was the director and that he would decide what was important and what was unimportant. So that's that.

I was disappointed that these discussions should have given rise to a bit of tension. However, the harm done was not entirely avoidable and in any case was not of such importance as could not be smoothed out very easily.

One of the problems involved is a clearer understanding of my job here. I had assumed that when an issue of scientific importance came up that I was to try to influence the thinking here along lines that seemed wisest. Of course I realize now the dangers involved in this attitude. It may be that Gamio viewed my job here as an alround [*sic*] clerk who would help with the translations and with answering letters in English. As a matter of fact he once told me that that was what he thought I had come for. But his attitude has changed. He seems delighted with the broader scope of the study and wants me to work hard on it. Gamio wants me to take complete responsibility for the results of the study. . . .

Gamio's enthusiasm reached a high peak today when he thought of the idea of introducing soybeans to Tepoztlán as part of our project. This came about after a discussion in which I suggested that we try to do something practical for the people of Tepoztlán, such as getting the government to pipe water to the village from a nearby source. His soy bean idea may be good. I prefer that it wait until we have collected some data on the food habits of the people. I also fear that it will mean taking the time of some of our workers from collecting psychological materials to teaching the Tepoztecans new food habits. However, far be it from me to cross Gamio on soybeans!

8. *Oscar Lewis to Robert Redfield, December 31, 1943*

Field work . . . in Tepoztlán began in early December. Six students are now in the field and are to be joined shortly by six others. Following your lead we have organized the research on a barrio basis, and a field worker has established residence with a family in each barrio. Your observation that the barrio differences may be of the same magnitude as the differences between Tepoztlán and [Ocotitlán] is very interesting. The fact of the road in Tepoztlán since 1935 may have changed the picture somewhat. I expect we shall soon have some data on this question. We have made considerable progress in the collection and analysis of data on population distribution, number and size of families, vital statistics, social and economic levels in the population, indices of acculturations, (all on a barrio basis) and other essential background data for selecting our families and individuals for more intensive psychological study.

9. *Oscar Lewis to Ernest Maes, January 12, 1944*

I was glad to receive your letter of Jan. 3rd and to learn that you liked the memorandum on the project. You were correct in describing the section on soy beans as an after thought for that is exactly how it happened. I had completed writing the memo when in discussion with Gamio the soybean idea came up. . . . However, the idea will certainly be thoroughly integrated with the rest of the program and will become a very important part of the project. I have just managed to get 50 kilos of soy bean free from Assistencia y Salubridad, as well as a doctor and a mid-wife who will go to Tepoztlán. The need for a doctor . . . was urgent. Their own curanderos charge exhorbitant prices and the people have no confidence in them. In addition to the beneficial services that the community will now receive our project will also gain for this should be proof of our intentions to help them. As I reported earlier, the lack of confidence on the part of the people is our greatest field handicap.

10. *Oscar Lewis to Ernest Maes, January 24, 1944*

We had our first meeting of the old men of the barrios yesterday and it was a tremendous success. The Tepoztecans are so eager to learn new techniques of all sorts. They responded beautifully to the plan to introduce soy beans. Dr. Gamio visited Tepoztlán on Saturday and attended a meeting of the workers. I believe he is very hopeful about the outcome of the study, despite all the handicaps we face.

11. *Oscar Lewis to Ernest Maes, February 11, 1944*

I suppose there are a number of factors that explain the enthusiastic response of the Mexican government agencies to our project. There are some good people in government departments who are aware of the needs of the Indians and how little is being done to help them at present. These people have realized the merit of our project and of the Institute and have pitched in enthusiastically. . . .

You say that you assume that I am keeping a minute description of all the difficulties encountered. There is no time for such procedures. It takes more time than I have got to solve problems as they arise. Personnel is still the *big* problem. Unfortunately I spent a great deal of my time running around to government agencies to get people for our project. I sometimes find this exasperating. The amount of time lost waiting to see Ministers and other jefes is shameful. But there is no getting around this procedure. Another difficulty is the way people don't keep their appointments, from students up to department heads. I have never been "stood up" so often in my life. . . .

There has been another last minute delay in getting the agronomists (two young students just out of agricultural school who have never had field experience) because of some internal difficulties in the Departmento Agrario. Then there was also a further delay in getting the doctors. This . . . is much more serious for we had promised the Tepoztecans doctors and each day they keep asking Ruth and the other workers, "When are the doctors coming? Is this another government promise?" I am still hopeful. It is only a matter of time. In short, any serious project in Mexico . . . must reckon liberally with the time factor. . . . The two month commission of the four students from Caso's Institute is up. Two of the four have left and I am trying to hold on to the other two for an additional month, but I doubt if I can. The promised social workers, who were officially commissioned three weeks ago and are theoretically at our disposal have still not begun work.

12. *Oscar Lewis to Ernest Maes, February 28, 1944*

Last week a delegation of five Tepoztecos came to the Institute to seek our help on a matter of great importance to them, a boundary quarrel. This was the first time a delegation of Indians came to the Inter-American Indian Institute and Dr. Gamio and I were quite thrilled about it. Its significance for the project was even more exciting for it indicated that we have won the confidence of the people. The extent to which we now have their confidence was shown by an incident which occurred in Tepoztlán. The agronomist who arrived . . . last week began to visit a few homes with a questionnaire I had prepared. After a few hours he returned very sad and depressed for he claimed that the people refused to give him the necessary data. We then revisited these families in the company of some of the other workers and explained that we were all of the same project, etc. The reaction was wonderful and the agronomist is now much happier.

I have finally gotten a doctor to begin the physical examinations of our subjects. He is going to Tepoztlán with me on Thursday. He will work only two days a week. I think the job will take about three months.

Let me list some of the minor difficulties I've run into this week.

1. One of the agronomists commissioned for us died three days before he was scheduled to begin work.

2. We lost two of the commissioned social workers (sisters) because one learned that she had a tumor on an ovary and has to be operated. She refuses to allow her kid sister to go out to the wilds of Tepoztlán alone.

3. The agronomist who is now working in Tepoztlán heard that there were guano deposits in the nearby hills and cooked up a scheme of going into business for himself. . . . He had to be straightened out and told in no uncertain terms that if guano did exist it would have [to] be exploited by and in the interests of Tepoztlán. Incidentally this would be a miraculous solution for the lack of fertilizer and the low production. An expedition was organized yesterday to investigate and I will tell you soon if there is gauno around.

4. The man who was hired on the recommendation of Chavez Orozco[1] to do some library research on the history of Tepoztlán hasn't showed up for three weeks. He was supposed to have a conference with me each Thursday. I have searched the city for him without success. . . .

5. One of the field workers . . . turned out to be a politician and soap box speech maker. He began to harangue the Tepoztecos on how grateful they should be that he was sacrificing his good time to study their way of life, etc.

6. A young man recommended to us . . . turned out to be a rabid Nazi, one of the past leaders of the Nazi youth movement in Mexico. We learned of this after he had been working for a few weeks in Tepoztlán . . . [and] he was dropped delicately so as not to offend his friend [the anthropologist who had recommended him]. . . .

1. Luis Chávez Orozco, Mexican historian and former Ambassador to Honduras, served as first President of the Executive Committee of the Interamerican Indian Institute.

13. *Ruth Lewis to Laura Thompson, March 6, 1944*

Dr. Lewis has managed to contact the man who was the informant for Malinowski and Julio de la Fuente in Oaxaca. We expect him to arrive some time next month. He will be a field worker here and will be valuable in giving us a comparative point of view. We also have a doctor who is willing to come here two days a week to examine the children in school.

So far we have given the Goodenough test, the free drawings, and two workers are giving the Grace-Arthur and the Thematic Apperception tests. Also, we broke down the Autobiography into 10 Themes and assigned them as compositions. The results are very interesting. Much delay has been caused in the giving of the Emotional Response and the Moral Ideology tests because of the necessity of translating and mimeographing the answer forms. We are still awaiting them. I devote myself to giving the Rorshachs and have completed 80 to date. Unfortunately many here are extremely slow in reaction time and also I have encountered a good number of anxiety and compulsive types, which as you know are very time consuming.

14. *Oscar Lewis to Ernest Maes, March 9, 1944*

Practically all of the 26 questions set down in the instructions for the agronomist which I sent you were suggested by problems in the field. We had learned in advance as a result of various meetings with the members of the barrios of Tepoztlán of certain specific difficulties they were having; they complained that their corn lasted only seven or eight months because of insects eating it away. . . . Their ciruela trees are infected with insects and other pests, etc. The job of the agronomist is therefore to examine these specific complaints, study the problems and make practical suggestions and demonstrations of how to deal with it.

I am troubled that you got the impression that the work assigned to the agronomist was not integrated with our total study. . . .

In going through the archives and files in the Dept. Agrario I learned that many problems of administration arose because of the failure to understand clearly the property concepts of Tepoztlán. It has never been clearly established whether each of the seven villages of the municipio owns its own communal lands or whether the municipio owns it. Two problems are involved here. One is the legal problem of titles, the other the traditional and functional use of the lands. It seems to me that [in] practice each village exploited the land in its vicinity and although theoretically a man from [a] village had the right to use any portion of the communal land this was not the case because of distances involved, etc. In 1930, for example, one of the villages organized a Forestry Coop., claiming that the nearby mts. belonged to the village. The Department of Forestry granted a license to this village without investigating the traditional concepts of communal land. At once a conflict began between the cabecera of the municipio and this village which lasted five years and ended in bloodshed. You see, then, that the data sought . . . is not an isolated bit of formal information but is related to special problems with which we are already familiar.

. . . Each plot of land in Tepoztlán has a name in [Nauhuatl]. I hope . . . to be able to 1) localize all the plots, establish distances between the homes of individuals and their land, which is in some cases . . . more than five kilometers; 2) reconstruct the history of land ownership and check the extent to which the prehispanic calpulli still survives. If for example we were to find that the larger portion of the plots of the barrio of Los Reyes are concentrated within a given area and are owned by related families it would indicate that [the] kinship basis of the old calpulli has still remained to the present. Such a fact would have importance on the administrational level. It would suggest that services of various kinds be organized on a barrio basis rather than a village basis, or that the two be better integrated.

These questions are also intended to yield data on whether wealth and possibly class differences (for class lines are very blurred) cut across barrios or have a barrio basis. There are three grades of land. . . . We hope to be able to find out how these types are distributed among the various barrios.

In the same manner the other questions [on the project outline] were asked with a definite frame of reference in mind and not as "catch-alls" [as suggested by Maes in criticizing the scope of Lewis's research plan].

The big news of this week is that we have finally gotten a doctor. He has an office in Tepoztlán and I have had a sign made saying: Consultario Medico, Instituto Indigenista Interamericano.

I am planning on forming a medical cooperative in Tepoztlán. I talked about this to the Coordinator of Medical Services of the State of Morelos. He was enthusiastic and agreed to render all help possible, for if it works he wants to introduce similar co-operatives throughout the State of Morelos. We have already had one meeting in Tepoztlán and have called a community wide meeting for Sunday. The plan is something like this. Each family will be asked to contribute one peso per visit, including medicine, injections, etc. This is a very modest sum compared to the fees of ten to 100 pesos charged by the curanderos. A committee of Tepoztecos representing each barrio will be formed. We will print tickets in duplicate which will be sold at our house. Each patient must present a numbered ticket to the doctor or rather to his Secretary, the idea being to have the administering [in] the hands of the Institute for the duration of our study and then pass it on to the committee. We will meet with the committee every two weeks to discuss the problems of finances and have them check income, expenses, etc.

We have already learned much about Tepoztecan concepts of disease, both from Redfield's work and from our own. One novel aspect of the set up will be that the doctor is to take down textually the patient's analysis of his disease. I am trying to get across to the doctor the importance of utilizing the native concepts in order to establish more confidence. Let me give you an example of how this might work. In Tepoztlán one classification of diseases is into "hot . . ." and "cold. . . ." The other day I took a very sick infant . . . to the doctor in Cuernavaca. The doctor injected the baby, while the mother watched her heat the needle to sterilize it. The next day the baby died and the explanation of the mother was simple. The baby had a "hot disease" and the doctor instead of injecting something cold to counteract the heat injected something "hot", so of course the baby died. In the future when our doctor knows that the patient has something "hot" he must explain that he will inject something very "cold", etc. If we can gain their confidence in this way we can later teach them more scientific rationalizations. . . .

Another addition to our study occurred to me and I am trying to get somebody to work on it. There is a colony of Tepoztecans here in Mexico City composed of about 200 families. Many of them came to Mexico during the Revolution, others have come since. From time to time these people visit their relatives in Tepoztlán. Visiting has increased since 1935 because of the good road. I want to study the influence of these "city people" on Tepoztlán and vice-versa. Furthermore, Mexico City now has a population of about two million. Of these at least a million are from the out-skirts, from rural areas. In this sense the colony of Tepoztecans may be representative of many country people who came to Mexico. We should know what happens to these people when they come to the city. . . . I have already been promised two workers from Asistencia to help me on this. We will begin with a simple questionnaire covering age, sex, address, occupation, date left Tepoztlán and why, number and names of relatives in Tepoztlán, land ownership in Tepoztlán (there is absentee ownership in some cases), social relations with . . . compadres, etc., occupation, size of family (in comparison with the size of families in Tepoztlán), no. of persons working in each family, material culture of household, type of food eaten, and a few other items. Tepoztlán has many proud sons in the city who are lawyers, doctors, dentists, etc. We must find out under what circumstances these people might consider going back and doing something for their people.

There has been some progress with the soy bean experiment. I took some soy beans out to Tepoztlán last week and started our cook and a few neighbors on making pinole, gordas, and tortillas. They turned out very tasty and the people showed great enthusiasm in learning how to make these products. We are planning to serve soy bean derivatives this Sunday at the meeting and to organize a soy bean dinner on Indian Day, April 19th. The agronomist with the aid of our other workers who know more about Tepoztlán by now, have chosen an experimental plot where soy beans will be planted. We may have to wait for the rainy season to begin, which means waiting until June. . . .

In rereading your letter I note your reference to methodology. This reminds me to tell you of the kind of anthropology we are using in just one sample case. Tepoztlán, like other municipalities has its own records. Unfortunately they go back only to the late twenties. Very early in our study we checked these records for property ownership and arranged the owners into lists according to barrio membership and into categories according to the size of ownership. It was immediately apparent that these figures could not be used without some further checking. [A] questionnaire was therefore made up, a copy of which I am enclosing. The field workers were asked to visit the same people listed as property owners in the town records and without telling the informants that we already had data on them, to ask for the various information we needed. We will then compare these two results and thereby determine the reliability of the written records. We have used similar techniques for other aspects of the investigation, and Mrs. Lewis is using similar scientific checks and cross checks in gathering personality data. . . .

The medical clinic and cooperative we are planning in Tepoztlán raises problems which are related to the program of teaching curanderos, which you have underway. Unlike conditions among the Navahos and other Indian tribes, the curanderos in Tepoztlán by and large have little or no prestige; many of them are hated for their exorbitant fees, and in the past a few have been killed. . . . They will no doubt resent our medical venture and will propagandize against it for it is a direct threat to their economic interests. In a community like Tepoztlán which is only 18 kilometers from Cuernavaca and 85 from Mexico, and has excellent roads it would be unwise to go in for the training of curanderos for three or six months. A medical clinic with a trained M.D. is much wiser. However, all depends upon how permanent this clinic will be. If after three or four months the doctor leaves it would put the curanderos in a new position of power, and would enable them to charge what they like. I think the State of Morelos should plan on a permanent set up in Tepoztlán. Otherwise we will have to play ball with the curanderos.

15. *Oscar Lewis to Ernest Maes, March 17, 1944*

The big news of the week is that we have formed a medical cooperative in Tepoztlán. Last Sunday we had a meeting of more than 150 Tepoztecan men and women and it was a great success. I wish you and the Commissioner could have been present on this occasion. It was a thrilling example of how democracy might work in this pueblo which has anything but a democratic tradition and which is at present in the throes of a local government imposed by the governor of the state. The meeting was not called by the municipal authorities despite the frequent promises of the president of the Municipio that he would. . . . Fact is he had called a meeting of the Union of Revolutionaries (Zapatists) and no one attended that very morning. The people had little confidence in their local government. Too often in the past meetings have been called only for the people to find that it was for propaganda purposes, to elect some local deputy, etc. However, I made a point of getting the president to attend our session, even though he sat up in front of the group, obviously uneasy and doing nothing.

A central medical committee was elected consisting of seven members, one from each barrio (note that we are utilizing the old barrio unit rather than the current political unit known as the demarcación) for within each barrio there is still some semblance of popular spirit, if not of true democracy. In addition sub-committees consisting of three members were elected in each barrio. A directive body consisting of Pres., Sec't Treasurer, and Vocals [was] also elected.

I had a long talk with Dr. Viniegra, head of the Rural Section of Salubridad. He is ready to help this cooperative and showed great enthusiasm for the work. However the aspect that interested him most was the idea of utilizing native therapeutic and medical beliefs as a means of gaining the confidence of the villagers. I showed him the form I had drawn up for use of the doctor . . . that is in addition to the clinical medical form. The form calls for a textual account of the history of the disease from the patient, whether or not he visited curanderos, the diagnosis of the curanderos, the fees paid them, the remedies used, whether or not the compadres were visited before going to the curanderos, etc. This will be followed by a thorough medical examination. We will then compare the diagnosis of the patient with that of the doctor and hope to . . . better understand the rationale behind native concepts. We will also have the doctor use native concepts wherever possible. . . .

Dr. Viniegra was so sold on this idea that he at once made the following offer. Medical students have to serve a six month training period in the field as a requirement for their degree, that is after they have completed their four year medical course. Each year about 300 students go into the field. Viniegra asked the Institute to draw up a list of Indian villages that needed medical attention and promised to assign students to these locations. The students would be asked to use the questionnaires I have prepared or better yet a fuller questionnaire. . . . It is imperative to get across to the doctors the importance of native concepts and to rid them of their attitudes of superiority as well as condescencion towards native beliefs. . . .

16. *Oscar Lewis to Ruth Benedict, anthropologist, April 26, 1944*

When I arrived in Mexico with Ruth and Gene last October, I was under the impression that my job would be a fairly easy administrative position, editing of the Bulletin, the pleasantries of a goodwill mission, siestas, Mexican beer, cocktail parties, etc. Instead, I soon found myself directing a large scale research project in Tepoztlán . . . and commuting back and forth to Mexico City each weekend. . . . My long awaited Latin American field trip certainly came with a bang. And what a wonderful way to do field work. Perhaps this is the way future field work should be done. Certainly the days of the anthropologist as a one-man expedition must be over. . . .

One of the most interesting and novel aspects of our project is the combination of a practical program of aid to the people with a scientific study. . . . These practical measures have been of great help in establishing rapport, but even more important, it has given us an opportunity to observe behavior in a more or less controlled experimental situation. The analysis of their reactions to our action program will, I am sure, yield some of the most important insights into the culture and psychology of Tepoztecans. The instances which provoked our greatest difficulties were the ones which taught us most. . . .

We are amazed at the diagnostic value of the Rorshach. The Thematic Apperception on the other hand seems most valuable for the incidental cultural material it yields. . . .

I now appreciate some of your comments at the lunch we had in Wash. [D.C.] before I left. Social science [here] is indeed years behind the States. Anthropology still consists primarily of archeology (tourist trade and American money are not to be sneezed at), physical anthropology and historical reconstruction of the good old Aztec days. This purely historical bent of anthropology is especially unfortunate in Mexico because of the immediacy and urgency of the Indian problem. A functional, cultural anthrop. could make a great contrib. on a national scale if only it began to study the living peoples. And they might very well begin in Mexico City. . . .

My work has brought me in contact with gov't officials, ministers, governors, senators, ingenieros, licenciados, reporters & students, and from it all I am trying to make up my mind about Mexico. But more of this when I see you. One thing is certain. I have found anti-American sentiment widespread & strong, from the liberals & leftists to the conservatives, reactionaries, Sinarquists, etc. Most alarming is that this sentiment is not just limited to the cities. You can find it in almost any campesino village. Nazi-Sinarquist elements have been & are playing upon the prejudice & ignorance of the peasantry. But it is especially griping to find so many anti-American teachers in the Instituto de Historia & Anthropologia, considering how much American dough is being pumped into this institution. Sometimes it makes me feel that we are suckers!

. . . Collier was down here for a few days and we had a swell time. He is a wonderful "boss." Whatever he may lack from the pt. of view of an academic anthrop. he certainly makes up for with good will & good intentions. The news which he brought about the internal domestic front at home was certainly depressing.

17. *Oscar Lewis to Ernest Maes, March 23, 1944*

I have been in Tepoztlán all of this week with a bad case of grippe that was first diagnosed as malaria. My presence . . . was a good thing for the project. I had felt for some time that I should be spending more time in the field checking up on the work and doing some field work on my own. This week gave me that opportunity, though somewhat inadvertently. The workers brought their reports in and I read them in bed in between shots of quinine and doses of aspirin.

I decided to use Tepoztecans as field workers in addition to informants. A few of them are turning out to be good field workers and some of them have the makings of sociologists. In some cases they are doing much better and more rapid work than some of our own field workers.

The two social workers are now in full swing and Ruth is simply delighted with their work. For the first time she is getting the type of case history material she has been yearning for. . . .

18. *Oscar Lewis to John Collier, U.S. commissioner of Indian Affairs, May 5, 1944*

I returned from my vacation somewhat rested only to find that Mrs. Lewis . . . had been ill for a week in Tepoztlán with very high fever and was being treated for malaria with no improvement. I brought her to Mexico where we learned that she had typhus and paratyphoid, a rare and dangerous combination. She still has a sort of undulating fever and is terribly weak but I believe the real danger is fortunately past. The doctor says she will have to be laid up for at least a month and must take it easy after that. What with my draft pending this further delay of our work is most unfortunate. . . .

19. *Ruth Lewis to Laura Thompson, July 13, 1944*

. . . The Thematics were sent to Mr. Maes by diplomatic pouch last week. You should have received them by now. I had to do all the translating, with someone's help, because no one knew Tepoztecan Spanish here. It took a great deal of time. Now I am translating and preparing some Rorschachs to send to Dr. Klopfer and Dr. Joseph, another time-consuming job.[1] We have begun the analysis of some of the other tests but because I was so occupied I couldn't do very much with them as yet. The Moral Judgment test has me somewhat stumped; I do not know exactly what to do with it. I hope one of the papers Dr. Havighurst sends will be helpful. . . .

In regard to the Thematics, I had thought that a group analysis of the majority, and an individual analysis of only those for which we have case histories, would be sufficient, especially if there is a shortage of time. If we could get a picture of general trends or tendencies which we could relate to cultural factors, it would fulfill our purposes well enough. . . .

My husband . . . had his physical two weeks ago but was not told definitely whether . . . he would be taken. The doctor who examined him said he would probably not be drafted but we are deliberately keeping ourselves up in the air until we hear from the draft board. . . .[2]

1. Alice Joseph studied the Papago Indians for the Indian Education Research Project.
2. Due to a scarred eardrum from a childhood accident Lewis was never drafted.

20. *Oscar Lewis to Robert Redfield, November 4, 1946*

. . . It seems to me that the study of wealth differences in simpler societies and its role in social organization has heretofore been neglected. I have been able to find no references in the literature to studies of wealth differences. Do you happen to know of any I could use for comparative purposes in my article ["Wealth Differences in Tepoztlán"]?

21. *Oscar Lewis to George Foster, anthropologist, October 16, 1947*

. . . I was especially interested and, I must admit, surprised to read your comments on the question of vertical mobility. As I see it, there are two aspects to the problem and I have put them in the form of two separate questions. First, what percentage of people in any society can manage to get to the top and, second, how did the people who are at the top at any one time get there? Now when I say that there is limited vertical mobility in Tepoztlán, I refer primarily to the first precept, namely, that only 4.4% of all heads of families had gotten to the top. This, to me, is a powerful index of the lack of vertical mobility, especially since I can prove that the great majority of the young people in the village today stand very little chance of getting into the top class. On the other hand, I have myself pointed out that of the thirty odd families now in class three, half of them have gotten there by their own hard work and the other half through inheritance of property. Now if one were to define vertical mobility only in terms of the question, how do the people on top (irrespective of how few) get there, then one could justifiably say that there is considerable vertical mobility in Tepoztlán. Indeed, I am making quite a point about the fact that there is much more vertical mobility now than there was before the Mexican Revolution. However, the wide range of wealth between the lower and the upper groups and the heavily weighted distribution on the lower ends indicates that few people can get to the top.

22. *Oscar Lewis to Carl Taylor, U.S. Bureau of Agricultural Economics, April 20, 1948*

. . . In your letter you asked for my opinion of Redfield's article on the Folk Society. I had read this article some time ago in mimeographed form and have been using it in my classes as one of the clearest and most systematic expositions of the concept of the ideal type. However, I believe that the ideal type concept has some serious weaknesses and one needs to be very careful in using it. For one thing, the concept of the folk society assumes a homogeneity and integration in primitive societies which is hard to find in real situations. Certainly Tepoztlán is not now and for the past four hundred years has not been a folk culture. I have documentary evidence to show the population of Tepoztlán back in 1550 was greater than at any time since then. In rereading Redfield's Tepoztlán I get the impression that he may have gone into the village with the preconceived notion that Tepoztlán was a folk culture and perhaps it was this that prevented him from realizing sufficiently the great range of custom and belief found in the village.

. . . I am becoming convinced that . . . family case studies based upon living with the family and using interviews as well as projective psychological testing techniques such as Rorschach and Thematic Apperception tests offers an excellent way to build up inductively a picture of the total culture. It may mean however that we anthropologists must be satisfied with writing monographs on single families before we write tomes on entire cultures. You know, the idea that the family is the mediator of culture is an old one, but I have searched through the entire anthropological literature and have been unable to find a single intensive study of a family unit. The closest that we have come to this in anthropology has been autobiographies of individuals. While these autobiographies have shed much light on family affairs they are no substitute for a complete family study.

23. *Oscar Lewis to Robert Redfield, May 17, 1948*

. . . I should explain that since I last spoke to you I have decided that I would like to publish my family studies together with the material on the life cycle and other psychological data in a separate volume under a title which might be "Family Life in a Mexican Village." I am taking the liberty of sending you the enclosed partially completed study of one of the three or four families that I am planning to present in this book. I do hope that you and Mrs. Redfield, if possible, will get time to read it.

. . . In talking with Ruben Hill, an anthropologist who has specialized in the study of family in our own culture, he suggested that the kind of data which I have on Tepoztlán might have a wider audience than anthropologists and he suggested that Cottrell of Cornell University might be interested in my manuscript as a possible publication in the Knopf Social Science Series. If you feel that you can recommend the manuscript to Cottrell I would appreciate it since I do not know him personally. If I could get a commitment from a publisher at this early date, I would complete the manuscript this summer. Otherwise, I would prefer to work on the other volume dealing with their history, economic, social and political organization, and cultural changes in the village.

24. *Oscar Lewis to Robert Redfield, June 11, 1948*
. . . The description of culture patterns as it has traditionally been done by anthropologists is after all a relatively easy job. What is really difficult is to get at the meaning which custom has for the individuals who carry out the expected behavior patterns of the group and to get at the emotional reactions of the individuals both to the expected behavior and to their own transgressions of that behavior. In sending you the manuscript of the Rojas family as I did I gave you the second step without having given you the first step. Apparently that is why the materials failed to get across to you my primary objective, namely, to portray the members of the Rojas family as thinking and feeling human beings who reacted to their culture patterns each in their own way and in accord with their individual personality needs and in response to a great variety of situations. I also tried to get across the effects of traditional forms of behavior upon the character development of the individuals and upon inter-personal relationships. I thought that the materials even as presented without an explicit analysis showed these points.

. . . I do think that much of the unity and bonds of family life in Tepoztlán flow from what might be called negative factors rather than positive ones. What I mean is that in a village where most people are withdrawn and suspicious and view the world as a hostile place to live in, the family unit by comparison with the non-family represents a relatively close in-group and in this sense is a haven. But it would be missing many of the crucial aspects of Tepoztecan family life and the quality of human relationships in Tepoztlán not to see the great amount of internal tensions and conflict that exist, as well as the frustrations and maladjustments. Nor do I believe that this is to be explained entirely in terms of the break-down of an earlier folk culture. The idea that folk cultures produce less frustrations than non-folk cultures or that the quality of human relationships is necessarily superior in folk-cultures seems to me to be sheer Rousseauan romanticism and has not been documented to my knowledge. It is something like the idealization of rural life that I have read about in the work of rural sociologists. Of course, implicit in all that I have said is my belief that it is possible to have valid standards which cut across all cultures without thereby being ethnocentric, by which the quality of human relationships can be measured and appraised. I think that Fromm's recent book "Man for Himself" represents a step in this direction. And incidentally I find that much of Tepoztecan personality falls within the category which he calls the hoarding type.

25. *Oscar Lewis to Professor J. Cara Baroja, anthropologist (Madrid), November 8, 1948*

. . . In the course of my work, I have become aware of the need for a much fuller knowledge of Spanish cultural backgrounds if we are to better understand the great contribution of Spanish culture to Latin American civilization. It is, of course, a commonplace that much of Latin American civilization is a fusion of Indian and Spanish cultural elements. However, in doing anthropological studies in specific Indian communities, we are continually faced with the question of what is Indian and what is Spanish. While we can answer this question in regard to some of the more obvious elements of material culture, such as domesticated animals, plants, and agricultural practices and techniques, we are frequently at a loss when we attempt to distinguish between the Indian and the Spanish in the field of social organization and the everyday customs, beliefs, and attitudes of the people. It seemed to me that our lack of knowledge of 16th century rural Spain is one of our serious handicaps. Most of our knowledge of Spanish influences in Latin America has been derived from the study of literature and historical documents. Don't you think that it might be extremely useful to supplement this knowledge with detailed and well-rounded field studies in rural communities in contemporary Spain? Is it possible to find rural communities in Spain today in which there still persists much of the 16th and 17th century beliefs and customs?

. . . I have proposed a research program to my University, based on the assumption that study of contemporary rural Spanish culture would be a useful addition to our general ethnographic knowledge and specifically might help us to better understand some of the processes in the fusion of Indian and Spanish elements in Latin America. I was planning to begin the research this summer in a preliminary way by selecting a single village in some rural area of Spain. I would want to live with a peasant family and participate in their daily activities to the fullest extent possible. I wonder whether you would care to help me select a suitable village for my purpose. I would want a village located in a region whose climatic and environmental conditions were somewhat similar to those of the mesa central of Mexico, where I have done most of my work. For this reason I thought perhaps a village in one of the sierra regions would be desirable. I would also like to select a region from which cultural influences have been diffused to Mexico during the colonial period. I would very much like to have your suggestions on these matters.

26. *Oscar Lewis to Irving Hallowell, anthropologist, November 11, 1948*
. . . In the course of my field work in Tepoztlán I did a number of family case studies. I first thought of this procedure in an attempt to get at the wide range of variation in custom found in a village as large and complicated as Tepoztlán. Out of this work I have come to the conclusion that family case studies of the kind I did can be a very useful technique when used by anthropologists interested in the problem of culture and personality.

27. *Oscar Lewis to Leonard Cottrell, psychologist, November 24, 1948*
. . . I realized soon after my arrival in the village that it was much too large and complicated to be adequately studied by the traditional informant method and so I organized the entire project in terms of studying intensively representative families. . . . One of the results of the method used is that it has revealed a much wider range of custom and personality types than one would have expected to find in a so called "folk-culture."
. . . I know that the sociologists and social psychologists have said a great deal about the importance of studying the family but to my knowledge the studies have been piecemeal and rarely based upon living with the family and treating the family as if it were the culture. It is my own feeling that we anthropologists have gone too fast and too furious. We discovered that there was such a thing as culture patterns and everybody that goes into the field looks for them without even beginning to do the necessary spadework for arriving at a sound view of what the culture patterns are. Its all part of the emphasis upon speed in research these days. It is interesting that perhaps the best monographs in anthropology were written by missionaries and political exiles in Siberia who had little formal training but who lived with their peoples for 20 or more years, and really got to know them. I am suggesting that we lower our sights just a little and be satisfied to understand a few families in a village thoroughly, as a stepping stone towards the understanding of the total culture.

28. *Oscar Lewis to Paul Radin, anthropologist, May 15, 1949*
. . . Please remember that I want to avoid any personal controversy with Mr. Redfield. I don't want it ever to get down to the level of a Redfield versus Lewis bout. I have therefore attempted to explain as best I could the reasons for our differences, for it is this after all which

is the important lesson to be learned for restudies. I suppose that one of the basic reasons, and one that perhaps I need to develop further than I have, is that the response that one gets from informants is in large measure a function of what one is seeking . . . , in addition, that is, to other factors, such as personality differences. In other words, if one goes out into the field with the grand intention of seeking to learn what are the problems facing the people, economic, social, political, emotional . . . and if this is made clear to the people themselves, they are bound to bare their innards so to speak and talk about what is troubling them. Since I was employed by an action agency which was concerned with the problem of what might be done to raise the standard of living of rural Mexicans, I was naturally concerned with getting at the problems of the people. This led me to use quantitative methods, among others, for when an administrator sees a report he wants to know out of how many cases is so and so true. Just how many people own land, sleep on the floor, have T.B., etc., etc. I submit that most anthropological monographs are of little use to administrators just because we have concerned ourselves with describing esoteric customs, costumes, etc. and have not concerned ourselves sufficiently with getting to know the character of the people as human beings and their problems, and how widespread these problems are.

Now obviously Redfield's approach was quite different. Since he told the people he was primarily after their traditions and customs he tended to get an idealized version of life. This is not to excuse his sloppy field work, of course. However, I am suggesting that our differences are not merely due to ideological orientations. I suspect that Redfield had rosy colored glasses about primitive or rural peoples, in the first place. You know the point of view, the desire to escape facing the real problems of our times by seeing heaven or something better at any rate in the noble savages. Rousseau come to life in neo-evolutionism, of the Park, Durkheimian school.

On the other hand . . . I am planning to add a section to the chapter in which I point out all the ways in which Tepoztlán even today has the characteristics of what Redfield means by his "folk society."

29. *Oscar Lewis to Kimball Young, sociologist, March 21, 1950*
. . . Individuals are always solving problems in new and original ways. The notion that culture gives us ready-made solutions to problems should not be pushed too far lest we reduce individuals to automatons. This in a nutshell is my criticism of the anthropological use of the culture concept and that is why I have reacted positively to what you call the personal-social factor. I am hoping to give some real

thought to this problem during this summer when I will be completing my book on *Family Studies in a Mexican Village*.

I am planning to make a list of all the aspects of family life which cannot be [classified] as cultural and which must be explained in terms of specific historical situations and the interactions of individuals who live and work within the family.

30. *Oscar Lewis to Florence Kluckhohn, anthropologist, June 20, 1950*

. . . And your suggestion that we need to relate the analysis of cultural profiles or the value systems to the analysis of social structure points to one of the most crucial problems in which the sociologist and anthropologist might cooperate.

. . . Tepoztecans, too, are a people without a past or a future, psychologically speaking.[1] This seems to me to be all the more remarkable for a village that is ancient and dates back to about the time of Christ! There is hardly a Tepoztecan who could tell you who his great grandparents were. But the Nahuatl names of house sites have not changed since 1580, as I have been able to show by a study of early colonial documents.

1. This appears to be a conscious paraphrasing of Marx's dictum that peasants are people without a history.

31. *Oscar Lewis to Edward Spicer, anthropologist, July 10, 1950*

. . . Originally our project was to have been solely a research project, i.e. a well rounded study of the community with special emphasis upon problems in the field of culture and personality and culture change. However, after field work began and meetings of Tepoztecans were called to explain why we were there, we learned that the villagers wanted something practical. They said they would cooperate with our study if we would prove our good intentions by aiding them with their problems. They asked for a medical doctor, agronomists, and a new school. They complained bitterly about decreasing corn yields and about their inability to preserve the harvested corn from one season to the next because of the plague of insects and corn bugs. As director of the project, I conveyed this information to the Mexican government agencies in Mexico City, which were sponsoring our project. After some discussions doctors and agronomists were sent to the villages.

. . . I must confess that I did not share Dr. Gamio's enthusiasm [for the introduction of soybean cultivation] and did not view soy beans as the salvation of the agrarian problem. Rather, I saw the experiment as an excellent way of establishing better rapport with the villagers for our anthropological study.

32. *Oscar Lewis to Oliver LaFarge, writer and anthropologist, November 21, 1950*

. . . At the suggestion of Leonard S. Cottrell, Jr. of Cornell, ["Two Family Portraits"] was sent for a reading to Knopf, but they turned it down on the grounds that a volume of this type could not sell sufficient copies to justify their expense in printing it.

. . . My own feeling is that Knopf is missing a good bet and that materials of this kind might well find a wide audience, particularly if there were some reorganization and some rewriting along more popular lines. Any suggestions that you might care to give me along this track would be very much appreciated. I would be interested to know if you find these materials interesting enough to be used for a novel. Is there any form halfway between a novel and an anthropology report which might be used in this case?

33. *Oscar Lewis to Francis Hsu, anthropologist, March 10, 1951*

. . . I am working on a paper in which I have suggested some new conceptual distinctions in the culture-personality field, concepts which may help clear up some of the current confusion and also save anthropologists from the recent strong criticism such as appeared in the *American Sociological Review*. I have just had [O. Hobart] Mowrer read my paper and he thought I had something "hot". In fact he invited me to do a joint paper with him, combining the two-factor learning theory with my approach. We may work something out together within a few months. In the meantime the paper will appear as part of one of my chapters in *Life in a Mexican Village—Tepoztlán Restudied*. I call the thing "Private and Public Personality."

34. *Oscar Lewis to Fred Eggan, anthropologist, May 22, 1951*

Won't you please look over the enclosed copy of my paper on Public and Private Personality and pass the paper on to Mrs. Eggan. . . . Hobart Mowrer has asked to collaborate with me on it, that is, he would like to document my concepts from his clinical experience.

. . . Both psychologists (also psychiatrists) and anthropologists will probably say they are interested in the total personality. However, after reading the paper I think you will agree that each of our disciplines emphasizes one aspect of the total personality more than another. As an anthropologist I am frankly most concerned with the public aspect, overt and covert.

35. *Oscar Lewis to Gitel Steed, anthropologist, December 5, 1952*

. . . Shortly before leaving [the] States, I was very pleasantly surprised by a very nice research grant for my personal research needs, from the Ford Foundation. It may, therefore, be possible for me to combine some intensive field studies of my own, with this Pilot Study for the evaluation programme. Specifically, what I have in mind is to do a few intensive family studies of the kind that I did in Mexico. Ruth and I are now completing a rather lengthy volume on two Mexican families, and it would be wonderful to have a comparable study of two Indian families. In fact, I wondered what you would think about the advisability of my studying intensively, two families from your Muslim village near Aligarh. My notion is that, family studies should come after, or form part of, a broader community study.

. . . I am fascinated by the many similarities and differences between Mexican and Indian villages. I must say, that Mexican peasant social organisation seems remarkably simple, compared to what you have here. However, I suspect that there are many similarities on the psychological level.

36. *Oscar Lewis to Helen Codere, anthropologist, March 21, 1952*
. . . I am now comparing the impression of the Kwakiutl given by Boas with that derived from [Clellan Ford's] *Smoke from Their Fires.* Since you have undoubtedly examined the Boas materials more carefully than I have, I am writing for your help on the subject.

. . . Would you consider the following comparison just and sufficiently accurate to use in my paper:

"The major differences in the portrayal of the Kwakiutl by Boas and by Ford is that Boas is literal, descriptive, and not analytic in any psychological sense, whereas Ford combines both approaches. Ford gives one a much better feeling of what it is like to be a Kwakiutl. Boas contains long textual descriptions of ceremonies and rites.

Boas gives a picture of a rather ruthless, violent people, competitive to the utmost, destructive beyond their own good. Ford gives a very different picture. His Kwakiutl are competitive, at times violent (covertly) but underlying all of the hostility and anxiety is an organization which will not allow too much physical manifestation of these feelings, except in the regularized channels of the potlatch, sorcery and the dance. And so one is impressed with the rather peaceful and unwarlike disposition."

I wonder to what extent these differences in interpretation are due to the changes which have occurred among the Kwakiutl between the time Boas and Ford were there? Moreover, can it be that Boas was describing a functioning culture while Ford was using the glorified remembrances of an old man living in a broken down society?

†37. *Oscar Lewis to Ruth Lewis, n.d. (sometime in April 1954)*

Redfield talked to me in his office for an hour—passionately, like a defense attorney addressing a jury—telling me "how embarrassed" and "disturbed" he has been in my critique of his folk society *model*. He claims I misunderstood the nature and role of a model. He says a model can't be wrong!—and if empirical data don't agree with or conform to the model this does not disprove the model. A model, he says, is simply a bundle of questions. I have a right to ask my own—but not thereby to take pokes at his model!! I am puzzled by all this but I did grant that his model—because I was critical of it—led me to a great deal of creative thinking which might otherwise not have transpired. . . . Redfield says that if the data don't fit the model—the model thereby has served a useful purpose! He agrees on the possibilities of alternative models—but won't brook criticism of *any* ideal type per se. What do you make of it?

38. *Oscar Lewis to Robert Redfield, April 25, 1954*

. . . I appreciated very much the discussion we had in your office on what you considered to be my misunderstanding of what a model is and how models are to be used. I have been thinking a lot about it and need time for even more thought on the subject in the light of your comments. If you think of a model as a set of questions or as you so well put it as embodying a bundle of questions, then models cannot be proven or disproven, are neither right nor wrong. But if you also see in a model a statement, explicit or implicit, about the relationship between variables, then checking with reality is in effect the testing of a hypothesis. In my criticism of what I saw as the folk-urban conception of social change I viewed the nature and function of models in both of the above senses. In lumping together these two somewhat different attributes of models or ideal types I have apparently attributed qualities to the model which you did not intend. Does this make sense to you?

But the two important points that I came away with after the discussion was a realization that first, I had not been sufficiently aware of the extent to which your models served as inspiration for a great deal of my own thinking even though it was of a critical nature. On the other hand I was using "models" of my own in my economic analysis and throughout most of the descriptive and analytic portions of the book. The second point I saw was that I had inadvertently given the impression that I was critical of your attempt to find broad generalizations about the processes of culture change and the forms of society from earliest times unto the present. This was brought home to me forcefully after reading your recent book on *The Primitive World and Its*

Transformations for I found myself in hearty agreement with most of what you were saying.

One thought more about models. The models one uses or the questions one puts do reflect that person's view of what are the significant problems, the significant dimensions to be studied, etc. Granted that models cannot be wrong per se does there not come a time when models should be modified in order to encompass a new way of looking at a problem or new substantive data which does not fit one model as well as it might another? Otherwise, how would we ever have gotten from the Newtonian conception of the universe to the Einsteinian?

39. *Oscar Lewis to Robert Redfield, May 13, 1954*

Many thanks for the copy of your sensitive and insightful paper on "The Peasant's View of the Good Life." It was a joy to read and reread. It also made me keenly aware of the shortcomings in my version of Tepoztlán with its accentuation of the negative aspects of life. It is true that I had often thought how far "we" had come compared to Tepoztlán, especially in terms of the potential of our civilization. But I was never really satisfied that I had conveyed the "wholeness" of Tepoztecan life and you have put into words and thoughts more beautiful than I had ever conceived the very aspects of peasant life that I had left out. In my next community study, if I should ever do another, I must strive for "the good and the bad" as you have put it.

40. *Oscar Lewis to Clyde Kluckhohn, November 15, 1954*

. . . You say that Redfield's discussion of "Civilization and the Moral Order" should destroy the superficial stereotype that has become accepted in some quarters of Redfield as a sentimental defender of "folk societies."

Having written on this subject I am naturally sensitive to your remarks. Please allow me to explain what I mean. I agree entirely with your evaluation of Redfield's book on *The Primitive World and Its Transformations.* I admire his book as I believe you do. But what impresses me is how much Redfield has changed in the past ten or fifteen years. This change became very noticeable in his *Chan Kom Revisited,* in which he no longer is testing his hypothesis on culture change but is giving a sensitive description of village life without reference to earlier hypotheses. In fact, his own data would suggest that his earlier hypothesis about disorganization was not confirmed by his revisit. In a recent paper of his on "The Peasant's View of the Good Life" he now sees both what peasants enjoy and what they suffer from, whereas in his early book on Tepoztlán and later on *The Folk Culture of Yucatan* he seemed primarily concerned with what they enjoyed.

. . . I am sorry to see the attempts of some people in anthropology to play up my critique of Redfield's earlier work because I admire Redfield as much as any man in anthropology today and I feel I have a great deal to learn from [him]. My talks with him have always been a great inspiration and a challenge. His capacity to change and grow is one of his most admirable traits. It seems to me that he has been moving away from a rather strict concept of science defined in terms of the testing of hypotheses to a broader and more humanistic emphasis which in terms of his great literary ability is his forte.

41. *Oscar Lewis to Irving Goldman, anthropologist, November 17, 1954*
. . . I have been thinking quite a lot about this article ["The Comparative Method"] and have decided there ain't no such thing as "the comparative method". All there is are comparisons.

. . . I have carefully re-read Boas's article on "The Limitations of the Comparative Method of Anthropology" and realize that he was at that time still thinking in terms of studying "customs" and "ideas" and their relation to the total culture, etc. Nowhere does he conceive (in this article) of studying culture complexes, economic systems, social systems, or total cultures. His notions of comparisons, though more careful and correct than that of the early evolutionists whom he was criticizing was still quite atomistic and primitive. You may reply that after all it was back in 1896. Yes, I suppose so, but there were some thinkers even earlier who had more dynamic functional conceptions on higher levels of integration.

As I see it what you have done for Polynesia is much more sophisticated than what Boas conceived of in his early emphasis upon studies within "small geographical areas". Am I correct in saying that based upon an analysis of the value systems plus the social and economic structures you have tried to derive trends and directions of development for the area? Schapera in his article on comparative method in the *AA* not long ago also seemed to stand for this kind of approach.

This approach is very appealing to me as one kind of study but I could hardly agree that no other kind of comparative studies are valid or fruitful. Studies of cultures as wholes in distant and unrelated areas of the world also have their use and often can lead to remarkable fertile insights. It seems to me that they may be especially useful to check upon the too early jelling of hypotheses which are based upon only one or two areas of the world.

42. *Oscar Lewis to Irving Goldman, November 28, 1954*
. . . I do have some questions about your piece ["Status Rivalry and Cultural Evolution in Polynesia"]. Perhaps the major one concerns

the preponderant weight you give to motivations in determining the trend of development. I equate motivation with values and this in turn seems to me to be part of the ideology or super-structure of a society. Are you saying that it is the super-structure, specifically that portion embraced by values, which is the crucial determining factor in evolution of social and economic systems. You politely say that of course the values are in turn related to the conditions, economics, etc. but you then go on to give priority to values. This came as a surprise for various reasons—but more important is the following observation. In my experience as a field worker and student of society, values are the most difficult thing to get at and spell out with any degree of accuracy. Moreover, we are familiar with the danger of assuming to[o] great an integration of cultures and selecting out a single dominant leitmotiv which explains everything. To this extent I think Opler's writing about themes in culture was a useful counterbalance to Benedict's emphasis upon a single theme or value. Now how did you conclude that status rivalry is the most important underlying motivation in all the Polynesian societies? What methodology did you use to arrive at this point, which may actually be so—but would I arrive at the same conclusion by reading the books you read? In other words how did you pull status rivalry out of the data and weight it as the most crucial? Are there not other sub-dominant themes or even counter themes? In my own reading of monographs I have found it very difficult to determine what the basic values of many people are because of the poor quality of the monographs. I would appreciate some enlightenment on this problem.

So much for the questions. However, I do see that your formulation, by including psychological factors carries out the idea of Boas that we need psychological laws for cultural development.

In reviewing the recent articles on comparative method I find that there is a tendency for each author to equate the comparative method with what he or she is especially interested in. . . .

Some time ago in my piece in *Anthropology Today* on controls, etc. I suggested that there is a split right down the middle in all the social sciences today on the issue of whether our discipline and others are more related to the sciences or to the humanities. The same thing applies to the study I am doing on "comparative method". Those who . . . like to think of anthropology as science [also like to think of] the comparative method in terms of establishing "the most rigorous conditions for formulating and testing hypotheses". Others think of comparative method in terms of any comparisons which lead to greater understanding of a problem or phenomenon of interest. I am myself trying to integrate both interests and views. I also believe that careful comparisons within a single community in order to establish the range of diversity in any particular aspect of the culture and the conditions with which this range is correlated is just as "scientific" and just as much of a contribution to the long term goal of understanding as are more difficult and ambitious comparisons between cultures in whole or in part. . . .

43. *Oscar Lewis to Florence Kluckhohn, November 28, 1955*
   . . . If ever you get yourself to read my Tepoztlán book, especially the chapters dealing with interpersonal relations and values, I would like to have some specific substantive criticism so that I might learn just where you think I have missed the boat on "Mexican character."

44. *Oscar Lewis to Morris Siegel, anthropologist, September 17, 1958* (The subject of this letter was the Lewises' "Family Dynamics in a Mexican Village," an article drawn from "Two Family Portraits.")
   I am no more a personality determinist than you are when it comes to explaining the growth of culture, culture change, basic social institutions, etc. However, the major theoretical point of my paper (or rather one of them) is that differences in nuclear family structure and the climate of family life in peasant families within a single non-class-stratified village have to be explained by personal, social, and psychological factors. Perhaps I shouldn't make this so general. Let us say that in the case of these two families I am thoroughly convinced of the truth of this position. Of course, it is more than just the personality of the husband and wife; it includes their family backgrounds, the order of birth of the children, i.e., sexual differences, the particular historical circumstances during which a child was born, the number of dead children, etc., etc. I consider these personal and even accidental factors. As you say, the fact that the only surviving son in the Rojas family was ailing since childhood influences the kind of family configuration that will develop. However, perhaps it was not made sufficiently clear that the mother's personality was influential in his "illness"—we have evidence of strong psychosomatic factors in his illness. Similarly, I wonder whether you got the point that Soledad Gomez, the mother in the Rojas family, has many psychosomatic symptoms—illness of anger, sick headaches of a migraine-like type, and frigidity. It is her negative image of men which has strongly influenced the family dynamics—it has delayed the marriage of the daughters, has tended to build up in the children negative attitudes toward the father, and has put a barrier between husband and wife, etc. These are psychological problems and processes which occur within a cultural context

but must be treated primarily on the level of psychological facts which are colored by the culture but not necessarily determined by it. . . .

The issue you raise about whether there are classes in Azteca is an important one. . . . In my opinion a great deal of harm and confusion has been brought into the social sciences by the almost indiscriminate use of "class". People like Lloyd Warner see classes under every bed. When the difference between being landless and owning land is one quarter of an acre, landownership is hardly significant from a functional point of view in the family economy. . . .

In a village like Tepoztlán one does not get the full spectrum of the Mexican class structure. I personally believe it is a serious distortion to maximize class differences in this situation. . . . one can speak of incipient social classes in Tepoztlán and in another 20 or more years these may become more clearcut, i.e., when the specialization of labor becomes sharper . . . and when the communal land become divided up into private parcels or ejidos. Please note that I have worked very hard to delineate difference in the village in housing, property ownership (including land and cattle), in diet, in clothing, in spending patterns, etc. But after having done all of this quite meticulously I concluded that there were no clear-cut social class differences in the village and that the value systems were remarkably similar. . . .

I did study about 30 families in all and it was on the basis of this study that I decided that most of the differences in family dynamics which I reported in two cases are not directly related to the factor of wealth or poverty, as these terms are defined by local conditions. Again, this is not to deny that wealth and poverty are influential forces in the history of each family. . . .

. . . I practically leave culture out because I consider it to be a constant in this village. This was the theoretical point of the paper, i.e., to show how personal and social factors lead to striking differences in family dynamics within a culture which is male oriented, authoritarian, Catholic, etc. . . .

P.S. I would agree that there are no classless societies. But this depends on what you include in the term "society". There are communities, like Tepoztlán, where most of the people belong to one of the classes which occur in the nation. I am suggesting that the small peasant is a class. . . .

I never intended to use the Rojas and Martínez families as representatives of the upper and lower class in Tepoztlán simply because I am convinced of the essentially one class (peasant) character of the social structure. Within this class the differences between poor and rich are significant but these are not yet class differences, at least as I define the term.

45. *Oscar Lewis to Jason Epstein, Random House editor, November 9, 1961*

From some points of view Pedro Martínez is one of the worst informants I've ever worked with. He has practically no interest in ritual or village custom and tradition, per se, and to this extent he may reflect the degree of breakdown of village culture even as early as pre-Revolutionary days. Of course, this should not be surprising in view of the generally destructive effects of the Spanish Conquest and the plantation system upon native life and institutions. His picture of poverty and suffering is certainly strong, almost traumatic, and he can be taken as a pretty good representative of the very lowest segment in the social structure of this village.

Mexico City

†46. *Oscar Lewis to Ruth Lewis, July 1957*

The material I am getting in Mexico City is exciting but it will mean more volumes. [Consuelo] has written a 150 page life story for me which is a first rate document and deserves publication in and of itself. . . . The interviews with Sr. [Jesús] are slow—he is a tough nut to crack. He refuses to even mention the name of [his wife]. . . . Angelica [Castro de la Fuente, his assistant] and I are planning to take Sr. [Jesús], his daughter [Marta] and [Roberto] to the O'Neill play this week and study their reactions to it! Don't you think this is a good idea. I thought this would help them see the level we are after. This family can be used to give a picture of Mexican culture.

47. *Oscar Lewis to Virginia Rice, literary agent, November 11, 1957*

. . . For a long time now I have been trying to find some way by which anthropological data might be presented to reach a wider audience without cheapening our materials or reducing its scientific validity. I believe I have found a possible solution through the medium of intensive family [studies] in the style of ethnographic realism.

I am now working on a volume to be titled *Five Days in Mexico* (a come-on for the tourist trade), which will deal with a day each in the lives of five Mexican families. These families represent different segments of the Mexican population. . . .

48. *Oscar Lewis to Maurice Halperin, April 11, 1958*[1]

. . . I am planning a full volume on this single family [Sánchez] and will let each member tell his or her own story. I will write an introduction giving the setting, the manner in which the data was collected and a short analysis of the personality and culture of this family. I face serious problems in regard to getting a publisher for this here because of the length of the document and because so many readers want to be entertained. These life stories are sobering and tragic accounts of an abandoned sector of the Mexican population. In Spanish I would like to call [it] "Los de Abajo—1958". I am searching for a title for the English volume. Yes, these vecindad families are part of the great mass of urban poor in the world who have few spokesmen. Novelists have tried to give us some picture of their lives but the social sciences have neglected them. I believe anthropology has a new historic task in reporting honestly and realistically the way of life of these people. I don't know how my colleagues will take to this idea but I am convinced that there is a job to be done as a social scientist and a humanist. Indeed, anthropology has always had these two aspects and family studies offers an ideal medium for their combination. . . .

. . . A great deal of flavor is lost in translation, even in your very good translation. I see no remedy for this and hope that some day I can publish a Spanish version staying quite close to the original. I sometimes think a movie on this stuff would be a natural—but that may come later. I am cutting the stories down a good deal in an effort to speed up the story and above all save space which is so important a consideration with the publishers.

1. Maurice Halperin is now professor emeritus of political science at Simon Fraser University. During World War II he was chief of the Latin American division of the O.S.S. He went to live in Mexico after coming under attack by the F.B.I. during the McCarthy era. The Lewises met him there and they became friends.

49. *Oscar Lewis to Robert M. Gomberg, Jewish Family Services, New York City, April 16, 1958*

. . . it now occurs to me that this [*Five Families*] is not a strait [*sic*] trade book and would probably do better if it were published by a house that would make an effort to reach social scientists and teachers. I would like your opinion as to how useful and marketable such a book of case studies on family life in another culture would be to social workers. Would there be any chance of getting sponsorship or some kind of blessing or support from social work circles. Could you be of some help on this score?

. . . How does this stuff I am doing differ from the reports on families you get from your case workers? Believe it or not, I've never read such a report.

50. *Oscar Lewis to Oliver LaFarge, July 31, 1958*

Seven years have passed since I wrote to you last about my ideas for anthropological family studies. In the meantime I have been to India and have written a volume . . . which has just come off the press. However, I have never given up my original idea of developing a style of anthropological reporting that gets away from our abstract and highly technical jargon. I have worked on the methodology of family studies and have learned that there are at least four separate ways of doing them. I call the general approach "ethnographic realism" in contrast to literary realism. . . .

I have finally come up with a manuscript which I call, tentatively, FIVE DAYS IN MEXICO, but which might better be called MEXICAN FAMILY PORTRAITS: A Day in Five Homes. The book deals with a day in the life of five families, each representative of a distinctive sector of the Mexican population. . . . All the days are based upon first hand observation and recording of conversations and actions as they occurred. But I have tried to give much more than the crude naturalism of the "slice-of-life approach" and have used flashbacks to give depth and meaning to the ordinary and often tedious details of daily life. . . . If this book takes it may mean a great deal for anthropology.

51. *Oscar Lewis to Gustavo Duran, Bureau of Social Affairs, United Nations, August 11, 1958*

. . . I am impressed by how little we know about the way of life and problems, and particularly the psychology, of the lower class in the large urban centers of underdeveloped areas of the world. It seems to me that social scientists are missing a bet here. With our present-day social science techniques we could get a much more profound and balanced picture of the life of the lower class than was provided us by Friedrich Engels and other 19th century researchers on these problems. The English anthropologists are finally waking up to the urgency of this task and are beginning to turn from the study of pre-literates to the study of illiterates in the London slums!

May I suggest that it would be a mistake to narrow the focus of urbanization studies to the question of migrants to the city . . . or even to make this the point of primary emphasis. Certainly this is an important gap in our knowledge. But the fact is that there are gaps wherever we turn in this field. It may be just as urgent to study the living conditions and problems and communities of old urban residents since it is to these "communities" that the migrants come and their adjustment is in large measure influenced by the culture of these older residents. Similarly, it would be most important to study the lower middle class and the problems incident upon upward mobility in these rapidly growing cities. The lack of field studies in all of these fields is amazing! There isn't a single field study of the lower class, the middle class or the upper class in modern Mexico.

52. *Oscar Lewis to Virginia Rice, New York City, September 14, 1958*

. . . In view of my decision not to try for a broad popular audience, I do not believe it would be wise to show the manuscript to the Atlantic Monthly Press. I am quite certain that they would want it cut down and revised in a manner which would make it more popular and I am not ready to do that. As I explained in my last letter, I plan to settle for a much more limited audience of social scientists and professional colleagues. . . .

53. *Oscar Lewis to John Steinbeck, writer, October 6, 1958* (from a letter asking Steinbeck to read and comment on the *Five Families* manuscript, which Steinbeck did)

I write to you as a cultural anthropologist who has been a student of Mexico since 1943 and a constant admirer of your work. You may recall that we met briefly at the Hotel Marik in Cuernavaca in the summer of 1947 or '48 when you were working on your Zapata book. . . .

For a long time I have been trying to develop a new kind of anthropological reporting which gets away from our abstract and highly technical jargon (culture patterns, roles, status, etc.) without cheapening our materials or robbing them of their scientific reliability. I believe I have found a possible solution through the medium of intensive family studies.

54. *Emanuel Schwartz, psychiatrist,*[1] *to Oscar Lewis, March 12, 1959*

I had occasion to discuss with the men at the Psychoanalytic Association your book and the question you raised about supplying a chapter analyzing the five families from the psychoanalytic point of view.

They will not cooperate if the book is published by the Fondo. They feel that [Erich] Fromm is the dictator of the Fondo and they wish to make no contribution to him or his work.

1. Emanuel Schwartz was a New York psychiatrist affiliated with the Psychoanalytic Association in Mexico City.

55. *Oscar Lewis to Arnie Sio, anthropologist, March 25, 1959*

. . . I have just gotten a small grant from the National Science Foundation to carry on my field research in Mexico City where I have already put in a few years of work. . . . I had been working with lower class families and Basic Books Inc. of New York is publishing my new book in May, titled FIVE FAMILIES: Mexican Case Studies in the Culture of Poverty. I want to do much more with this new concept "the culture of poverty". At any rate my project will last eight months beginning in June and I will concentrate on a study of the emerging middle class using the family as my basic unit of study. I plan to study family life, the effect of mass media, kinship depth and social participation, the tensions engendered by upward mobility, the compadre system with lower class–middle class comparisons, etc. etc. I plan to use questionnaires, sentence completion, open ended interviews, life histories, problem analysis, and may get some Mexican psychoanalysts to cooperate for some intensive studies of sample families. Projective tests will also be used.

. . . I will also be continuing my lower class study.

. . . look at my FIVE FAMILIES when it comes out. You are in for quite a surprise—but I'm not sure you will like what I have done. That remains to be seen. Fact is, I didn't write this book for sociologists or anthropologists even though some of them will read it and like it. . . .

56. *Oscar Lewis to Oliver LaFarge, March 31, 1959*
   . . . In retrospect I am sorry I did not take more time to sum up in my introduction some of the positive aspects in the lives of these families. In such a summary I would probably have pointed out the great devotion of Lupita to her children and grandchildren (and to the animals), Antonia's love of her children (albeit that of a protective mother), Jesús's love of his grandchildren who gave meaning to his harried life, and Juana's devotion to Guillermo and family. And certainly Esperanza was a loving wife to Pedro Martínez.
   I was therefore surprised by your generalization about the lack of love among the poor, their inability to afford the more tender, warmer emotions, etc. . . . I understand what you were getting at but I just don't see it as the whole story.
   I gather that you thought the Castro family was the best done. It seemed to me that the Gutíerrez family was the most successful in illustrating the possibilities of my method and in getting across the flavor of lower class vecindad life—the disorder, the endless hours spent in cleaning a single room, the constant coming and going of people, the strong belief in sorcery and faith healing, the lack of privacy, the web of compadrazgo, the partial and distorted views of what was going on in the larger society, the passive acceptance of misery, and the inability to plan far in the future for themselves or their children. . . .

57. *Oscar Lewis to Margaret Mead, anthropologist, May 7, 1959*
   . . . I am eager to have your reaction to the materials on lower class daily life and to my approach [in *Five Families*], which is one kind of "chunk ethnography", to use a favorite expression of yours. I believe these are the first anthropological portraits of lower class urban life in an underdeveloped country. I wish I could get to India to do some comparative studies. India would be a good test of my concept of "the culture of poverty" because India and Mexico are so very different in most ways.
   I am convinced that the intensive studies of families highlights the universal human element—much more so than does the study of whole cultures or other larger units. Indeed, it may be that our traditional anthropological emphasis upon cultural differences has been due in part to the unit of study and the methods used. In describing total culture patterns there is an almost inevitable neglect of range of variation in custom and personality which may lead to overdrawn

configurations that play up differences between cultures rather than emphasize human similarities. In stressing the importance of studying the range of variation in family types and in other aspects of culture I do not intend to suggest that the attempt to describe total culture patterns or to search for core values which may distinguish one culture from another is useless or unimportant. Obviously both types of research are valuable and each can contribute to the other. . . .

58. *Oscar Lewis to Dr. Arnaldo Orfila Reynal, director, El Fondo de Cultura Económica, September 22, 1960* (translated from the Spanish)

The more I think about the problem of the fifth family—the Castros —the more uneasy I am, and I am more convinced that it would be better not to publish it in Spanish. I'm afraid that the publication could bring trouble for them if the book reaches their hands. If you agree with me I am ready to change the introduction and we could change the title to *The Culture of Poverty—Four Mexican Families.*

59. *Oscar Lewis to Conrad Arensberg, anthropologist, November 3, 1960*

Your letter of comment (May 10th) on FIVE FAMILIES, or more accurately on my concept of the culture of poverty, was much appreciated because you were so critical of the concept. . . .

Of course, since the culture of poverty is a sub-culture, its members although poorly integrated into national institutions nevertheless share many cultural values of the larger society—in Mexico it would include machismo, belief in a Christian God, in saints, etc. . . . But again there is a local reinterpretation of some of these beliefs.

One point in your letter of May 10 seemed way off the beam, that is, your reference to inter-personal relations in the families described, reveal a mixture of American Indian–Mediterranean influences. This would be true, at best, only in the village family—the Martínez family. I see nothing Indian in any of the other four.

The crux of your criticism was as follows: "Hunger and coping with it, or bad housing and crowding, and coping with it, are not cultural phenomena, any more than cold, and coping with cold, and though they are part of the lives of the places, cultures, societies experiencing these phenomena, the copings do not make culture until we can show them to be patterned differently from one society to the next, sanctioned and transmitted as collected, evaluated, distinctive habits of more than individual or immediate-group provenance, symbolized within and articulated into the other values and relationships of a living whole culture, with its full structure of status running from top to bottom." Wow, what a beautiful statement!

This touches so many points I don't know where to begin without

having to write a tome. I can see that most of the points would apply quite well to the concept culture when used for small, isolated
primitive societies. I wonder how you would apply it to the modern
world civilizations. But this is beside the point. Fact is that the crucial meaning of the term culture, as I see it, is that it is a way of life
which is passed down from generation to generation. These two criteria hold for the life of the poor I describe. Poverty, and all that goes
with it, is literally stable, persistent and passed down from generation
to generation along family lines. Can all the many cross-cultural similarities I have noted be the result of accident or coincidence? I've been
reading some novels on the Gorbals of Glasgow and on the slums
of Copenhagen (see Martin Anderson Nexo for example) and again
I'm so impressed by the similarities with Mexico City. Can this be
no more than Mediterranean diffusion or the fact that all three cases
share Christianity? Perhaps.

Of course, still another possibility is that perhaps what you have
called the social or external-environmental conditions in and of themselves make for important similarities. I believe it is more. Uniones
libres, for example, are sanctioned by the parents in the vecindad even
though they are ambivalent about it and would prefer a church or civil
marriage for their children. . . .

P.S. You'd love my book on THE CHILDREN OF SÁNCHEZ. I'd hate
to spoil it with questionable models like the culture of poverty. But
I've found nothing better to explain the similarities.

60. *Conrad Arensberg to Oscar Lewis, November 19, 1960*
. . . If your "culture of poverty" is a lower or proletarian subculture
or class culture in the urban-metropolitan Western civilization, fine,
I have no quarrel. That is certainly what the Tepoztecans are moving
into. But Bott for London, Harris, etc. for housing tracts, and many
others show that by no means full acculturation takes place in the
move. . . .

As for counter-culture, an idea I have long played with in social psychology and sociology is the notion of the "contrast phenomenon",
angry inversion and rebellion on the part of the lower class against imposed middle class morality, *also*, the well attested phenomenon that
in a stratified society the lowest-class or pariah group (Harijan, Eta,
Southern Negro, Riverbrooker (see Warner's *Yankee City*), midwestern rivershanty dweller, etc.) [are] forced into exemplifying, though
only part of the time, (and in much mixed ambivalence of feeling on
their part) into acting out in their own persons the stereotypes of badness; they are the living representations of the things disvalued, the

living examples of the traits and behaviors regarded in the value system as wrong and bad. . . . The point is that they do not do these things much, try to be as respectable as others, but know they have the name for doing these bad things, agree they are bad or low, and occasionally, out of disgruntlement or poverty or both, do do them, too. . . . I learned long ago with Warner that there is always in a stratified society a lowest class, a pariah, outcaste group, exemplars of the disvalued, contrast phenomena. . . . you, by dipping into the slums, see the lower edge, not the outer edge, which you might also see in Calcutta or Hongkong or might have seen in Lwow (Lemberg) in the years up to 1914. Outer-edge revolt, involving arty Bohemians, [goes] hand in hand with these lower-class poverty-placed inversions, two facets of the same acculturation process.

. . . Peasant cultures may be a category of culture, but as your own India article well attests, there is blessed little resemblance between Tepoztlán and [Rampur]. . . . Villages and cities do not make cultures, cultures use such settlement patterns. The reactions to poverty are many: Middle Eastern, Arab austerity, Puritan frugality, Chassidism, the lazzaroni of Naples, etc. etc. show that poverty, even with urbanization, does not produce similarities of culture. . . .

61. *Conrad Arensberg to Oscar Lewis, December 5, 1960*
. . . Your introduction is beautifully done . . . so well argued and so persuasive I haven't the heart to disagree. Your statement of the problem, your evocation of its likeness round the world of city-slum poverty, through the reaches of the immense urbanization of our age . . . is so clear and strong that no one, much less I, will argue the point whether "culture of poverty" is good metaphor or imperfect theory. I still have the bad taste to think that you have mixed up Mediterranean urbanism . . . and our common humanity, with a new culture. . . . Your Indios are swept into a Spanish-Mediterranean city life, heir to Rome, and Naples, and Alexandria, and that life in turn is being swept, at its higher reaches, onto Norteamericano civilization, if only peripherally. . . . The strictures of poverty damage and destroy human beings, whether in London, Hongkong, or Mexico. But city life and slums do not make culture, any more than [Julian] Steward's tobacco or his sugar. . . . The urbanization of our day is a terrible and insistent phenomenon, sweeping all before it from about 1750 to God knows what future date, but it is still, like any other culture wave, datable and locatable in the story of mankind.

But who cares, I will never open my mouth again. You are so right, in human terms, so eloquent in argumentation, and so pure in mastery of the forms of literary art and human feeling just now that it does not matter what I counter-argue, or any body else. The culture of (urban) poverty is as good a way to call attention to the insistencies of our day as many another, and you do it superbly. . . .

62. *Oscar Lewis to Frank Tannenbaum, historian, January 6, 1961*
. . . Many thanks for your prompt and generous letter of comment on the [*Children of Sánchez*] manuscript. . . . You seem troubled by the fact that I suggest that all is not well in the world when over a billion people are still members of what I call the culture of poverty. Aren't you also troubled by this fact. Because poverty is widespread and ancient does not make it any more ideal or acceptable at least in the modern world, when we have the knowledge, skills and resources to eliminate it and thereby help to integrate the poor into the larger national cultures of which they form a part—but only in a marginal sense.

I have accused no one in my introduction because the problem is terribly complex and no one person or group or class can be blamed, as such. But I do lament the failure of present day Mexican institutions and leadership to elicit a greater equality of sacrifice in the tremendous task of building a modern nation. . . .

In some ways the Mexican brand of the culture of poverty seems less grim and depressing than the British brand of the 19th century. This raises some very interesting questions which psychoanalysts would probably explain in terms of the nature of the mother-child relationship in Mexico as compared to 19th century British.

63. *Oscar Lewis to William Foote Whyte, sociologist, March 4, 1961*
. . . When I find time to elaborate upon this concept I plan to show the range of rural-urban differences as well as the differences between what one might call ancient and stable poverty versus modern and perhaps temporary poverty.

64. *Oscar Lewis to Jason Epstein, March 17, 1961*
I am not too sanguine about the reaction of my anthropological colleagues to the book [*The Children of Sánchez*]. There are so few humanists left now that Benedict, Kluckhohn and Kroeber are gone. Most of the younger generation are going in for scientism and tend to judge things in terms of their rather narrow and preconceived categories.

65. *Oscar Lewis to Nathan Whetten, anthropologist, April 12, 1961*
After spending a number of years of field research in Mexico City, I have decided to go back to my first love and have selected a small village of 500 people, San Andres de la Cal, in the municipio of

Tepoztlán. San Andres is about an hour and a half off the road and has no tourists, no electricity and no running water. One of my objectives is to systematically compare the institutions and belief systems in this village with that of the Cabacera, Tepoztlán. I will be taking a group of six graduate students from the University of Illinois in order to give them their first field work training.

66. *Oscar Lewis to Bernard Shiffman, Welfare Council of Metropolitan Chicago, April 16, 1961*

. . . I haven't had time to draw up a list of the implications of this paper [a lecture entitled "The Culture of Poverty," using excerpts from *The Children of Sánchez*] for social workers but even in its present form I trust that some of the implications will be clear. For one thing, the similarities in the culture of poverty in different national contexts suggests that social workers everywhere are faced with remarkably similar problems. Second, the insights and generally high quality of expressiveness in these excerpts is not atypical or idiosyncratic but is a common characteristic of people who live by oral tradition. Of course, this point is much more striking if you read the entire volume. In any case, I wonder whether the paucity of such striking materials in the published case materials of social workers may not reflect a lack of deep rapport with the poor! I realise that this is a sacrilegious suggestion for social workers and I wonder whether I even dare say this in public. However, it is also based upon my experience with Mexican social workers who tried to assist me in my study of the slums.

Once we conceive of "a culture of poverty" rather than just "poverty" it becomes more clear that we are not dealing only with economic deprivation but with a whole complex of inter-related attitude and value systems at the core of which is a feeling of marginality of not belonging. Certainly the concept of a culture of poverty should make us look hard and critically at some of the old slogans such as "the war against poverty", "let's wipe out poverty". Can one make war on a culture or sub-culture? Can one wipe it out? Or is it a problem rather to change the constellation of traits which constitute it and in this process transform the culture of poverty. In our own society where the culture of poverty is a relatively small segment of the total national population, the effort has been to transform its values and ways of life into middle class values and ways of life. But in many of the underdeveloped nations of the world the "sub-culture of poverty" accounts for the majority of the population. Can such people truly be incorporated within the middle class way of life or are there other solutions, such as reducing the sense of marginality and provincialism of the poor by giving them political power in a restructured social and economic system. But such an alternative implies basic revolutionary changes with heavy emphasis upon education in addition to material gadgets and comforts. Where this occurs the members of the culture of poverty undergo a spiritual change and show a great sense of loyalty to the new social system and its rulers, even though there may be no rapid change in the standard of living. It is my impression that this sort of thing happened with the Cuban people under Castro.

67. Oscar Lewis to Berenice Hoffman, Random House editor, April 19, 1961

The galleys arrived this morning and I got to work on them at once. After reading the introduction it occurred to me that it was much too academic and might stop some readers. It also seemed inconsistent with the spirit of this work to begin in the usual way. I phoned Jason and he agreed. So we are putting it in an Appendix: Notes on the Setting, Methods, and the Culture of Poverty. In place of the Introduction there will be a very short PREFATORY NOTE. . . . Believe it or not, it is quite upsetting to make a change of this kind at this late date. But I believe it is right. Hope you agree. Won't you think about it and let me have your reactions. Imagine all my work on a conceptual model for the culture of poverty going into an appendix! Such is life.

68. Oscar Lewis to Thomas Gladwin, sociologist, May 23, 1961

. . . I am writing to ask for your advice and possible assistance on a project that I have had in mind for some time now. In the fall, Random House is [to] bring out my new book, *The Children of Sánchez*. . . , and I thought it would be a good idea to get together a small group of experts from various fields—a psychiatrist, a social psychologist, a sociologist, and perhaps another anthropologist in addition to myself—to attempt a formal analysis of the autobiographical materials presented in my volume, plus an evaluation of the Rorshach and thematic apperception protocols which I have on each of the members of the Sánchez family but which I have not included in the book because I did not want to load it down with technical materials.

It seemed to me that a small volume might result from such an undertaking. . . . One of the proposals of this projected seminar would be to come up with specific testable hypotheses on psychological and social mechanisms at work in what I have called "the culture of poverty."

†69. Oscar Lewis to Carolina Luján, psychologist, November 15, 1961

. . . I am not a psychological determinist and cannot accept your thinking on that score. Nor am I an economic determinist. I see economic institutions as part and parcel of social organization and I suppose I would consider myself a social determinist, one who places great emphasis upon certain forms of economic institutions and technology within the social organization. I suppose I would say that I am also a historic [sic] determinist, but at any rate I think it is quite impossible to explain the great variety of forms of technology, social organization, economic institutions, religion, art, etc., in terms of individual psyches and their dynamisms. . . .

I don't feel it's so much that I have thought of you as a conservative as that I have disagreed with your psychologism and the tremendous emphasis that you place upon individual psychology to the relative neglect of the social, economic, and technical factors which play so great a role in the history of humanity. I also feel that politics is a much more important factor than you have given it credit for. Simply to say that politics is dirty and to reject it as such plays into the hands of the dirty politicians and leaves us with no out. Perhaps I am too sanguine, but I do believe that politics can be cleaned up just as everything else, provided we have an intelligent, educated and more politically conscious populace. Perhaps when I state it this way there is less disagreement between us than appears on the surface.

. . . I, too, have great faith in science, but I would want to make very careful distinctions between the predictive process and the reliability and validity of the propositions in the different social sciences. And despite all my readiness to see good in psychoanalytic approaches, I apparently do not share the degree of faith which you exhibit in the scientific status of those propositions at the present time. . . .

I am making some progress in my attempt to get comparative data on the culture of poverty from a reading of autobiographies and novels dealing with poverty. The single most exciting thing I have come upon so far is the autobiography of . . . Ethel Waters, HIS EYE IS ON THE SPARROW, published in 1951. I wish the Fondo de Cultura Economica would translate this into Spanish so that Mexicans would finally have an opportunity to get a realistic image of some of the conditions of poverty which have existed and still persist in the United States. Her story has very much of the quality of the Consuelo story and it was a best seller in this country when it was published.

You might mention . . . that Abraham Kardiner, Nathan Ackerman, [Eric] Erickson and Santiago Ramírez have professionally agreed to write a chapter each of analysis of the individual and family psychodynamics of THE CHILDREN OF SÁNCHEZ. I will write the introductory chapter and final summary analysis of their points of view.

70. *Oscar Lewis to Eric Wolf, anthropologist, January 19, 1962*

I should like to make a sharp distinction between the "culture of poverty" and the culture of the poor. While poverty is one of the traits in the total configuration which I have defined, there are many poor who do not have a culture of poverty. For example, middle class people who are impoverished during a financial crisis such as the great depression etc. They may even have to sell apples but their mental outlook is so different. They usually are hopeful about the chances of upward mobility, especially in the U.S. where it is difficult, even for many intellectuals to realize that poverty may be an age old, stable phenomenon which has characterized many generations in particular family lines. This is one of the conditions for my culture of poverty. Another one, which you did not mention, is the marginality of these people, even though they are in a numerical majority. . . . By the culture of poverty I have in mind all of the more than forty variables which I give in my introduction. It would be a distortion of my meaning to equate "poor people" with "the culture of poverty". I am now working out more refined subtypes of "the culture of poverty" according to historic periods. Serfdom and slavery share many of the traits but are different from the urban culture of poverty which I was trying to illustrate. A crucial difference is the much greater freedom of the slum dwellers under modern capitalism.

Once the poor begin to identify with larger groups or with larger causes, once they become class conscious or become socialists or Communists they rapidly begin to lose some of the crucial aspects of the culture of poverty. They begin to take on an internationalist rather than a provincial, locally oriented world view.

It is certainly flattering to have my book listed along with Frazer, Benedict, and Mead. . . . However, I should like to point to one important difference between the *Children of Sánchez* and the work of Benedict and Redfield. Although both of them talked and wrote a good deal about the humanistic component in anthropology, it has seemed to me that their work lacked the crucial humanist component, namely a vital concern with individuals, with the everyday reality. One does not find human beings in the work of Ruth Benedict, instead there are cultural configurations. It is almost as if Benedict found it difficult to come down to the hard road where humans walk and had to rise to an Olympian height. The same is doubly true of Redfield with his high level abstractions or ideal types, folk, peasant, urban. It was to get away from this kind of thing, or rather to show some different dimensions, that I have been trying to develop the family approach in anthropology. I had hoped you would have responded to the crucial methodological innovation, namely family studies. Autobiographies have been used often in anthropology and to excellent effect. However, when the multiple autobiography within a single family is used it raises the autobiography to an entirely different level.

71. *Oscar Lewis to Lee Rainwater, sociologist, January 24, 1962*

I have enjoyed reading your paper on "Marital Sexuality and the Culture of Poverty" and thank you for sending it to me. It seems to me that you have done a good job with the materials available.

In defining and conceptualizing the culture of poverty I had not included Tepoztlán within this category and was therefore taken aback, at first, by your use of the Tepoztlán data. Actually, Tepoztlán was markedly wealth stratified and over 80 per cent of the families fell in Group I or what I called the lowest and poorest group. However, the presence of communal lands and the fact that over a third of the families owned some land, eliminated them from the culture of poverty in terms of the economic criteria I had set up.

Of course, this in no way invalidates your handling of the data and your findings. . . .

72. *Oscar Lewis to Carlos Fuentes, writer, January 26, 1962*

Have you seen the article on my book *Antropologia de la Pobreza* titled "La Pobre Antropologia de Oscar Lewis". . . . I wish you would read it and give me your reaction to it.

. . . [Ricardo] Pozas quite misleadingly equates Anthropology with Science exclusively neglecting its humanistic aspects. Actually anthropology is a discipline which has . . . scientific and humanistic and artistic aspects. . . .

. . . Pozas criticizes my book because it does not provide the reader with an analysis of the social, economic, political and technological causes of Mexican poverty. He uses an old trick of criticizing an author for not writing a book on the subject that the reviewer would have him write on. Indeed, *Antropologia de la Pobreza* quite frankly sets out to record a single average day in the lives of five families, and no more. It is presented as an experiment in anthropological field technique and reporting. These crucial aspects of the book are ignored by Pozas. . . .

73. *Oscar Lewis to Fernando Cámara, anthropologist, March 9, 1962*

. . . Have you seen the stupid and nasty review of my book [*Five Families*] by Ricardo Pozas? He took advantage of the Spanish title, which wasn't my choice in the first place, to criticize me for not having written an analysis of the causes of poverty in Mexico. It seems to me that any intelligent ten-year-old already knows the answer to that question. How ironical that . . . [he] should have completely by-passed, and ignored, the humanistic content of my work and made a "sacred cow" out of science. . . .

74. *Oscar Lewis to John Paddock, anthropologist, March 19, 1962*

Thank you for your letter of March 5, and for the copy of your most recent review of FIVE FAMILIES and THE CHILDREN OF SÁN-CHEZ. I was delighted to note the much friendlier tone in this last review.

. . . I understand from *El Fondo de la Cultura Economica* that FIVE FAMILIES sold out the first edition and is therefore considered by them as a best-seller. I must say that I have somewhat ambivalent reactions to this wide distribution of the book in Mexico, because I still dread the possibility that some ill-intentioned person, who can spot some of the vecindades that I described, may want to cause trouble and bring the book to the attention of the residents. In changing the street names and the given and surnames of all the characters in the book, I have done all that I possibly could do to protect them. However, were I to do this thing all over again, I am certain that I would now publish this kind of research under a pseudonym, thereby adding further protection to the people with whom I have worked, and for whom I have such great respect and affection.

. . . in stressing what you consider to be my over-pessimistic view of Tepoztecans, you were probably referring to my chapters on the quality of interpersonal relations which was, of course, only one part of the book. I had the impression that you were underplaying some of its other contributions, such as the emphasis upon an historical approach, the use of national archives and village records, the emphasis upon quantification and sampling in areas where this is feasible, particularly in the study of the economic system, the conception of hoe culture and plow culture as separate systems, and in general the emphasis upon the social and economic problems faced by the people. As you must know, all too often anthropologists' ethnographic reports are of very little use to administrators and action anthropologists, because they contain practically nothing on the felt needs of the people. In my own evaluation of my first Tepoztecan study, I would underscore the fact that it was probably one of the first studies to take exception to the then prevalent concept of basic character structure. Recently [A. F. C.] Wallace and others have come up with more explicit critiques of the Kardiner scheme. But if you read Part II on the people and Chapter 20, "General Observations of the Life Cycles," you will note that I nowhere use the basic character structure approach, because it seemed to me that what it really referred to was what I called the public personality, which is simply the other side of the culture coin.

I have recently reread Octavio Paz's book, *The Labyrinth of Solitude*, and am impressed by the tremendous similarity between his depiction of what he considers to be the Mexican national character, and my own description of the quality of interpersonal relations in Tepoztlán. But whereas my frame of reference would always allow for important and even basic changes in the quality of interpersonal relations in response to changing culture, the national character approach tended to give to character a stamp of stability which I would question.

. . . If I understand you correctly, you tend to idealize the Mexican middle class, and assume that as soon as people get into it they become ideal or wonderful human beings, in contrast to the so-called damaged people in the culture of poverty. I most certainly do not agree with this view judging from my reading of Mexican psychiatrists, and the novels of Carlos Fuentes, among others.

75. *Oscar Lewis to Frederick Wyatt, psychologist, June 14, 1962*
. . . I have in mind the preparation of another volume which might be called "A Guide to the Children of Sánchez," consisting of independent contributions by two Mexican and two United States psychiatrists, each of whom will be asked to write a chapter of analysis of the individuals in my book and of the family as a whole. I should also like to make available to these scholars an analysis of the Rorshach and T.A.T. protocols. It should be interesting to see whether the differences in the cultural backgrounds will appreciably affect their interpretations. I am also curious to see the relative weight that will be given the elements of pathology and health as reflected in the life stories and in the projective tests. In my own experience I have found that psychiatrists and clinicians generally tend to emphasize pathology, especially in dealing with lower class subjects.

. . . Among the names I was considering as contributers are Nathan Ackerman, Abraham Kardiner, Eric Erickson, Santiago Ramírez, Ramon Parres, Alfonso Millan, and, possibly, Eric Fromm, if I can get him to take time off from his travels and speech making. I would appreciate it if you would be willing to suggest a few names of outstanding United States clinicians who might be available and interested in this kind of task.

. . . I plan to ask the National Science Foundation for financial assistance. If you are interested in participating in this project and preparing a chapter of analysis of the five Rorshachs and T.A.T.s I would appreciate some suggestions from you as to your fee for this work. The test protocols are now in Spanish but I could translate them into English if necessary. . . . When all of the contributions are in my hands, I would have the analysis mimeographed and circulated to all the participants and we would then hope to have a one day meeting at which we could have some final discussion of the different points of view.

76. *Oscar Lewis to Dorothy Terry Carlson, executive secretary, Mental Health Small Grant Committee, National Institute of Mental Health, September 21, 1962*

The essential accomplishment of my summer research based upon research grant M-5556(A) consisted in collecting life histories and psychological testing on twelve grandchildren in the families that I have studied over many years. I found working with young children terribly time consuming and difficult, and I have filed my research data for use as a base line in a future study about five or ten years hence, when most of these children will be in their teens and a few in their early twenties. In accord with the original research design the analysis of this base line material will have to wait until the second stage of the study is undertaken and completed some years hence. I therefore do not anticipate any immediate publications based upon the data I collected. . . . However, this data should prove invaluable for the long time objectives that I have in mind with these families.

†77. *Oscar Lewis to Carolina Luján, November 20, 1962*

. . . I am still struggling to improve the manuscript of my volume on PEDRO MARTÍNEZ. The editor with whom I deal at Random House likes it very much. He went so far as to say that in many ways he found it a more moving document than my Sánchez book. However, I cannot agree with him at all. Moreover, I am convinced that my new manuscript is not sufficiently powerful to stand alone. I believe it needs a part II which will deal with the village culture, the general historical setting and analysis of the family and of the individuals. This will make for a 700 page manuscript and more work for me.

As it stands, the volume shows very clearly the effects of severe deprivation upon the character and the lives of a peasant family.[1] I realize that not all poor landless peasants lose their father at three months [nor] are [they] practically abandoned by their mothers at 18 months, right after the end of nursing, as occurred to Pedro Martínez. Many many poor peasants are lucky enough to have a mother and a father until they are grown. On the other hand, I suspect that poverty in peasant villages with their high mortality rates, often produces situations of the kind I have studied, and perhaps to this extent, I am dealing with a phenomenon of widespread occurrence. How do you feel about this?

When I first began to do family studies my objective was to do much more than provide a portrait of individuals within a family. I had hoped that the life story of a family would reflect the local village culture and also the broader events going on in the nation. Since Pedro Martínez was born in 1889 I hoped that the story of his life would tell us something about the life of a peasant under Diaz, the meaning of the Mexican Revolution to the villagers, their attitudes toward Zapata, Carranza, etc., and the vital events of the post-Revolutionary period in Mexico. Unfortunately, my manuscript doesn't accomplish all of this on a very high level because of the serious limitations of my major character, Pedro—limitations in intelligence, in his power of description. He is much too egocentric to be truly sensitive to a great deal of what was happening around him, even within his own family. A comparison of his version of the first night of their marriage with the version of his wife reveals this very clearly. Also, a comparison of his son [Felipe] with the father shows how insensitive Pedro was. There is the further drawback that Pedro like most peasants [has] little desire or ability to be introspective and [is] much too inhibited to probe the realities of [his] inner world, of [his] deepest feelings. It is here that the slum dwellers of the city have a great advantage. They are so much more voluble and expressive, their language is so much more colorful. Both are of the culture of poverty but what a difference! How would you explain these differences in terms of your theoretical frame of reference? How much weight would you give to the constricting forces of small village life with its ancient traditions of conformity? Or does this have deeper roots?

Another weakness of my manuscript with which I am trying to cope is the fact that most of the characters are not very good story tellers. The result is therefore quite uneven and choppy in terms of human interest. There are relatively few peaks of intensity. Most of it, like their very lives is in a rather low and dull key, especially when compared to *The Children of Sánchez.* . . .

   1. Here Lewis was referring to emotional as well as economic deprivation, but he saw the emotional deprivation as a consequence of the family's poverty and his mother's need to work. I have no reason to believe that Lewis was influenced by his Marxist readings in this position, but it is similar to what Marx wrote about the consequences of working women and child labor in *Capital*, chapter 15, "Machinery and Modern Industry" (see section 3).

†78. *Oscar Lewis to Carolina Luján, December 12, 1962*

   . . . I am fascinated by how much emphasis you give to Pedro's TAT responses on the dangers of working for others. It may be that his mother was a courtesan or a loose woman, certainly, she had many lovers, and this enraged Pedro, so he tells us. Can he be getting the idea of "working for others" as dangerous from this early experience of his mother with many men. Can he have viewed her affairs as "working for others". This doesn't quite explain his imagery of the door being closed if one arrives late at work. Most interesting to me was your suggestion that he identified working for others with being feminine, with the threat of homosexuality. As I see [it], on the social level there is a very important aspect here. When Pedro worked on the plantations prior to the Revolution (along with hundreds of other poor peons) he was beaten and downtrodden. He describes a scene in which the foreman, *el capitaz*, rides his horse toward a group of men eating their tortillas and the horse stomps on the tortillas while the foreman threatens the group with his whip. Certainly here the masculine figure on the horse is a threatening one, perhaps a castrating one as you might say. In other words working as landless peons for low wages under objectively poor and exploitative conditions is a demeaning experience which threatens a man's dignity and self-respect. I would say this was true for almost all peons. But if I follow your line of thought, you would argue that the way a peon reacts to such a situation is a function of his earlier experience at home with mother and father. I wish you would try to expand on this point. The two explanations are not irreconcilable. However, my tendency would be to emphasize the social and economic determinism because few peons stand up to their masters and the few that do usually get beaten up or killed as many were killed under [former Mexican president] Diaz. I might argue that irrespective of one's view of his mother and relationship with her, peonage is a degrading, demeaning experience. In the case of Pedro, it must have been even more traumatic because of his problems with his mother. Do you agree?

I can't wait to see the rest of your interpretation. . . .

79. *Oscar Lewis to Berenice Hoffman, December 15, 1962*

I am glad to have your reaction to the PEDRO MARTÍNEZ manuscript and want to thank you for your kindness in doing such a helpful job.

. . . I am quite disturbed at your suggestion for me to break in at various points of the narrative or at the beginning or end of sections. I am inclined to reject this possibility because it would violate the form which I have slowly and patiently been building. If you want to see an example of what such a mixed style can lead to look at Sidney Mintz's *Worker in the Cane, A Puerto Rican Life History* . . . which . . . is . . . something I want to keep away from. He even listed a few of his own questions to the informant to keep it "scientific". I realize this is far from what you had in mind but the very thought of going towards such a "mixed" style, i.e. back to formal anthropology frightens me. Instead, I believe I can lick the problems you raised by a good introduction and perhaps a part two of analysis.

80. *Carolina Luján to Oscar Lewis, December 15, 1962*
   . . . I find it difficult to evaluate the psychological versus the socio-economic aspects in man's struggle to attain maturity and independence. Perhaps the closest thing to an answer would be any socio-economic system that can preserve, foment, and stimulate family life, and make boys and girls conscious of the importance of their nature established roles. However it seems that this consciousness comes precisely from having experienced the right kind of relationship with one's own parents. This kind of relationship makes for the right kind of internalization of social norms and moral standards, so that they might become part of the ego, and not foreign bodies as in the case of cruel, persecutory objects, where the 'superego' is too often only a caricature of authentic goodness and morality, and often makes for paranoid pathology. Certainly conditions of extreme misery and cruelty are not favorable to mental health. But the answer is not as simple as having a radio and television set in the home. It seems like a vicious circle, but I believe man follows a line of progression with occasional regressions. . . .

81. *Oscar Lewis to S. C. Dube, director, National Institute of Community Development, Government of India, February 8, 1963*
   . . . As you may know, I have developed the concept of a subculture of poverty with a series of some fifty traits, most of which I believe exist in the large cities of modern nations. India should be crucial as a test case for the hypothesis. Indeed, it is a rare hypothesis in the Social Sciences which can also be confirmed by Indian materials. The combination of a caste system and a planned system as predominant social forms of a modern nation does havoc to most Social Science generalizations emanating from Western culture.
   UNESCO has repeatedly asked me to head up a Social Science Center in India for research in rural communication systems, but I've had to turn it down because I am completing another book on Mexico, and I have just received a research grant for a comparison of lower class family life in Puerto Rico and New York City, i.e. of Puerto Rican families who have migrated to New York. It seems to me high time that some of us American anthropologists study the culture of poverty in

our own backyard. It seems unlikely, therefore, that I shall be visiting India in the near future. . . .

82. *Carolina Luján to Oscar Lewis, March 28, 1963*

. . . I don't think I make Pedro 'more sick' than he is at all. I simply don't see any reason in the world for carefully avoiding the use of patho-terminology when there is pathology. I don't think of pathology as something degrading or shameful or unmentionable. I think of pathology as something to be recognized, understood, and helped. I read the first part of Professor [William E.] Henry's book 'Analysis of Fantasy' when I received . . . Professor Henry's interpretation of [Pedro's] T.A.T., and notice that he speaks of the need of a theory of personality for normal people. There is no such thing. There is no different 'theory of personality' for Normals and Psychopathology. The Normal is an 'Ideal', and any one with problems, conflicts, and anxieties, will have some kind of deviation from this ideal. There is no such thing as a Theory of Personality that does not comprehend a thorough knowledge of psychopathology, the dynamics of psychopathology, psychotic thought disorganization, etc. I think this 'touchiness' about calling a spade a spade is most ineffectual and does more harm than good. You can't cure cancer or tuberculosis by calling it pretty names. And you can't cure psychopathology by describing it in the language of 'normal' personality theory. Sick people *are* normal human beings, whatever affliction they struggle against, and I have little patience with these differentiations, as though psychopathology were disgraceful! . . .

I don't think I make Pedro any more sick by using psychopathological terms which are very useful, than by describing a very sick personality in 'personality' terms. In fact I think Professor Henry makes Pedro as sick as a human being can be by considering him the essence of passivity. Passivity is the worst prognosis in psychiatry! Analysts are very loth to take extremely passive patients. And I believe Pedro has enough fight in him to have been a good candidate for psychotherapy at an earlier time in life.

†83. *Oscar Lewis to Carolina Luján, April 30, 1963*

. . . Because I am writing for a general audience, I find it difficult, indeed impossible, to utilize your psychoanalytic concepts, particularly regarding the importance of Pedro's latent homosexuality as a key motivating force in his character and his personal development. People in the field of clinical psychology, and especially those of a psychoanalytic bent, would not consider the presence of latent homosexuality in a man as a terribly negative or devastating phenomenon, however, to write about this for a lay audience might very well have the effect of blackening their image of Pedro Martínez. I am, therefore, settling for a mere statement of the absence of adequate male figures in his early life, and a statement about his ambivalence towards his own mother and later towards his wife. I wish there were some way in which I could convey the latent homosexuality in a simple, non-technical language that would not prejudice the reader or be too demanding upon his value system.

84. *Oscar Lewis to Ruth Landes, anthropologist, May 9, 1963* (postscript to a letter in which he asked Landes to read the Martínez manuscript)

The unusual success of my Sánchez volume has made it very hard for me to finish the book that I am now working on. It's a very different kind of a book even though the technique used is quite similar, but peasants are not slum dwellers. In a way, I suppose it's a sadder and more terrifying book, especially when you think that approximately sixty-five per cent of the world's population are peasants. In the past, peasants have played a much more important role in history and have toppled many more kings and kingdoms than have urban slum dwellers. In this sense, perhaps the political message of my new book is more weighty, but the urban poor may still have their day.

85. *Carolina Luján to Oscar Lewis, May 17, 1963*

. . . Pedro's conversion, like his activities and his 'ideals and causes' *must* be interpreted in the context of his personality if the interpretation is to be psychologically sound, and not convey a drastically wrong impression, which I believe is what you have done in your paper on 'Seventh Day Adventism in a Mexican Village: A Study in Motivation and Culture Change.' My dear, your conclusions on this are sheer blah. Why in heaven's name don't anthropologists stick to Anthropology, and not go around making gratuitous, unfounded statements, or at least take time out to learn something about psychodynamics and psychopathology and personality theory, before going in for 'psychological' interpretations? You simply cannot make psychological interpretations with a complete disregard for personality theory and psychological rationale. Whatever theory you use, psychological rationale is a *must*, though I recognize from the samples you have sent me, that your American psychologists do a pretty good job at dispensing with psychological rationale and internal coherence. . . .

To go back to Seventh Day Adventism. It is psychologically unsound to say or believe that with Pedro's psychological make up, he could, by adopting Seventh Day Adventism, or any other religious system, become a different character, acquire all sorts of critical abilities, become a 'modern Western man' and a Christian 'in a more universal sense.' This is terrible! Pedro's disorganized thought processes are every bit as disorganized in his evaluations of Protestantism as they are in his 'folk Catholicism'. Only more so! His Biblical acquisitions only make the rather nice syncretism of pre-hispanic pagan beliefs with Catholicism more confused. In his 'folk catholicism' Pedro shares the beliefs of his community and favors communication. His rejection of erstwhile good objects represents an increase in paranoid projection. What Pedro's 'conversion' really represents is an intensification of superego threat by the archaic, irrational superego and a concomitant need to become propitiative. What better means than the Scriptures!

. . . I have almost given up hope that you will ever take the time to follow the psychological rationale which I very painstakingly work out for you. I hope you will reciprocate by doing so on this occasion. Otherwise it is only a waste of time for both of us. . . .

†86. *Oscar Lewis to Carolina Luján, May 31, 1963*

. . . Although the Martínez family lived much closer to a subsistence level than the children of Sánchez and although the former actually suffered chronic hunger, it is striking that Pedro produced three school teachers whereas Jesús produced none. In this sense Pedro's life has realized a good deal of his aspirations for education and progress and has not been such a failure after all.

What you say . . . about Pedro not *really* being interested in ideals and social causes and justice raises a more general question. Would you grant that anyone's interest in justice, social ideals, and causes and the readiness to sacrifice oneself (and/or one's family) for such goals is good mental health? Can you point to any historic figures who have done so? Remember that the best analytic studies of Jesús claim that he was a very sick man who suffered from all kinds of delusions, believed in magic, etc. Do you know any truly great revolutionary figures, true heroes, of whom you would not say what you have said about Pedro. It may certainly be true that all men who seek . . . ideals and causes are doing so in fulfillment of their own needs. But so do the people who do not seek goals and causes try to fulfill their own needs. Need fulfillment per se does not explain the difference between the idealists and the non-idealists, the reactionaries and the radicals or revolutionaries. . . .

87. *Carolina Luján to Oscar Lewis, June 5, 1963*

. . . I must say my reaction to your evaluation of Pedro's conversion was one of shock. I felt you were most unjust in attributing it to 'strong and deep Catholic values and resentment against all forms of Protestantism as being anti-Mexican and bad.' I certainly *don't* think of Protestantism as anti Mexican and 'bad'. . . . I have great respect for the beliefs of others as long as those beliefs are not used to fustigate others who do not share them, and as long as they do not interfere [with] understanding and communication with others. I was amazed that you could say such a thing because I felt my interpretation to be a strictly psychological one such as I might have made of any religion. . . .

And I wouldn't be too sure about your statement that 'not being a Protestant yourself, you have no axe to grind in favor of Protestantism'. In fact, my impression on reading your conclusions was that you were definitely biased and were taking this indirect way of showing prejudice. You may not have had an axe to grind in favor of Protestantism, but perhaps, as a Jew, you *do* have an axe to grind against Catholicism as the original Christian religion. It is not at all improbable that you are more sympathetic towards Protestantism as an ally against the common foe: Catholicism. . . .

I was almost forgetting: I am very appreciative of your thought to perhaps use my analysis of Pedro as an Appendix. I have no objection, but since I certainly didn't write it with a view to publication . . . I would like to rewrite it myself and do my own cutting out of repetitions. . . . I am perfectly willing to accept corrections on my English, but would not like to have psychological meaning changed.

88. *Oscar Lewis to Ruth Landes, June 7, 1963*
   . . . Regarding more on my methodology in working with informants, I believe this would be out of place in this kind of introduction and might better appear later in a professional journal, except that I do not feel highly motivated to delve into this data for my colleagues.

89. *Oscar Lewis to Richard King, psychologist, February 20, 1964*
   [In *Pedro Martínez* I] tried to show that the Mexican Revolution eliminated the culture of poverty in village Azteca by making accessible to the landless peasants their own communal land resources, and in so doing, the Mexican Revolution created a peasantry in villages where a landless, somewhat proletarianized group had existed earlier.

90. *Oscar Lewis to Hyman Rodman, sociologist, July 26, 1965*
   . . . I like your idea of "The Lower Class Value Stretch" and I find it fits quite well with my own thinking on the culture of poverty. The culture of poverty is exactly that sector of the lower class which has

very little stretch. More accurately, it refers to the way of life at that sector of the lower class which has very little value stretch. I have never equated the culture of poverty with the lower class as such. Within the lower class there are many sub-groups with somewhat distinctive patterns.

I enclose a short piece I did a few years ago on "The Culture of Poverty". Actually, the children of Sánchez are not the best examples of this concept because they have quite a lot of value stretch, i.e. they were more influenced by the values of the larger society than many other poorer families I have studied. . . .

The question as to the prevalence of personal pathology among people with a culture of poverty is a difficult one. My own suspicion is that it is widespread. In part it may be a reaction to the deprived conditions of slum life, particularly the harsh treatment of children and the lack of love; but it is also probably something that many migrants to the slums bring with them from rural areas. Increasingly I tend to lean toward the view that urban slums attract people with deep psychopathology.

I shall look forward to reading your forthcoming book on lower class families. Again, I find the rubric of power class much too broad and undefined for analytical purposes. I can readily conceive of a lower class that is not poor at all, certainly not by the standards of under-developed countries. My own concept of a culture of poverty has the advantage that it focuses directly upon poverty as a core constellation and seeks to find other traits that correlate with it. On the other hand, poverty per se does not always produce some of the key traits of the culture of poverty. When poverty is associated with the other key traits you find a culture of poverty.

91. *Oscar Lewis to Frederick Johnson, Robert S. Peabody Foundation for Archaeology, October 29, 1965*
. . . I am very grateful for your kindness in sending me the Second Annual Report of the Tehuacan Project and the reprint of the article "Domestication of Corn." I find this work some of the most exciting that I've seen in archaeology.

When archaeologists and botanists discover that maize is a few thousand years older in Mexico than was heretofore known, it brings great glory to the nation and helps the Mexicans in their own self-image. However, when an anthropologist studies the slums of Mexico City and discovers the persistence of great misery and suffering fifty years after the Mexican Revolution, it creates a scandal. I sometimes wish that I were an archaeologist.

92. *Oscar Lewis to Richard Morse, historian, November 23, 1965*

. . . Your comment on the culture of poverty is well taken. Indeed, one of the crucial aspects of the culture of poverty is the poverty of culture. Marx's inversion of the philosophy of poverty to "the poverty of philosophy" was intended as a critique and deprecation of Proud-homme. However, I have myself suggested that the inverse of my phrase is one aspect of its definition. . . .

I am afraid there has been some misunderstanding and misuse of the concept "the culture of poverty" which I presented for the first time [in English] in 1959 in the introduction to my book *Five Fami-lies*. As I understand it, Michael Harrington reviewed that book and took up the concept in his own volume *The Other America*, without a sufficient understanding of what I had in mind. Undoubtedly this is due to my much too brief statement on the subject at that time. I have been too busy gathering data on particular families to devote my-self to theoretical formulations and model building. However, I have given thought to the "culture of poverty" and have tried to elabo-rate, modify, and sharpen it conceptually. I enclose a list of sixty-two traits which together constitute the configuration I call the culture of poverty. Although poverty is only one of the traits, I have used it to name the total configuration because I consider it terribly important. Now this may make for some confusion because the other traits, and especially the social and psychological ones, are also important, but I can't think of a better title for the complex. . . .

. . . The distinction between poverty and a subculture of poverty is basic to my way of thinking. There are degrees of poverty and there are many kinds of poor people. The culture of poverty refers to one way of life shared by poor people in given historical and social contexts. The economic traits which I have listed . . . are necessary but not sufficient to define the phenomena I have in mind. . . .

Puerto Rico

†93. *Oscar Lewis to Muna Muñoz Lee, principal translator for the Puerto Rico and Cuba projects, May 24, 1965*

I am now working on the introduction to the book [*La Vida*] and am trying to present some generalizations on our findings based on the 200 families we have studied. It is my thesis, however, that a careful study of a single extended family by the methods we have used reveals a great deal about the history and culture of the country, i.e., in addition to what it tells us about the specific families. The data we have on the [Ríos] family and other families can only be understood in the light of Puerto Rican history and it seems to me that it is an unusually sad history, a history of isolation and abandonment, a history with few glorious moments. Of course, in my evaluation of some of the highlights in Puerto Rican history I am comparing it with Mexico. The Mexicans had attained a much higher pre-Hispanic civilization than had Puerto Rico and the Mexicans fought the conquerors with greater zeal than did the natives of Puerto Rico. Most urban slum dwellers of Mexico know about the great Cuahtemoc who fought against Cortez and gave his life in the struggle. I wonder how many Puerto Ricans know about their Indian heritage. In Mexico the Indian heritage has persisted and is a point of great national and personal pride [in] that it gives the people a sense of a great past, a sense of historic continuity which seems absent in Puerto Rico. As I have once told you, for most Puerto Ricans whom I have studied history begins and ends with Muñoz Marin—and only a few recall Muñoz Rivera.

Perhaps one of the greatest differences between Mexico and Puerto Rico can be seen in their very different reaction to oppression and exploitation. The Mexicans were fighters and revolutionaries. Their wars of Independence against Spain were bloody and prolonged and heroic. Father Hildago, Father Morales, Vincente Guerrero, those are names which continue to live in Mexico—even among the poor and illiterate. The Puerto Rican heroes, men like Betances, seem to have less heroic, less dramatic stature. In the 19th century Puerto Ricans who tried to wrest a few concessions from Spain, who tried to get just a bit more autonomy for Puerto Rico are the heroes. And finally, Mexico has produced one of the great revolutions of the 20th century when it overthrew Diaz and I don't see anything comparable in Puerto Rico, even though I admire and applaud the great progress made since 1940.

I am suggesting that Puerto Ric[ans] as a people were more broken by the Conquest and the colonial period than was Mexico and that somehow this has left a distinctive mark on the family and personal lives of many of its people, especially the poorest segments who as usual, have suffered the most. Almost 90 per cent of the heads of families of our study came from rural areas where they were the children of *agregaos*—tenants or share croppers.

Mrs. Luján has the impression from my materials that the Puerto Rican people of the culture of poverty, unlike the Mexicans, are essentially not depressives. They have never received enough love as infants and children to produce depression. She sees them as closer to the schizoid pole of the continuum. Does this make any sense to you?

†94. *Muna Muñoz Lee to Oscar Lewis, May 25, 1965*

Insofar as I understand your statements about P.R. history and its effects on P.R. personality, I tend to disagree where I don't doubt. That is, I disagree with the specific statements on our history (or rather with their interpretation) and don't really understand how the connections between having been an abandoned colony of Spain and having such a high incidence of material indifference and hostility in at least one group of our population can be worked out in detail.

As regards the specific statements and their interpretation:

Our feeling about our knowledge of our alleged "Indian background" as compared to Mexican's [*sic*] reactions to theirs, seems to me totally irrelevant. There is not one single individual in our present day population who can be identified by himself or anybody else as having any proportion of Indian blood, who speaks any Indian language, or who has the remotest reason to identify himself with the tribes who, for an undetermined time before the Conquest and for less than a century afterwards, lived in the land we now occupy. It would be far more relevant in our case to try to trace the importance of African cultural elements, survival of African customs (however modified) etc. and the importance given to them (although I doubt there is much knowledge of the actual history of these) but certainly they are valued traits in our culture. To attribute any deficiency in our personalities to lack of knowledge of our Indian background is equivalent to interpreting the personalities of New Yorkers on the basis of their ignorance of their "Indian background."

In the second place, what P.R. finally got from Spain, one year before the American conquest, was not a "wresting of a few more concessions" nor "a bit more autonomy" but full status as a Province of Spain, with representation in the Cortes. To call this "a bit more autonomy" is like saying Hawaii and Alaska "wrested a bit more autonomy from the U.S." when they were made States of the Union. (I hope this doesn't make me sound like an Estadista—lagarto sea!)

In general, I tend to disagree that a bloody history is glorious per se. Mexicans have a great deal more to be proud of than their revolutions—art (both Indian and Hispanic), literature, the building of more than one great civilization—in artistic and intellectual achievement. About the revolutions, their sources, the way they were fought and their effect, I know only what I have read in your own books, especially *Pedro Martínez*. The account given there of the motivations, the leaders and followers of the Revolution does not impress me as heroic—bloody, yes! As to the effects—basing my opinion on the same source—they do not seem to have been far-reaching.

Going back to Puerto Rican's [sic] reactions to the Conquest: to their being "more broken" and for that reason less overtly hostile to Spain: the Puerto Ricans who were for so many years neglected by Spain were not an indigenous group fighting against foreign oppressors. They were, initially, the colonizers themselves; they were neglected by their own countrymen, not conquered by an outside group. The other main element in the population, the Africans, were either sold by their own people to slavers or captured, rather than conquered. The treatment of both groups is extremely significant to our history and, no doubt—but just how?—to our personality. But it seems to me that trying to fit it into a Mexican framework (which is not exactly the same thing as comparing it to Mexico) can only produce distortion.

†95. *Oscar Lewis to Muna Muñoz Lee, June 1, 1965*

I enjoyed your reaction to some of my statements about Puerto Rico and its history. I wish I knew what Puerto Rican Negroes were taught about their past, about Negro civilization in Africa, etc. Here in the U.S. there has been a major trend to portray the great achievements of the Negro people of Africa in pre-European conquest times. Has the same thing been happening in Puerto Rico? I would like to have a set of the Puerto Rican history books for the elementary . . . and . . . high schools. . . .

. . . I agree that the absence of Indians in your population makes the question of the knowledge of the pre-Hispanic Indian background less germane in Puerto Rico than in Mexico. However, it does not really violate my point, namely that by comparison to Mexico [sic], Puerto Ricans have less of a sense of historic continuity, their knowledge of history is more truncated and is shallower. And for God's sake, don't generalize my comments on lower class slum dwellers to all Puerto Ricans. I have never suggested that middle class Puerto Ricans are superficial or more superficial than middle class Mexicans or *gringos*.

. . . To me there is a great difference between trying to achieve autonomy or commonwealth status or its equivalent as did Muñoz

Rivera and struggling for independence. I understand that de Diego was critical of Muñoz Rivera on this point, that is, de Diego wanted independence.[1] I must do a great deal more reading on these matters before I go into print. I am now reading a history of slavery in P.R. which claims that even slavery was very mild, that emancipation was easy and without violence and the transition period peaceful and gradual. Were it not for the few nationalists we might conclude that gradualism was genetic to Puerto Ricans!

1. José de Diego headed, with Muñoz Rivera, the Unión de Puerto Rico.

†96. *Muna Muñoz Lee to Oscar Lewis, June 4, 1965*

There is no denying that we Puerto Ricans are very ignorant of our own historical background, whether Spanish or African. My point was that an "Indianista" approach throws no light upon any of our historical or psychological problems and that, while the term "Colonialism" is a key word in the discussion of these, the term "Conquest" is irrelevant to either.

. . . We know very little about specific historical events, African civilizations and so on. Your way of putting the question—this is an aside—"how Puerto Rican Negroes are taught about their past" is an interesting illustration about a very fundamental difference between the U.S. approach, even in the case of liberals. A Puerto Rican would have spoken of what "Puerto Ricans are taught about their Negro background." A Puerto Rican without Negro blood must be a statistical rarity. . . . It would never occur to anybody here, if they started to teach about African civilization, which I believe they unfortunately do not, to think that only *one* group of the population would have an interest in it! But the point I really had in mind was a more general one: accepting the fact that an ignorance of history is an element of the culture of poverty, can we take it as a cause of any of the other factors? Are roots to be found only in knowledge of specific "heroes" or historical events. Or can they also be found in a continuance and appreciation of customs, crafts, beliefs, etc. known by the people who practice them, to have come from a culture which has contributed largely to the formation of ours?

. . . There is certainly a difference between trying to achieve independence, autonomy or some sort of federation. There is also a difference between sulfa and penicillin. And a good thing too, because neither by itself could cure all ills. True, de Diego disagreed with Muñoz Rivera. And what did de Diego ever achieve for P.R.?

It is a pity and a crying shame that in P.R. "even slavery was very mild . . . emancipation easy and without violence . . . the transition period peaceful and gradual." We are bad masters, not being tyrannical enough; and bad slaves, never really (in spite of colonialism) having learned to be individually subservient enough. Think of all the fun we are missing now by not having made the institution of slavery all it ought to have been. But no matter, if we want excitement we can always take the next plane to Alabama.

"History shows many instances of the ruin of states by measures ill-suited to the temper and genius of their people . . . whence a total separation of affection, interests, political obligations and all manner of connections, necessarily ensues, by which the whole state is weakened and perhaps ruined forever." This, from Benjamin Franklin, only a few years before the Revolution! [Muñoz goes on to quote from Samuel Adams's resolutions for the Massachusetts Assembly.]

If I had the right books around, I could give you the same ideas as expressed by Jefferson and several others, a few years before the American Revolution, in protest of the practices the continuance of which finally precipitated the Revolution! The men seem to have been gradualists—obviously broken by colonialism. If Britain had granted a few reforms (among which some of these men would have included representation in the House of Commons . . .) there might not have been a Revolution at all and the U.S. might be a Dominion, like Canada and Australia.

Driving me to look up things in order to answer a letter is the limit!

†97. *Muna Muñoz Lee to Oscar Lewis, May 25, 1965*

The analyses of [Fernanda Ríos—*La Vida*] and [Gladys—from an unpublished manuscript] were fascinating and provided a kind of consistent framework for their subject's actions which Freudian-oriented interpretations do, whether you accept their accuracy or not. To me they both sounded not only consistent but convincing. There is one point, repeatedly stressed in [Fernanda's] analysis, mainly, it seems on the basis of the life-history material and the "day" which seems to me somewhat doubtful: that is the often-repeated statement that [Fernanda] is completely incapable of giving in return for what she gets. Granted that [Fernanda] could hardly be classified as a generous, giving kind of person, she is far from being totally incapable of giving. Witness her detailed account of the way she keeps [Junior's] clothes always clean, ironed and ready to wear by washing and ironing everyday. She is obviously very proud of this as well as of her husband's neat appearance. In the day while she did boss [Junior] around, I do not remember getting the impression that "he did all the work." In fact, I had an overall impression that [Fernanda] was a hard and efficient worker and proud of the fact. Then there is the case of the lame . . . girl who had been seduced and abandoned by her lover, then beaten and thrown out of the house by her stepmother. The very fact that she turns to [Fernanda] who has not the remotest shadow of a duty to help her, shows that [Fernanda] is not regarded by her neighbours as an unsympathetic or ungenerous woman. And the material help and reassurance [Fernanda] so readily gives shows that the neighbours are not completely wrong in their estimate.

As for our superficiality—this may be true but I do not feel your materials prove it. After all, you worked in Mexico for twenty years, did much more of the interviewing (both in terms of time, number of interviews and proportion of the total of interviews made) than you have in P.R. In at least the case of the "Sánchez" and "Martínez" families you did all the interviewing. While it is an obvious truism that a person who has no inner life at all (if there be any such) can give no account of his inner life, it is equally true that a person who values his inner life and tends to live inwardly is very much less likely to be ready to reveal it than a more outgoing type. Actually, my own impression tends to correspond to yours—that on the whole we Puerto Ricans are more preoccupied with outward events than with inner ones—but the statement of Dr. Luján that Puerto Ricans tend more to the schizoid end of the scale would seem to contradict this— or doesn't it? Anyway, the point I am trying to make is that it is risky to state that people you know only superficially are superficial.

†98. *Oscar Lewis to Muna Muñoz Lee, June 1, 1965*
. . . I would take sharp exception to your comment that my study of Puerto Rican families has been superficial. Certainly this is not true of my study of the [Ríos] family which I believe I know as well as any one can know a family. When you read the book I believe you will agree. Nor can I agree that they may have a very profound inner life which they have managed to withhold from me and my assistants. The projective tests suggest the very opposite. But I hardly need projective tests after the mass of data I have on hand—over 6,000 pages of data on a single extended family. And so many hours of direct observation! You can't really be serious.

†99. *Muna Muñoz Lee to Oscar Lewis, June 4, 1965*
I never said the [Ríos] family had unplumbed depths. . . . However, I will now make a remark which I may have to spend the next quarter century explaining away: the, admittedly peripheral, studies of [Benedicto, Arturo, and Flora] do seem even slighter than is strictly necessary. In none of these cases was there the slightest penetration of the informants defenses. . . . [Benedicto and Arturo] seem as superfi-

cial to me as their in-laws. In the case of [Flora] I have a feeling—and that is all it is, I can't even recall what gave it to me, that there is a lot more going on inside than in any of the others who are in any way related to the family. If a projective test is ever done on [Flora], I would love to see the analysis.

†100. *Oscar Lewis to Muna Muñoz Lee, June 5, 1965*
  I tend to agree with your point about [Fernanda's] capacity for somewhat more generosity than Mrs. Luján's report would suggest. I have discussed this with Luján who agrees also but she would not give such acts too much importance in the total view of [Fernanda's] character. Mrs. Luján has personally retested [Fernanda] and has concluded that she is even more "psychotic" than we believed her to be. It would seem that the slum provides a very therapuetic environment for disturbed people because of the great tolerance for pathology and the permissiveness for acting out. In a middle class environment, people with such pathologies would get much sicker and eventually be institutionalized.

†101. *Oscar Lewis to Muna Muñoz Lee, June 16, 1965*
  Did I tell you that I have finally resolved the problem about how to phrase the matter of the abandonment of children by P.R. mothers. In a culture in which mothers have a great readiness to give away their young children to relatives or friends and in which women have an equally great readiness to accept young children, the children involved in these transactions (forgive the word) will probably develop a feeling that they have been abandoned. From studies of foster children we know that formally adopted children often feel great hostility towards their true parents and also a feeling of abandonment. I presume this must occur also in Puerto Rico. To phrase it as I have above seems to fit the situation much more accurately than to talk about mothers abandoning their children—a practice which is culturally taboo in a society which tends to glorify motherhood.

†102. *Carolina Luján to Oscar Lewis, June 25, 1965* (discussing the projective tests given to members of the Ríos family)
  . . . The test material of both is definitely psychotic, [Flora's] those of a deteriorated psychotic, and [Broco's] those of a paranoid. The fact that they are out in the world in a tolerant environment may allow them to function apparently better than in an institution, but it doesn't make them any less psychotic. Perhaps this should be the starting point of social endeavour: giving children homes and environments

that will keep them mentally healthy. Otherwise, I suppose we go on living in a near psychotic world.

103. *Oscar Lewis to Kenneth Brown, psychologist, July 2, 1965*

. . . I have found the Rorshach and Thematic Apperception Test useful but by no means essential to the kind of work I have been doing. Indeed I have come to the conclusion that our concepts of mental health are thoroughly middle class and therefore of limited value for cross cultural analysis. Perhaps this is an overstatement of my true feelings on the subject but at least it reflects the difficulties I have encountered whenever I have tried to make careful analysis, cross culturally. . . .

104. *Oscar Lewis to Joseph Finney, psychologist, October 15, 1965*

I've read your comments on my "Culture of Poverty" paper and I am inclined to agree that there is probably a high incidence of dependency and orality and little compulsivity among people with the culture of poverty.

I am a little worried about the broad characterizations of entire peoples and cultures as "hysterical" (you cite Spain in this connection) or "compulsive" (you cite Japan). I believe I have already indicated to you that it is my impression that there is a higher incidence of hysterical symptoms among the San Juan slum dwellers that we studied than among the Mexico City slum dwellers and yet they both have a Spanish component.

I am also troubled by the underlying assumption in your paper that the inability of individuals to move out of the culture of poverty is essentially a result of their personality failures. Implicit in your model is the notion of a laissez faire system with free mobility and so the people who don't make it are either sick individuals or don't have the proper personality traits. It is interesting that this view of the poor dates back at least a few hundred years. It could be that the old stereotypes are now being scientifically validated; but it may also be that you are not giving sufficient attention to the nature of the social structure, the built-in obstacles to upward mobility, and the inherent limitations in the system which would make it difficult, if not impossible, for more than a small number of the poor to move out of their present situation, irrespective of their personality traits.

. . . It is clear that we should have some careful studies of the psychological aspects of people in the culture of poverty. It is my hunch that we would find quite a number of personality types but their statistical distribution may turn out to be distinctive and, therefore, significant.

105. *Oscar Lewis to Lola M. Irelan, Division of Research, Welfare Administration, Washington, D.C., October 28, 1965*

. . . Not all people who live in poverty develop the 62 traits which I find go together in joined bundles and which constitute a way of life which I have designated as the culture of poverty. I am [enclosing] a list of these traits which we are now examining in some detail in my graduate seminar.

. . . In my own experience with slum children in Puerto Rico, I find that some of them are remarkably verbal and capable of a considerable amount of abstraction.

The usual generalization about the concrete mindedness of slum dwellers has never really been sufficiently validated and the few studies that we have on the language of slum dwellers reflects a weakness in methodology and rapport. Certainly the characters in *The Children of Sánchez* reveal a remarkable gift for language and they have lived in the slums all of their lives.

106. *Oscar Lewis to Lloyd Ohlin, sociologist, January 3, 1966*

. . . The phrase "culture of poverty" is a catchy phrase and has been used in ways I had not intended. I am now working on a further elaboration and refinement on the concept. . . .

I am afraid my new book on the Ríos family will be a shock even to social workers whose middle-class values and experiences will probably make the "Ríos" family seem "animal-like" and unreachable. It is true that, compared to the Puerto Rican families I've studied the children of Sánchez seem stable, highly motivated, repressed—in short, almost middle class. I sometimes suspect that the success and popularity of *The Children of Sánchez* was due in part to the reflection of middle-class values in the lives of some of the characters, values with which middle-class readers could identify. Marta, the one character who was truly representative of the culture of poverty, has been the least understood and has evoked less compassion and sympathy from readers. . . .

107. *Oscar Lewis to Helen Harris Perlman, professor of social work, January 4, 1966*

. . . It is interesting to me that you, along with other readers, found Marta "dull and without conflict." She is one of the best representatives of the true culture of poverty. . . . In a sense, I suppose Consuelo would be a social worker's dream because she was so aware of the values of the larger society and in effect she was saying—if only I could be like the middle class. But as you say, the Ríos family is different and they are not alone in this. They are more typical than one would like to believe. The style of life of the Ríos family is a challenging one because they are not trying to be like us and show relatively little of what has been called the lower class value stretch.

It may very well be that social workers can do very little for people like the Ríos family unless they are willing to approach them with very few preconceptions as to the good life and with considerable empathy and compassion for them as human beings. Perhaps the most that can be done is to provide them with additional income so that they will not be forced into prostitution. Certainly the social worker wouldn't get very far if he or she tried to change their love-life pattern.

I find your over-all evaluation of Fernanda and Soledad much more negative than my own evaluation; or perhaps to put it another way, while I realize the depth of the pathology, I also see many redeeming factors. My over-all reaction to them is one of acceptance rather than rejection. Perhaps this is why I have found it possible to relate to these people to the point of getting them to confide in me these intimate and often negative aspects of their lives.

It seems to me that they do have an inner core of personality, albeit on a rather primitive level, and it is this inner core which accounts for "the inexorable repetitions, verbal and motor, that reveal the iron entrenchment of patterns of behavior," to quote from your letter.

They have a great deal of staying power or else how could we possibly explain their survival in the face of their difficult and sometimes brutalized existence. My general reaction to people like this is one of marvel that they are doing as well as they are given their life experiences. They have their own sense of morality and a sense of dignity and they are capable of kindness and consideration. . . .

108. *Oscar Lewis to Fr. Joseph P. Fitzpatrick, sociologist, January 17, 1966*
The life story of the son Simplicio [Ríos] has a distinctive quality and shows more hope [than those of Fernanda and Soledad]. One can sense that his horizons are broadening and he is reaching out for new ideas and new frames of reference. Moreover, his story—like those of most of the men in the book—contains very little obscenity or vulgarity. This is in striking contrast with the women. . . . I believe it reflects a basic difference between the personality of the men and women. The latter are much more aggressive and seem to care less about middle-class standards, perhaps because they have been less exposed to personal relationships with middle-class people. This difference in language may have an even deeper significance but I haven't quite figured it out. . . .

It seems to me that the Ríos family is an example of terribly hurt human beings and, unfortunately, the world is full of them. . . .

The Ríos family has to be understood against the background of Puerto Rican history with its slavery, colonialism, and poverty. Clearly, twenty years of the Commonwealth is not nearly enough to overcome the profound damage that has been done in the past and which unfortunately continues into the present.

. . . In its pure abstract form as an ideal type, the subculture of poverty can be defined as a way of life of poor people (I think of it in terms of families rather than individuals) who live in urban or rural slums in countries with a cash economy, wage labor, production for profit—in short, a capitalist system. The core characteristic of this subculture is the lack of effective participation in the major institutions of the larger society and the absence of membership in any organizations beyond that of the bilateral nuclear and extended family and the local slum settlement. Most of the sixty traits which I have listed for the subculture . . . flow from the above proposition or are intimately related to it. It is the primitive level of organization which gives the subculture of poverty its marginal and anachronistic quality. Most primitive peoples have achieved a higher level of socio-cultural organization and participation than many of our modern slum dwellers!

. . . I believe it is important to distinguish between different profiles in the subculture of poverty depending upon the national context in which these subcultures are found. If we think of the culture of poverty primarily in terms of the factor of integration in the larger society and a sense of identification with the great tradition of that society, then it may follow that slum dwellers with a lower per capita income may have moved farther away from the core values of the culture of poverty than others with a higher per capita income. In Mexico, for example, even the poorest slum dweller has a much richer sense of the past and a deeper identification with the great Mexican tradition than do Puerto Ricans with their tradition.

. . . In terms of my present thinking, I would say that while there is still a great deal of poverty in the United States, there is relatively little of what I would call the culture of poverty. My rough guess would be that only about 8% of the families in the United States have characteristics which would justify classifying their way of life as that of a culture of poverty and probably the largest sector within this group would consist of very low income Negro families. The relatively small number of people in the United States with a culture of poverty is a positive factor because it is much more difficult to eliminate the culture of poverty than to eliminate poverty.

It seems to me that the uniqueness of a phenomenon is in many ways just as revealing and just as important as its generality. I would not want to play down the uniqueness of the Ríos family. In a sense, all families are little worlds unto themselves. But on the other hand, I am convinced that in broad outline the way of life of the Ríos family is very similar to that of most families in La Esmeralda. I say this with the knowledge that only approximately one-third of the families in La Esmeralda have some history of prostitution. . . . prostitution per se does not drastically transform most of the other traits and other aspects of life. . . .

109. *Oscar Lewis to Stanley Diamond, anthropologist, January 21, 1966*
. . . [the Puerto Rico] project represents one stage in my long-term research plans to test and further develop the concept of a subculture of poverty. I believe there is an urgent need for solid comparative data of this type to help us arrive at significant cross-cultural regularities. In addition to the theoretical insights that this research may yield, I also am hopeful that some of the findings on the culture of poverty and the obstacles to urbanization will be of use to educators, social work agencies, and all others who are deeply concerned with multiple-problem, lower class families.

†110. *Carolina Luján to Oscar Lewis, January 25, 1966*
. . . I am not quite happy about including the Ríos family in 'The Culture of Poverty' because prostitution *is* their way of life and colors every aspect of their experience. *This* I do not believe to be a trait of The Culture of Poverty. I feel very strongly that the Ríos family et al. are beyond the Culture of Poverty.

Whether your material should or should not be presented in the raw hinges on a more philosophical than on an ethical or utilitarian issue. It is surely true that it will provoke in middle class minds, and by this I don't mean middle class people but middle class minds, many an unfavorable reaction. It is also true that your material may be used or misused as a legitimized form of sexual stimulation. So may the Dictionary. Yet I haven't heard anyone clamoring for censorship of Noah Webster and even First Grade children have access to him. Humanity, at this point in its history and development, has a right to knowledge of facts and the censorship of truth seems to me far more harmful than any ill effect produced by its promulgation. Our fear of words is no doubt a remnant of 'magical' thinking and the magical power ascribed to words. . . .

. . . Soledad and Fernanda are near psychotics. I use the word 'near' as a concession to some of your well founded objections. I would say they are psychotics, but with a difference. They are at home with their psychosis. And they have not given up, they are still searching, struggling, maintaining themselves in a hostile world against impossible odds.

111. *Oscar Lewis to Elizabeth Herzog, chief, Child Life Studies Branch, Division of Research, HEW, Washington, D.C., March 10, 1966*

. . . I am now finishing a new statement on the . . . subculture of poverty. . . . It is the fullest and most systematic statement that I have put together so far. I have been hesitant to expound on the level of research designs and theoretical concepts because of the paucity of intensive comparative data on whole family studies and I don't like to let the theory get too far ahead of the facts. If I had fifty or sixty volumes like *The Children of Sánchez* or *Pedro Martínez* from countries all over the world, including the socialist countries, we would be in a much better position to come up with some meaningful conceptual models and typologies. . . .

112. *Oscar Lewis to Lloyd Ohlin, March 22, 1966*

. . . One of the crucial practical and theoretical issues raised by my new book is the extent to which the life styles presented therein are typical of the culture of poverty and, therefore, cross-cultural and the extent to which they are distinctively Puerto Rican. I am sure that both elements are involved and I plan to try to discuss this problem in my introduction. The impact of my book on the Puerto Rican image would be less damaging if I could sustain the thesis that what we are dealing with is essentially a universal condition rather than a distinctively Puerto Rican one. . . .

†113. *Muna Muñoz Lee to Oscar Lewis, March 22, 1966*

As regards the paragraphs for which you ask for "my forthright comments," undoubtedly many of the problems Puerto Ricans face in New York are due to the fact that they were desperately poor, illiterate and not even trained—in most cases—for semi-skilled jobs, too ignorant to be able to defend themselves from thieving landlords, etc. This, of course, is true of most immigrant groups: were you to get a mass migration of white, Anglo-Saxon, Protestant millionaire PhD's they would not meet with so much prejudice, nor would their children find growing up in a strange country so hard. Nor do I believe that the "onus for the situation has been thrown on New York," on the contrary, it is my impression that New Yorkers place the blame for being poor and ignorant on the victims of poverty and ignorance, that New York schoolteachers—and there is a great deal of evidence by North American writers on this—discourage even the most modest ambitions of even the few P.R. students who manage, against what seem to be the almost overwhelming odds of the situation, to become superior students. And this seems to me the cruellest aspect of prejudice. Not that Puerto Rican teachers on the Island are not prejudiced against P.R. slum children. It would seem to me, that the prejudice of N.Y. is of a harsher and more crushing kind but so far as I know nobody has raised this problem in regard to P.R. schools so this is only an impression—and no doubt a prejudiced one—on my part.

In short, I quite agree with what you say but think there is something very disturbing in the way you say it . . . that it may leave an impression that you mean that there's no point in trying to do anything for Puerto Ricans in New York until Puerto Rico is as prosperous as the U.S.! And, by the way, in my experience, when people talk or write about the progress of P.R.—and there has been progress—they do not deny that P.R. is poor (twice as poor as Mississippi, the most backward State of the Union, we have been told until we know it by heart) or that there is a great deal still to be done, and that it will not be easy to do it. Except in the Tourist Bureau ads, and it isn't fair to count these!

On the whole it seems to me that the onus for the situation should fall equally on New York and Puerto Rico. Take the drug traffic for instance—it is supposed to be mainly in the hands of Puerto Ricans (as far as the lower-down, actual peddlers are concerned, anyway). In P.R. it is popularly supposed that the great increase there has been in P.R. in past years is due to returning migrants who got into the racket in N.Y. Take the P.R. juvenile gangs in N.Y.—that is a U.S. pattern which even yet does not exist in P.R. I don't know how accurate the idea about the drug traffic is. As regards gangs, they are certainly a symptom of even deeper problems than slum adolescents find here (in spite of all the individual violence which exists in the slums in P.R.).

Maybe I'm being chauvinistic, but if you substitute the name of any oppressed group for that of Puerto Ricans, my reaction would be the same. I quite agree with you that the harm done by the Ríos families in the world is much less than that done by world leaders and that it is largely the ambition, limitations, etc. of the leaders of all countries, great and small, that create the environment in which so much misery, ignorance and human waste is possible. But then they are products of a middle-class environment for which I hold far less of a brief than even you sometimes do.

†114. *Carolina Luján to Oscar Lewis, March 23, 1966*

I don't care for the 'prostitute' in either title or subtitle of your book. . . . I don't believe we should be called names for our afflictions, certainly not by our friends, and these people think of you as a friend.

I certainly can't agree with you (or Manny Schwartz) that there is little difference between the prostitutes in a culture and other women of the culture of poverty in the same culture. As far as I'm concerned, you're way off. They do not represent two points on a continuum, but entirely different psychological constellations. . . .

As far as presenting a denigrating image of the Puerto Rican, I believe you can avoid this by avoiding generalizations in your introduction. It is not easy because people on the whole like jumping to generalizations. If you can put it across that your study is a study of prostitution *in* a culture of poverty, and not a characteristic of the culture of poverty, this would seem convenient. There is prostitution in every walk of life and I don't believe you can consider it a characteristic of the culture of poverty, but a characteristic of poverty in internalized objects.

†115. *Oscar Lewis to Muna Muñoz Lee, March 23, 1966*

I found your forthright comments on my provisional statement of the Puerto Rican problem in New York extremely helpful and I heartily agree with your way of putting it. Moreover, it occurs to me that in my earlier writing on the culture of poverty I have not stressed sufficiently the factor of exploitation and of the imposition of this way of life by the institutional setup of the larger society—by the social, economic, and class discrimination which is an important factor.

116. *Oscar Lewis to F. K. Lehman, anthropologist, March 28, 1966*

. . . It occurred to me that I might put the speculative sections [of the 1966 "The Culture of Poverty"] toward the end. I refer especially to my hunch about the absence of a culture of poverty in Socialist countries and the relatively small number of families with a culture of poverty in the United States. I am also thinking of putting in a small section on the conditions and mechanisms which perpetuate the culture of poverty from generation to generation. What I have in mind here is the element of imposition by the dominant classes in terms of social and economic discrimination and the manner in which the values of the culture of poverty are passed on through children who by age of six or seven already have a clear-cut model of a way of life to which they are remarkably well adapted and which they are bound to re-enact in their own lives—even in the face of changed and improved economic conditions.

117. *Oscar Lewis to Elizabeth Herzog, March 29, 1966*

. . . I see no short cut in terms of checking the trait lists. I believe family studies are essential to determine the presence or absence of a subculture of poverty and to distinguish between the latter and simple poverty, per se.

. . . [in Puerto Rico] we decided to concentrate on the study of families with an annual income of $1200 or less because it was in these families that we found the greatest concentration of culture of poverty traits.

. . . In this book I have combined two techniques which I had used separately in my earlier work. . . . The biographies provide a subjective view of each of the major characters whereas the days give us an objective view of their actual behavior. The two types of data supplement each other and, indeed, there is a counterpoint which develops between them. On the whole, the observed days give a more positive, likable, and warmer portrait of these people than do their own biographies. The days also tend to give a picture of greater organization and orderliness to their lives than do their own autobiographies.

. . . One of the fundamental theoretical and practical questions raised by this first volume is the extent to which the Ríos family, its relatives, friends, and neighbors, reflect a universal culture of poverty and the extent to which they reflect something which is distinctively Puerto Rican. I have no doubt that there are both elements here but it is difficult to say which is the predominant one.

. . . I am faced by a very important and difficult theoretical decision. Does the presence of prostitution in this family make the Ríos family a very special case within the culture of poverty or is it a pretty good example . . . in spite of the existence of prostitution? A friend of mine, a Mexican clinical psychologist . . . who has read the entire manuscript and the Rorshach and T.A.T. protocols, leans very heavily toward the special case interpretation and she believes that this would limit the generalizations that I might derive from this family study. Indeed, she urges me to emphasize in my introduction that this is not a typical culture of poverty family because of the prostitution factor. My own tendency goes in the other direction. I would very much like to have your thinking on this intriguing problem. . . .

†118. *Muna Muñoz Lee to Oscar Lewis, May 9, 1966*

. . . I would like to know more about the statement in your first paragraph [that the situation in Puerto Rico in 1960 was worse than in 1950; made in the introduction to *La Vida*]. A statement like that, without the comparative figures leaves one up in the air. As this is not a book on economics, one can't really ask for an analysis of the reason for this (larger population? less migration? more automation? increasing concentration of wealth in fewer hands? return of more migrants because of fewer employment opportunities in the States? or whatever). In regard to this last, which I have heard occurs (i.e. more migrants return here as employment opportunities for unskilled labor decrease in the U.S.) I have always wondered why that doesn't tend to make people stay where relief is more adequate.

As to the degree of aggression shown between the sexes, perhaps you do not overemphasize the aggressiveness of the women but you do overlook that of the men (excluding Fernanda, who is so far from accepted feminine behavior that even her non-psychologically oriented relatives and neighbors say that she is like a man, and excluding also Soledad who is more like her mother than either of her sisters). For instance: "women take the initiative in breaking up marriages"—both Felicita and Cruz were cruelly beaten by their first husbands before they "took the initiative" by leaving them; "in calling the police"—it seems to me that in any subculture of the Western world, a man who called on outside help would be held to show not male aggressiveness but feminine weakness and would surely make himself a laughing stock; "taking husbands into court for non-support of the children"—aside from the fact that, under existing law, that is an initiative not open to a man (who is not likely to be the one to keep the children anyway) it seems to me you overlook two very important factors here, (1) that a desire to keep their children from starving may be a much stronger stimulus than hostility in this, at least in many cases, (2) the great amount of hostility displayed (both against the children and against the ex-wife) by a man who refuses to help support his children (displayed, I mean, by the bare fact of the refusal, considering especially, that unless he has some means of support, there is nothing the court can do about it).

About the conclusion that P.R. women (regardless of social class) are aggressive, I have no arguments—too many outside observers have agreed about this. Also, there are some indications that Puerto Rican men think so too! A few years ago the jury for a short-story contest sponsored by the Ateno commented that of sixty-odd stories submitted, *more than sixty* dealt with a man being psychologically destroyed by a woman. (However, Hopi men project a great deal of suppressed aggression on Hopi women who are not, by the standards of outside observers, aggressive).

Oh, by the way, the ideals of the larger society in this respect are not all in favor of submissive women but quite ambivalent. While it was quite common in former (but not very remote generations) for a woman to put up with unfaithfulness, physical violence and unlimited neglect, the many women who did so were more despised than admired. I have heard many women of every generation I have known, from my grandmother's contemporaries to girls only a few years older than my own, express contempt for a "mujer aguantona" (one who will "put up with things"). True, people will often say that a woman who puts up with those things "es una santa," but nobody is ever called a saint in P.R. without a strong undertone of contempt! Men will call a woman like that "muy comprensiva" but are apt to boast that their wife has more spirit than that! (This all refers to the middle class).

119. *Elizabeth Herzog to Oscar Lewis, May 20, 1966*

The most fascinating question . . . you raised in your letter of March 29 [is] the extent to which the characters in this book represent a universal culture of poverty or something distinctively Puerto Rican—or . . . the idiosyncratic patterns of the Ríos family, or . . . the occupational characteristics of prostitution. I begin to think that no matter how carefully one formulates an answer to that kind of question, it will require reformulation in the next round. If you give more weight to the universal subculture of poverty this time, then next time you will find you want to play up the national differences and exceptions to both national and cross-national patterns. You can't win, but that doesn't matter because the game itself is so rewarding. I suspect that in the end the "universal" traits will be reduced to very few, but those few are well worth recognizing. . . .

I must confess to a problem in relation to family life patterns among the very poor. I cannot wholly forget that unvarnished reports, however accurate, may . . . play into the hands of a subtle sort of racism, in this country, at this time. . . . What I settle for is to be extra sure that reports are accurate and if they are, then that is that. But in cases of doubt, I suppose I would take special pains to avoid something that might *not* be fully accurate and also is bound to have a negative impact. . . .

I *would* emphasize that this is not a typical subculture-of-poverty family, and would also emphasize that in spite of that it displays typical subculture-of-poverty traits.

†120. *Oscar Lewis to Muna Muñoz Lee, July 28, 1966*

I had lunch with my publisher who has finally read the entire manuscript [*La Vida*]. His major objection is to Part I, Fernanda. He is afraid parts of it are heavy reading and that it will stop too many readers from going on to the rest of the manuscript which he believes will be fascinating but shocking reading. His idea is that Fernanda is unable to serve as an introduction to the rest of the book because she isn't sufficiently articulate and intelligent to set the stage and so he wants me to help her out in italics every now and then and explain to the reader what is going on, etc. I can't agree with him at all. He has yet to cite chapter and verse but he promises to come up with some specific criticism within a few days.

For me the inherent weakness of part one is the superficial view Fernanda gives of the men she has lived with. Her picture of her relationship with them is so utterly one-dimensional—sex and violence. She seems incapable of describing them as people with feelings and thoughts, with problems or yearnings, or frustrated ambitions, bitterness etc. I suspect this is not my shortcoming as an interviewer but is really the way Fernanda sees other human beings and even herself. However, I may put everything aside and try to spend a few days doing intensive interviews with her before she returns to P.R.

†121. *Oscar Lewis to Carolina Luján, September 27, 1966*

I have just read an excellent article by Manuel M. Marzal, *El Fenomeno Religioso En "Los Hijos De Sanchez"*. . . . I understand that Marzal is a priest, but I am not sure. In any case I was very pleased and impressed by the article and I am glad that some people are finally discovering that my work contains a great deal of basic research data which is crying out for further analysis. It is a pity that I did not have time to do something along these lines myself. . . .

Reassessing

†122. *Oscar Lewis to Carolina Luján, June 28, 1965*

I am back at work . . . after a very pleasant three days in the company of some fascinating psychiatrists with strong research interests. . . .

The reaction to [Gabi Ríos] was incredibly enthusiastic. They seemed to fall in love with the child, and they found the portrait unforgetable. They suggested that I publish it separately in a psychological journal. Most present commented on how well this child had adapted to a very pathological environment and speculated on the cost of this adaptation. A few wondered whether a good adaptation to a pathological environment could be considered good mental health. This seems to me a philosophical question but a fascinating one.

. . . They seemed very reticent to accept your diagnosis that he was a very disturbed child! I found considerable division among them on the value of projective tests but a few were in favor of them.

†123. *Oscar Lewis to Carolina Luján, June 30, 1965*

. . . I am impressed [by] how well the child [Gabi Ríos] has done in his poor and inadequate family environment. The resiliency of some children is remarkable. It takes a lot to get them down. . . . If only there were more time so that I could study the child or at least be with him for a while each day.

†124. *Carolina Luján to Oscar Lewis, July 1, 1965*

I can't help but feel that these psychiatrists were reacting to Oscar Lewis, after having been unduly influenced by Oscar Lewis as to [Gabi's] good functioning in his environment. I consider this a thoroughly unfair presentation.

We have often discussed the greater tolerance for psychopathology in an individual who develops in a medium where psychopathology is endemic. You can't send an entire slum to a mental institution. But the fact that it is cultural does not convert psychopathology into mental health. There is simply greater tolerance for it *because* it is cultural. . . .

I don't believe you are at all an impartial judge of [Gabi's] functioning. You have a very subjective need to find that every subject you study is "functioning very well". According to your standards, or needs, [Fernanda] functions very well, [Soledad] functions very well, [Simplicio and Flora] function very well. . . .

Why do Americans in general have this need to be noble in making allowances for people in so called underdeveloped or underprivileged environments? Can't human beings even become sick because they don't belong to the Great Society? Should we say rickets are normal because they occur in a culture whose diet is deficient in Vitamin D? . . .

†125. *Oscar Lewis to Carolina Luján, July 3, 1965*
. . . It may be that many of the characteristics of the [Ríos] family are rather widespread and not distinctively Puerto Rican. To formulate these characteristics and to decide which are Puerto Rican and which are more general—this is the next big job.

My impression about the [Ríos] family is that the personality of their members is rather simple rather than complex. Moreover, it is said that these "hard core poverty" families are hard to reach and to understand. Well, I've certainly reached them and I believe we understand them. In commenting on the communication style of such families the analysts have written that content seems less important than interpersonal relations. I don't know what this means. As I read more perhaps I shall begin to understand.

I hope you are not annoyed by my report of the reaction . . . regarding the [Gabi] test results. For me your work has been very very helpful and I wish you will find it possible to continue to work with me in the future.

†126. *Oscar Lewis to Carolina Luján, July 5, 1965*
. . . You are undoubtedly right . . . in thinking that I had unduly influenced the audience in favor of thinking of [Gabi] as of pretty good mental health. I pointed out to them (in all fairness) that my organization of the story gave [Gabi] just the quality that he lacked and for clinical or rather psychological analysis, this was a distorting factor. At any rate, I now have another analysis of the Rorshach. . . . There are a few discrepancies which I should like to have your reactions on. If anything, Dr. [Dorothy] Huntington sees him as even more disturbed than you do. At one point she suggests he may have a tendency for suicide. . . .

My impression that [Gabi] is functioning quite well is truly a superficial impression. I have never given the time that would be necessary by my own standards to study [him]. But even if I did, you and I would probably not agree entirely on this subject. . . . If I had my way, I would set up a well designed scientific experiment to test the predictive value of tests like the Rorshach, T.A.T., C.A.T., etc. . . .

127. *Oscar Lewis to John Fischer,* Harper's *magazine, September 6, 1965*
. . . The most remarkable thing about Gabi is how well he manages to cope with a difficult, pathological environment. Those who define

mental health as the ability to adapt would have to conclude that Gabi has excellent mental health. Actually, Gabi's adjustment is achieved at a high price. Psychological tests suggest that he is a lonely, confused and frightened child who is pushing himself hard to survive in his hostile and overwhelming world. So far he shows no manifest symptoms of psychological disorders. His own dream in which he sees himself at age twenty foretells his destiny with considerable accuracy. . . .

128. *Oscar Lewis to Helen Icken Safa, anthropologist, December 14, 1966*
    . . . In looking through the early part of your report, I have the impression that you don't subscribe at all to the idea of a subculture of poverty. You seem to think that the people I describe have middle-class values and that the only problem is that they don't achieve them because of barriers in the larger society. . . . Actually, the reality which I have described is much too complicated for any single conceptual model like the subculture of poverty. And although most of the reviewers have lauded the introduction and find the model very exciting, my own feeling is that the major contribution is the rich ethnographic data. . . .

†129. *Oscar Lewis to Carolina Luján, April 21, 1967*
    . . . I am trying to decide what should be my next book on Puerto Rico. I am tempted to produce a relatively short book dealing with the lives of three women. I would also like to include [Gladys] but I hesitate because she is a prostitute, and if I go on at this rate people may think I am becoming a specialist in prostitution! I have most of the material for a full-size volume on another family ["Six Women"], but that too would mean including two sisters who were prostitutes and whose husbands in some cases were pimps. There are also other characters in the family who are quite interesting. I can't afford to publish anything which would sound too repetitious of *La Vida*. I wish you could read some of these new materials so that you could give me your reaction to them and perhaps this would help me to make the best decision possible in the light of what I have.
    . . . I received another three-year research grant to continue work with Puerto Rican families in San Juan and in New York and I am planning to spend part of my time in San Juan to finish up the field work. . . . However, I am looking forward to the possibility of spending six months or a year in Mexico after I have completed my next two Puerto Rican volumes. I want very much to finish my follow-up study of the grandchildren of Sánchez and 1968 or 1969 would be just about right.

130. *Oscar Lewis to Carolina Luján, May 9, 1967*

. . . I am not very enthusiastic about the usefulness of applying middle class "objective" tests of any kind to lower class people. So many articles have shown that middle class values are built into the tests that there are no culture-free tests.

131. *Oscar Lewis to Ruth Lewis, May 25, 1967*

. . . Barrington Moore's review [of *La Vida*] is quite interesting. I've thought of all the points he made in his analysis of the apolitical nature of the Ríos family but I've never published on this. Someday, if there is time, I shall elaborate on this analysis. Most of what he says is in my introduction. I very much like his idea that the slum poor are but a poor imitation of some of the values of the larger society, i.e. they reflect the values of the larger capitalistic and materialistic system—they want the same things and have no basis for developing an independent set of critical values. In this sense, one might argue, they have no real sub-culture of their own—their sub-culture consists of the same values—but *watered down* and poorly integrated. His point that they produce little and are mainly consumers and have a consumer's ideology is quite good, etc. On the whole, I'd say it was the most thoughtful review so far, the only Marxist analysis I've seen. Too bad I didn't do it myself.

†132. *Oscar Lewis to Carolina Luján, October 3, 1968*

. . . As you will see . . . the design of this book ["Six Women"] is intended to provide the reader with a contrast between three generations in the lives of a poor and landless family, most of whom have been *agregaos* in the coffee country in the hills . . . of Puerto Rico. . . .

One of my motives [was to provide] a comparison between Gloria, age 26, and her "milk sister," Sofia, also age 26, [as] an excellent controlled experiment in the effects of environment and upbringing upon two children born to the same family but raised in different settings. Actually, Sofia and Gloria are aunt and niece. . . .

. . . to my great surprise, Gloria turned out to be much more like her mother [who gave her up for adoption] than I had anticipated. It makes me wonder whether we social scientists haven't been neglecting the genetic factor.

. . . I hope this book will throw some light on the social conditions and the family backgrounds of lower class illiterate people, whose traditionally rural culture breaks down in the city slums and leads to the development of a subculture of poverty. If this book will truly contribute to our understanding of the process involved, I will have achieved one of my major goals. . . .

It seems to me that, in many ways, the women in my new book, all except Gloria, are much better representatives of the subculture of poverty than were the children of Sánchez or Pedro Martínez. [Their] lives seem so much more circumscribed than those of my Mexican subjects. In reading PEDRO MARTÍNEZ, and even THE CHILDREN OF SÁNCHEZ, one learns not only about the private lives and the family histories of a few individuals, but also a great deal about Mexico, its institutions and its history. In the case of ["Six Women"] I am afraid there is much less payoff on this score. One learns so little about the major events of Puerto Rican history in the last 70 years in reading their lives. It's almost as if history has passed them by. . . . You will recall that provincialism and limited horizons are one of the key characteristics of the sub-culture of poverty. It therefore follows that the closer the individuals studied are to the theoretical model the less one can learn from their lives about the larger society. . . . In spending so much of my time in the study of the humble lives of these people, I feel that I myself am rapidly becoming illiterate, isolated and out of touch with the great pressing and frightening, but important, events of our time. This distresses me. But it seems to be part of the price that I have to pay for having decided to specialize in the sub-culture of poverty. Perhaps my future study in Cuba will once again bring me into touch with more complex, more advanced, and more developed human beings—human beings whose lives have presumably been touched or influenced by the magic of revolutionary, socialist ideals, by conceptions of international solidarity and the brotherhood of man. If the conception of the brotherhood of man is to be anything but rhetoric, the first prerequisite is for the abolition of illiteracy and ignorance, breakdown of barriers between nations, and the awareness on the part of poor people of the existence of their brethren in other parts of the world. The Puerto Rican experiment of [former governor Luis] Muñoz Marin has obviously not succeeded in bringing this new elementary knowledge to the people that I have studied. Of course, the tradition of the brotherhood of man is an old one and, I understand it was central to Christianity. And certainly the family that I am writing about is Catholic but somehow the doctrine just remained a theoretical ideology and was never translated into a reality or into action for the poor that I have gotten to know. . . .

†133. *Oscar Lewis to Carolina Luján, November 8, 1968*
. . . It strikes me that *doña* Carmen ["Six Women"] has some of the qualities which I described for "Manly-Hearted Women Among the Blackfoot" [*sic*] many years ago. . . . It strikes me that Carmen was just enough of a rebel and a deviant from her traditional rural culture

to prepare the way for the later deviation and breakdown which is represented by the sub-culture of poverty. It is my hunch that if Santa [Carmen's sister] had had daughters, and if her daughters had come to the slums of San Juan, they would have adjusted quite differently from Carmen's daughters. Of course this is hard to prove. . . .

†134. *Oscar Lewis to Carolina Luján, November 12, 1968*

. . . In reading this manuscript ["Six Women"] I would appreciate it if you would keep in mind one of the major objectives that I had in mind in selecting and studying this particular constellation of relatives. I thought I could show the process of change from a traditional essentially father-oriented or patriarchally-oriented rural culture to the more matrifocal sub-culture of poverty characteristic of the slums. In the past, most explanations of the origins or ideology of the sub-culture. . . , with its matrifocal emphasis, have been primarily in terms of the specific social and economic conditions presented by urban slum life, with emphasis upon the factors of high rates of unemployment for the males; more stable income, either through Relief or work, for the females; a high rate of desertion of females by males who have had a bad image of women and of themselves, which is in part a function of their own lack of economic opportunities and a consequent inability to fulfill the expected male role of provider. What I am suggesting, however, is that there is a selective factor at work in the migration to urban slums, whereby there is a unduly high proportion of migrants who come from poor rural families who already showed signs of deviation from the cultural norm even in the country, and specifically, from families where the mother, as in the case of Carmen, had begun to develop a spirit of independence and autonomy, and an ability to stand up against men and not take it in the submissive way that the tradition required. Children raised by such mothers as Carmen had a model which inclined them towards the further development of female dominance, or at least not the total expected submission to males. . . . In any case, I don't have the time at this moment to further substantiate and document from my own case material the general proposition which I have stated. I would very much appreciate your giving serious thought to this proposition and sharing with me any reactions, pro or contra, which may occur to you. . . . In essence I am arguing that there are selective psychological factors among migrants which predispose them toward the deviation of the traits of the sub-culture of poverty in urban slums, because they come from rural families where the traditional forms of control were already weakening or breaking down in the country. I would have to argue, therefore, that had the children of Santa ended up in [La Esmeralda], they would have retained the more stable family patterns of their mother than did the children of Carmen. Incidentally, whereas Santa had only one husband, married by law and church and never remarried after his death, *doña* Carmen, after the death of her first husband, had two free unions and a daughter by her cousin . . . who was probably her secret lover. This exemplifies what I call the beginning of deviant patterns. On the other hand, I suspect that there were many poor landless women in [Vega Baja] who lived in free union—indeed, were seduced by plantation owners, etc., and thereby were developing some of the sub-culture of poverty traits. . . .

135. *Oscar Lewis to Steven Polgar, anthropologist, December 9, 1968*

I understand from some colleagues that you raised some critical objections to my concept of a subculture of poverty. I would very much appreciate having you spell them out for me if you are interested and can find the time. . . .

On the basis of my own studies of families over three generations I have clear-cut evidence to support the contention that under circumstances of slum life, the subculture of poverty may be self-perpetuating. However, to say this by no means ignores the factors of neglect and exploitation involved in the creation and perpetuation of this phenomena. Indeed, one of the six basic preconditions for the development of the subculture of poverty is a capitalist system. . . .

Cuba

136. *Oscar Lewis to Arnaldo Orfila, September 22, 1960* (translated from Spanish)

. . . After living in Mexico fourteen months, living in Urbana is a somewhat rude change in environment, not only in the sense of geography and climate, but also in a moral sense, if I can put it that way. The great majority of people and of my colleagues are anti-Castro and speak of him with hatred and fear, as if he were a personal danger to each one of them. Sometimes their reactions seem a little hysterical to me.

In spite of this I would like to visit Cuba in order to get a look at socio-economic realities, and if they want it, to give some seminars in the University on new trends in modern anthropology, covering among other topics, my studies of poor Mexican families and playing some tapes of my interviews. . . .

137. *Oscar Lewis to C. Wright Mills, sociologist, December 17, 1960*

. . . It must be an unusual opportunity to be in the midst of a great social revolution of the kind that is going on in Cuba.

All great revolutions seem to me to be a miracle. Perhaps that is why there are so few, despite the misery and oppression throughout the world and perhaps throughout history.

As you may recall from our conversation in Mexico, I studied a sugar hacienda in Cuba in 1946 during the regime of Grau San Martín. I'd love to go back to do a restudy of the same place but more important, I'd like to use the family study techniques I've used in Mexico and do a few intensive family studies of peasants and city people who are living through this epocal change. I had been expecting an invitation from the Minister of Education, Armando Hart, but have had no word. Orfila from El Fondo de Cultura Economica was supposed to have arranged it.

. . . If more Americans knew what it means to live and grow up in the slums of a modern Latin American city they would understand that conditions are ripe for great social changes even without Communist influence.

I was especially pleased with your evaluation of the Mexican situation. For a moment, in Mexico, I was afraid you were being taken in by some of the intellectuals who serve as apologists for the present regime and whose slogans become more revolutionary with every retreat from the Revolution. . . .

271

138. *Oscar Lewis to Arnaldo Orfila, January 2, 1961* (in Spanish; written a little more than two months after Orfila wrote to Cuban Minister of Education Armando Hart asking him to invite Lewis to Cuba to do research; a copy of Orfila's letter to Hart was sent to Lewis)

. . . Not long ago C. Wright Mill's LISTEN, YANKEE came out. It is formidable and is one of the few works which expresses the point of view of Cuban revolutionaries. The fact that a book of this kind could be published and reach the public in my country in spite of the reigning hysteria, gives me hope that there is still some feeling of community and freedom in my country. What a pity that Dr. Mills has had a heart attack, quite a serious one I believe, and is still in the hospital in New York.

Since having received your letter, I have been waiting for news from Cuba, but it never comes, and each day it seems less likely that I will be able to do anthropological research in Cuba. I hope to spend two or three days in Mexico in the middle of February and I hope that we will be able to talk more about this then.

139. *Oscar Lewis to Arnaldo Orfila, March 10, 1961* (translated from Spanish)

. . . When I was in Cuba in the summer of 1946, I did a small study of living conditions on the Merceditas *central*, in Melena del Sur. . . . I also studied El Zapote *batey* on this *central*. I would like to return to this same sugar plantation to do a re-study and in this way investigate the changes that have occurred since the Revolution. I could also use my stay there to give some seminars on my Mexican family studies.

I would like to have the opportunity to see with my own eyes life in Cuba.

(On March 18, 1961, Orfilo wrote to Lewis to say that he had met with the eminent Cuban historian Dr. José Antonio Portuondo, who was then serving as ambassador to Mexico. Orfila gave a letter to Portuondo asking him to help arrange an invitation for Lewis to go to Cuba to work; the letter [a copy of which was sent to Lewis] quoted directly from Lewis's letter of March 10, giving the focus of his intended research.)

140. *Oscar Lewis to Arnaldo Orfila, May 6, 1961* (translated from Spanish)

. . . The invasion of Cuba has frightened us and now we are afraid that our administration in Washington is preparing other strikes in the future. I hope that Mexico and the other Latin American countries will show unity in support of the principle of national sovereignty.

I understand that C. Wright Mills and his family have left to live in Europe for a year because Mills can no longer tolerate the insults and the strain he felt in the New York [political] climate. . . . a short time ago Mills published a statement saying that if his health had permitted, he would have fought with Fidel to defend Cuba.

141. *Oscar Lewis to Gordon Ray, The Guggenheim Foundation, New York, October 16, 1961*
     . . . I enclose a copy of a letter of arrangement from John Fischer of Harper's Magazine, for work in Cuba. I believe this should be enough for permission from our State Department and in view of the length of my proposed stay, I am hopeful they will allow my family to accompany [me]. I certainly would not want to go alone.

142. *Oscar Lewis to Arnaldo Orfila, October 26, 1961* (translated from Spanish)
     . . . Three weeks ago I received an invitation from the University of Havana telling me that I could return to Cuba to continue my anthropological studies in Melena del Sur. . . . I have already taken the necessary steps with those in charge here at the University of Illinois, asking for a year's leave beginning in June, 1962. Ruth doesn't want to leave sooner. At the same time I have applied for a Guggenheim Fellowship. It seems to me that things are moving along very well.
     . . . Almost all of my colleagues here advise me not to go to Cuba for fear that the North American public is not disposed to read anything objective about Cuba.
     . . . I am sending a check with this letter for copies of . . . *Antropologia de la Pobreza* with the hope that you could send them to Cuban writers and intellectuals who are interested in this type of study. You can pick the names better than I.

(In a letter written to Lewis by Orfila on January 24, 1962, Orfila said he had spoken to Hart and Raul Roa about the possibility of UNESCO "intervening" to ask for Lewis's collaboration in some of their work in Cuba. Orfila wrote that the two Cuban officials approved this idea and he asked for Lewis's reaction to the plan. A few days later the Fondo sent Lewis a copy of a letter from Celia Sánchez acknowledging that Castro received a copy of *Antropologia de la Pobreza.*)

(Joseph McDaniel, Jr., secretary of the Ford Foundation, wrote to Lewis on February 26, 1962, refusing funding for research in Cuba: "Your proposal has raised problems which bear rather on Foundation policy in the management of its programs than upon the merits of your particular proposal." McDaniel also wrote that the proposal "falls outside the scope of the Foundation's program policies. . . .")

143. *Oscar Lewis to Robert Taber, journalist, February 22, 1963*

Yes, I suppose that Castro is the one great leader in recent years of people with a culture of poverty. The problems involved in working with such people must be terrible, and the obstacles to be overcome just in terms of their own backgrounds would seem to be so formidable as to make unlikely the transformation of Cuba into a showplace for Latin America for many years to come, even under the best of circumstances, i.e., even if they didn't have to cope with the additional problem of the opposition and destructive efforts of the U.S.

. . . You may be interested to know that the Guggenheim Foundation has offered me a fellowship for a year's study in Cuba, but I'm afraid that there would be too many difficulties in my way, particularly from our own State Department, and so I have decided to study Puerto Rican slum families in San Juan and their relatives in New York City.

(In February 1968 Lewis made a trip to Cuba, on a reporter's visa, and while there gave several talks for La Casa de las Americas, Cuba's leading cultural institute. La Casa was founded and directed by Haydée Santamaría Cuadrado until her death by suicide in 1980. Santamaría was a principal supporter of Lewis's bid to do research in Cuba. In 1968 the Book Institute of La Casa, without securing rights, published Spanish-language editions of several of Lewis's books.)

144. *Oscar Lewis to Lowry Nelson, sociologist, March 27, 1968* (Nelson and Lewis met in Cuba in 1946)

. . . I spent about seventeen days in Cuba looking over the possibilities of my own future research there. My major concern was to find out whether I would have complete freedom to do my kind of intensive family studies, which demand complete anonymity of the subjects investigated. I was given assurance by many men in high places that these conditions would be respected and I am now thinking seriously about the possibility of going to Cuba for a year. However, I should probably begin my studies of Cuban families in Miami, because I consider their experiences to be a crucial part of my overall objective, namely to investigate the effects of the Cuban revolution on family life and family structure.

At this point, I am not sure that I could be very helpful to you on advising you how to get to Cuba. I have no contacts or influence there. My own trip was the result of an assignment by Harper's Magazine to do an article on poverty in Cuba. I believe the Cuban government issued a visa for me because they like my books, and, indeed, are pirating THE CHILDREN OF SÁNCHEZ, PEDRO MARTÍNEZ and LA VIDA.

145. *Oscar Lewis to Harry E. Wilhelm, Ford Foundation, November 1, 1968* (This is the only proposal or "design" that existed for the Cuba project. I have deleted the two-page summary budget for the first three-year period [$294,903] and several lines on travel plans and budgetary matters.)

In accord with our talks of September 23, I am now writing to make formal application for financial assistance to help me do a comparative analysis of the culture of poverty and its transformation in the changing Latin American scene. I propose to begin with the study of the effects of the Cuban Revolution on the lives of lower-class Cubans in a number of cities and rural areas in Cuba. I believe it is terribly important to learn more about the nature and meaning of poverty in a socialist context.

My interest in doing comparative work in Cuba grows out of my earlier experience in that country and my hope that careful research in Cuba can make an unusually significant contribution to the social sciences, to policy makers, and to the general public. Most of the reporting on the Cuban Revolution has been on a political and macroscopic level, by people who have spent very little time in that country and, with few exceptions, have had little or no background in the study of Latin American cultures. A good deal of the reporting has, therefore, been of a superficial and rather poor quality. It seems to me that what is needed is patient, rigorous field investigation, in a number of spots throughout the island, to determine what the revolution means in terms of the daily lives of the people, particularly the peasants and urban slum dwellers who have been my special interest for many years.

In 1946 I spent approximately four months in Cuba as a visiting professor of anthropology at the University of Havana for the U.S. State Department. As part of my assignment, I gave field work training to a group of Cuban students during a two-month's survey of social and economic conditions on a sugar plantation at Melena del Sur, approximately ninety miles southeast of Havana. We collected data on both the town and the *municipio* (county) of Melena del Sur, on the sugar *ingenio*, and on some of the surrounding rural settlements (*bateys*) of sugar workers. I also spent some time in a reconnaissance survey of lower-class slum settlements in Havana and traveled throughout the island gathering impressions of regional differences in rural Cuba.

In August, 1961, I returned to Cuba on assignment from *Harper's Magazine* to do an article and to explore the possibilities of continuing my earlier research. In this connection I revisited Melena del Sur, where I found some of the same families I had known back in 1946. I was given a warm reception and received offers of cooperation for any further study. Even this short revisit revealed many changes and lack of changes (the physical conditions of the Havana slums seemed very much like what I had seen in 1946) which deserve careful investigation if we are to have a better understanding of what is going on in Cuba today.

In February, 1968, I visited Cuba again, this time for two weeks. The major purpose of my visit was to explore with Cuban intellectuals and government leaders the feasibility of my doing research there under present conditions. In my talks with a number of professors at the University of Havana, with José Llanusa, Minister of Education, and with Fidel Castro, I was assured that I would have complete freedom and privacy to carry out my studies. I have also talked with Mr. Frederick Smith, Jr., Deputy Administrator, Bureau of Security and Consular Affairs, Department of State, Washington, D.C., and have assurance of Department approval for my trip. In short, I seem to have the blessings of both the Cuban Government and our own for this project.

In the course of my visit with Fidel Castro in February, I was surprised and pleased to learn that he was thoroughly familiar with my book, THE CHILDREN OF SÁNCHEZ, which he had read in the Spanish version, and which we discussed at some length. He had his favorite characters and made astute comments on the reliability of the accounts of the various informants. For example, he thought that Manuel was a classical picaresque type and such a good story teller that it would be difficult to know when he was describing events and when he was just making up a good yarn. On the other hand, he felt that Marta, although less colorful, spoke with greater sincerity, from the heart, and with less fantasy and distortion.

When Fidel Castro invited me to undertake similar studies of poor families in Cuba, I explained in some detail the conditions that would have to be met for my work, namely, complete freedom of investigation, including my selection of sample families without interference and, above all, assurances from the government that the subjects that I selected for study would not be investigated or otherwise harrassed. In this connection I recalled that during my study of a village in Spain in 1949, the peasants were called up for questioning by the local police, at which point I left the village and terminated my study. I also explained that I would have to be able to assure the people who cooperated in the study that they would remain anonymous and that my taped interviews with them would not be subject to examination or seizure. Finally, I said I would want to bring my own secretary and research assistants.

Mr. Castro agreed to these conditions. He said that he and his government were not interested in the particular individual families that I studied but rather in the general results of the study. He went on to say that there was nothing to hide, that Cubans were the most talkative people in the world and there were probably no complaints or grievances that people would tell me about which he hadn't already heard from the counter-revolutionaries. Then he paused and added, "You know, come to think of it, we are probably the only Socialist country in the world that would allow you to do your kind of study." He said that although my study would be of no help to the Cuban revolution, it was important for the historic record to have some idea what the people feel and think at this particular point in the progress of the revolution. He then suggested that I work out the details of my plans for the study with the Minister of Education and with the head of the Book Publishing Institute, both of whom were present [José Llanusa and Rolando Rodríguez].

I propose to spend three years on the Cuba study, beginning in January, 1969. My research project will include a rural and an urban phase: (1) a restudy of the *municipio* of Melena del Sur in the province of Havana; (2) a study of some sample families from the Las Llaguas slum which I had studied earlier—the slum has been completely eliminated and all the Las Llaguas families have now been relocated in six housing projects in Havana; (3) a comparative analysis of families in three types of housing settlements in the city of Santiago, in Oriente Province. The first type will be an inner-city *cuarteria*, or slum-like settlement. The second type will be in the new Martí high-rise apartments on the outskirts of the city, and a third will be the new single-dwelling units of the Colonia Nuevo, which is inhabited by former slum dwellers, primarily Negroes; (4) a sample of families living on a state-controlled farm enterprise; (5) some sample families who work in factories; and (6) some Cuban exile families in New York City, Miami, and Puerto Rico and some of their relatives in Cuba. [1]

I should like to apply the same methods of study which I have used with some success in my anthropological community study of a Mexican village (1943–48), in my studies of lower-class settlements in Mexico City (1951, 1955–56, 1959, 1960), and in San Juan and New York City (1963 to date). The emphasis in the Cuban studies will be upon a combination of community studies and intensive family studies which will provide us with comparative data on the culture of poverty in another Latin American country.

The Cuban Revolution provides an unusual opportunity to study the effects of drastic social, economic and political transformations on personal and family life. I will attempt to determine the change or stability in some of the basic traits of the culture of poverty such as consensual marriages, illegitimacy, alcoholism, the abandonment of mothers, authoritarianism, mother-centered families, present-time orientation, fatalism, etc. I will also try to evaluate the degree of success or failure in achieving some of the national objectives of the Castro government, such as the elimination of illiteracy, raising the standard of living, agrarian reform, and the development of revolutionary ideals, as seen from the vantage point of daily observation and participation over a two or three year period in each of the areas selected for this study.

I am aware that there are many problems and risks involved in undertaking a study in Cuba at this time. Asking hundreds of questions and prying into life histories always creates some suspicion of motives and may be particularly dangerous for a *norteamericano* or *yanqui* at this time. However, as indicated earlier, I have assurance of cooperation from the Cuban government and the University of Havana that I would be given the necessary freedom to carry out this study and I'm willing to risk it.

. . . I am planning on three or four trips to the United States to bring back data, to get necessary equipment, and to supervise my study of Cuban exiles in this country. During [each of] the first two years of the project I am planning to spend approximately seven months in Cuba and five months in the United States. However, this may have to be changed in accord with the needs of the project. During the third year of the project I plan to spend four or five months in Cuba.

1. Lewis, with the assistance of José Saenz de la Peña, a Cuban exile, did interviewing with seventeen Cubans living in New York and New Jersey, during 1968–69.

146. *Oscar Lewis to Joseph Casagrande, anthropologist and director, Center for International Comparative Studies, University of Illinois* (sponsor of the Cuba Project), *April 17, 1969*

I am writing to advise you that my Cuba research program is off to an excellent start. The Cuban government has been very cooperative and has provided me with a lovely home, an office, and space for my research assistants. They have also helped with a car and a chauffeur.[1] Even more important, I have complete freedom for my research and I have already selected for study two housing projects inhabited by former residents of Las Llaguas. I have also managed to locate most of the rural families that I had studied in 1946 in Melena del Sur.

1. The Lewises *rented* the space and equipment from the Cuban government.

†147. *Oscar Lewis to Muna Muñoz Lee, September 2, 1969*

I returned from Cuba about two weeks ago and I had hoped to write to you sooner but I have been overwhelmed with work, which is about the usual state of my existence.

. . . This is the largest staff that I have ever worked with and it certainly has its drawbacks. Sometimes I feel that the more people that I have working for me the less I can get done. Ten of my staff are young Cubans who have had very little background in the social sciences, but all of them are eager to learn my fieldwork techniques and they have reached the point where they are making a real contribution to the project. Eight of them are graduates of pedagogical institutes and two are university graduates. Most of these young people volunteered their services during the literacy campaign in 1960–61, when they left their homes and went to live with peasants in the hill country. I have tried to reconstruct their experiences but most of them were so young and had so little background at the time that I haven't been able to do much with this.

I selected 100 families for study—an entire housing project. Most of these families formerly lived in the Las Llaguas slum which, as you may recall, I had visited and studied prior to the revolution. On purely theoretical grounds I had expected to find that these families would show much less incorporation into the revolutionary process than non-slum families. Our results so far indicate that in approximately 35% of the homes one or more individuals [are] actively participating in some kind of revolutionary organization. When you consider that the degree of participation in the slum was about zero this figure shows considerable progress. However, it is also clear that many of the traits of the culture of poverty persist in this housing project. I believe I was overly optimistic in some of my earlier evaluations about the disappearance of the culture of poverty under socialism. However, there seems to me to be no doubt that the Cuban Revolution has abolished the conditions which gave rise to the culture of poverty.

I am impressed by the degree to which the government has been able to organize large masses of people for its many crash programs. The entire economy is now geared to agricultural production, specifically to the production of ten million tons of sugar in 1970. The most that Cuba ever produced in pre-revolutionary days was 6.4 million tons. Production for the year 1969 didn't quite reach five million tons, so you can see that a ten million ton goal is really pushing hard. Many of the shortages in the large cities and the poor services are due to the all out effort to get people working in agriculture. In most stores and shops and restaurants about one-half of the employees are out cutting sugarcane, or doing some other agricultural task. This is quite disruptive for urban life; nor is it very efficient, because it takes about four or five seasons for a man to get enough experience to become a good sugarcane cutter, and I doubt that the great majority of volunteers get this experience. However, I think there is a very good chance that they will reach their goal of ten million tons and this will be a tremendous boost to the morale of the country. The Cubans, like so many of us, perform well under crisis conditions and in emergencies, and life since the revolution has been one crisis after another.

The rationing system has been a great equalizer and has made for a basic kind of social justice. The Cubans have to make-do with what they've got but, at least, they have the satisfaction of knowing that they're all in it together and that the entire nation is paying the price of development and industrialization without any single group getting rich in the process. I admire the heroism of the Cuban people in this effort to overcome underdevelopment, and certainly the U.S. blockade is not helping them.

I am planning to be here [in Urbana, Ill.] until about October 10 when I return to Cuba to begin the rural side of my study. This should be the most fascinating part of the work because most of the progress has been made in rural areas. In picking former slum dwellers as subjects for the first phase of my study I was aware that this would be a severe test of the progress of the Cuban revolution. Had I begun with people in rural areas the results would probably have been very much more dramatic and encouraging.

The Cubans have made tremendous progress in the fields of education and health but there is still a great deal to be done and it will be an uphill struggle for a long time to come. This was to be expected, and yet it tends to depress me. It must be that I am getting old very fast.

148. *Oscar Lewis to Marvin Harris, anthropologist, September 12, 1969* (from a postscript)

Do you believe that you can predict the outbreak of a major revolution by your techno-economic-determinism, or do you consider such an event outside the deterministic universe that you are concerned with? This is a question of great practical and theoretical importance. Fidel Castro generally distinguishes between what he calls the objective and subjective conditions necessary for a successful revolution. The objective conditions stated by Castro are very similar to those enumerated by Lenin. However, under subjective conditions he stresses the importance of revolutionary leadership, courage, and the readiness of the people to give their lives in aggressive and violent attacks against the existing regime.

One of the major criticisms of the Communist Parties in Latin America is that they sit back and wait for the objective conditions to be just right rather than making their own history and changing objective conditions by their own revolutionary efforts. Of course, any good study of revolution would have to try to explain under what conditions the Castro approach develops and under what conditions the Communist Party approach develops within the Latin American scene. To date, Anthropologists have made little or no contribution toward the understanding of this kind of a problem. It is an intrinsically difficult problem. Similarly, the environmental, technological and economic conditions in Cuba and Puerto Rico seem to me to have been remarkably similar during the nineteenth century when both were colonies of Spain. How then can we explain the presence of a revolutionary tradition in Cuba and the absence of one in Puerto Rico? When I asked Fidel Castro this question, he said it was simply historical accident that there were some courageous men in Cuba who decided to fight against Spain and that their struggle then established a tradition which clearly was a deterministic factor in the evolution of the Castro approach. This kind of an explanation does not satisfy me, and I am still searching for other factors that might provide a profounder understanding of Puerto Rico vis-a-vis Cuba.

When I suggest that your formulation does not give enough weight to the personal or human factors, I have in mind the example I cited above. . . .

†149. *Oscar Lewis to Muna Muñoz Lee, July 3, 1970*
. . . I have had very serious problems in Cuba and am quite depressed right now. I hope things will clear up. I've worked terribly hard and want to do some good books. The recent publication of two books on Cuba, one by Karol [the Polish expatriate journalist], the other by Dumont [the French rural sociologist], both in French, both quite critical, have done incalculable harm to my research project.[1] The government is now worried about my books on Cuba and this has created problems for me. It is not easy to do my kind of research during a Socialist revolution—or in a Socialist state. It's almost a miracle that I've done as well as I have.

1. The English-language editions of these books are K. S. Karol, *Guerrillas in Power* (New York: Hill and Wang, 1970); and René Dumont, *Is Cuba Socialist?*, trans. Stanley Hochman (New York: Viking, 1974; originally published in 1970 by Editions du Seuil as *Cuba est-il Socialiste?*).

†150. *Oscar Lewis to Muna Muñoz Lee, August 6, 1970*
. . . This [Nicolás Salazar (*Four Men*)] material is dynamite in the sense that it portrays the persistence of many of the characteristics of

the culture of poverty in a Socialist context. I am afraid I was over optimistic about the possibility of eliminating the culture of poverty so rapidly.

†151. *Oscar Lewis to Muna Muñoz Lee, August 17, 1970*
. . . I am reading the new book on Cuba by Karol, and I find it fascinating. However, it is extremely critical of recent political trends in Cuba. For Karol, Fidel's support of the Soviet Union in the invasion of Czechoslovakia marks a turning point in the political philosophy of the Cuban regime. Karol explains the high absen[tee rate] and the general low level of productivity in all fields as a function of a system which does not give the people very much of a voice in the decision making process. He claims that fundamentally it is a one man rule and that, moreover, Fidel has very little faith in the rank and file. No wonder Fidel was furious. I hope to have something to say on this matter when I am ready to publish.

†152. *Oscar Lewis to Jason Epstein, September 11, 1970*
. . . I can't seem to get the Cuban problem out of my mind. It has had a terribly depressing effect upon me and it is slowing up my work on all fronts. However, I am planning to have the Puerto Rican manuscript ["Six Women"] ready for you before the end of November. . . .

153. *Oscar Lewis to Joseph Casagrande, December 12, 1970* (four days before Lewis died)
. . . Field work in Cuba was carried on over a period of sixteen months, from March 1, 1969 through June 25, 1970. During this time I made eight trips back to the States and I managed to get 30,000 pages of research data which are now in my files here in Urbana.

The first six months of 1970 were spent in intensive field work in Havana, with special emphasis upon three areas: 1) the Buena Ventura urban renewal settlement; 2) an apartment house with five families in Miramar, and 3) a number of families of middle class background selected at random. . . .

. . . The termination of the field work on June 25, 1970 occurred because of circumstances beyond my control. One of the results of this unfortunate and unforeseen development is that I will not be able to complete the rural phase of my original research plan. I am negotiating with the Cuban government for special permission to finish up my field work. Because of the delicacy of these negotiations, it is essential that this matter receive no publicity and that it remain strictly confidential for the present. . . .

This has been a most difficult year for me. For a number of years I have had a heart problem—angina pectoris—but I had managed to keep up with my work quite successfully. During my last two months in Cuba . . . my symptoms became more severe. I had planned to leave Cuba in late June for a two month period for a careful checkup here in the States, and I had hoped to return to Cuba in September to continue my field work. On September 17, 1970, I was hospitalized here in Urbana with an acute myocardial infarction. . . .

I plan to return to Cuba in early February in an effort to resolve some of the problems which arose in connection with my research project and thereby enable the finishing up of the field research.

Policy and Ethics

154. *Oscar Lewis to Ward Shepard, U.S. Public Affairs Institute, December 13, 1949*

. . . I think my study has some direct implications for the Point IV program for I have tried to show what happens to a rural Mexican village as a result of changes in technology and means of communication.[1] I am afraid that there has been a lot of wishful thinking on the part of some of the planners of Point IV. I confess that after a long and thorough study of the village and Municipio of Tepoztlán I would be hard put to sit down and write up a program for this country which might lead to a fuller and richer life. . . . My implications [in "Husbands and Wives in a Mexican Village: A Study in Role Conflict"] concerning the poor quality of human relations has definite bearing upon any planning for backward or colonial areas. It is difficult to know whether the program should begin with a psychological clinic or with improving agricultural techniques. Of course what is needed is an over-all integrated program rather than the kind of blind piecemeal fumbling around that has characterized most welfare programs with which I am familiar.

1. Point IV was the Truman administration's program for providing scientific and technical aid to developing nations.

155. *Oscar Lewis to Clyde Kluckhohn, January 1, 1953*

. . . I have been doing brief reconnaissance surveys of [Indian] villages in some of the 55 community development projects and have also been interviewing social scientists at the major Universities, to build up an inventory of personnel resources which might be available for collaboration with the community development projects. I have met and talked with anthropologists, sociologists, and economists at Delhi, Lucknow, Bombay, Poona, Allahabad, Madras and Hyderabad. Everywhere I have found keen interest in learning about developments in social science in the United States.

. . . My main job is to help along with the evaluation in my capacity as advisor to the National Planning Commission. . . . I find that there is just as much of an educational job to be done within our own organization, particularly in regard to the need for basic research. . . . I sometimes think that the real hurdle for anthropologists on Point Four programs is not so much the resistance of natives as that of our own personnel, administrative and otherwise. Some administrators, sensitive to the growing prestige of anthropology, are willing, even eager, to employ anthropologists as window-dressing to validate their programs, without having any real understanding of what it is that anthropologists have to contribute, nor the conditions under which they can do their best work.

. . . As an anthropologist, I am expected to come up with relatively simple techniques which can be reliably applied by untrained workers, most of whom will not have had a single course in cultural anthropology. But I am hopeful that some good work can be done. Most of the reporting will be on the level of program analysis rather than that of culture change. However, it may be possible to make each evaluation officer responsible for an intensive study of at least one village within his project area, in addition to the over-all reporting. With guidance and good luck we may be able to get some pretty good community studies from twenty different regions in India, covering all the major cultural diversity of the country. At any rate, this is one of our goals.

It is a pity that in the early planning stage of this program no adequate provision was made for . . . competent social scientists [to be] imported along with extension agents, if necessary, to do baseline studies in a few sample communities of the project areas before the action began. Indeed, it is somewhat ironical that one of the best conceived community development programs (at least on paper) should have begun without the benefit of even a single well-rounded modern community study to serve as a basis of departure. But such are the exigencies of our times!

156. *Oscar Lewis to Douglas Ensminger, Ford Foundation, November 6, 1953*
. . . In my opinion the major value of the piece on factions is . . . to show the relevance of this kind of material for action programs and to help set up a baseline from which change can be measured.[1] This was the emphasis in my talk to the Development Commissioners and this is what they responded to so favorably.[2] The first objective, namely to develop relatively simple and reliable methods for the study of values, social organization, and leadership is one about which I have never felt sanguine. Wade [Jones] and I had discussed this at great length and he knows how doubtful I was about this matter. However, since he thought it was important and for the sake of harmony I included it [in the article].

. . . One of my major motives in getting the research going in village R. was to get some first hand familiarity with Indian village culture so that I could be better prepared for the big job of visiting and advising the twenty evaluation officers with whom I had intended to work closely. It seemed to me then as it does now that the most effective way to help the young evaluation officers was through first-hand contacts with them, through on the spot mutual observations and discussions—the kind of thing we did for Carl Taylor [U.S. Department of Agriculture] in the 71 county study.

1. "Group Dynamics in an Indian Village: A Study of Factions," *The Economic Weekly of Bombay* 6 (1954): 423–25, 445–51, 477–82, 501–6.
2. Lewis also met with Indian prime minister Jawaharlal Nehru to discuss the utility of anthropological research for development planning.

157. *Oscar Lewis to Philip E. Mosley, Council on Foreign Relations, New York City, May 25, 1959*

. . . I simply haven't had the time to do justice to the preparation of a statement of policy suggestions on U.S.-Mexican relations—and how to improve them. This is a terribly complicated business and frankly, my anthropological training doesn't help much when it comes to policy matters in international relations. Most of what I would have to say on this score would probably strike you as naive, wild-eyed, and academic—the kind of things professors are noted for.

In view of my interpretation that most of the tensions in U.S.-Mexican relations are a function of the Mexican sense of dependence upon the United States it would follow that U.S. policy must seek to do everything possible to help Mexico become more independent. This would involve encouragement of the growth of Mexican heavy industry, the assurance of a stable price structure for Mexican exports, the provision by the U.S. of government to government loans at low rates of interest, and U.S. backing for the development of a Latin American international trade community which will make possible the free flow of goods and money and personnel.

I would recommend that we expand our present cultural exchange programs with Mexico both on the government to government level and the university to university level so that more professors and students can spend time in each other's country. A number of U.S. universities have successfully sponsored a Junior Year Abroad program. This might be extended to include Mexico. We might also respond to the eagerness of Mexicans to learn English by sponsoring English classes in the larger cities of Mexico through the increase of U.S.-Mexican cultural institutes. At the same time we might organize English classes for *braceros* who come to work in the U.S.

Something more should be done to give the [six] hundred thousand American tourists who visit Mexico each year a better understanding of the way of life of the great mass of Mexicans—their problems, how they think and feel, what they worry about, argue over, anticipate or enjoy. For this to happen more Americans must learn to speak and read Spanish. In the meantime I would like to see some of the fine contemporary Mexican novels and short stories translated into English and made available in low priced paperbacks.

Perhaps our most impressive potential contribution as a good neighbor could be in the field of encouraging greater social justice. My study of the changes in Mexico since 1940 has shown that although the Mexican national wealth has greatly increased its distribution has become [more] unequal than before. In other words the Mexican poor have been paying for the costs of industrialization and national progress. This is not a new pattern; the same thing happened in the history of western European nations. In Mexico this can be seen most dramatically by comparing the housing and living conditions of the ever-increasing slum districts of Mexico City with the lovely modernistic homes of the nouveau riche in Lomas de Chapultepec. The rise in the wealth and standard of living of the upper class . . . is occurring at a much faster rate than the improvements in the lower class. This makes the contrasts between rich and poor more striking than before even though there has been some progress for all strata of the population. I am suggesting that U.S. aid programs be broadened to cover not only improvements in production but also to deal more directly with improving standards of living. If the U.S. (either through government, private or international agencies) could take the lead in making available to the Institute for Public Housing . . . large low-interest bearing loans earmarked for housing projects for the poor, this might have a considerable impact in building a positive image of the U.S. in the popular mind. I mention this as one example of what might be done. The improvement of housing in Mexico is a key point because of the many implications of crowded living upon family life and mental health. In terms of modern psychological concepts it would seem impossible for good mental health to develop in a situation where an entire family must eat, live and sleep in a single room—a condition that is experienced by millions of Mexicans. In this connection it is interesting to note that Mexican psychiatrists claim that a great deal of anti-gringoism is rooted in deep psychological factors which are produced by difficulties in Mexican family life—particularly the ambivalent attitude toward the father image.

Well, I doubt that this is what you want but it is the best I can do at this time. . . .

158. *Oscar Lewis to Chester Bowles, undersecretary of state, March 7, 1961*

It has been seven years since we talked over lunch in your home in New Delhi about India and Indian problems. . . .

It seems to me that the Peace Corps plan has some real possibilities provided there is careful selection of volunteers and an adequate training program, and some administrative provisions for keeping in touch with the young people in the field. . . .

. . . I have a specific proposal which I should like to submit. I am taking a group of graduate students from the University of Illinois to a small, fairly isolated village in Mexico for a two-month summer research study. It occurred to me that it might be feasible to have a few members of the Peace Corps join us in this village to teach English and otherwise help the villagers. In this way we would be combining a program of scientific study with a program of services, and I am sure that this would be mutually beneficial.

It might be worthwhile to consider the possibility of some such joint endeavor between anthropological research groups and the Peace Corps throughout the world. This would make possible some field training and supervision of the young volunteers by professionally trained anthropologists without any additional cost. It might prevent some young people from committing blunders and perhaps help keep them from getting into serious troubles. It would also provide an opportunity for the Peace Corps workers to learn something about native culture in a systematic and disciplined way.[1]

1. Lewis sent the same proposal in a letter written the following day to Philip Mosley of the Council on Foreign Relations. In the summer of 1965 the Peace Corps asked Lewis to spend a month in South America evaluating their urban slum work, but the pressures of the Puerto Rican project kept him from accepting the assignment.

159. *Oscar Lewis to Arnaldo Orfila, October 26, 1961* (translated from Spanish)

. . . A short time ago I received a letter from Carballo telling me a little of the reaction to my book [*Five Families*]. Please tell me how the Mexican public has received my book. How many copies have been sold? Some of the reviews seem excellent to me and others very negative. But even in the good ones I feel there is some resentment of the fact it was a Northamerican, a gringo, who has acquainted the world, and even Mexicans, with a little of the misery in which so many families live.

I regret it very much if I have offended some Mexicans with my work. It was never my intention to hurt Mexico or Mexicans because I have so much affection for them. Yes, I admire very much the Mexican people and the ideals of the Revolution and furthermore I have noted how much the Revolution has achieved in spite of so many difficulties. Nevertheless I know that there are still many Mexicans who live in misery and to me has fallen the good fortune to know them and to study them. For this reason I could not be content with only praising the achievements of the Revolution, as the politicians there and even in my country already do very well. If the picture of the poor that is portrayed in my book stimulates discussions that bring some change in the conditions and institutions that sustain this misery, then I will feel my book has been a great success.

The fact that poverty still exists in the United States is no secret to anyone whose eyes are open, and our playwrights and novelists have illustrated this many times.

Many times I have suggested that it would be good if some Mexican anthropologists would be willing to leave their Indians for a while and come to my country to study the Neighborhoods of New York, Chicago or of the South. I have even offered assistance in getting grants for them.

160. *Oscar Lewis to Vera Rubin, anthropologist and director, Institute for the Study of Man, November 12, 1965* (an identical letter was sent to several other people)

In light of the Camelot scandal and the various questions raised both here and in Latin America about the future of research by American scholars in Latin America, it seems to me that my experience with the Mexican reactions to *The Children of Sánchez* may have some important lessons for anthropologists. Actually, the problems raised by the reactions to my book are of an entirely different order from those of the Camelot affair and the two should not be confused.

The story is relatively simple. The first Spanish edition . . . was published in October, 1964 (6,000 copies), was well received in the press in Mexico, and sold out in the first six weeks. The second edition (6,000 copies) appeared sometime in December and was attacked in early February at a meeting of the Mexican Society of Geography and Statistics.

The attack consisted of the following points:

(1) The book was obscene beyond all limits of human decency;
(2) The Sánchez family did not exist. I had made it up;
(3) The book was defamatory of Mexican institutions and of the Mexican way of life;
(4) The book was subversive and anti-revolutionary and violated Article 145 of the Mexican Constitution and was, therefore, punishable with a twenty-year jail sentence because it incited to social dissolution;
(5) The Fondo de Cultura Económica, the author, and the book were all cited for action by the Geography and Statistics Society to the Mexican Attorney General's office; and

(6) Oscar Lewis was an FBI spy attempting to destroy Mexican in-
    stitutions.

Another problem raised by my book was related to the traditional
image of what anthropology is. Anthropology in Mexico has been
almost exclusively identified with the study of Indians and rural communities. It came as a surprise to some Mexicans to find that a study of
urban slums was being done by an anthropologist. Indeed, one of the
points raised by the minority who attacked the book was that this was
not traditional anthropology and they couldn't quite place it. Moreover, the novelty of the approach, namely intensive family studies,
was also a bit disorienting to some of the Mexicans. They wondered
whether family studies were as scientific as community studies and it
was difficult for them to grant that a book with literary quality could
also be scientific. Nevertheless, the whole affair was really a great
victory for anthropology in Mexico. I believe that some of the factors
responsible for the defense of the book were:

(1) I had invited some leading Mexican intellectuals to one or two
    of the slums during the study; and
(2) I had played the tapes in my home for Mexican writers, one or
    two anthropologists, and for a few people in the movie industry.

In short, I had taken the Mexicans into my confidence as the work
progressed so that they knew that a book of this kind was forthcoming. I also played the tape for some of the leading economists and
historians and the head of the publishing house which later published
the book in Spanish. These people were able to refute the absurd
charge that I'd written a book of fiction.

These charges were a grave threat to freedom of scientific investigation and freedom of press and were, therefore, taken up by leading
Mexican writers and intellectuals as a threat to Mexico. Over 500 clippings from Mexico City newspapers are in the file of the Fondo de
Cultura Económica and I have the most important ones.

These issues were discussed on radio and on television and in
the press, in editorial columns, in cartoons, and at special meetings
arranged at the University [of Mexico].

. . . the members of the Sánchez family and my friends at the University tell me that the scandal has had a very beneficial effect and
that it has defeated the forces of reaction who were using my book
as a first move in a campaign designed to eventually censor, if not
silence, some of the contemporary young writers whose novels and
short stories dealt with some of the pressing unsolved problems of
the Mexican revolution.

I was also told that the government is giving much more attention to the slums of Mexico City and is spending more heavily on improvements since my book was published. If this is true, even in part, then I shall have been successful beyond my wildest dreams because I strongly identified with the slum dwellers and I hoped that bringing their way of life and their problems to the attention of readers might eventually do some good and might lead to some amelioration of these conditions. Judging from my informants in Mexico, the book has had exactly this effect.

The single grave concern raised by this scandal is the fact that a number of newspapers sent out their reporters to track down the *vecindad* of the family and [name deleted] was successful in this venture, identified and photographed the slum, and identified one of the family members, Manuel Sánchez of the book. All the other members of the family had left the *vecindad* and were scattered in different parts of the city, and indeed, in different parts of the Republic.

I had made three trips to Mexico with the specific purpose of getting Manuel out of the slums before the appearance of the Spanish edition. He was not enthusiastic to leave and he seemed to welcome the idea of eventually being identified as one of the characters in my book. After much insistence on my part, he agreed that he would move if I could get him into some low-priced public housing. I made a number of efforts to accomplish this, particularly since the head of the Instituto de la Vivienda was a personal friend of mine of many years. However, the promises to do something never materialized so Manuel was still living in the same slum when the scandal broke.

To my knowledge, the true names of the family appeared in only one edition of [name deleted] and after that, due to some unknown cause, the newspapers seemed to withhold this information almost as if they sensed the indecency of what they had done and certainly the violation of my intent and pledge to the family to do everything possible to maintain their anonymity.

Of course, the family was aware, beginning with the early stages of the study . . . that I was writing a book about them and they signed releases allowing me to publish all the data they had given me individually with the understanding that their names and those of their friends and relatives would be changed. All the members of the family except Manuel have tried to keep their part of the bargain and have denied consistently their identity as characters in my book. [Jesús, Roberto, and Consuelo Sánchez identified themselves only after Lewis's death.] Manuel, however, for a variety of motives—one of which was his belief that he was helping me disprove the charge that I had made everything up, identified himself. Moreover, he made a tape recorded statement available to a Mexican professor of sociology and this tape was played at a very crucial meeting of students at the National University which was attended by a great overflow crowd and featured a leading anthropologist, a writer, a sociologist, and one of the men from the Geography and Statistics Society who had originally attacked the book—Sr. [Luis Cataño] Morlet [in a speech given at the Society's headquarters on February 9, 1965].

I have a tape recording of this meeting and a number of clippings from the newspapers. It is clear that the students gave Sr. Morlet a very rough time. Ricardo Pozas, a Mexican anthropologist who had written a very critical review of my earlier work *Five Families* when it appeared in Spanish, publicly defended *The Children of Sánchez* and attacked the Geography Society for its stand.

In April [1965] the Attorney General's office issued a statement clearing the book, the author, and the publisher of all charges and reaffirming the freedom of investigation and freedom of press as a [sic] basic Mexican value. However, despite this ruling the publisher [Orfila] was unable to get his Board of Directors to approve the third edition. . . .

I have the detailed story of the politics of this decision but I do not feel at liberty to publish these details. As you can see, this issue was carefully considered by people who were very high up in the government. The members of the Board of Directors of the Fondo de Cultura Económica who failed to approve a third edition included the novelist and the present Minister of Education, Augustino Yañez; Carrillo Flores, present Minister of Foreign Affairs; and Ortiz Mena, the present Minister of Hacienda. The first two men were all in favor of a third edition but apparently they did not consider it politic to oppose Ortiz Mena who controls the purse strings.

Fortunately, a nongovernment controlled publisher, Joaquín Mortíz has just published a third edition of 12,000 copies. The official statement of the Mexican Attorney General is included as an appendix so that, in effect, the book now has government approval.

Throughout the entire affair the Sánchez family has continued their friendship and sense of loyalty and identity with me. For this I am most grateful and I am deeply moved. Nevertheless, this case does raise the more general question about the possibility of doing this kind of intimate research on the lives of people. Is it really an invasion of privacy when one has the permission of the subjects as I had in this case?

Fortunately in this case the government ruled in my favor. Had they found me guilty on the charge of social dissolution, I suspect that further tape recording research anywhere in Mexico, particularly by

American anthropologists, would have been an impossibility. Even as is, some of my colleagues are afraid that the Sánchez affair may adversely affect their own research plans in Mexico.

The study of slums and poverty by Americans in Latin American countries—particularly in a country like Mexico with its strong anti-gringo tradition—is fraught with dangers of a kind that archaeologists, for example, working in Mexico would not be troubled by. The American archaeologist who can show that corn is 2,000 or 3,000 years older in Mexico than has heretofore been known becomes a hero. The social anthropologist who describes the misery of people who live in the slums automatically steps on many toes of men in high places.

161. *Oscar Lewis to Arnaldo Orfila, March 21, 1965* (translated from Spanish)

. . . I feel very bad about the trouble this scandal of *Los Hijos de Sánchez* has brought to you and the Fondo. You will remember that I had anticipated something like this and once offered to pay for a delay in the publication of this work in Spanish. I was afraid that someone was going to identify the family and hurt them. Just today I received two letters from Roberto and Consuelo and it seems that they are living in great fear that the government is going to imprison them for having given information to a North American! The ability to protect my informants always has been the moral base (prerequisite) of my research. If it is not possible to assure the anonymity of my families, I cannot continue with my research technique. What has happened in Mexico is a threat to all anthropologists, be they Mexican or North American, who study urban problems, that is to say, a threat to the development of the new field of urban anthropology.

I have suffered during all of this, first because of my preoccupation for the family, and also because of the misunderstanding of my work and the calumnies that have been made against me in the press. I have received some letters from Latin American professors with newspaper clippings announcing: "Anthropologist Oscar Lewis accused of being an FBI agent," and asking me for explanations. How terrible! I spoke with the President of the American Anthropological Association and they are going to send a letter to you explaining my professional status, my work in anthropology, etc. What a shame that only the few negative and absurd reviews have reached them through the Latin American press, while the articles of Fernando Benítez and other serious writers haven't reached them. I hope that you, as my editor, can help to clarify this point to colleagues in Latin American universities and correct this bad impression.

I hope that a third edition of *Los Hijos* will come out soon. I can't write a prologue for it, first because of lack of time, and second because of the absurdity of the charges. I am certain that these things are not worth taking seriously and I prefer to let them die by themselves. This whole campaign against my book has defamed what is good about Mexico, its revolutionary spirit, its progressive tradition, its courage in facing life's realities. . . .

. . . I am sorry that the Fondo never has published my principal work on Tepoztlán. I want to suggest the possibility of publishing the four or five chapters on economics and the agrarian problem in Tepoztlán, and on the distribution of wealth in this town. And if the Fondo can't do it or does not want to, I would like to ask Jesús Silva Herzog to publish it in his review as an example of a research technique in micro-ethnology (?) that still is used as a model at Harvard and other universities in the world. I am not recommending publication of the chapters on the quality of human relationships in Tepoztlán because with this the scandal would begin all over again. Only a Mexican like Octavio Paz could escape it. Many things that he has said about the Mexican character in general in his book *The Labrynth* [sic] *of Solitude*, written from pure intuition and genius, I have written about a small town after many years of research. . . .

162. *Oscar Lewis to Carolina Luján, February 28, 1965*
. . . Of course, the most dreadful aspect of the entire affair is the way the press has been hounding the families I have studied. Yesterday I received a letter from [Guillermo] Gutiérrez . . . in *Antropología de la Pobreza*. He complained that he is being visited daily by newspapermen who ask questions and he doesn't know how to answer. He asked for money to move out.

. . . the father in the Sánchez family has not been bothered so far. He is a cautious man and has shown great astuteness in staying away from the [Casa Grande] etc. The Sánchez family has been very loyal in this entire scandal. . . .

The basic ethical premise of my research has been the possibility of maintaining the anonymity of the subjects studied. If this is not possible it raises serious questions in my own mind about my future research along family lines. I feel that family research is important but I must find some better safeguards for the families. Unlike a psychiatrist who works alone with his patient in his office, I have to work with many families in the vecindades or arrabales of P.R. and many people get to know me. I studied 71 families . . . in the "Sánchez" vecindad and it was probably some neighbor who fingered the Sánchez family. . . . In retrospect, it might have been better to have published under a pseudonym. . . .

In the case of the Puerto Rico volume, I had better ask three or four Puerto Rican intellectuals to read the manuscript and get their advice before I send it to the press. I haven't been able to work during the past week.

The big mistake was my allowing publication of the Sánchez book in Spanish. You may recall that I once offered Orfila a thousand dollars to tear up our contract and he laughed at my worrisome nature etc. Now he is charged with social dissolution for publishing it. I certainly don't want to have a Spanish edition of my work on the P.R. families. None of the family members read English.

163. *Oscar Lewis to Carolina Luján, March 20, 1965*

. . . The manuscripts [the Ríos interviews] are quite interesting but at times depressing and very obscene! Or at least it strikes me as obscene. In the light of the recent Mexican experience I have become sensitive to the problematic reactions to obscenity. I therefore went to San Juan to discuss this problem at a round table with leading Puerto Rican intellectuals and writers and they assured me there would be no scandal in Puerto Rico. Indeed, they suggested that what I thought of as obscene was not necessarily obscene to them. They thought some of my data was vulgar but not really obscene by Puerto Rican standards! I would like to explore the cultural variations in the definitions of obscenity.

I understand that the Sánchez affair has quieted down in Mexico but I was alarmed at the nasty piece in *Siempre* on Pedro Martínez. The selections from the book distorted what I had done and in some places even made up phrases which are not in the book. In over 250,000 words the strongest word used is *caray* and yet the *Siempre* article warned that the book was even more obscene than the *Children of Sánchez.*

164. *Oscar Lewis to Michael Kenny, anthropologist, June 7, 1965*

. . . I am afraid that my first volume on Puerto Rican families will cause a scandal here in New York among Commonwealth officialdom who are so desperately and understandably trying to build a positive image of the Puerto Rican, stimulate community organization and solidarity, etc. I am sympathetic to their goals but find that they are out of touch with a large sector of their own people. Either that, or they manage to conceal even from themselves the knowledge of the serious problems of Puerto Rican family life. American readers will find my new book much more upsetting than *The Children of Sánchez*, who, after all, were Mexicans and foreigners. But the children of Sánchez seem like a decent, stable, upright middle class family compared to the [Ríos] family and their relatives who are the leading characters in this volume. Moreover, Puerto Ricans are United States citizens, our friends and neighbors. They live and work among us. Both our sense of responsibility and our sense of guilt for the conditions of their lives will be greater than in the case of the Mexicans. In short, this is a serious political problem and how can urban anthropologists deal with such problems? I would appreciate your own reaction to this question. . . .

165. *Oscar Lewis to Luis Muñoz Marín, governor of Puerto Rico, January 7, 1966*

. . . My big problem is to place my materials on this one special sector of the population which I studied (i.e. 100 families from Greater San Juan slums) within a meaningful historical, and national context, and to carefully delineate what is distinctively Puerto Rican and what is universal in the culture of poverty.

. . . I know that an intensive study focused on poverty and its multiple facets and problems, particularly its effects upon character, runs the risk of offending Puerto Ricans who have dedicated their lives to eliminating poverty and to generally improving the conditions of the masses. However, I am trying to make it perfectly clear in my introduction that the sixteen Puerto Ricans who tell of their life experiences in my volume represent only one style of slum life and are not typical of the entire Puerto Rican lower class, much less of Puerto Rico as a whole.

There is no question in my mind that since 1940, and especially since the Commonwealth, great improvement has been brought about in Puerto Rican life. Unfortunately, this has not reached down to many of the slum families who seem to have been bypassed by the industrial progress. Moreover, industrialization and the rapidly changing culture has itself created some new problems.

Now that we have finally discovered the widespread persistence of poverty in the United States, one of the richest and most powerful countries in the world, it cannot come as a surprise or as a shock to find large pockets of concentrated human misery in countries which are so much poorer than the United States. In the case of Puerto Rico, there has been so much publicity given to the great strides made in such a short time that it may be a positive contribution to the Puerto Rican cause to present a few dramatic instances of family life which indicate how much there is yet to be done.

In my study in San Juan and New York I have found an intense degree of internal conflict and disorganization within families, an abysmal ignorance of Puerto Rican tradition and history, a lack of a sense of identity, a predominant present-time orientation, a tremendous impulsivity and acting out, with little effort to defer gratification and plan for the future, an emphasis upon violence and sexuality, and a general quality of emotional and intellectual superficiality which compares unfavorably with my earlier studies of slum dwellers in Mexico City. I am afraid this will not make a pretty picture but I believe it is an accurate one.

Because of my identification with the cause of Commonwealth and my love for Puerto Ricans, I am deeply disturbed by some of my own findings, and especially that these . . . may be misinterpreted or used to support and justify highly prejudiced and stereotyped negative attitudes still held by some Americans about Puerto Ricans. However, in the long run, I believe that the publication of my studies will do more good than harm. As I have said before, we know a great deal about the statistics and economics of poverty but we still know too little about the style of life of the poor, how they feel and think, how they manage to cope with problems which would be completely overwhelming to middle-class people. On the other hand, some of the people in the anti-poverty programs have a Rousseauan tendency to play up the courage, dignity and capacity for leadership of the very poor, without sufficient realization of the terribly destructive consequences of extreme poverty upon the character of the poor, consequences which sometimes lead to serious and irreversible pathology. Certainly my findings will serve as an antidote to this Rousseauan point of view. . . .

166. *Oscar Lewis to Rosa Celeste Marín, director, School of Social Work, University of Puerto Rico, May 6, 1966*
. . . I have tried to anticipate the sense of outrage which some Puerto Ricans may feel in reading this book. I understand that Samuel Quiñones, the president of your Senate, gave a talk in New York City on February 7 to the Puerto Rican Cultural Institute at which he denounced my two articles in Harper's and called for the condemnation by all Puerto Ricans of my forthcoming book. All this without having read it, so you can see that the fireworks may be brighter than in the case of *The Children of Sánchez*. I suspect that it would be a good thing for Puerto Rico to create such a reaction. I just hope that I can take it. I tend to get upset by this kind of unreasonably blind hostility and the incapacity to see the positive motives behind my work. . .

167. *Oscar Lewis to Rosa Celeste Marín, September 20, 1966*
. . . Just the other day I finally got around to reading LA CHARCA by Manuel Zeno Gandia and I happened to pick up an edition with an introduction by Samuel Quiñones who praises the author's courage

in presenting the sordid and pathological facts of Puerto Rican family life in this volume. Certainly the scene in which the motherly Landra urges her daughter Silvina to yield to the advance of Landra's husband in free union and the ensuing seduction in the presence of the Mother, indeed in the same bed, is more sordid than anything in my articles, or in my new book. But, whereas Samuel Quiñones saw fit to praise the realism of the Puerto Rican writer he now attacks the same kind of realism in my own work. How this man has changed. Someday you must explain this to me.

168. *Oscar Lewis to Herbert Gans, sociologist, November 23, 1966*

I have just returned from a hectic time in New York where I met with some members of the press and with a few officials of the Commonwealth government who were unduly defensive and protesting too much about *La Vida*. I certainly understand their sensitivity and the dangers inherent in publishing on the seamy side of life, etc., etc. By concentrating on the negative characteristics of the Ríos family, those Puerto Rican leaders are actually denigrating their own people. In any case, I shall be very interested in your reaction to *La Vida*. I expect you will find it quite a shattering document. Few middle class social scientists can match the toughness of the people of the culture of poverty and I am afraid that many of them just can't take it. . . .

P.S. I can't understand how both you and Michael Harrington so misunderstood my sentences and my intention regarding the possibilities of a social work and psychiatric solution to the culture of poverty. Actually I was trying to be a little cynical, but apparently it was missed. I think we need much more than a social work approach. At the very minimum, active community development programs are needed, but even that isn't enough to provide . . . the impact that is necessary to really make a difference and to really make for some changes in the long run.

169. *Oscar Lewis to Edgar L. Owens, special assistant to the director, USAID, American Embassy, Saigon, April 13, 1967*

Many thanks for your letter of March 22 [in which Owens asked for Lewis's reaction to an AID plan for "political development" in South Vietnam] and for the report you enclosed. I have looked through it hurriedly and hope to give it the attention it deserves as soon as [possible]. . . .

However, I have a few preliminary reactions on a rather general level. Given the overall context of the war which the United States is waging on North Vietnam, I doubt that my conception of the culture of poverty would have much relevance or be of any great aid to you.

As you may know, I am bitterly opposed to our war efforts in Vietnam and I believe that the work we are doing in South Vietnam is a tragic mistake, given the war context.

It seems to me that every social scientist must make a personal decision as to the moral issues involved in a matter of this sort. If peace were to come tomorrow, I would be more inclined to take seriously the efforts of you and your group to really get something positive done. However, to try to accomplish something within the negative context you are working in seems to me to be a contradiction of terms. To napalm villages and to try to improve welfare services in the same breath is too much for me to take. Incidentally, may I recommend the fascinating article by Mary McCarthy which appeared in *The New York Review of Books*, April 20, 1967 (Volume 8, no.7)?

(Owens wrote a courteous response to this letter which further explained the government's logic in the AID program and reiterated that the culture of poverty thesis had relevance for Saigon and parts of the central lowlands and that Lewis's writings were "of immense value in formulating our hypothesis.")

170. *Oscar Lewis to Corrine Schelling, American Academy of Arts and Sciences, February 5, 1968* (Lewis had participated in an academy-sponsored seminar on race and poverty)

. . . In a letter of January 17th Pat [Daniel Moynihan] asked if I could send him a short statement on some of the policy implications of my research on the Culture of Poverty. I've touched upon a few of these points indirectly in my *Redbook* dialogue with Senator [Robert] Kennedy and I enclose a copy for you.

The policy implications might be summarized as follows: First there is a great danger in lumping all the poor together and in generalizing about the ghettos and the slums. In my own experience I have found considerable range in income, in family structure, in educational level, and in degree of participation in institutions of the larger society, etc., among slum dwellers. I believe that the failure to take into account the distinctive sectors among the poor may explain some of the apparent contradictions in the literature and also some of the failures of the Anti-Poverty Program.

It seems to me that there is an urgent need for basic research on the nature of slums and ghettos with special emphasis upon delineating the specific sub-groups that live therein so that programs can be tailored to the needs of these sub-groups. One of the sub-groups that is found in most slums can be distinguished by a style of life which I have called the subculture of poverty. To make any significant changes or improvements in the lives of people in this sub-group will take more time, more money and more trained personnel than is anticipated in most anti-poverty projects. Indeed jobs, occupational retraining and an annual minimum family income, though all highly desirable, will in themselves not eliminate the pathology associated with the Culture of Poverty; it will not eliminate poor mothering, free unions, illegitimacy, alcoholism, gambling, wife-beating, present time orientation, impulse spending, and provincialism, to mention only a few traits.

Research and action directed to this sector of the population will have to take a long time perspective and should be organized in terms of five or ten year plans at the very minimum. Carefully designed pilot projects combining both action, research and evaluation could produce helpful leads for policy makers. . . .

PUBLICATIONS OF
OSCAR LEWIS

Books

1942. *The Effects of White Contact upon Blackfoot Culture, with Special Reference to the Role of the Fur Trade*. Monographs of the American Ethnological Society, no. 6. Seattle: University of Washington Press.

1948. *On the Edge of the Black Waxy: A Cultural Survey of Bell County, Texas*. Washington University Studies (New Series) in Social and Philosophical Sciences, no. 7. St. Louis.

1951. *Life in a Mexican Village: Tepoztlán Restudied*. Urbana: University of Illinois Press.

1958. *Village Life in Northern India*. Urbana: University of Illinois Press.

1959. *Five Families: Mexican Case Studies in the Culture of Poverty*. New York: Basic Books.

1960. *Tepoztlán: Village in Mexico*. New York: Holt, Rinehart and Winston.

1961. *The Children of Sánchez: Autobiography of a Mexican Family*. New York: Random House.

1964. *Pedro Martínez: A Mexican Peasant and His Family*. New York: Random House.

1966. *La Vida: A Puerto Rican Family in the Culture of Poverty—San Juan and New York*. New York: Random House.

1968. *A Study of Slum Culture: Backgrounds for La Vida* (with the assistance of Douglas Butterworth). New York: Random House.

1969. *A Death in the Sánchez Family*. New York: Random House.

1970. *Anthropological Essays*. New York: Random House.

1977–78. *Living the Revolution: An Oral History of Contemporary Cuba*, 3 vols. (with Ruth M. Lewis and Susan M. Rigdon). Urbana: University of Illinois Press (*Four Men* and *Four Women*, 1977; *Neighbors*, 1978).

Articles, Chapters, and Reports

(includes only those book reviews cited in the text)

1941. "Manly-Hearted Women among the North Piegan," *American Anthropologist* 43:173–87.

1944. "Social and Economic Changes in a Mexican Village: Tepoztlán 1926–44," *América Indígena* 4:281–314.

1944, with Ernest Maes. "Base para una Neuva Definicion Practica del Indio," *América Indígena* 4:107–18.

1946. "Bumper Crops in the Desert," *Harper's Magazine*, December, pp. 525–28.

1947. "Wealth Differences in a Mexican Village," *Scientific Monthly*, August, pp. 127–32.

1948. "Rural Cross Section," *Scientific Monthly*, April, pp. 327–34.

1949. "Aspects of Land Tenure and Economics in a Mexican Village," *Middle American Research Records*, May 30, pp. 195–209.

1949. "Husbands and Wives in a Mexican Village: A Study in Role Conflict," *American Anthropologist* 51:602–10.

1949. "Plow Culture and Hoe Culture: A Study in Contrasts," *Rural Sociology*, June, pp. 116–27.

1950. "An Anthropological Approach to Family Studies," *American Journal of Sociology*, March, pp. 468–75.

1952. "Dynamics of Culture Patterns—Summary," in *Problems in Social Psychology: An Interdisciplinary Inquiry*, ed. J. E. Hulett, Jr., and Ross Stagner. Urbana: University of Illinois, pp. 222–27.

1952. "The Effects of Technical Progress on Mental Health in Rural Populations," *América Indígena* 12:299–307.

1952. "Urbanization without Breakdown: A Case Study," *Scientific Monthly* 75 (July): 31–41.

1953. "Concepts of Health and Disease in a North Indian Village." Program Evaluation Organization, National Planning Commission. New Delhi: Government of India.

1953. "Controls and Experiments in Anthropological Field Work," in *Anthropology Today*, ed. A. L. Kroeber. Chicago: University of Chicago Press, pp. 352–75.

1953. "A Preliminary Guide to the Use of Village Patwari Records." Program Evaluation Organization, National Planning Commission. New Delhi: Government of India.

1953. "Tepoztlán Restudied: A Critique of the Folk-Urban Conceptualization of Social Change," *Rural Sociology*, June, pp. 121–36.

1954. Discussion of G. K. Yocorzynski's "The Nature of Man," in *Aspects of Culture and Personality*, ed. Francis L. K. Hsu. New York: Abelard-Schuman, pp. 183–84.

1954. Discussion of Otto Klineberg's "How Far Can the Society and Culture of a People Be Gauged Through Their Personality Characteristics?," in ibid., pp. 35–39.

1954, with the assistance of Harvant Singh Dhillon. "Group Dynamics in an Indian Village: A Study of Factions," *Economic Weekly of Bombay*, April 10, pp. 423–25, 445–51, 477–82, 591–606.

1955. "Comparisons in Cultural Anthropology," in *Yearbook of Anthropology*, ed. William L. Thomas, Jr., with the assistance of Jean Stewart. New York: Wenner-Gren Foundation for Anthropological Research, pp. 259–92.

1955. "La Cultura Campesina en la India y en Mexico," *Ciencias Sociales* (Unión Panamericana, Washington, D.C.), August, pp. 194–218.

1955. "Medicine and Politics in a Mexican Village," in *Health, Culture, and Community*, ed. Benjamin Paul. New York: Russell Sage Foundation, pp. 403–35.

1955. "Peasant Culture in India and Mexico: A Comparative Analysis," in *Village India*, ed. McKim Marriott. Chicago: University of Chicago Press, pp. 145–70.

1956. "The Festival Cycle in a North Indian Jat Village," *Proceedings of the American Philosophical Society* (Philadelphia) 100:168–96.

1956, with Ruth M. Lewis. "A Day in the Life of a Mexican Peasant Family," *Marriage and Family Living*, February, pp. 3–13.

1956, with Victor Barnouw. "Caste and the Jajmani System in a North Indian Village," *Scientific Monthly*, August, pp. 66–81.

1957. "Urbanización sin Desorganización: Las Familias Tepoztecas en la Ciudad de México," *América Indígena* 17:231–46.

1958. "Mexico desde 1940," *Investigación Económica* (Mexico City: Universidad Nacional Autónoma de México), 2d trimester, pp. 185–256.

1959. "La Cultura de la Vecindad en la Ciudad de México," *Ciencias Políticas y Sociales*, July–September, pp. 349–64.

1959. "Family Dynamics in a Mexican Village," *Marriage and Family Living*, August, pp. 218–26.

1960. "The Culture of Poverty in Mexico City: Two Case Studies," *Economic Weekly of Bombay*, June (special issue), pp. 965–72.

1960. "Dinámica Familiar Comparada en un Pueblo Mexicano," *Tlatoani* (Escuela Nacional de Antropologia e Historia), August, pp. 7–14.

1960–61. "Some of My Best Friends Are Peasants," *Human Organization*, Winter, pp. 179–90.

1961. "Mexico since Cardenas," *Social Change in Latin America Today: Its Implications for United States Policy*. Council on Foreign Relations. New York: Vintage Books, pp. 285–345.

1962. "Preliminary Guide for the Study of Village Culture in Northern India," *Journal of the Pakistan Academy for Village Development*, July (special issue on rural social research), pp. 26–47.

1962. "Visit to a Holy Shrine," *Holiday Magazine*, October, pp. 52–62.

1963. "The Culture of Poverty," *Trans-action*, November, pp. 17–19.

1964. "After the Revolution," *Reporter*, April 19, pp. 34–36.

1964. "The Culture of Poverty," in *Explosive Forces in Latin America*, ed. John T. TePaske and Sydney Nettleton Fisher. Publications of the Graduate Institute for World Affairs, no. 2. Columbus: Ohio State University Press, pp. 149–73.

1964. "In New York You Get Swallowed by a Horse," *Commentary*, November, pp. 69–73.

1964. "The Tender Violence of Pedro Martínez," *Harper's Magazine*, February, pp. 54–60.

1965. "Further Observations on the Folk-Urban Continuum and Urbanization with Special Reference to Mexico City," in *The Study of Urbanization*, ed. Philip M. Hauser and Leo F. Schnore. New York: John Wiley, pp. 491–502.

1965. "Mother and Son in a Puerto Rican Slum," *Harper's Magazine*, December, pp. 71–81.

1966. "La Cultura de la Pobreza," *Mundo Nuevo*, November, pp. 36–42.

1966. "La Cultura de la Pobreza," *Siempre!*, October (supplement).

1966. "The Culture of Poverty," *Scientific American*, October, pp. 19–25.

1966. "Even the Saints Cry," *Trans-action*, November, pp. 18–23.

1966. "I'm Proud to Be Poor," *Commentary*, August, pp. 44–47.

1966. "Un Paysan et Sa Famille," *Les Temps Modernes*, April, pp. 1783–1816.

1966. "Portrait of Gabriel: A Puerto Rican Family in San Juan and New York," *Harper's Magazine*, January, pp. 54–59.

1966. "A Thursday with Manuel," *New Left Review*, July–August, pp. 3–21.

1967. "A Redbook Dialogue: Oscar Lewis and Robert Kennedy," *Redbook*, September, pp. 73ff.

1967. Reply to book reviews of *The Children of Sánchez, Pedro Martínez,* and *La Vida,* in *Current Anthropology*, December, pp. 480–500.

1968. "The Culture of Poverty," in *Man in Adaptation: The Cultural Present,* ed. Yehudi Cohen. Chicago: Aldine Press, pp. 406–14.

1968. "Ghetto Education," *Center Magazine*, November (special supplement), pp. 46–60.

1968. "Love in El Barrio," *New York Magazine*, December 9, pp. 33–46.

1969. Book review of Charles Valentine's *Culture and Poverty,* in *Current Anthropology*, April–June, pp. 189–92.

1969. "La Cultura Material de los Pobres," *Pensamiento Crítico*, July, pp. 159–202.

1969. "A Death in the Sánchez Family," *New York Review of Books*, September 11 and 25 (special supplements), pp. 31–36, 34–39.

1969. "The Death of Dolores," *Trans-action*, 6:10–19.

1969. "One Can Suffer Anywhere," *Harper's Magazine*, 238:54–60.

1969. "Portrait," in *Breakthrough,* ed. Robert E. Yarber. Menlo Park, Calif.: Cummings, pp. 100–104.

1969. "The Possessions of the Poor," *Scientific American*, October, pp. 945–991.

1970. "La Cultura Material de los Pobres," *América Indígena*, October, pp. 945–91.

1970. "Gloria and Spiritism," *New York Magazine*, February 9, pp. 32–39.

1970. "Reminiscences of an Aging Puerto Rican," *Caribbean Review*, Fall, pp. 1–3.

SELECTED BIBLIOGRAPHY

Books, Documents, and Periodicals

Allport, Gordon. *Becoming: Basic Considerations for a Psychology of Personality.* New Haven: Yale University Press, 1955.

———. *Pattern and Growth in Personality.* New York: Holt, Rinehart and Winston, 1937.

———. *Personality: A Psychological Interpretation.* New York: Henry Holt and Co., 1937.

American Anthropology: The Early Years. Proceedings of the American Ethnological Society, ed. John Murra. St Paul, Minn.: West Publishers, 1974.

América Indígena: 40 Años Indice General. Instituto Indígenista Interamericano, Serie Sedial 1. Mexico, 1980.

Benedict, Ruth. *Patterns of Culture.* Boston: Houghton Mifflin, 1959 (first published 1934).

Boas, Franz. *General Anthropology.* Lexington, Mass.: D. C. Heath, 1938.

———. *Race, Language and Culture.* New York: Macmillan, 1940.

Borgatta, Edgar, and William Lambert, eds. *Handbook of Personality Theory and Research.* New York: Rand McNally, 1968.

Butterworth, Douglas. *The People of Buena Ventura: Relocation of Slum Dwellers in Postrevolutionary Cuba.* Urbana: University of Illinois Press, 1980.

Cohen, Yehudi, ed. *Man in Adaptation.* 2 vols. New York: Aldine, 1968.

Finney, Joseph C., ed. *Culture Change, Mental Health and Poverty.* Papers and proceedings of a 1965 conference on ethnopsychology and cross-national psychiatry. Lexington: University of Kentucky Press, 1969.

La Gaceta. Issue of the Fondo's monthly magazine devoted to the publication of *Los Hijos de Sánchez.* Mexico City: Fondo de Cultura Económica, March 1965.

Goldfrank, Esther. *Notes on an Undirected Life: As One Anthropologist Tells It.* Flushing, N.Y.: Queens College Press, 1978.

Goslin, David A. *Handbook of Socialization: Theory and Research.* Chicago: Rand McNally, 1969.

Hall, Calvin, and Gardner Lindzey. *Theories of Personality.* New York: Wiley, 1957.

Himmelfarb, Gertrude. *The Idea of Poverty.* New York: Vintage Books, 1985.

Honigman, John. *Culture and Personality.* New York: Harper and Bros., 1954.

———, ed. *Handbook of Social and Cultural Anthropology.* New York: Rand McNally, 1973.

Hsu, Francis C. K., ed. *Aspects of Culture and Personality.* New York: Abelard-Shuman, 1954.

Kaplan, Bert, ed. *Studying Personality Cross-Culturally*. Evanston, Ill.: Row, Peterson and Co., 1961.

Kardiner, Abram. *The Individual and His Society*. New York: Columbia University Press, 1939.

———. *Psychological Frontiers of Society*. New York: Columbia University Press, 1945.

———, and Edward Prebble. *They Studied Man*. Cleveland: World Publishing Co., 1961.

Keesing, Roger M., and Felix Keesing. *New Perspectives in Cultural Anthropology*. New York: Holt, Rinehart and Winston, 1971.

Klopfer, Bruno, and D. M. Kelly. *The Rorschach Technique*. Yonkers, N.Y.: World Book Co., 1942.

Kluckhohn, Clyde. *Culture and Behavior: Collected Essays*. Glencoe, Ill.: Free Press, 1962.

———, and Henry Murray. *Personality in Nature, Society and Culture*. New York: Alfred A. Knopf, 1948.

Kroeber, A. L., ed. *Anthropology Today*. Chicago: University of Chicago Press, 1953.

———, and Clyde Kluckhohn. *Culture: A Critical Review of Concepts and Definitions*. Papers of the Peabody Museum of American Archeology and Ethnology, Harvard University. Cambridge, Mass., 1952.

Leacock, Eleanor Burke, ed. *The Culture of Poverty: A Critique*. New York: Simon and Schuster, 1971.

Liebow, Elliot. *Tally's Corner: A Study of Negro Streetcorner Men*. Boston: Little, Brown, 1967.

Lewin, Kurt. *A Dynamic Theory of Personality: Selected Papers*. trans. Donald K. Adams and Karl E. Zener. New York: McGraw-Hill, 1935.

———. *Field Theory in Social Science*. trans. Dowin Cartwright. New York: Harper and Bros., 1951.

Lindzey, Gardner. *Projective Techniques and Cross-Cultural Research*. New York: Appleton-Century Crofts, 1961.

Linton, Adelin, and Charles Wagley. *Ralph Linton*. New York: Columbia University Press, 1971.

Linton, Ralph. *The Cultural Background of Personality*. New York: Appleton-Century Crofts, 1945.

———. *Culture and Mental Disorder*. Springfield, Ill: Chas. Thomas, 1956.

———. *The Study of Man*. New York: Appleton-Century Crofts. 1936.

Mayhew's London: Selections from "London Labour and the London Poor" by Henry Mayhew. ed. Peter Quennel. London: Spring Books, n.d. (*London Labour and the London Poor* was first published in 1851.)

Mead, Margaret. *An Anthropologist at Work: Writings of Ruth Benedict*. New York: Atherton, 1966.

———. *Blackberry Winter: My Earlier Years*. New York: William Morrow and Co., 1972.

———. *Ruth Benedict*. New York: Columbia University Press, 1974.

Moynihan, Daniel P., ed. *On Understanding Poverty*. New York: Basic Books, 1968.

Ohlin, Lloyd. "Implications of the Concept Culture of Poverty for Social Action." International trade union seminar on low-income groups and methods of dealing with their problems. Organisation for Economic Cooperation and Development, Paris, n.d.

Problems in Social Psychology. Papers and proceedings of the Allerton Conference on Social Psychology. ed. E. L. Hulett and Ross Stagner. Urbana: University of Illinois Press, 1950.

Public Law 87-415. "Manpower Development and Training Act of 1962," enacted March 15, 1962.

Public Law 88-452. "Economic Opportunity Act of 1964," enacted August 20, 1964.

Public Law 89-15. "Manpower Act of 1965," enacted April 26, 1965.

Public Law 89-792. "Manpower Development and Training Amendments of 1966," enacted November 7, 1966.

Public Law 89-794. "Economic Opportunity Amendments of 1966," enacted November 8, 1966.

Redfield, Robert. *The Primitive World and Its Transformations.* Ithaca, N.Y.: Cornell University Press, 1953.

———. *Tepoztlán: A Mexican Village.* Chicago: University of Chicago Press, 1930.

Riessman, Frank, Jerome Cohen, and Arthur Pearl, eds. *Mental Health of the Poor.* New York: Free Press, 1964.

Sargent, S. Stanfield, and Miriam W. Smith, eds. *Culture and Personality.* New York: Viking Fund, 1949.

Sundquist, James, ed. *On Fighting Poverty.* New York: Basic Books, 1969.

Valentine, Charles. *Culture and Poverty: Critique and Counter-Proposals.* Chicago: University of Chicago Press, 1968.

Wallace, Anthony F. C. *Culture and Personality.* New York: Random House, 1961.

Warner, W. Lloyd, Marcia Meeker, and Kenneth Eells. *Social Class in America: A Manual of Procedure for the Measurement of Social Status.* Chicago: Science Research Associates, 1949.

Winter, J. Alan, ed. *The Poor: A Culture of Poverty or a Poverty of Culture?* Grand Rapids, Mich.: Wm. B. Eerdmans, 1971.

Articles and Book Chapters

Allport, Gordon. "Scientific Models and Human Morals," *Psychological Review* 54 (1947): 182–92.

Allport, Gordon, and Henry S. Odbert. "Trait-Names: A Psycholexical Study," *Psychological Monographs* 47 (1936): v–37.

Benedict, Ruth. "Configurations of Culture in North America," *American Anthropologist* 34 (1932): 1–27.

Book reviews of *The Children of Sánchez, Pedro Martínez,* and *La Vida,* in *Current Anthropology,* December 1967, pp. 480–500.

Book reviews of *Culture and Poverty: Critique and Counter-Proposals,* in *Current Anthropology,* April–June 1969, pp. 181–201.

Davis, Allison. "The Motivation of the Underprivileged Worker," in *Industry and Society*, ed. William Foote Whyte. New York: McGraw-Hill Co., 1946, pp. 84–106.

Gladwin, Thomas. "The Anthropologist's View of Poverty," *Social Welfare Forum* 88 (1961): 73–86.

Gordon, Milton. "The Concept of Sub-Culture and Its Application," *Social Forces* 26 (1947): 40–42.

Herzog, Elizabeth. "Some Assumptions about the Poor," *Social Service Review* 37 (1963): 389–402.

Inkeles, Alex. "Sociology and Psychology," in *Psychology: Study of a Science*, vol. 6, ed. Sigmund Koch. New York: McGraw-Hill, 1963.

Kaplan, Bert. "Personality and Social Structure," in *Review of Sociology*, ed. Joseph B. Gittler. New York: Wiley, 1957, pp. 87–126.

Kelly, Lawrence. "Anthropology and Anthropologists in the New Deal," *Journal of the History of the Behavioral Sciences* 16 (1980): 6–24.

Kluckhohn, Clyde, and O. H. Mowrer. "Culture and Personality: A Conceptual Scheme," *American Anthropologist* 46 (1944): 1–29.

La Barre, Weston. "The Influence of Freud on Anthropology," *American Imago* 15 (1958): 275–328.

Maslow, A. H. "Personality and Patterns of Culture," in *Psychology of Personality*, ed. R. Stagner. New York: McGraw-Hill, 1937, pp. 408–28.

Mead, Margaret. "Some Relationships between Social Anthropology and Psychiatry," in *Dynamic Psychiatry*, ed. Franz Alexander and Helen Ross. Chicago: University of Chicago Press, 1952, pp. 401–48.

Miller, S. M., and Frank Riessman. "Implications of Lower-Class Culture for Social Work," *Social Problems* 9 (1961): 86–97.

———, and A. Seagull. "Poverty and Self-Indulgence: A Critique of the Non-Deferred Gratification Patterns," in *Poverty in America*, ed. L. Fermin et al. Ann Arbor: University of Michigan Press, 1965, pp. 416–32.

Miller, Walter. "Subculture, Social Reform and the Culture of Poverty," *Human Organization* 30 (1971): 111–25.

Nadel, S. F. "The Typological Approaches to Culture," *Character and Personality* 5 (1936–37): 267–84.

Moore, Barrington. "In the Life: Review of *La Vida* by Oscar Lewis," *New York Review of Books*, June 15, 1967, pp. 3–4.

Opler, M. E. "The Psychoanalytic Treatment of Culture," *Psychoanalytic Review* 22 (1935): 138–57.

"Oscar Lewis: Los Hijos de la Pobreza," interview with Oscar Lewis by Lorenzo Batallan for *El Nacional*, Caracas, Venezuela, November 6, 1967.

Parker, Seymour, and Robert Kleiner. "The Culture of Poverty: An Adjustive Dimension," *American Anthropologist* 72 (1970): 516–27.

Peattie, Lisa R. "Anthropology and the Search for Values," *Journal of Applied Behavioral Sciences* 1 (1965): 362–72.

Podfield, Harland. "New Industrial Systems and Cultural Concepts of Poverty," *Human Organization* 29 (1964): 29–36.

Rainwater, Lee. "Marital Sexuality in Four Cultures of Poverty," *Journal of Marriage and Family Living* 26 (1964): 457–66.

Redfield, Robert. "The Folk Society," *American Journal of Sociology* 52 (1947): 293–308.

————, Ralph Linton, and Melville J. Herskovits. "Memorandum for the Study of Acculturation," *American Anthropologist* 38 (1936): 149–52.

Roach, Jack, and Orville Gursslin. "An Evaluation of the Concept 'Culture of Poverty'," *Social Forces* 45 (1967): 383–92.

Sapir, Edward. "Cultural Anthropology and Psychiatry," *Journal of Abnormal and Social Psychology* 27 (1932): 229–42.

Schorr, Alvin. "The Nonculture of Poverty," *American Journal of Orthopsychiatry* 34 (1964): 907–12.

Smith, Brewster. "Anthropology and Psychology," in *For a Science of Social Man*, ed. John Gillan. New York: Macmillan, 1954, pp. 32–66.

Spiro, Melford E. "Culture and Personality: The Natural History of a False Dichotomy," *Psychiatry* 15 (1951): 19–46.

Turner, Ralph H. "Life Situation and Subculture," *British Journal of Sociology* 9 (1958): 299–320.

Wagley, Charles, and Marvin Harris. "A Typology of Latin American Subcultures," *American Anthropologist* 57 (1955): 428–51.

Whyte, William Foote. "Social Organization in the Slums," *American Sociological Review* 8 (1943): 34–39.

Yinger, J. Milton. "Contraculture and Subculture," *American Sociological Review* 25 (1960): 625–35.

Unpublished Proceedings

Conference on the Culture of Poverty. Transcript of general sessions. Temple University, Philadelphia, October 10–11, 1969.

Conference on the Puerto Rican Child in His Cultural Context. Transcript of general session. Department of Education of the Commonwealth of Puerto Rico, San Juan, November 18–20, 1965.

Seminar on Race and Poverty. Minutes of monthly sessions, October 1966–November 1967. American Academy of Arts and Sciences, Boston, 1966–67.

INDEX

Abel, Theodora, 38, 42, 64, 115
Ackerman, Nathan, 82, 86n28, 230, 234
Adams, Lucy Wilcox, 45n3
Allport, Gordon, 58, 116, 127, 130n10
América Indígena, 36, 45n1
American Academy of Arts and Sciences, 154, 299
American Anthropological Association, 293
American Council of Learned Societies, 19
American Philosophical Society, 37
Anthropological Essays, 37, 43, 105
Applied anthropology. *See* Lewis, Oscar
Arensberg, Conrad, 59, 60, 113, 118, 131n20; correspondence with, 224–27
Arriaga family study. *See* "Six Women"
Asch, Solomon, 12
Asociación Psicoanalitica. *See* Psychoanalytic Association (Mexico)

Basic Books, 222
Bartlett, Hull, 146–47
Batallan, Lorenzo, 7
Bateson, Gregory, 134n37
Beatty, William, 45n3
Beckmann, Matilde, 25n8
Beckmann, Max, 25n8
Bell County, Texas (research site), 20, 21
Beltrán, Alberto, 29, 135
Benedict, Ruth: as teacher, 11, 12, 14, 25n6, 26n12, 180, 215, 227; comparison with work of, 6, 7, 8n7, 13, 25n6, 112, 130n12, 131n23, 173, 176, 181n5, 231; correspondence with, 200–201; culture and personality school, 24n3, 25n4, 28, 38; fieldwork with, 14, 25n10
Bettelheim, Bruno, 156
Biele, Harry, 25n9
Blackfoot Indians: fieldwork among, 12, 14–15, 17, 19, 268
Boas, Franz, 12, 14, 25nn6–7, 211, 214

Borbolla, Rubén, 186, 187n1
Borden, Viviana Muñoz, 84n4
Bowles, Chester: correspondence with, 287
Bram, Joseph, 13
Brocton Reservation. *See* Blackfoot Indians
Brooklyn College, 12, 17, 18, 28
Brown, Kenneth: correspondence with, 252
Buñuel, Luis, 145–46, 149n5, 175
Bunzel, Ruth, 12
Bureau of Agricultural Economics (BAE; U.S. Department of Agriculture): employment by, 20–21, 22, 37, 203, 286
Butterworth, Douglas, 74, 75, 84n4, 101, 112, 175

Calabresi, Renata, 38, 42
Cámara, Fernando: correspondence with, 232
Camera Three: television adaptation of *Five Families*, 135
Campos, Vicente, 188
Caplow, Theodore, 172n37
Cara Baroja, J.: correspondence with, 206
Carlson, Dorothy Terry: correspondence with, 235
Carter, James: administration of, 167
Casagrande, Joseph: correspondence with, 278, 282
Casa Grande *vecindad* (Mexico City research site), 51, 52, 55, 57, 69n11, 97, 98, 119, 131n25, 160
Caso, Alfonso, 185, 186, 189, 194
Castro, Fidel: and Cuba project, 98, 108n36, 167, 168, 169, 276–77, 278; views on, 169, 170n3, 229, 271, 272, 274, 280, 281, 282
Castro de la Fuente, Angelica, 219
Chase, Stuart, 35
Chávez Orozco, Luis, 195

311

A Note on the Author

Susan Rigdon grew up in Galena, Illinois, and attended the University of Illinois at Urbana-Champaign. In 1971 she received a Ph.D. in political science and since then has taught comparative and international politics at four universities. Her primary teaching and research interests are in the area of political development.